THE BIBLICAL
and
HISTORICAL
BACKGROUND
of
JEWISH CUSTOMS AND
CEREMONIES

THE BIBLICAL
and
HISTORICAL
BACKGROUND
of
JEWISH CUSTOMS AND
CEREMONIES

BY
ABRAHAM P. BLOCH

KTAV PUBLISHING HOUSE, INC.
NEW YORK
1980

Library of Congress Cataloging in Publication Data

Bloch, Abraham P
  The Biblical and historical background of Jewish
customs and ceremonies.

  Bibliography: p.
  Includes index.
  1. Jews—Rites and ceremonies. 2. Fasts and
feasts—Judaism. I. Title.
BM700.B54   296.4   79-26007
ISBN 0-87068-658-5

MANUFACTURED IN THE UNITED STATES OF AMERICA

This book is affectionately dedicated to
My wife, Belle
My children,
A. Zachary and Liebe M. Apfel
Raphael S. and Dorothy Bloch
My grandchildren,
Stuart, Mark, Howard and Bruce Apfel
David and Joel Bloch.

Contents

Preface

The object of this book is to trace wherever possible the date of origin of various religious customs and to follow their development through the centuries. This project is of more than academic interest. The perspective of time is frequently invaluable in the discovery of the rationales of various rituals. These inevitably reflect socio-religious conditions of the period when the customs came into existence.

The emergence of the synagogue, the dispersal of the diaspora, the encounter with Christianity and Islam, the Crusades, the change of the economic base of East European Jewry, the Holocaust and the rebirth of Israel have all inspired and left an imprint upon the development of Jewish customs.

For the purposes of this book only standard practices have been included for discussion. Occasional references are made to differences between the Ashkenazic and Sephardic rituals. Odd and exotic ceremonies of isolated Jewish communities do not come within the purview of this work.

A review of most religious practices, which are part of the Jewish tradition, is included in each chapter. The review of the customs serves as a background for the discussion of their development. This book is not a guide to religious practice and no legal conclusions are to be drawn from opinions expressed therein.

Abraham P. Bloch

1

The Life-Cycle

I.
BIRTH

"THE WHOLE WORLD rejoices when a child is born" (*Midrash Samuel* 23). In ancient times this joy was tinged with a deep concern for the survival of mother and child. The high rate of mortality incidental to the delivery of children justified a sense of grave anxiety.

According to talmudic statistics, "the majority of women bear healthy children" (*Yevamot* 36a). However, inadequate knowledge of proper postnatal care was responsible for the death of many infants. Indeed the viability of the average newborn was put in question. Accordingly, Rabbi Simon b. Gamliel (2nd cent.) ruled that infants are not legally viable until they reach their second month of life (*Niddah* 44b).

Despite their lack of viability, newborn infants enjoyed all the rights and protection accorded to viable people. Rabbi Simon b. Gamliel pronounced the following legal dictum: "The Sabbath may be desecrated for a day-old infant" (*Shabbat* 151b): This principle was reiterated in another talmudic statement: "All the laws of the Sabbath may be suspended to preserve an infant's life" (*Yoma* 84b).

Even a fetus was entitled to similar rights. If a mother dies in labor, a surgical procedure may be performed on the Sabbath in an effort to

1

save the unborn child (*Arachin* 7a). A heathen who destroys a living fetus is guilty of a capital offense. The issue of the viability of a victim is legally immaterial in a crime committed by a heathen (*Sanhedrin* 57b). However, a fetus is not an independent living organism. In the words of a talmudic legal maxim: "The fetus is a thigh of the mother" (*Gittin* 23b). Since the fetus derives its life from its mother, it cannot assert claims which are in conflict with the mother's interests. If a mother is endangered during labor and she can be saved only by the destruction of the fetus, the guiding principle is : "Her [the mother's] life takes precedence over its [the fetus's] life" (*Ohalot* 7:6). However, from the time that the head of the fetus emerges from the birth canal, it is considered a born child and it may no longer be sacrificed to save the mother, despite the child's questionable viability.

Tradition, cognizant of the extreme care required by infants, took them under its protective wings. It promoted and praised the instinctive love of parents for their offspring. "Upon emergence from the mother's womb, an infant is slimy with fluid and blood. Nevertheless, it is immediately smothered with hugs and kisses" (*Lev. Rabbah* 27:7).

The Talmud made practical provisions for the safety of children. An infant may nurse for two years, thereafter it must be weaned (*Ketubot* 60a). A mother's vow to withhold breast-feeding from her child is inoperative (ibid. 59b). A nursing widow or divorcee may not remarry until her child is two years old (*Yevamot* 42a). A widower left with young children is exempt from the traditional waiting period and may immediately remarry for the sake of the children (*Moed Katan* 23a). Infants may lie in a cradle in the daytime but must be transferred to the mother's bed for the night. Couples were cautioned against cohabitation in a bed where a child is asleep, for fear of injuring it (*Pesachim* 12b).

Public concern for the welfare of children was expressed through special prayers by members of the Maamad (lay representatives of the public who attend Temple rituals). "The men of the Maamad assemble in the synagogue and observe four fasts. . . . On Wednesday [they fasted] that croup may not attack children. On Thursday . . . that nursing mothers be capable of nursing their children" (*Taanit* 27b).

It was generally believed that the first week after birth was the most crucial period in an infant's life. This belief was bolstered by the fact that the Torah had postponed the rite of circumcision to the eighth day. Prior to the eighth day, infants are apparently susceptible to sickness and mishaps (*Deut. Rabbah* 6).

Medieval superstitions were responsible for the introduction of various customs designed to safeguard mother and child. Sundry amulets were affixed to the walls of the birth-room. The One hundred and twenty-first Psalm (*Shir HaMaalot*) was posted over the mother's bed. The names of protective angels were added to the poster under kabbalist influence. In some communities there were nightly gatherings at the home of the new child to give moral support to the parents and to recite the *Shema*.

SHALOM ZACHAR

The medieval celebration of Shalom Zachar on the first Friday night after the birth evolved into an enduring custom (Rema, *Yoreh Deah* 265:12). There is no record of a similar celebration in the talmudic era. However, the medieval custom was based on an obscure festivity mentioned in the Talmud under the name of Yeshuah Haben ("the salvation of the son"; *Baba Kama* 80a). Rashi identified this celebration with Pidyon Haben (the redemption of the firstborn), which is held on the child's thirty-first day. Rabbenu Tam disagreed and suggested that Yeshuah Haben was a celebration observed after the birth of a son. Josephus, however, stated: "The law does not permit us to make festivals at the birth of our children" (*Against Apion* 2:26).

Yeshuah Haben was discontinued in the post-talmudic era. However, Shalom Zachar, a similar celebration, was introduced in the Middle Ages. The event was held on Friday night because people were free and able to attend the celebration. The durability of the custom of Shalom Zachar is due to the approval given to it by Rema (16th cent.) in his annotations to the *Shulchan Aruch* (*Yoreh Deah* 265:11).

Beginning with the thirteenth century, the night preceding the circumcision assumed special significance. There was a common superstition that evil spirits seek to harm a child on that night to prevent the circumcision from taking place. To counteract their designs, friends gathered at the home of the newborn to maintain a vigil and spend the evening in prayer. In time the occasion assumed a festive and social character, with lavish refreshments served to the guests. In the German-Jewish communities this night later became known as Wachnacht ("a night of watchful vigil").

The eve of a circumcision lost its special significance in modern times. The custom lacked the sanction of the *Shulchan Aruch*. Furthermore, the superstition which had originally inspired the event lost its credibility. Historical research, however, seems to indicate that the custom had a precedent in talmudic times in a celebration called Shevua Haben.

SHEVUA HABEN

There are four references in the Talmud to an occasion called Shevua Haben ("the week of the child" or "the week-old child"). The name appears twice in tannaic passages (*Baba Batra* 60b, *Sanhedrin* 32b) and twice in amoraic passages (*Baba Kama* 80a, Jer. *Ketubot* 1:5). Rashi identified Shevua Haben with the rite of circumcision, which is performed after the child has passed its first week. This translation is open to question. Circumcision is performed on the eighth day. Would not Shemini Haben ("the eight-day child") be a more appropriate designation? Furthermore, why did the name refer to the date of the circumcision rather than to the rite itself? We may therefore conclude that Shevua Haben was observed on the seventh day to mark the conclusion of the child's first week and to make preparations for the forthcoming berit.

The *Baba Batra* text quotes the reaction of Rabbi Ishmael b. Elisha (1st–2nd cent.) to the Hadrianic decree proscribing the rite of circumcision. "And from the day that a government has come into power which issues cruel decrees against us and forbids us the observance of the Torah and the precepts and does not allow us to enter the Shevua Haben, we ought by right to bind ourselves not to marry and beget children . . ." The fact that the authorities prohibited the observance of Shevua Haben indicates that it was not merely a social occasion but a preliminary to the circumcision.

The *Sanhedrin* text is more enlightening with regard to the character of Shevua Haben. "It has been taught: 'The noise of grindstones [in the preparation of medicinal powders for the circumcision] at Burni announces the holding of a Shevua Haben.' " Obviously, it was a preliminary gathering for the making of preparations for the circumcision. Since it was considered commendable to circumcise a child as early in the day as possible, the necessary powders had to be prepared on the previous evening.

The text in Jerusalem *Ketubot* makes it clear that the sound of grindstones was not confined to the town of Burni. Similar sounds in any city were a sign of an impending circumcision. The text informs us that Shevua Haben was also an occasion for feasting. "A sound of grinding in a city, there is a festival, a festival." We are also told that the people of Beror Hail introduced the custom of lighting candles at a Ben Shevua to enhance the festive character of the event.

The *Ketubot* text, much later than the one in *Sanhedrin*, traces the gradual development of Shevua Haben. It began as a functional working session during which all preparatory details were taken care of, and gradually it developed into a celebration of the completion of the first week. From the text in *Baba Kama* we learn that Shevua Haben was still observed in the third century.

Nachmanides mentions a celebration of Shevua Habat ("the week of the daughter"; see Soncino, *Baba Batra* 60b, note 8). There is no record of such an event in the Talmud. All indications point to the association of the occasion with a forthcoming circumcision.

After a hiatus of about a thousand years, the festivity at the end of the seventh day was reintroduced in some medieval Jewish communities. The belief that the child needed added security on that night motivated the gathering of the family's friends. In communities where no festivities were held on the evening of the seventh day, a special feast was served on the morning of the eighth day, prior to the circumcision (*Machzor Vitry* 506).

THE NAMING OF A CHILD

Girls are named on the Sabbath following their birth, when the father is called to the Torah. Initially, the ceremony was postponed until such time as the mother was in condition to appear in the synagogue. However, since this practice delayed the naming of a girl for an indefinite period, it was eventually abolished.

The naming of boys is part of the circumcision ritual. Rav Saadiah Gaon (9th cent.) included in his siddur an Aramic prayer (*Tishtlach asusa*) for the health of the child. The child's name was announced in the prayer. A Hebrew prayer (*Kayem et hayeled*) was substituted in the Middle Ages.

The custom of naming boys at the time of circumcision dates from the talmudic period. There is a midrashic reference to Moses' original Hebrew name, which was allegedly given to him when he was circumcised (*Pirke deRabbi Eliezer*). Rabbi Natan HaBavli (2nd cent.) mentioned several instances when boys were named after the circumcision (*Shabbat* 134a). There are also references to this practice in the New Testament (Luke 1:59, 2:21).

The custom of naming children for ancestors, or other kin, was not widespread in the talmudic era. The practice of the Patriarchate family

(the descendants of Hillel) to name infants for grandparents (Gamliel
–Simon–Gamliel–Simon; Judah–Gamliel–Judah–Gamliel–Judah–
Hillel–Gamliel–Judah–Gamliel) was an exception, probably due to the
princely rank of the office of Patriarch (see *Moed Katan* 25b, Rabbi
Chanin).

Rabbi Jose (2nd cent.) discussed the difference between the adoption
of names in biblical times and in his period. "The ancients were familiar
with their genealogy and therefore coined names to commemorate
events. We are not familiar with our genealogy and hence adopt names
of ancestors" (*Gen. Rabbah* 37). By the adoption of "names of ancestors," Rabbi Jose implied the adoption of previously established names
as opposed to the creation of new names.

The practice of naming a child for a close relative began to take root
among the Oriental Jews of the geonic period (6th–11th cent.). It
became widespread in the Egyptian Jewish community. Maimonides
departed from the local custom when he named his son Abraham, in
honor of the patriarch. He was motivated by a desire to focus his son's
attention upon Abraham, whose noble character was to serve him as a
model. Maimonides' grandson was named David in memory of
Maimonides' younger brother, David, who had perished at sea. The
famous Rabbi Isaac Alfasi (10 cent.) named his son Jacob in memory of
the child's grandfather, Jacob. There are numerous similar illustrations.

The custom of the Oriental Jews gradually spread to the Ashkenazic
community. Initially, Ashkenazic Jews named their children for distinguished individuals worthy of emulation. Rabbi Judah HeChasid
(12th–13th cent.) stressed the importance of naming children for
righteous and God-fearing people (*Sefer HaChasidim* 244). However, it
is evident that the custom of commemorating names of close kin was
already in vogue in his time. Thus he discussed the propriety of
naming a girl for a deceased sister (ibid. 477).

Ashkenazim named their children only for deceased kin. There was
no such tradition in the talmudic period. In the case of the Patriarchate
family, mentioned above, some of the grandfathers were surely alive
when grandchildren were named for them. There are talmudic accounts of children who were named for Rabbi Natan HaBavli in his
lifetime (2nd cent., *Shabbat* 134a) and for Rabbi Elazar b. Simon in his
lifetime (2nd cent., *Baba Metzia* 84b). However, no son was ever named
for his father in his lifetime (see below, chap. 2, "Honor of Parents").
Rabbi Judah HeChasid even cautioned against marriages in which

mother-in-law and bride or father-in-law and groom have similar names (*Tzavaat Rabbi Judah HeChasid* 254).

The tradition of naming children for a deceased relative was rigidly followed until the onset of the emancipation, when the adoption of non-Jewish names became the vogue. As a concession to custom a dual system was established. The child was given a Jewish name to be used at religious functions, but for all other purposes, including official birth registry, a popular name was used. There was little or no affinity between the two names.

In modern times, under conditions of total acculturation and growing assimilation, the old tradition for the naming of children has been increasingly neglected. Commemoration of ancestral names is no longer an urgent consideration for many young parents. This is particularly true when boys are circumcised by physicians and when girls are named in the hospital rather than in the synagogue.

Modern Israel has witnessed a revival of the ancient biblical custom of creating new names in commemoration of events or geographic locations. This development is not an outgrowth of assimilation but of a desire to break with old practices which were closely associated with life in the diaspora. Biblical names which have not been used in the diaspora have also come into vogue (Gideon, Yael, Amnon, Bilhah, etc.). Among the names commemorating significant events are Nili (an underground group which opposed the Turks), Yigal ("he will redeem"), and Derorah ("freedom"). Among the names commemorating geographic locations and flora are Carmela, Sharon, Ilanah, and Erez.

CIRCUMCISION

The rite of circumcision is based on a biblical injunction addressed to Abraham (Gen. 17:9–14). It preceded the Sinaitic revelation by four centuries and for that reason was not restated in Deuteronomy. Josephus took note of the antiquity of this ritual. "And they circumcised him [Isaac] upon the eighth day, and from that time the Jews continue the custom of circumcising their sons from that number of days" (*Antiq.* 1:2).

The practice of circumcision was common among some Western Semites but not among the Eastern Semites. In Judaism circumcision became a symbolic token of a covenant between God and the Hebrew people (Gen. 17:13).

Various rationalizations have been offered for the rite of circumcision. According to Josephus and Maimonides, it is a sanitary measure. According to Philo, it was designed to aid procreation. Some ancient non-Jews regarded it as an act of consecration. The literal sense of the scriptural text appears to stress circumcision as a physical distinguishing mark of Jewishness.

Jewishness is identified by marks attached to garments *(tzitzit)* and to homes *(mezuzah)*. The mark in the flesh is indelible and constitutes a permanent reminder of one's descent and religion. The rabbis viewed circumcision as a deterrent to sex crimes and intermarriage. "The Torah decreed the circumcision of the genitals so that the fear of God may deter one from committing a sin" *(Yalkut, Shofetim* 42).

Despite all rationalizations, the real purpose of circumcision has remained obscure. Such was the conclusion of a midrash: "Only to Abraham did God reveal the mystery of circumcision" *(Tanchuma, Lech Lecha* 19). Rav Tzemach Gaon (quoted by Avudrahim, *Hilchot Millah)* said: "We do not know the reason for the mitzvah of circumcision and we practice it because it is a divine decree."

The rite of circumcision was widely observed by Jews from time immemorial. The Talmud noted: "Every mitzvah for which Jews had been willing to sacrifice their lives they continue to observe it wholeheartedly" *(Shabbat* 130a).

There were a number of exceptions to this rule in the pre-exilic history of the Jewish people. According to a talmudic tradition, Jews did not practice circumcision in Egypt because of their desire to imitate the Egyptians *(Exod. Rabbah* 1). Only the children of the tribe of Levi were circumcised (ibid. 19). As a priestly tribe they might have followed the custom of Egyptian priests who practiced circumcision. Children born in the desert were not circumcised due to the danger of sandstorms *(Yevamot* 72a). However, entry into Palestine was contingent upon circumcision *(Gen. Rabbah* 46). After the division of the Jewish state into two kingdoms, the Ephraimite kingdom abolished circumcision *(Pirke deRabbi Eliezer* 19). This provoked the wrath of the prophet Elijah, who gained a reputation in Jewish lore as a champion of the rite of circumcision (ibid. 29). There was also a brief interlude during the Hellenistic period when some Hellenized Jews abandoned circumcision.

The proscription of circumcision by King Antiochus IV (2nd cent. B.C.E.) and Emperor Hadrian (2nd cent. C.E.) provoked major uprisings backed by the majority of the Jewish people. These uprisings demonstrated a determination to resist, even at the cost of life, any interference with the right to observe the Sabbath and the rite of circumcision (see below chap. 3, "Sabbath and Circumcision").

Rabbinic Judaism extolled the merit of circumcision and classified it as a central pillar of the faith. "Great is circumcision, which is as weighty as all the mitzvot of the Torah" (*Nedarim* 32b). "Whosoever is circumcised will not suffer gehinnom" (*Tanchuma* 20). "The Jewish people was saved by God thanks to the merit of circumcision" (*Yalkut Mishle* 964). Similar rabbinical maxims established circumcision as a basic fundamental of Judaism.

Even an alienated Jew like Spinoza noted, in a letter to his Christian friend Henry Oldenburg, the importance of circumcision in the survival of the Jewish people: "The symbol of circumcision . . . is, I believe, so potent that I am convinced it alone will keep this nation alive forever" (Kobler, *Treasury of Jewish Letters*, p. 535).

THE CIRCUMCISER

In view of the delicate nature of the surgical procedure, there was obviously a need for trained circumcisers. There is no record in the Bible of the existence of specialists in this field. In ancient times surgeons may have performed the rite for the children of wealthy families. When King Izates of Adiabene (1st cent.) converted to Judaism, he had himself circumcised by a surgeon (*Antiq.* 20:2). However, most circumcisions of children of the biblical era must have been performed by a member of the family.

According to the Talmud, the obligation to have a child circumcised rests upon the father (*Kiddushin* 29a). It is conceivable that most circumcisions were performed by fathers. Yet there are some vague indications that it was the mother who performed the operation as part of her normal routine of caring for the early needs of the baby. Moses' son Eleazar was circumcised by his mother (Exod. 4:24–26). Even in the Hasmonean period it was the mothers who circumcised their sons in defiance of Antiochus' decree and were executed for their disobedience (I Macc. 1). There are also references in the Talmud to religious problems relating to the rite of circumcision which were presented by mothers to rabbinic courts (*Yevamot* 64b).

There is definite proof of the existence of trained circumcisers in the second century. A tannaic passage refers to them by the term *uman* ("technician"; *Baba Batra* 21a). The same passage also lists specialists termed *rofe* ("physician"). Rashi identified *uman* with a bloodletter and *rofe* with a circumciser. Elsewhere in the Talmud, Rashi identified *uman* with a circumciser (*Shabbat* 133b, *Baba Metzia* 109a). We may therefore question Rashi's identification in *Baba Batra* of *rofe* with a circumciser. The latter was most likely a medical practitioner.

The term *gozer* ("cutter") was used by a third-century rabbi who was also a circumciser (*Shabbat* 130b). Apparently, an *uman* performed bloodletting and circumcisions, while a *gozer* specialized in circumcisions exclusively.

Beginning with the fourth century, the term *mohel* (*mohela* in Aramaic) appeared for the first time as the title of a circumciser (*Shabbat* 156a). To make sure that a mohel's surgical expertise is matched by his proficiency in the religious aspects of the ritual, the Talmud urged all scholars to learn the skill of circumcising (*Chulin* 9a).

Circumcisers were not paid for their services because performing a circumcision was considered a mitzvah of great merit. Due to economic conditions in the Middle Ages, volunteer circumcisers were replaced by professionals who exacted a fee for their services. Contemporary rabbis were greatly displeased with this development, particularly when it imposed a hardship upon poor families. Rabbi Solomon b. Adret of Barcelona (13th cent.) had harsh words for such men. "The rabbinical court should criticize such practice. It has been the custom of many circumcisers to seek out an opportunity for performing this mitzvah. If the mohel remains adamant, and the father is unable to pay the fee, the rabbinical court must assume jurisdiction and compel the mohel to perform the circumcision" (quoted by Rema, *Yoreh Deah* 261).

Opposition to the remuneration of religious functionaries was not shared by most laymen. The organized medieval Jewish community required a religious leadership which could devote its full time to the needs of the people. In time all religious officials, including rabbis, were compelled to accept a salary.

The profession of mohel was combined in many communities with that of the shochet, thus providing a more secure economic base. The circumcision of children of poor families was never neglected for want of money. Public charitable organizations provided financial assistance to help with the increased expenses attendant upon the birth of a child. This included a modest fee for the mohel and the expense of the traditional meal tendered after the circumcision.

In our time, the arrival of large numbers of uncircumcised Russian Jews in Western Europe, Israel, and America has elicited the cooperation of many mohelim who have generously contributed their services.

THE RITUAL

In the talmudic era, circumcisions were performed at home. In the geonic period (6th–11th cent.), the ceremony was transferred to the synagogue. Medieval custom honored the father by providing a minyan at his home on the morning of the circumcision (Avudrahim, *Milah Ubirkotehnah*).

The principals of a circumcision ceremony—the father, the sandak (derived from the Greek for "godfather"), and the mohel—are called *baale berit* ("the principals of the berit"). Beginning with the tenth century, the function of the sandak was to hold the infant on his knees during the circumcision. The custom of holding the baby in the lap was based on a talmudic description of a circumcision: "Today he [the infant] sits in the lap of Abraham" (*Kiddushin* 72b). The term *sindiknos* is mentioned in talmudic literature (*Yalkut Tehillim* 723; *Shochar Tov* 35).

The number of principals was gradually increased in the Middle Ages in order to accommodate the great demand for participation in the ceremony. The wife of the sandak was given the privilege of carrying the infant to the synagogue (Maharil). Another principal, known as *kvater*, was introduced in the fourteenth century in German-Jewish communities (*Minhage Maharak* 174:15). The kvater (derived from the German for "father") placed the child in the lap of the sandak. In the event that the father was absent, the kvater recited the father's benediction. In time grandparents were added to the list of honorees, each of whom was given a chance to hold the infant.

Two ceremonial chairs were prepared prior to the circumcision. One chair was for the sandak. The other chair, known as *kisse shel Eliyahu* ("the chair of the Prophet Elijah"), was placed on the right of the sandak's chair. This medieval custom was based on midrashic lore regarding God's promise to Elijah that he would be privileged to attend all circumcisions (*Pirke deRabbi Eliezer* 19). A beautifully decorated Chair of Elijah was acquired by many synagogues for use at berit ceremonies.

Another medieval custom was the lighting of candles in the synagogue prior to the circumcision. A similar custom prevailed in the talmudic era (*Sanhedrin* 32b; Tosafot, *Or haner*).

Tradition requires the presence of a minyan at a berit (*Pirke deRabbi Eliezer* 19). However, if none is available the ceremony may be performed without it.

When the infant is brought into the synagogue, the mohel greets him with the traditional salutation *Baruch haba* ("Blessed is the one who comes"). In medieval times, the guests responded with *beshem HaShem* ("in the name of God"). The mohel recites next the biblical declaration of God's covenant of peace (Num. 25:10–13). He then takes the infant and pronounces *Hineni muchan* . . . (his preparedness for the performance of the mitzvah). Next, the infant is placed on the Chair of Elijah and the mohel declares: "This is the throne of Elijah . . ." This declaration is based on a text in the Zohar (Gen. 13). He then places the infant in the lap of the sandak and recites the benediction *Al hamilah* ("who has given us the command concerning the circumcision"). The *milah* (the cutting off of the end of the upper prepuce) is then performed. In medieval Ashkenazic communities it was customary to place the removed prepuce in a container of sand. The sand symbolized the biblical prediction of the proliferation of the Jewish people like the sands of the sea.

Following the milah, the father recites the benediction *lehachnito* ("who commanded us to admit him into the covenant of Abraham"). In the Sephardic rite, and the current custom in Israel, the father also recites the benediction of *Shehecheyanu*. The benediction is omitted in the Ashkenazic rite in the diaspora because medieval scholars deemed it inappropriate at an occasion when the infant suffers pain. The guests respond with a prayer: "Even as the child has entered into the covenant may he be initiated into Torah, marriage, and good deeds." The ultimate goal of a religious education is thus stressed at the very outset.

The second stage of the circumcision, *periah* (the slitting of the inner lining of the prepuce), is performed after the father's benediction. Periah, according to one talmudic opinion, is of post-Sinaitic origin (*Yevamot* 71b).

Metzitzah (the staunching of the blood in the wound) is the final stage of the circumcision. The mohel then recites a benediction over a cup of wine and offers a prayer for the welfare of the parents and child. The name of the child is announced in the course of this prayer. It is customary to moisten the child's lips with the wine when the verse "Yea, I said unto thee, in thy blood live" is recited. The cup is handed to the sandak, who drinks some of the wine, and the rest is sent to the mother.

Most of the prayers in the text of the ceremony date from the second century (*Shabbat* 137b).

According to a custom prevalent in medieval Ashkenazic communities, ten men visited the infant after the circumcision. One of them placed a Bible near the child and declared: "May this one fulfill what is written herein" (*Machzor Vitry*). Once again the preeminence of education and piety was given prominent display.

A circumcision banquet *(seudah)* is an important feature of the celebration (*Ketubot* 8a; *Tanchuma, Tetzaveh; Pirke deRabbi Eliezer* 29). The *Birkat HaMazon* (Grace) following the seudah is amplified by the insertion of additional prayers in honor of the occasion.

THE RECOVERY OF THE MOTHER

Biblical law decreed a period of ritual impurity following the delivery of a child. During that time the mother may not cohabit with her husband. The length of the period varies, depending upon the sex of the child: seven days after the birth of a boy, and fourteen days after the birth of a girl. This period was followed by a second postpartum stage. In the second stage, cohabitation is permitted but the mother may not eat sacred food or enter the Temple. The length of this stage also depended upon the sex of the child: thirty-three days for a boy, and sixty-six days for a girl. At the end of the second stage, the mother brought sacrificial offerings and "the kohen shall make atonement for her and she shall be clean" (Lev. 12:1–8). The second stage became inoperative after the destruction of the Temple.

The reason for the variance in the length of the period of impurity is obscure. In the absence of a physiological explanation, Rabbi Simon b. Yochai (2nd cent.) offered a psychological reason. It was assumed that most women in the agony of giving birth secretly vow to reject all future sex relations with their husbands. However, when the pain has subsided, women retract their vows. In the case of a boy, the joy and festivity attendant upon a circumcision accelerate a woman's retraction and she is willing to resume normal relations soon thereafter (*Niddah* 31b).

The alleged secret vow of women is also taken to be the reason for the mother's need for sacrificial atonement (ibid.). However, biblical law required two sacrifices, a burnt-offering and a sin-offering. The burnt-offering was apparently a thanksgiving ritual exclusively for the mother.

Rabbi Simon b. Yochai's rationalization links the length of the period of impurity to the mother's state of mind and readiness to return to a normal routine. In effect, the period of "impurity" is actually a period of rest from a husband's sexual demands. While she is not isolated, the wife is accorded the treatment due a person who is recovering from an illness. There might have been practical reasons for terminating the period of "rest" when the boy reached his eighth day. Mothers of the biblical era were very much involved in the arrangements for the berit and most likely performed the circumcision. Since no such demands were made of mothers upon the birth of girls, the mother was permitted a much longer period of rest.

The link between the period of impurity and the impending circumcision of a boy is clearly indicated in the scriptural text. The twelfth chapter of Leviticus deals with the impurity of a postpartum mother. Normally, one would not expect the law of circumcision to be interpolated into a chapter dealing with the mother's impurity. The second verse informs us that the period of impurity after a boy is seven days. This verse should have been followed immediately by a provision for the second stage of impurity (33 days), exactly what was done in the case of a birth of a girl (v. 5). The abrupt interposition of the law of circumcision after the provision of eight days of impurity appears puzzling. The Talmud read a legal connection into this sequence (*Shabbat* 135a), but one cannot excape the impression that the law of circumcision was interposed as an explanation for the termination of the mother's period of impurity at the end of seven days.

There were no special thanksgiving rituals for mothers in the talmudic and post-talmudic eras. A modern Prayer of Thanksgiving for new mothers was introduced in England by Rabbi Nathan Adler (Hertz, *Daily Prayer Book*, p. 1038).

PIDYON HABEN

A male-child who is his mother's firstborn (Exod. 13:15) must be redeemed with five selaim upon reaching his thirty-first day (Num. 18:16). If the thirty-first day falls on a Saturday or holiday, the ritual is postponed to the following day. The redemption ceremony is called Pidyon Haben. If the mother is the wife of a kohen or levi, or the daughter of a kohen or levi, no redemption is required (*Bechorot* 46a, 47a).

The ritual of Pidyon Haben is based on a biblical injunction: "And all the firstborn of man shalt thou redeem" (Exod. 13:3). Redemption releases the child from the kohen's jurisdiction, which he had acquired by virtue of the command: "The firstborn of thy sons shalt thou give to me" (Exod. 22:28). In the words of Maimonides: "We redeem from the kohen, as if he had already acquired a title to him" (*Sefer HaMitzvot*, mitzvah 80).

The Bible links the rationale of the Pidyon Haben to the tenth plague: ". . . the Lord slew all the firstborn in the land of Egypt, both the firstborn of man and the firstborn of beast; therefore I sacrifice to the Lord all that opens the womb, bearing males, but all the firstborn of my sons I redeem" (Exod. 13:15). Pidyon Haben, like the paschal lamb, commemorates the escape of the Jewish firstborns from the plague when God passed over their homes in Egypt.

Biblical injunctions are seldom bracketed with rationalizations. In the case of Pidyon Haben, the rationale is offered within the context of a response to a child's inquiry: "What is this?" (Exod. 13:14). The link to the tenth plague places the ritual within the framework of the educational objectives of the exodus, which mandate detailed explanations.

The reason for limiting the rite of Pidyon Haben to the firstborn of mothers is not indicated in the Bible. The limitation is generally attributed to the fact that the firstborn of animals are also sanctified. It is impossible to determine the first issue of a male animal.

We may also suggest a social explanation. Firstborn are dedicated to the service of God at the moment of birth, unless redeemed from a kohen. Mothers are the principal mentors of children in the early years of life. The task of consecrating the child therefore rests on the mother. For this reason, the mother's firstborn was chosen for a special mission. Thus it was Hannah who dedicated her firstborn, Samuel, to God (I Sam. 1:11).

There is another ritual that was linked to the tenth plague, the post-talmudic Fast of the Firstborn (see below chap. 13, "Taanit Bechorim"). This fast is not related to the sanctification of the firstborn and was therefore imposed upon all firstborns, maternal and paternal. Indeed, in some communities even females observed the fast.

Despite the pivotal role of the mother in the law of Pidyon Haben, the obligation to redeem the child rests solely upon the father (*Kiddushin* 29a). In the event that the father fails in his duty, the obligation devolves upon the firstborn when he reaches maturity (ibid.). The Talmud based the exemption of the mother upon legal technicalities. We must also take into account the fact that the responsibility for implementing all the religious and social functions attendant upon the different stages of a growing child has been placed upon the father, the head of the family. The father must attend to the circumcision, redemption, education, marriage, and professional training of his child (ibid.).

THE KOHEN

Any kohen is qualified to perform the rite of Pidyon Haben. Parents have naturally always preferred to obtain the services of a kohen with a reputation for piety and scholarship. Rabbi Tarfon (2nd cent.), a kohen, was in great demand by parents (*Bechorot* 51b). Rabbi Chanina (2nd–3rd cent.) was another popular kohen (ibid.), and so was Rabbi Kahane (3rd cent., *Kiddushin* 8a).

Redemption money was one of several sources of revenue provided in the Bible for kohanim. Most priestly revenues came to an end after the destruction of the Temple. Kohanim had to turn to other occupations to derive a livelihood, and many of them prospered. Redemption money is one of the few priestly remunerations which have survived the destruction of the Temple. For some poor parents the payment of five selaim, or its equivalent, constituted a great hardship. This situation is reflected in a mishnaic halachah: "Therefore if the kohen wants to give him [back the money] as a gift, he may do so" (*Bechorot* 51a). Rabbis Tarfon and Chanina routinely returned all redemption fees (ibid.). Medieval scholars, desiring to protect the interests of poor kohanim, ruled that the fee may be returned only if the parents are in need.

THE REDEMPTION RITUAL

The modern text of the Pidyon Haben ritual is of post-geonic origin. In the talmudic era, the text consisted only of the recitation of two benedictions and the transfer of the redemption fee. The benediction of *Al pidyon haben* ("who has commanded us concerning the redemption of the son") was recited by the father. There was uncertainty as to who should recite the benediction of *Shehecheyanu*, the father or the kohen. It was finally resolved in the time of Rabbi Simlai (ca. 3rd cent.) that the father should recite both benedictions (*Pesachim* 121b).

Rav Saadiah Gaon (9th cent.) retained the brief talmudic text but added a few embellishments. After the benedictions, the father hands the money to the kohen and states: "I hereby give you the five selaim in redemption of my son." The kohen accepts the money and pronounces a blessing: "Just as you have fulfilled this mitzvah may you fulfill all the mitzvot of the Torah." There were some lengthy texts current in Rav Saadiah's time but he dismissed them as improper.

A more elaborate text made its appearance in medieval Europe. The child was handed to the kohen, and the father informed him that the infant was his firstborn. The mother followed with an assertion that the infant was her firstborn. The kohen then inquired whether the father wished to give up the child or redeem him. The father responded that he wished to redeem the child and handed the money to the kohen. The child was returned to the father, who then recited the two benedictions. The kohen held the money over the head of the child and intoned: *Zeh tachat zeh* . . . ("this is instead of that, this is in exchange of that . . ."). He then pronounced a benediction over a cup of wine and concluded with biblical blessings.

The modern ritual has retained the medieval text, with some modifications. In the Ashkenazic rite, the mother is no longer required to make any statement. The father states that the infant is the mother's firstborn. The mother's statement is still part of the Sephardic rite. The kohen's recitation of *Zeh tachat zeh*, reminiscent of the ritual of Kapparot, (see chap. 5, "Kapparot"), has been eliminated. In the Ashkenazic rite in Israel, all the Aramaic verses of the text have been translated into Hebrew.

The post-geonic elaboration of the text was designed to dramatize the redemption through an exchange of questions and answers between the kohen and the parents. The scenario serves an educational purpose but in two instances carries an implication that is contrary to the law. The father's assertion that the infant is his firstborn (in the medieval text) is immaterial. The mother's testimony that the child is her firstborn would make him subject to redemption even if he were not the father's firstborn. The kohen's question whether the father wishes to give up the child presumes an option which does not exist. The child must be redeemed.

Another medieval innovation was the seudah, a festive meal tendered after the ceremony. According to Rashi, this custom was in practice in the talmudic era (*Baba Kama* 80a; Rashi, Yeshuah Haben).

THE FIRST HAIRCUT

The first haircut of a boy, which marks his emergence from infancy, was considered an event of great significance in many Jewish communities, particularly in the Orient. Beginning with the sixteenth century, Jews came to Meron, the traditional site of the tomb of Rabbi Simon b. Yochai (2nd cent.), on Lag B'Omer to commemorate the yahrzeit of the legendary rabbi. One of the features of the celebration is the cutting of the hair of boys who have reached their fourth birthday. The ceremony is called Chalakah (derived from the Hebrew for "smooth," Gen. 27:11). Guests of the family are invited to participate by snipping off a few hairs. The conclusion of the operation is climaxed with a festive seudah.

The significance of the first haircut stems from kabbalist mysticism. The concurrence of Lag B'Omer, the day on which the Sefirah restriction of haircutting is lifted, and the yahrzeit of Rabbi Simon b. Yochai, the source of kabbalist inspiration, enhanced the spiritual aspect of the first haircut. The custom is based on the law of Orlah (forbidden fruit of a newly planted tree). The fruit is forbidden for the first three years. The fruit of the fourth year is "holy, for giving praise [*hilulim*] unto the Lord" (Lev. 19:24). The yahrzeit of Rabbi Simon is known in the Zohar as Hilula deRabbi Simon b. Yochai.

Chasidism has retained the formality of the first haircut. The age when the child's hair is cut for the first time varies among different groups.

SCHOOL AGE

The obligation to provide an education for one's children rests upon the father (*Kiddushin* 29a). In ancient Israel, prior to the establishment of elementary schools, it was left to the fathers to instruct their own young. Such an arrangement did not bring satisfactory results. In the words of Rav (3rd cent.): "If a child had a father, his father taught him, and if he had no father the child did not learn at all" (*Baba Batra* 21a). The first effort to raise the educational standard was made in the first century, when an elementary school was established in Jerusalem. The school was open to students from all over the country, but parents were reluctant to send young children away from home. As a result most beginners were in their late teens.

To remedy this situation, schools were established in the capitals of several districts and the age of beginners was lowered to sixteen. The expansion of the school system attracted a greater number of students, but disciplinary problems continued to plague the officials. Disgruntled adolescents frequently quit school and returned to their homes. It was not until the appointment of Joshua b. Gamala to the high priesthood (in the last decade before the destruction of the Temple) that order was brought to the chaotic school system. Schools were established in all cities, permitting the lowering of the school age to children of six or seven (ibid.). At the age of thirteen, students were transferred from the elementary school to the Bet HaMidrash (an intermediate school; *Yalkut, Ruth* 600).

In medieval Europe the school age was lowered to five, in keeping with the advice of Rabbi Judah b. Tema (*Avot* 5). A child's first day at school was a festive occasion and special initiation ceremonies came into being. The day when a child began to study Torah was even more festive and parents tendered a holiday meal in honor of the boy (see below chap. 8, "Religious Education").

II.
BAR AND BAT MITZVAH

In modern usage the term Bar Mitzvah denotes the religious ceremony in the synagogue which marks a boy's attainment of his religious majority. This perception dates from the thirteenth century.

There were no special rites in the talmudic and geonic periods to mark a boy's reaching of his thirteenth birthday. As a new adult he was quietly integrated into the congregation and automatically entitled to participate in all functions from which minors are excluded. One of the prized privileges of adulthood was the right to be called to the Torah. Although this honor was generally reserved for scholars and the elderly, we may assume that a new adult was initiated with an aliyah soon after his birthday as a public demonstration of his coming of age.

The term *bar mitzvah* is mentioned once in the Talmud (*Baba Metzia* 96a). In the talmudic lexicon *bar mitzvah* is a legal definition of an adult Jew, from thirteen to the end of life, who is under obligation to perform mitzvot. The secular counterpart of *bar mitzvah* is *gadol* ("grown-up"), a biological designation devoid of any religious connotation. A non-Jewish adult is a *gadol* but not a *bar mitzvah*.

The age of majority differs for boys and girls. Boys attain their majority at the age of thirteen and a day, girls at twelve and a day (*Yoma* 82a). The distinction hinges upon the time of the onset of puberty. According to an ancient tradition, allegedly dating back to Sinai, puberty is established by the growth of at least two pubic hairs. The Talmud estimated that the appearance of pubic hair generally coincides with the beginning of the fourteenth year of a male and the thirteenth year of a female.

The determining condition of adulthood is puberty, not age. In the absence of pubic development one remains a minor. On the other hand, pubic symptoms prior to the age of twelve or thirteen are considered premature abnormalities which do not signify adulthood.

A minor male (*katan*) enters directly into adulthood upon reaching the required age. A minor female (*ketanah*), however, passes through an intermediary stage of adolescence (*naarah*) before reaching adulthood. This stage lasts six months. During the intermediary period a girl is obligated to observe mitzvot (such as fasting, etc.) and acquires some legal rights which she did not enjoy as a minor.

A girl's earlier physical maturity is not necessarily matched by a corresponding intellectual precocity. A twelve-year-old girl is socially more sophisticated than a boy of the same age but their intellectual levels are on a par. This is probably why a girl of twelve, despite her attainment of religious majority, is not yet ready for adulthood.

The peak of intellectual development, according to the Talmud, is reached at the age of twenty in both sexes. Hence its assertion that heavenly punishment is not inflicted on young people under the age of twenty (*Shabbat* 89a).

PRE–BAR MITZVAH RITES

It was customary for boys of twelve in ancient Jerusalem to fast the whole day of Yom Kippur. At the end of the fast, the boy was taken by his father to each elder in the congregation to receive his blessing. The elder prayed that the boy grow to become a scholar and a performer of good deeds (*Masechet Soferim*, chap. 18). The fasting anticipated the boy's thirteenth year and consituted a pre–Bar Mitzvah rite.

Another pre–Bar Mitzvah custom is the wearing of tefillin one month before the thirteenth birthday. This practice is based on a talmudic statement: "A minor . . . who is competent to care for tefillin, his father should procure him a set" (*Sukkah* 42a). A longer period of training is allowed for orphans.

THE BAR MITZVAH CEREMONY

The earliest mention of a Bar Mitzvah in the modern sense of the term appears in a thirteenth-century manuscript of a German rabbi. Several factors may have contributed to the emerging prominence of the rite. In the face of spreading massacres in Western Europe in the thirteenth and fourteenth centuries, parents sought divine protection for their children through religious ceremonies which evoked congregational good wishes and blessings. It is also possible that growing anxieties and dangers produced a yearning for happy days in the family calendar as an escape from the dismal realities of existence.

The Bar Mitzvah rite has not changed with the passage of the centuries. An aliyah to the Torah is at the heart of the ritual. Initially, boys were taken to the synagogue on a Monday or Thursday following

Bible reflects the process by which marriage evolved from its initial primitive stage to its emergence in Judaic tradition. For the purpose of this discussion, we will confine the study of the various stages in the development of the institution of marriage exclusively to an analysis of biblical sources.

Adam's reaction to the appearance of Eve, and the scriptural postscript to his statement, is couched in terminology which clearly depicts the perceptions of primitive society. Adam's first words upon seeing Eve were as follows: "This is now bone of my bones and flesh of my flesh; she shall be called woman [*ishah*] because she was taken out of man [*ish*]" (Gen. 2:23). A casual reading of his words conveys the impression of a cordial statement of welcome and a declaration of Eve's fitness to be his mate and companion because both were built in the same image. Upon rereading the sentence one cannot fail to note a different nuance. Adam seems to be asserting a husband's superior matrimonial position and the legal rights appertaining thereto.

Adam emphasized the fact that Eve was built out of one of his ribs. This formed the basis of man's proprietary claims to a woman. When an individual retrieves a lost article, there is no need for securing another party's consent. It is likewise unnecessary for a rite or bilateral agreement to precede the establishment of a family unit. Marriage is an acquisition established by the legal right of repossession, devoid of a status of sanctity. A wife's transgression, such as adultery, constitutes an assault upon man's proprietary rights rather than a breach of the sanctity of the marital status. This summation, I believe, is a fairly accurate description of the primitive concept of marriage.

Our analysis is corroborated by the succeeding verse, which begins with the conjunctive "therefore." "Therefore man will leave his father and mother and he will cleave to his wife and they shall be one flesh" (Gen. 2:24). How does the practice of cleaving to one's wife relate to Adam's preceding declaration? What is the significance of the term "cleave" *(vedavak)*? Why was the traditional biblical word for marriage *(kichah)* omitted from this sentence?

The Hebrew term *vedavak* is ambivalent. It describes either a sense of strong emotional attachment (Gen. 34:3, II Kings 18:6, Ruth 1:14) or a state of extreme physical closeness (Deut. 28:60, Ps. 102:6). It is obvious that the phrase "cleaves to his wife" falls into the second category and is a euphemism for cohabitation.

The sequence of the two verses becomes apparent if we take the primitive perception of marriage into consideration. Adam had defined marriage as an act of reclamation of man's property. "Therefore" man leaves his parental home and takes possession of a woman for the purpose of cohabitation. By restoring his missing part man becomes whole again (one flesh). The traditional expression "taking a wife" was omitted because there was no rite or "taking" in primitive marriage, only cohabitation.

According to a midrashic statement, the phrase "and he shall cleave unto his wife" conveys a legal implication. It suggests that in the early period of Genesis man was not authorized to divorce his wife because he was under a permanent injunction to "cleave to his wife." On the other hand, the wife was exempt from this injunction and therefore was not restrained from divorcing her husband (*Gen. Rabbah* 18). It is hard to conceive of such a situation, except in a matriarchal society. Some anthropologists believe that mankind began as a matriarchal society.

The traditional expression "taking" is also absent from the account of Cain's marriage, which was recorded in a brief report that "Cain had intercourse with his wife" (Gen. 4:17). We are thus indirectly informed that the ancient perception of marriage persisted beyond the generation of Adam. The first indication of a new development is alluded to in the marriage of Lamech, the seventh generation since Adam. This stage is introduced through the first pentateuchal mention of the rite of "taking": "And Lamech took unto him two wives" (Gen. 4:19).

TAKING A WIFE

The phrase "taking a wife" could conceivably mean the physical transfer of a wife to her husband's home or the performance of a rite of marriage. That the latter is correct is made clear in several biblical passages. Thus Isaac's marriage to Rebecca was spelled out in three stages: "And Isaac brought her into his mother Sarah's tent [physical transfer], and he took Rebecca [marriage rite], and she became his wife [consummation]" (Gen. 24:67). The three stages, albeit in a different sequence, also appear in the description of Jacob's marriage to Leah: "And he took his [Laban's] daughter [marriage rite], and he brought her to him [physical transfer], and he cohabited with her" (Gen. 29:23). Leah's marriage took place at her father's home. That was standard procedure. The marriage rite therefore preceded the physical transfer of the wife.

This definition of "taking a wife" is further supported by the fact that the term "taking" is omitted in the Bible from any description of a matrimonial union which did not require a marriage ceremony. Thus Sarah did not propose that Abraham "take" Hagar but merely that he "cohabit" with her (Gen. 16:2). A sexual relationship with a female slave was a master's prerogative and did not require a prenuptial rite. The "taking" is also significantly missing from the account of Jacob's unions with Bilhah and Zilpah, the maidservants of Rachel and Leah (Gen. 30:4, 9).

With the introduction of a wedding ceremony, known as "taking," the primitive perception of marriage marked its second stage of development. Marriage was no longer a man's unilateral privilege but the culmination of a bilateral agreement for the assumption of mutual obligations. Lamech's son Yuval is described in the Bible as the "father of such as dwell in tents and have cattle" (Gen. 4:20). We may therefore assume that the new perception of the marital status became part of the heritage of the nomadic Semites, the ancestors of Abraham.

Changes in the perception of the institution of marriage did not necessarily effect immediate innovations in the method of establishing the marital status. For a long time cohabitation remained the only proof of marriage (*Sanhedrin* 57b, *Gen. Rabbah* 18).

A vestige of this practice lingered on in ancient Hebrew society. An alien female captive of war, whom a Hebrew warrior wished to marry, was granted a thirty-day delay to mourn her kin. "After that you may go to her and cohabit with her and she shall be your wife" (Deut. 21:13). According to a rabbinic comment: "There is nothing left for you [the soldier] to do but the mitzvah of cohabitation" (*Sifre,* loc. cit.). This statement, in the view of Nachmanides, restricted the rite of that marriage to cohabitation (ibid.), possibly reflecting the fact that the marriage was sanctioned only as a concession to a soldier's sexual temptations under war conditions.

Another vestige of the ancient practice of establishing matrimony lingered on in the law of levirate marriage. The brother of a man who died without issue was enjoined to marry the wife of the deceased. The marriage was established only by cohabitation (*Kiddushin* 14a), a restriction possibly intended to emphasize the objective of levirate marriage, the continuation of the lineage of the deceased through offspring born of the union.

ERUSIN

The first stage of a traditional Hebrew marriage is known as *erusin* ("betrothal"; Exod. 22:15, Deut. 20:7, 22:23). A betrothed woman was in fact a married woman who remained for a period of time in her father's home and custody before her transfer to her husband's home. The etymological connotation of *arushah* is "a desired woman." The groom signified his desire to make her his wife by performing a religious ceremony known in the Talmud as *kiddushin* ("holiness"). A betrothed woman, like holy property owned by the Temple *(hekdesh)*, is forbidden to all men *(Kiddushin* 2b).

The Talmud lists three methods of betrothing a woman: financial consideration given to the bride, a written bill of betrothal, and cohabitation *(Kiddushin* 2a). Any of these methods had to be coupled with the groom's declaration: "You are betrothed unto me with this money (or document or cohabitation) in accordance with the laws of Moses and of Israel."

The method of cohabitation, a relic of Semitic custom, was rarely used by Jews even in biblical times. Most betrothed women remained virgins until the second stage of the marriage. The Bible refers to an *arushah* as "a virgin betrothed to a man" (Deut. 22:23). Even in the exceptional cases, when a groom cohabited with his bride to establish a state of betrothal, the early rabbis prohibited further contacts between them until the completion of the marriage. The method of cohabitation was outlawed in the third century *(Kiddushin* 12b).

A husband was under no obligation to support his betrothed bride unless he delayed the marriage beyond twelve months *(Ketubot* 57a). Betrothals could be dissolved only by divorce or death *(Kiddushin* 2a).

Betrothal ceremonies generally took place at the home of the bride's parents *(Ketubot* 7b). The occasion was climaxed by an appropriate banquet. Witnesses were required to be present at the ceremony but there was no need for a minyan (ibid.). The text of the betrothal benediction was published in the third century (ibid.). It includes the rabbinical proviso prohibiting cohabitation of bride and groom.

The need for a period of betrothal arose from social conditions prevalent in ancient times. There was no engagement as we know it today. When an introductory meeting of both families resulted in mutual agreement, the young couple was immediately betrothed. This precluded hasty breaking of the agreement or possible consideration of other matches. However, the bride, who was generally very young, needed a little more time for maturing, and she also had to acquire a trousseau, an elaborate kit of cosmetics, and appropriate jewelry. The groom also needed time to establish a home, to see to his financial independence, and to make arrangements for a lavish wedding banquet.

Betrothal periods were open-ended. If need be, the betrothal could last for several years, if mutually agreed to by both parties. However, bride and groom both had the right to terminate the period by serving notice of an intent to have the marriage consummated. The wedding date then had to be set within a twelve-month period. It was assumed that it takes at least a year to complete all the wedding preparations and for the bride to become expert in the application of cosmetics. Curiously, the Persian maidens who were chosen to appear before King Ahasuerus were allowed a similar period to perfect the process of beautification (Esther 2:12).

Betrothed widows needed less time to put things in order. Their betrothal period was generally limited to one month after notification of intent of marriage (*Ketubot* 57a).

A trend favoring shorter periods of betrothal emerged in the third century. According to Rav Huna, a girl who was betrothed after she had passed the age of twelve and one-half years was entitled to delay a wedding for only thirty days. Rav Papa (4th cent.) agreed with this ruling, but only if the girl had passed the age of thirteen and one-half years at the time of the betrothal (*Ketubot* 57b). The new trend was probably the result of a rabbinical decree, enacted in the third century, prohibiting the betrothal of minor girls (*Kiddushin* 41a).

The interval between betrothal and marriage was totally eliminated in the Middle Ages, when the current practice of combining the betrothal and marriage ceremonies was instituted. Several factors contributed to this development. Due to unsettled conditions and the uprooting of Jewish communities, it was no longer expedient to separate the bride from the groom for any length of time. Furthermore, frequent confiscation and looting of property put in question the long-range ability of parents to meet financial commitments.

TENAIM

The elimination of extended betrothal periods gave greater prominence to the custom of *tenaim* ("conditions" listed in the prenuptial agreement). In the talmudic era this practice was known as *shidduchin* (from the Aramaic *shadacha* for a state of peace or agreement; *Targum Rav Yosef*, I Chron. 4:40). Financial arrangements and other stipulations were spelled out in an oral or written contract, known as *shetar pesikta* (*Ketubot* 102a).

The execution of *shidduchin* agreements generally preceded the performance of the betrothal and was considered an adjunct to the ceremony (*Ketubot* 102a). The agreement served as a deterrent against hasty and unstable marriages. It also assured the involvement of both sets of parents. Rav (3rd cent.) inflicted physical punishment on grooms who betrothed girls without the benefit of a prenuptial agreement (*Kiddushin* 12b).

The signing of *tenaim* in the Middle Ages took place a considerable time before the wedding. The *tenaim* created a relationship akin to the modern connotation of an engagement. The contract set forth the parental financial commitments and the date of the wedding. It also provided for penalties in the event of a breach of its terms. Although the occasion lacked religious significance, it took on an air of formality and festiveness. A late medieval custom injected a religious element into the transaction with the breaking of a plate upon the signing of the agreement, in memory of the destruction of Jerusalem. The breaking of a plate distinguished the ritual from the practice of breaking a glass under the chuppah.

In some communities, a second document of *tenaim* was drawn up prior to the wedding. The "latter *tenaim*" set forth commitments by the groom which were to be incorporated in the ketubah.

MARRIAGE OF MINORS

Despite talmudic objections to the betrothal of minor girls (*Kiddushin* 41a), the restriction was relaxed in the Middle Ages. Small, isolated Jewish communities occasionally faced the problem of a shortage of available brides. The demand for qualified girls produced a pressure for early marriages and an abundance of child brides. A child bride had the legal right to reject her husband prior to reaching majority by declaring her refusal to be his wife (*miun; Gittin* 65a). In the late Middle Ages, the practice of marrying minor girls and their exercise of the right of *miun* was discontinued.

THE SABBATH BEFORE THE WEDDING

It is customary for a groom to be called to the Torah at the Sabbath service on the Saturday preceding the wedding. This occasion is known as *aufruf* (from the Yiddish for "calling up"). The practice was based on an ancient tradition that King Solomon had erected near the Temple a chamber for grooms to receive the congratulations of family and friends (*Masechet Soferim* 19).

In medieval Europe, the principal congregational welcoming of a groom took place on the Sabbath after the wedding. An additional biblical portion (Gen. 24:1–7) was read in his honor. The regular Haftarah was supplemented with a special passage from Isaiah (61:10–62:5).

THE DAY OF THE WEDDING

The wedding day is an eventful occasion for the young couple, their families, and, to some extent, the entire community. Some medieval congregations honored the groom on the morning of his wedding day by providing a minyan for the Shacharit service at his home *(Kol Bo)*. In the Sephardic community, the festivity began on the preceding evening when the attendants of the groom tendered him a dinner at his home Avudrahim). The bride's attendants spent the evening with the bride at her home.

Bride and groom fast on their wedding day. This custom originated in the sixteenth century (Rema, *Even HaEzer* 61:1). It was based on a talmudic assertion that the sins of a bridal couple are forgiven on the day of their marriage (Jer. *Bikkurim* 3). A more prosaic explanation for the fast was the practical need for keeping the couple from tasting intoxicating drinks on that day.

In the talmudic era, virgins were married on Wednesdays and widows on Thursdays (*Ketubot* 2a). The choice of Wednesdays was influenced by the fact that rabbinic courts were in session on Mondays and Thursdays. In the event that a husband discovered that his bride was not a virgin, as she had been represented to be, he could have immediate recourse to a court.

One must not assume that there was a high incidence of false claims of virginity, requiring instant judicial intervention. The demand for court action did not come from outraged husbands but from the rabbinic leadership, the zealous guardians of family purity.

First-marriage brides were assumed to be virgins *(betulah)* and were referred to as such in the prenuptial agreement and ketubah. If the facts proved otherwise, there was ground for suspecting that an indiscretion had been committed during the extended period of betrothal. A voluntary transgression would, according to the religious law, bar the couple from further cohabitation. Even an involuntary transgression would prohibit her to her husband if he were a kohen. Considering the high standard of Jewish morality, the incidence of deception was undoubtedly very low. However, the rabbis deemed it important that judicial facilities always be available to prevent any violation of a strict biblical prohibition.

The need for immediate rabbinical adjudication was eliminated in the early Middle Ages, when the rituals of betrothal and marriage were joined into a single ceremony. If any indiscretion had occurred it could only have happened prior to the betrothal. That might warrant financial claims or possibly a divorce, but the legality of the cohabitation was not put in question. As a result, the talmudic dates for weddings were no longer of any consequence. The general medieval custom was to celebrate weddings on Fridays because of the proximity of the Sabbath, when people are free and able to join in the festivities.

The subject of a bride's virginity came to the fore once again in the ninth century. Curiously, it inspired the composition of a special benediction to be recited by the groom on the wedding night (*Siddur Rav Amram Gaon*). The groom expressed his gratitude that his bride had been spared from mishap and was able to preserve her chastity. This short-lived custom sadly reflected the organized assaults upon Jewish communities which occasionally brought dishonor to some Jewish women. The benediction was eventually discontinued for lack of precedent in the talmudic literature.

PRENUPTIAL POMP AND CEREMONY

Brides of the Temple era were borne on a palanquin to the wedding house, to the accompaniment of strains of music and much jubilation. The Talmud refers to the wedding premises as Bet Chatanim, "the house of bridegrooms" (*Ketubot* 7b). Bet Chatanim is not necessarily synonymous with the home of the groom. The reference to a "house of bridegrooms" rather than "houses of bridegrooms" seems to point to a single place where many bridegrooms celebrated their weddings. This supports our conjecture that there were public wedding halls in ancient times.

The merit of entertaining a bride and groom was greatly extolled in the Talmud (*Ketubot* 7a; *Even HaEzer* 65:1). Ancient weddings undoubtedly attracted large crowds, who joined in the festivities even if they were not dinner guests. Wealthy families built new homes, including a chuppah chamber, for their sons (*Megillah* 5b). The average family, however, could hardly accommodate the crowd of well-wishers. They probably used the facilities of the Bet Chatanim. The chuppah chamber was most likely an adjunct of this institution.

Brides and grooms of antiquity wore diadems and crowns. After the destruction of the Temple, the wearing of crowns was prohibited and so was the ceremonial palanquin (*Sotah* 49a). Instrumental music at weddings was also outlawed (ibid.). Much of the ancient pomp and ceremony was restored, however, in the Middle Ages. The bridal garland made its reappearance. As a concession to ancient restrictions, olive leaves, known for their bitter taste, were added to the garland as a symbolic reminder of Jerusalem. In the fifteenth century, the locale of wedding ceremonies was shifted to the synagogue (for a first marriage) or the open court of the synagogue (for second marriages).

COVERING A BRIDE'S FACE

The custom of covering the bride's face (*badeken*) has come to assume great importance. The groom, escorted by his attendants and parents, is taken to the bride and he lowers the veil over her face. This practice is based on the precendent of Rebecca, who "took the veil and covered herself" (Gen. 24:65) prior to her meeting with Isaac. After the "covering" of the bride, the people respond with the blessing which was bestowed upon Rebecca: "Our sister, be thou the mother of thousands of ten thousands" (Gen. 24:60).

THE WEDDING RING

The custom of using rings in marriage ceremonies began approximately in the seventh century. Due to the popularity of the practice, the use of the ring was officially incorporated into the groom's declaration of betrothal: "You are betrothed unto me with this ring . . ." The ring is placed on the index finger of the bride's right hand, where it has prominent visibility.

Medieval rabbis prohibited the use of rings with gems. If the bride misjudged the worth of the gem and consented to the marriage under the false impression that she was the recipient of a precious stone of great value, the validity of the marriage might be affected (*Kol Bo*). Wedding rings may come in any shape and design and have inscriptions on them. Medieval wedding rings were occasionally inscribed with the words "Mazal Tov."

THE ORIGIN OF THE CHUPPAH

The association of the term *chuppah* with the wedding rite can be traced to the Bible. However, the physical appearance of the chuppah and its religious significance have undergone many changes.

The etymological meaning of *chuppah* is "cover." Thus *chafu ish rosho* (II Sam. 15:30) means "every man covered his head." Isaiah applied the term *chuppah* to a canopy formed by a cloud (4:6). Chuppah also meant a covered place or a chamber. In time, as an extension of this connotation, the word also came to designate a bridal room.

Unlike the chuppah of the talmudic era, which was used for the purpose of consummating the marriage after the wedding ceremony, the chuppah of biblical times was a room where either the bride or the groom whiled away the time prior to the ceremony. The rising sun was poetically compared to "a bridegroom coming out of his chuppah" (Ps. 19:6). This simile obviously portrayed the impatience and vigor of a groom emerging from the chuppah to meet his bride. The prophet Joel, bearing an important message, urged the groom to come out of his room and the bride from the chuppah (2:16). This clearly indicates the prenuptial use of two separate rooms by bride and groom.

The chuppah of the talmudic era was a beautifully appointed chamber, "covered" with curtains and ornaments (Jer. *Sotah* 9:16). Bridal couples did not enter the chuppah immediately after the ceremony. They first spent an hour together in an ordinary room so that they could get used to one another (*Ketubot* 12a). The bride then entered the chuppah by herself. Etiquette dictated that the groom obtain the bride's permission before joining her in the chuppah (*Lev. Rabbah* 9).

The legal and religious significance of the chuppah chamber played a decisive role in the establishment of matrimony. A betrothed couple who had entered a chuppah chamber were considered legally married, even if the preceding ceremony had been omitted. The required Sheva Berachot could subsequently be recited at the wedding banquet or other meals.

The use of a chuppah chamber was discontinued in post-talmudic times. The name *chuppah,* however, was retained to designate the cloth or tallit which was spread over the heads of the couple, a "cover" which created the semblance of a room. A tallit is still used in the modern Sephardic rite.

Initially, no special significance was attached to an open-air ceremony. In time, however, a ceremony under the stars took on great importance due to a symbolic association with a biblical blessing: "I will multiply your seeds as the stars of heaven" (Exod. 32:13). Rema's inclusion of this custom in his annotations to the code (*Even HaEzer*

61:1) gave the practice great prominence and widespread acceptance.

Ready-made chuppot, consisting of four poles and a canopy, came into use in the sixteenth century.

THE KIDDUSHIN RITUAL

The groom is led to his place under the canopy. The bride is then escorted to her place near the groom, symbolizing her arrival at her husband's home. Some rabbis found a precedent for this custom in the biblical narration of the creation of Eve. God was her escort "and brought her unto Adam" (Gen. 2:22). The choice of her place, on the right side of the groom, was based on a verse in Psalms: "At the right hand does the queen stand" (45:10).

It is customary for the bride to circle the groom three times. This practice is based on Jeremiah 31:21: "A woman shall go around [or court] a man." The three circles match the three expressions of betrothal mentioned in Hosea: "And I will betroth thee unto me forever, and I will betroth thee unto me in righteousness . . ., and I will betroth thee unto me in faithfulness . . ." (2:21–22).

The religious ceremony begins with the recitation of the benediction over wine. This is followed by a second benediction ("who sanctifies his people Israel by the rite of the chuppah and kiddushin"; *Ketubot* 7b). The groom then drinks from the cup and offers some to the bride. The wine, like the ring, becomes part of the bride's consideration which establishes the state of betrothal (*Machzor Vitry* 476).

Following the drinking of the wine, the groom holds the ring close to the bride's index finger and declares his intent to betroth the bride with the ring (*hare at* . . .). The declaration precedes the slipping on of the ring so that the bride may understand beforehand the purpose of the ring. By accepting it, the bride indicates her assent.

There is no official text prescribed in the Talmud for the groom's declaration of intent. It was most likely confined to a brief statement: "You are betrothed unto me." In the Middle Ages the phrase "in accordance with the laws of Moses and Israel" was appended to his declaration. There is some indication that part of this phrase was used in ancient times. According to the Book of Tobit, Raguel gave his daughter, Sara, to Tobias and declared: "Behold, take her after the law of Moses" (7:13).

The first part of the wedding ceremony ends with the giving of the ring, which establishes the betrothal. This part theoretically does not require a chuppah since the chuppah is the symbolic home of the groom. Betrothals, however, were performed in the home of the bride in the talmudic era. Even after the betrothal ritual and the wedding ritual were combined into a single ceremony in the early Middle Ages, there was a time when the tallit was spread over the heads of the couple after the completion of the kiddushin (*Kol Bo* 75). However, with the introduction of ready-made chuppot which were set up beforehand, the entire ceremony was conducted under the canopy.

THE READING OF THE KETUBAH

The custom of reading the ketubah upon the conclusion of the rite of betrothal is attributed to Rashi (11th cent.). According to the Talmud, no bride may come to live with her husband unless she possesses a ketubah (*Kallah* 1). Since ancient marriages were consummated shortly after the wedding ceremony, it was imperative to have the document executed prior to the beginning of the second rite.

The reading of the ketubah serves two purposes. It marks the brief interlude between betrothal and marriage. It also demonstrates the availability of the ketubah so that the marriage ceremony may proceed as planned. When the reading of the ketubah is finished, it is given to the bride for safekeeping.

THE ORIGIN OF THE KETUBAH

Prenuptial agreements were common in ancient Israel long before the emergence of the ketubah. The earliest-known marriage contract, dating from about 440 B.C.E., is a covenant between the groom and his prospective father-in-law (Sayce and Cowley, *Aramaic Papyri Discovered at Assuan*). It is a comprehensive document which combines several elements of what came to be subsequently known as *tenaim*, *shetar erusin*, and ketubah. One of the major provisions of this document is contrary to biblical law. The Book of Tobit (ca. 3rd cent. B.C.E.) mentions an "instrument of covenant" written by the bride's father (7:14). The father had made some financial commitments and apparently put them in writing.

A ketubah (written document) records the groom's financial obligations to his bride. It is signed by witnesses who act in her behalf. The Talmud credits Rabbi Simon b. Shotach (1st cent. B.C.E.) with the introduction of ketubot (*Shabbat* 14b). This does not imply that ketubot were unknown prior to his time. According to Rabbi Simon b. Gamliel (2nd cent.), ketubot date back to biblical times (*Ketubot* 10a). Rabbi

Simon b. Shotach was given the credit of authorship because of his important contribution in making the ketubah a practical and enforceable document (*Ketubot* 82b).

The need for a ketubah arose from the biblical law which grants a husband the right to divorce his wife without her consent. This left the wife in an insecure financial position. The ketubah was designed to remedy the situation by providing a financial settlement to the wife in the event of the husband's death or a divorce. In effect, the ketubah was presumed to act as a deterrent against hasty divorces (*Ketubot* 82b).

The early ketubot brought little relief to the wife. Heirs of the husband's estate managed to defeat the wife's claims by a transfer of title. In the reign of Alexander Jannai (d. 76 B.C.E.), a fervent Sadducee, the position of the wife became even more precarious. The Sadduceans followed a strict interpretation of biblical law, and the Bible does not specifically provide for the payment of a settlement upon the husband's death or a divorce.

Rabbi Simon b. Shotach was the leading rabbinical figure who succeeded in restoring rabbinical authority. The financial insecurity of married women was one of the problems which claimed his attention. Since various remedial measures enacted by other rabbis had proven ineffective, many girls took matters into their own hands and refused to enter into matrimony. To put an end to the boycott, Rabbi Simon decreed that a woman's claim under the ketubah forms a lien upon her husband's property which cannot be alienated (*Ketubot* 82b).

THE MARRIAGE RITUAL

The second part of the wedding ceremony, marking the transfer from betrothal to marriage, is known as *nisuin* ("marriage") or *birkat chatanim* ("benedictions of grooms"). It consists of seven benedictions (*sheva berachot*): (1) wine, (2) *Bara lichevodo* (a call upon the guests to glorify God), (3) *Yotzer haadam* (the creation of Adam), (4) *Asher yatzar* (the union of Adam and Eve), (5) *Sos tasis* (restoration of Jerusalem), (6) *Sameach tesamach* (prayer for a happy marriage), (7) *Asher bara* ("may the sounds of conjugal joy fill the land of Israel").

The text of the *sheva berachot* was published in the third century (*Ketubot* 8a). The presence of a minyan is required for the performance of this ceremony (ibid. 7b).

Upon the conclusion of the ceremony, the groom breaks a glass in memory of the destruction of Zion. Some medieval congregations had a special stone built into the exterior of the synagogue wall so the groom could hurl the glass against it. (For a discussion of this custom and other mourning practices at weddings, see below chap. 14, "Avele Zion.")

The custom of throwing wheat and rice in the path of the bridal couple, a symbol of prosperity and fertility, dates back to the talmudic era (*Berachot* 50b).

Ever since the elimination of the talmudic chuppah, marriages are no longer consummated immediately after the conclusion of the wedding ceremony. In place of the bridal chamber, the custom of *yichud* ("privacy") has been instituted. The couple is taken to a room where they have complete privacy, symbolizing the intimacy between husband and wife.

MAZAL TOV

No sooner does the groom break the glass than a rising crescendo of exclamations of Mazal Tov fills the hall. It would come as a jolting shock to the guests if they were to realize that they had just uttered a prayer that a favorable planetary constellation bestow prosperity and bliss upon the young couple. Of course, all that the guests wanted to do was to wish the bride and groom good luck.

The Hebrew word *mazal* means "zodiac." The belief in astrology, the decisive influence of heavenly planets upon the affairs of man, was pervasive in postbiblical times.

Some rabbis of the talmudic era subscribed to the view that heavenly bodies influence human behavior, but they limited the scope of this impact in order to reconcile the conflict between the principle of fate and the tradition of free will. According to Josephus' assessment of the doctrine of rabbinical Judaism, stars may determine a man's poverty or wealth, his wisdom or foolishness, but the choice of good and evil, virtue or immorality, is left to human discretion (*Wars* 2:8). In contrast to this opinion, some rabbis categorically denied any interaction between the stars and men. Rabbi Yochanan (3rd cent.) dismissed astrology in a three-word statement: *Ein mazal leyisrael* ("Israel is not subject to planetary influences"; *Shabbat* 156a).

In time the word *mazal* lost its original connotation and took on the meaning of "luck." Chance is a vital factor in the fortunes of man and is most significant in the choice of a mate. Marriage is a serious gamble, fraught with unpredictable consequences. It is not surprising that the exclamation of Mazal Tov has been the most popular greeting extended to newlyweds.

Astrological terms have long since attached themselves to ketubot as a comforting assurance to concerned parents. The phrase *besiman tov* ("under a good sign") regularly appeared in the artistic frame of seventeenth-century ketubot. The Aramaic version of Mazal Tov, *bemazla maalya,* made its appearance in the eighteenth century. As we have already noted, Mazal Tov was engraved on some medieval wedding rings.

THE FESTIVE BRIDAL WEEK

Wedding festivities have always extended beyond the wedding day. According to the Talmud, it was Moses who ordained seven days of festivities (Jer. *Ketubot* 1). This parallels the length of the major biblical festivals. A festive week became standard practice. Laban delayed Rachel's wedding until the completion of Leah's festive week (Gen. 29:27; Jer. *Moed Katan* 1). However, there seem to have been some variations. Tobias' first wedding celebration, at the bride's home, lasted fourteen days (Tobit 8). The second celebration, at his father's home, lasted seven days (ibid., chap. 11).

In the first week of marriage, the Sheva Berachot are recited daily after Grace, whenever new people are present. One may extend the festivity for an entire month or even a year (*Ketubot* 8a). The Bible designated the first year of marriage a period of marital joy during which the husband is exempt from military service (Deut. 24:5).

JUDAIC ATTITUDE TO MARITAL SEX

A rigorous code of morality normally tends to frown upon untrammeled indulgence in marital sex. Judaism, despite its strict laws of morality, is free from such a restrictive attitude. Husbands are enjoined in the Bible not to neglect the sexual needs of their wives (Exod. 21:10). Such concern is particularly understandable in a society in which polygamy was permissible. A flexible schedule of minimal sexual activity was published in the Talmud (*Ketubot* 61b). The husband's sexual obligation is one of the commitments mentioned in the ketubah (*Nachalat Shivah* 12:33).

The Song of Songs is a paean of love, colored by nuances of the joy of marital sex. Ecclesiastes proclaimed "a time to love" (3:8). It also urged men to "enjoy life with the wife whom thou lovest . . ." (9:9).

The Talmud noted that men and women express their sexual desires in different ways. "A woman demands with her heart, a man demands with his mouth" (*Eruvin* 100b). Men were therefore instructed to recognize the subtleties of behavior which signal the wife's state of mind. The Talmud listed specific occasions when conjugal love is appropriate. The night when a wife immerses in the mikveh is a time for affection. Another occasion is the night prior to a husband's departure on an extended journey (*Yevamot* 62a).

A husband's explicit sexual obligation is matched by a wife's implicit duty to engage in sex. However, no husband may force his attention upon his wife without her consent. Despite Judaism's progressive attitude to marital sex, the Talmud cautions against overindulgence (*Berachot* 22a), for excess deprives sex of its romanticism and dehumanizes an important privilege of marriage.

Rabbinic Judaism never regarded marital sex as an impure or evil function which is tolerated only for the sake of procreation. A husband's sexual obligation is not suspended during a wife's pregnancy. Widowers and divorced men are urged to remarry, even if they have already fulfilled the mitzvah of procreation (*Yevamot* 61b).

Curiously, the nonrabbinic literature of the talmudic era, under Essenic influence, links marital sex to the exclusive purpose of reproduction. In his review of the biblical law of marriage, Josephus stated: "That law allows no other mixing of the sexes but that of a man with his wife, and that this be used only for the procreation of children . . ." (*Against Apion* 2:25). He repeated the same opinion in his discussion of the law of the rebellious son (Deut. 21:18). The parents, he said, must first attempt to reform their son by pointing to their own virtuous life. They tell him "that they cohabited together, not for the sake of pleasure . . . but that they might have children" (*Antiq.* 4:24). A similar intent was proclaimed by Tobias in his postnuptial prayer: "And now, O Lord, I take not this my sister for lust" (Tobit 8:7).

The stringent moralist inhibitions of medieval Jewry tended to introduce an element of primness and restraint in the sex act. According to *Kol Bo* (ca. 14th cent.): "It is a positive command of the Torah that a man take a woman to be his wife for the purpose of bringing children into the world. His intent shall be the perpetuation of the species rather than the derivation of pleasure" (75). In another place the treatise said: "The less one indulges in sexual activity, the more praiseworthy he is, provided there is no infringement upon the sexual prerogatives of his wife" (ibid.). Despite the moralist tone, there is no intimation that intercourse is intrinsically evil. Considering the *Kol Bo's* sanction of extensive sexual foreplay, it is clear that the importance of sex in promoting marital harmony was not overlooked by the medieval sages.

PROCREATION

The biblical injunction of procreation devolves, according to the prevailing talmudic opinion, solely upon the man (*Yevamot* 65a). Since the initiative of establishing a marriage is traditionally in the hands of the man, it would be unfair to charge the woman with a duty over which she has no control.

The mitzvah of procreation is based on the biblical mandate which commanded: "Be fruitful and multiply" (Gen. 1:28). According to the School of Shammai, this mitzvah is fulfilled only when one sires two sons. Apparently they felt that the greater attrition of men through war requires a compensatory replacement through birth. The School of Hillel expressed the prevailing opinion that the mitzvah of procreation is fulfilled with the birth of a boy and a girl. Thus the biological needs of the succeeding generation would be met (*Yevamot* 61b).

The biblical command of procreation comprises two distinct parts, "be fruitful" and "multiply." The first part can conceivably be satisfied even with the birth of a single child, the "fruit" of a marriage. However, "multiplication" implies an increase in population, which can be achieved only through a high birth-rate, exceeding the minimum of two children per family. Even to maintain zero population growth, 2.1 children are required per woman of childbearing age. A much higher rate was needed under the primitive sanitary conditions of antiquity.

Jews managed to maintain their numbers, and even register an increase from time to time, despite prolonged homelessness and not infrequent massacres. Religious restrictions on most forms of contraception and early marriages were responsible for the physical survival of the Jewish people. The elimination of both factors has posed a serious threat to the modern Jewish community.

FAMILY PURITY

Sexual relations are prohibited beginning with the onset of the menstrual cycle (Lev. 18:9, 20:18). Biblical law extended the restriction for a period of seven days after the end of the flow (Lev. 15:28). Rabbinical law decreed a minimal period of five "impure days" and

seven "clean days." White undergarments must be worn during the
"clean days," and the woman must examine herself twice daily to
confirm the end of the flow. The ritual immersion takes place on the
evening of the same day of the week that the "clean days" began.

A hot bath, trimming of the nails, and rinsing of the hair are
prerequisites to immersion. Bandages and jewelry, which prevent the
contact of water with the entire surface of the body, must be removed.
A benediction, "Blessed . . . who commanded us concerning the
immersion," is recited after the immersion.

The laws of family purity were widely observed in ancient times.
Indeed, in one important respect, women are said to have voluntarily
added to the severity of the law without rabbinical prompting. Biblical
law imposes seven clean days only if preceded by a full menstrual flow.
Women, however, came to regard even a stain as evidence of the onset
of menstruation (*Berachot* 31a).

Ritual immersion was prohibited in the period of the Hadrianic
persecution (2nd cent.; *Meilah* 7a). Apparently, the family purity laws
were regarded as being as fundamental to Judaism as the Sabbath and
circumcision, which were also proscribed. It is possible that the
Romans contemplated the genocide of the religious element of the
people by stopping their sexual activities.

Despite widespread observance of the purity laws, there was
enough neglect to provoke rabbinic strictures. Women were warned
that failure to observe the law contributed to death in childbirth
(*Shabbat* 31b), and that children conceived during the menstrual period
were afflicted with a skin disease (*Kallah Rabbati* 1). On the other hand,
the rabbis asserted, the reward of scholarly children could be expected
by those who were meticulous in their observance of the law (*Shevuot*
18b). Whatever neglect of the law existed, it was probably due to the
lack of mikveh facilities in many parts of the country.

To lessen sexual temptation, the rabbis prohibited couples from
sleeping in the same bed during the menstrual period (Num. Rabbah
10:22). Wives were also cautioned against performing personal services for their husbands of the type which might stimulate affection
and sexual desires (*Ketubot* 61a). An extreme view that wives should
refrain from using cosmetics during the menstrual period was over-
ruled by Rabbi Akiva (2nd cent.) on the ground that a wife should
always appear attractive to her husband (*Ketubot* 64b).

There is an allusion in talmudic literature to an ancient custom of
menstrual women moving out of the home for two or three days

(*Eichah Rabbati* 5:18). Such is still the custom of some Falasha women in Ethiopia.

The Talmud offered two rationales for the sexual restrictions during the menstrual period, sanitary and psychological. One rabbi alleged that intercourse at that time causes skin disease in the offspring (*Tanchuma, Metzora* 1). Another rabbi compared the menstrual period to the three years of Orlah (fruit of a newly planted tree which is considered unhealthy; *Lev. Rabbah* 25:8); still another rabbi regarded the period of sexual abstinence as a boon to marital bliss by keeping the romantic flame alive (*Niddah* 31b). (For a further discussion of the significance of ritual immersions, see chap. 2, "A Symbol of Consecration.")

LEVIRATE MARRIAGE

It is the duty of a man to marry his deceased brother's widow if he died without issue (Deut. 25:5). This law applies alike to widows who had merely been betrothed and to those who were already married (*Yevamot* 13b). Samaritan tradition limits levirate marriages to the former only.

Levirate marriages were practiced by some ancient peoples prior to the Sinaitic covenant. Tamar's effort to woo her father-in-law, Judah, into marriage (Gen. 38) conformed to provisions of Hittite law. Whereas the Bible limits levirate marriage to brothers of the deceased, some ancient codes included all next of kin. Article 193 of the Hittite code provides: "If a man takes a wife and then the man dies, his brother shall take his wife, (then) his father shall take her."

According to Josephus, the first son of a levirate marriage is named for the deceased and inherits the latter's estate (*Antiq.* 4:23). This interpretation was rejected in the Talmud (*Yevamot* 24a). By marrying the widow, the brother perpetuates the name (estate) of the deceased within the family.

If the brother refuses to marry the widow, he must release her so that she is free to marry any other man. The religious procedure of releasing the widow is known as *chalitzah* ("removal"). The widow disgraces the brother-in-law by removing the shoe from his right foot and spitting on the ground in front of him (Deut. 25:9). A special ritual "shoe" is used for this religious ceremony.

Despite the biblical preference for levirate marriage over *chalitzah*, the Talmud gave priority to the latter. Normally, a marriage between a

man and his brother's widow is prohibited, except when the man died
without issue. Compelling agricultural reasons in the biblical era
dictated the need to preserve the estate of the deceased. With the
elimination of those reasons in the postbiblical era, levirate marriage
lost its attractiveness. The rabbis rationalized their change of the
biblical priorities. Said one rabbi: "The mitzvah of levirate marriage
was preferred at first [in the Bible] over the mitzvah of *chalitzah* because
there was a desire [on the part of the surviving brother] to fulfill the
intent of the mitzvah. Now that they do not desire to fulfill the intent of
the mitzvah, the mitzvah of *chalitzah* comes first" (*Bechorot* 13a).
Another rabbi expressed reservations about the morality of levirate
marriages in his day: "If one marries his sister-in-law because of her
beauty, for sex, or for other reasons, it takes on the appearance of incest
and I look at the child of this marriage as if he were illegitimate"
(*Yevamot* 39b). Despite these bold assertions of the rabbis of the
Mishnah, the Amoraim of the succeeding generations hesitated to
adopt such daring views in contradiction to the Bible, and refused to
assign priority to either rite.

When Rabbenu Gershom outlawed polygamy (beginning of the 11th
cent.), levirate marriage could no longer be practiced because in most
cases the surviving brother had a wife. Thereafter, *chalitzah* became the
sole acceptable rite.

IV.
DIVORCE

Biblical divorce law flows directly from the Bible's perception of the
establishment of marriage. A marital state is effected when a man
"takes" a wife and the wife consents to be "taken." In the event of the
dissolution of a marriage, the man has to give up what he previously
took. Theoretically, the consent of another party is not required for an
act of surrender. A wife cannot initiate a divorce proceeding because
she did not "take" the husband and consequently cannot give him up.

While the legal theory behind this reasoning is sound, biblical law in
effect created a situation in which the husband has all the advantages
and the wife none. A husband can divorce his wife against her will. He
may adamantly refuse to divorce his wife despite her unhappiness. If
he disappears his wife becomes an *agunah* ("bound woman"), barred
from ever marrying another man.

The biblical concept of marriage was designed to protect the woman under the conditions prevailing in ancient society. Women enjoyed neither political nor economic equality. A woman's safety and happiness depended upon the protection of a man, first her father and then her husband. Such conditions, of course, no longer prevail in most civilized countries.

Rabbinic Judaism contributed much toward the elimination of the legal disadvantages of wives, but it could not go outside the framework of the biblical concept of marriage. The Talmud interpreted biblical statutes but it could not abrogate them. Had it attempted to do so, it would have destroyed the very basis of Rabbinic Judaism, the belief in the divinity and immutability of the Bible. The perception of marriage as a status created by the "taking" of the husband is too firmly established in the Bible to permit rabbinical amendment.

The process of ameliorating the wife's legal position began in the first century B.C.E. with the introduction of the ketubah (a binding financial settlement) by Rabbi Simon b. Shotach (*Ketubot* 82b). The ketubah served as a deterrent against capricious and hasty divorces.

The legal right of a husband to divorce his wife against her will was not questioned in the Talmud. However, the rabbis severely criticized individuals who divorced their wives without justifiable grounds. The need for such grounds was indicated in the Bible: "And when it comes to pass, if she finds no favor in his eyes, because he discovered an indecency in her conduct . . ." (Deut. 24:1). The Schools of Shammai and Hillel differed in their interpretations of this verse. The former considered immoral conduct to be the only justifiable grounds. The latter deemed incompetency as a housewife sufficient reason for divorce. Rabbi Akiva was even more liberal, favoring divorce whenever a marriage fails to provide a base for happiness (*Gittin* 90a).

Rava made it clear in the fourth century that the validity of a husband's divorce is not affected by the absence of justifiable grounds (*Gittin* 90a). Even the School of Shammai's insistence on charges of moral misconduct did not deprive the husband of his intrinsic power to divorce his wife at will. There is therefore no similarity between the opinion of the School of Shammai and the ruling in the New Testament which outlawed divorces except in the case of a wife's adultery (Matt. 5:32).

While the right of the husband to divorce his wife was not curtailed, the Talmud corrected the imbalance by listing grounds justifying a wife's demand for a divorce. Since she lacked the power to initiate such an action, the rabbis resorted to their prerogative of applying coercive measures to force recalcitrant litigants to comply with their directives. If there were sufficient grounds, the rabbis forced the husband to divorce his wife.

The following justifiable grounds, entitling a woman to a divorce, were published in the second century: the husband's development of major physical defects, conditions under which cohabitation is impossible, engagement in a malodorous trade, chronic bad breath, etc. Rabbi Ami (3rd cent.) ruled that a husband's addition of a second wife is ground for a demand for a divorce by the first wife (*Yevamot* 65a). If a wife is childless and the husband is the cause of that condition, she may demand a divorce (ibid.).

The concern for the plight of the wife was further indicated by a post-mishnaic regulation that the wife pay the fee of the scribe who writes the divorce. According to the Bible, "he [the husband] shall write the bill of divorcement" (Deut. 24:1). That was interpreted in the Talmud as the placing of the obligation to secure a scribe and pay him for his services upon the husband (*Baba Batra* 168a). Unfortunately, some husbands refused their wives' demands for a divorce because they did not want to incur the expense. Is it legal for a wife to pay the scribe? One may argue against it because the divorce document has to be the husband's property, which he transfers to his wife. The rabbis overcame this objection by a juridical transfer of the title to the wife's money to her husband.

The most far-reaching regulation which brought a large measure of equality to women was the enactment of Rabbenu Gershom (beginning of 11th cent.) requiring a wife's consent to a divorce. In effect, rabbis refused to preside over a divorce proceeding without the wife's consent, thus preventing the husband from exercising his legal right. The trend toward improving the wife's position continued throughout the medieval period. A husband's intolerable temper and wife-beating were added to the grounds justifying a wife's demand for a divorce (Rema, *Even HaEzer* 154:2).

In the eighteenth and nineteenth centuries, the end of Jewish communal autonomy deprived rabbinic courts of their power to employ coercive measures. This resulted in a setback to the cause of equality of women because the rabbis could no longer compel a husband to grant a divorce.

Rabbinic courts in Israel have jurisdiction over divorce proceedings. They wield greater power than the medieval rabbinic courts, yet they too cannot relieve a woman's plight in all instances. They cannot help a woman if her husband is missing. A stubborn husband can still refuse to divorce his wife, if he is willing to take the punishment.

Orthodox women who are active in the feminist movement have repeatedly brought to the attention of the rabbinate the legal disadvantages of a wife. Reform rabbis recognize civil divorces. Conservative rabbis require a religious divorce, but solved the problem of the agunah by inserting a clause in the ketubah in which the husband authorizes the rabbinic court to act in his behalf if an occasion for instituting a divorce proceeding should arise. The legality of this clause, or of a previous proposal for the institution of conditional marriages, has been disputed by most Orthodox rabbis. In view of the sensitive nature of this problem, it is unlikely that an innovative solution, acceptable to all, will emerge in the near future.

BILL OF DIVORCEMENT

The biblical term for a divorce is *sefer keritut* ("a document of severance"; Deut. 24:1). The talmudic term for a divorce is *get peturin* ("a document of conclusion"; *Gittin* 85a) or simply *get*. It is assumed that the term *get* is derived from its numerical value, 12. There are twelve lines in a traditional divorce. The rabbinical reluctance to use the term *sefer keritut* was probably due to its common application to the punishment of extirpation inflicted by heaven (from the Hebrew *karet*). The talmudic tractate dealing with that subject is called *Keritut*.

The Bible spells out three basic steps essential to the implementation of a divorce: (1) there must be a written document; (2) the husband must transfer the divorce to the wife; (3) the wife must leave the husband's premises (Deut. 24:1).

The text of a divorce did not have to conform to a specific formula. According to a mishnah, the core of the text is the sentence: "You are free to marry any man" (*Gittin* 85a). It is likely that this sentence comprised the full text of an ancient divorce. In a time when people spent most of their lives in one location, and residents of a town knew each other, such a document was adequate. In the talmudic era, when people frequently moved from place to place, and husbands, separated from their wives, occasionally sent divorces by messengers from distant countries, it was essential to make sure of the identity of the parties to the divorce. By rabbinic decree the divorce document must clearly identify the parties, the residence of each party, and the name of the river which borders the town. The document must be dated and bear the signatures of attesting witnesses.

The discovery of the so-called Assuan Ketubah, dating from the fourth century B.C.E., brought to light the practice of an isolated Jewish community in ancient Egypt which was at variance with the biblical divorce procedure. Women, like men, had the right to institute divorce actions. A divorce went into effect through an oral declaration in the congregation. However, if the wife initiated the divorce, she forfeited the dowry and the financial settlement which she had received from her husband. On the other hand, if the husband divorced his wife, he kept the dowry and reclaimed his financial settlement.

The religious practices of the Assuan Jewish community had an admixture of idolatrous elements derived from contacts with non-Jewish neighbors. The right of women to initiate a divorce action was one of the borrowed practices.

Curiously, the talmudic literature alludes to the non-Jewish practice of imposing a financial penalty upon a wife who divorces her husband. According to a midrash, women of prediluvian society had a legal right to divorce their mates. However, they were penalized by a provision which required them to pay double the amount of the marriage settlement (*Gen. Rabbah* 18).

V.
BIKKUR CHOLIM

The traditional practice of visiting the sick (*bikkur cholim*) has been part of the voluntary health service offered by Jews to the sick. These visitations were not mere social calls for the purpose of cheering up a patient. A visitor was expected to look after the patient and attend to his needs (*Nedarim* 39b). In an age when hospitals were unknown and professional nursing unavailable, the mitzvah of bikkur cholim frequently spelled the difference between life and death. Rabbi Akiva (2nd cent.) stressed the sanitary significance of the custom by stating: "He who does not visit the sick is [as guilty] as if he had shed blood" (*Nedarim* 40a).

The practice of visiting the sick is as ancient as Jewish history. In its early stages the custom was principally confined to calls on dying persons to help complete any unfinished business, make last-minute arrangements, or bid a final farewell. Jacob's last illness brought Joseph to his bedside to secure a blessing for his children (Gen. 48:1). The illness was also the occasion for Jacob's summons of his sons to his bedside to receive his last instructions (Gen. 49:1). King Joash called on the prophet Elisha when the latter "had fallen sick of the sickness whereof he was to die" (II Kings 13:14). Isaiah visited King Hezekiah when the latter "was sick unto death" (II Kings 20:1). However, the Bible also records visits to the sick as a sign of respect (II Kings 9:16).

The Hebrew word *bikkur* means "inquiry" or "examination" (Lev. 13:36, 27:33). It has a common root with *boker* ("morning" or "shine"). An examination gets the best results if it is carried out in the light of day or sunshine. In biblical usage, *bikkur* did not have the connotation of a sick call. David prayed for the privilege of "visiting his temple," i.e., to examine the magnificence of the structure (*levaker behechalo*; Ps. 27:4). In the time of the Mishnah, however, *bikkur* became a technical expression for visiting the sick (*Nedarim* 38b, *Berachot* 28b, *Sanhedrin* 68a, *Gittin* 61a, et al.). The adoption of this term reflects the development of the custom of bikkur cholim into a mission of inquiry into the condition of the patient.

In addition to the sanitary significance of bikkur cholim, the rabbis also sensed the value of this humane gesture in the promotion of interfaith harmony. They therefore urged Jews to disregard faith in visiting the sick (*Gittin* 61a).

Amoraim of the third century enhanced the importance of bikkur cholim by attributing great merit to this act of kindness. The social and economic conditions of the period may have contributed to the greater rabbinic emphasis on the need for visiting the sick. Rabbi Yochanan declared that bikkur cholim is one of six deeds "the fruits of which man eats in this world, while the principal remains for him in the world to come" (*Shabbat* 127a). His statement was an elaboration of a mishnah which had listed only four deeds; bikkur cholim was not among them (*Peah* 1:1).

Abaye (4th cent.) extended the practice of visitation to include sick children (*Nedarim* 39b). Rava (4th cent.) declared that the mitzvah of bikkur cholim is not fulfilled with a single visit. If the patient requires more attention, one should repeatedly visit him on that day (ibid.).

Despite the promotion of bikkur cholim, the rabbis did not lose sight of its practical limitations. Thus it was declared that in the first three days of illness, visitation rights be limited to members of the family (Jer. *Peah* 3). People were also advised not to visit a patient during the first and last three hours of the day (*Nedarim* 40a). According to Maimonides, these two periods are normally devoted to the medical care of the sick (*Hilchot Avel* 14:5). The Talmud also lists some categories of illnesses which are very debilitating and make conversation burdensome. Such patients should be visited only if and when it is essential.

One of the important functions of bikkur cholim is the offering of a prayer at the patient's bedside. Rabbi Jose (2nd cent.) published the text of a brief prayer: "May the Almighty have compassion upon you in the midst of the sick of Israel" (*Shabbat* 12b). It was presumed that a prayer interceding for all sick people was more likely to be answered.

Bikkur Cholim societies have been established since the thirteenth century. They raised funds to provide medical and financial assistance to indigent patients. Similar societies in modern times visit hospitalized patients to take care of their religious needs. An organized chaplaincy service is provided in the City of New York by the New York Board of Rabbis. Individual rabbis render a similar service in all Jewish communities.

VI.
MOURNING RITUALS

Judaic mourning rituals are based on ancient customs, many of which antedate the Sinaitic code. The Bible records the following mourning practices of the patriarchal era: weeping and eulogizing (Gen. 23:2), rending of garments, the wearing of sackcloth (Gen. 37:34), and the offering of condolences (Gen. 37:35). Jacob was mourned for seven days (Gen. 50:10). A thirty-day mourning period is mentioned later in connection with the death of Moses (Deut. 34:8).

The Pentateuch did not prescribe any specific mourning rituals. Ancient customs were well established by that time and apparently there was no need for restating them. There are, however, references to heathen rites which Jews were forbidden to practice. These included the "making of baldness upon the head," the shaving of the corners of the beard, and "the making of cuttings in the flesh." The first admonition against such practices was addressed to kohanim (Lev. 21:5). The injunction was repeated later to all Jews (Deut. 14:1) on the ground that such rites are incompatible with holiness (Deut. 14:2).

These prohibitions were apparently forgotten or ignored due to pervasive heathen influences. Some Jews were still practicing the forbidden rites at the time of the destruction of the First Temple (Jer. 16:6, 41:5).

The pentateuchal silence on the subject of mandatory mourning rituals led some rabbis to the conclusion that the detailed talmudic laws of mourning are of post-pentateuchal origin. According to

Maimonides, the biblical mourning period is limited to a single day (*Hilchot Avel* 1:1). On the other hand, the law of *aninut* (mourning rites prior to burial) appears to be based on a specific biblical reference (Lev. 10:19).

The Prophets and Hagiographa list additional ancient mourning customs: dust on the head (Josh. 7:6, Esther 4:3), mourner's garments (II Sam. 14:2), removal of shoes (Ezek. 24:1), abstention from using cosmetic oils (II Sam. 14:2), the covering of the head and upper lip (II Sam. 15:30), silent grief (Lev. 10:3, Amos 5:13, Lam. 3:28), sitting down and weeping (Neh. 1:4), visits of condolence (Eccles. 7:2), a condolence meal (Jer. 16:7, Ezek. 24:17), a condolence cup of wine (Jer. 16:7). All these customs laid the groundwork for the religious practices subsequently enacted into law by the Talmud.

ONAN

A mourning relative, prior to the burial of a deceased, is called an *onan* (from the Hebrew for "grief"; Gen. 35:18, Deut. 26:14). An onan may not eat meat, drink wine, or engage in sexual intercourse. He is exempt from the performance of mitzvot so that he may devote his entire time to the making of funeral arrangements (*Moed Katan* 23b, *Berachot* 17b).

The first ritual of an onan is *keriah* (the rending of garments; Lev. 10:6, *Moed Katan* 15a). The left side of the garment is rent upon the passing of a parent, the right side for other relatives (spouse, child, sibling). The Talmud prescribed a benediction to be recited by members of a family upon an occurrence of death: "Blessed . . . the true judge" (*Berachot* 59b). The wording may have been inspired by a verse in Jeremiah: "But the Lord is the true God, at his wrath the earth trembles . . ." (10:10). The talmudic benediction was not initially associated with keriah. However, since keriah is the first rite following death, the benediction was linked to it.

An onan is charged with the prime responsibility for making the required preparations for the funeral and burial—*taharah* (the washing of the body; *Shabbat* 151a), the procurement of *tacharichim* (shrouds of white linen; *Moed Katan* 27b), the digging of a grave, and the burial.

Burial societies *(chevrah kadisha)*, first established in the Middle Ages, assumed some of the preparatory tasks (Abrahams, *Jewish Life in the Middle Ages*, p. 357). Modern commercial undertaking establishments provide all the services required of an onan, but his exemption from performing ˙mitzvot has not been lifted because he still has the responsibility for making all the arrangements.

Jewish tradition mandates burial on the day of death (*Sanhedrin* 46a). A delayed burial degrades the body and contaminates the environment (Deut. 21:23). This was particularly true in the damp, hot climate of Israel. Exceptions are made when a delay is called for in the interest of honoring the deceased (*Yoreh Deah* 357:1).

It is considered disrespectful to leave a body unattended. It is the duty of an onan to procure the services of a watchman (*Ketubot* 18a).

Traditional Judaism objects to autopsies (and embalmment) for two reasons: mutilation of the body is disrespectful, and a removed organ may not be buried in time or at all. Some rabbis permit autopsies if the deceased gave consent in his lifetime or if there are definite grounds for belief that an autopsy might save another patient whose life is in danger.

Rabbinical law prohibits cremation (Jer. *Ketubot* 11:1). Cremation is deemed disrespectful to the deceased, and it is also regarded as a denial of the principle of resurrection.

Funeral eulogies are omitted beginning with the eve of Sabbaths, holidays, minor festivals, and the entire month of Nisan (Jer. *Moed Katan* 5). Eulogies were traditionally part of the process of weeping and wailing for the dead, which is muted in deference to the spirit of the holiday.

The entire community is under an obligation to pay respect to a deceased. This duty has priority even over the paramount mitzvah of studying Torah (*Ketubot* 17a). The establishment of burial societies did not relieve a community of its obligation to honor the dead.

No burials are permitted on a Sabbath. On the first day of a holiday only non-Jews may take care of the burial. On the second day of a holiday Jews may perform all the rites.

AVELUT

All the customs of *avelut* ("mourning") go into effect immediately after the burial. The Talmud fixed the length of the initial period of mourning at seven days, a practice said to have been ordained by Moses (Jer. *Ketubot* 1:1). Another talmudic source based the length of the period on a verse in Amos: "And I will turn your feasts into mourning" (8:10). The prophet appears to have indicated an equal duration of time for both occasions. The seven-day period (*shivah*) became standard even prior to the talmudic era (Judith, chap. 16).

The term of shivah is divided into two parts. The first three days are a time of intense grief, designated in the Talmud as "the three days of weeping" (*Moed Katan* 27b). The second part of the shivah period continues to be regulated by all the restrictive laws, but it is considered a time for "eulogizing" rather than weeping (ibid.). A mourner is not permitted to engage in any type of work in his home during the first part of shivah, even if his livelihood depends upon it.

The following activities were banned during the shivah week by rabbinic law: bathing, anointing, sexual intercourse, the wearing of freshly laundered garments, the cutting of hair, the study of Torah, the putting on of tefillin (on the first day only), exchange of greetings, and participation in a festive occasion. Mourners may not go outside of the home.

In addition, the following customs were observed in the talmudic era: beds and couches were turned over on their sides, mourners sat on the overturned couches or on the ground, a cloth was wrapped around the head and most of the face. These customs were discontinued in the Middle Ages. Mourners were permitted to sit on low stools and sleep in their beds.

The mourners' first meal, upon their return from the cemetery, is provided by friends. This is known as the "condolence meal."

There is no public display of mourning on a Sabbath. Mourners may join the congregation for services, but to reflect the change that has come about in their lives, they do not occupy their regular seats.

The thirty-day term of mourning (*sheloshim*) is free from all restrictions except for the prohibition of "rejoicing." One may not attend wedding feasts and similar occasions, or visit places of amusement, or give or receive gifts. The mourning ends upon the conclusion of sheloshim, except in the case of the loss of a parent, for whom one mourns an entire year.

When a festival occurs in the midst of shivah or sheloshim, the balance of the period is canceled together with all the restrictions pertaining to it.

THE RATIONALE OF MOURNING RITES

Due to their antiquity, some Judaic mourning rituals appear archaic in the light of modern standards of behavior. To get a better insight into the significance of these customs, it is essential to inquire into the purpose of the mourning laws and the symbolism of the various rites.

The twin functions of mourning rites are to pay respect to the memory of the deceased and to guide the mourner through the period of bereavement. Tradition acts to contain rather than suppress normal grief so that it does not overwhelm or destroy a mourner.

Mourners react in many ways to the loss of a beloved kin. The traditional rituals permit the mourner to act out his multiple reactions and thus rid himself of negative and destructive impulses.

The emotional composition of a state of mourning is a blend of love, grief, guilt, and a sense of isolation. The impulse of love, frustrated by the mourner's helplessness in the face of death, explodes into grief and an overpowering desire to shower praise upon the memory of the deceased.

Tradition recognized the importance of the eulogy and gave it preeminence among the rites attending a death. This satisfies a mourner's deep craving to honor the departed. His sense of grief is similarly appeased by his submission to traditional restraints which deny him all pleasurable activities. The classification of pleasurable activities includes bathing, anointing, fresh garments, cohabitation, haircuts, study of Torah, and merrymaking.

The other ingredient of mourning is a sense of guilt. Survivors of the Holocaust have repeatedly admitted to a sense of guilt. Why did they survive while their friends perished? Did they abandon their friends? A similar unwarranted sense of guilt clouds the outlook of many a mourner, even when the departed died a natural death. An unchecked, rampant sense of guilt may promote suicidal tendencies.

The heathen rite in which a mourner cut his own flesh was an act of self-destruction short of death. The Bible condemned such violence. The ritual of keriah sublimates the self-destruction impulse by taking the sense of guilt into account and giving vent to it, but the act of cutting is limited to a garment worn close to the flesh. In time the garment will be mended.

The prohibition of shoes, which normally cushion the feet from the discomforts of walking, is another rite which falls into the category of affliction. It too is a response to the sense of guilt.

The condolence meal, served by friends upon the return of the mourners from the cemetery, is another custom devised to minimize the effect of the sense of guilt. An astute rabbinic observation explained the need for this meal as follows: "The mourner is concerned and depressed by the death and he has no desire for food for he would rather die. He was therefore enjoined to eat what others provide for him" (quoted in *Ach LeTzarah,* p. 203).

Nachmanides took note of the existence of two classes of mourning rites, those which deny pleasure and those which afflict. In his view only the former are of biblical origin. He felt that the Bible did not impose affliction upon a mourner and therefore all restrictions which come within that classification are of rabbinical origin *(Torat Adam)*. With due deference to his opinion, the Talmud based all restrictions on biblical verses, thus giving them all equal status. Furthermore, there is ample reason for the imposition of afflicting rites in their therapeutic effect on the sense of guilt.

The third category of mourning rites is based on the mourner's sense of isolation and ostracism from the rest of the functioning community. A mourner, reeling under his loss, assumes that he was punished by God. This creates a sense of rejection and continuing apprehension of further punishment. This view found expression in the Talmud: "Rabbi Levi [2nd–3rd cent.] said: 'A mourner during the first three days should look upon himself as if a sword is resting between his shoulders [a reasonable chance that he too may die]; from the third to the seventh, as if it stands in the corner facing him [a lesser chance of death]; thereafter as if it is walking alongside of him in the marketplace [a remote chance]' " *(Moed Katan* 27b).

A mourner who assumes that he is being punished may justly conclude that he has incurred the displeasure of the Almighty. People who incur the displeasure of a mortal rabbinic court are placed under a ban *(nidui)*. Such individuals are isolated from the rest of the community. No one may visit them or engage them in conversation.

There is a tendency in the Talmud to draw a legal analogy between mourners, lepers, and persons who have been placed under a ban *(Moed Katan* 15a). There is, of course, no moral implication intended in this analogy, only a factual comparison between the situations of these three categories. Some of the restrictions applying to each of these classes of people are strangely similar. An individual under a ban may not wear freshly laundered clothes, cut his hair, or wear shoes. He is also excluded from a minyan.

A mourner's rite of wrapping his head, in effect hiding his face in shame, is in a way an expression of a sense of isolation. The same is true of the prohibition of his exchanging greetings and engaging in distracting conversation. Ritva (13th cent.) explained the prohibition as a reflection of the fact the "God had removed his mantle of peace from them due to their sins" *(Chidushe HaRitva, Divre Chibah, Megillah* 15a).

The mourner's sense of isolation is allayed by the traditional rites. He does not exchange greetings in the first three days when the apprehension of further punishment is at its highest. Thereafter he may respond to people's inquiries. After shivah he resumes normal social intercourse with his friends. Unlike the person under a ban, a mourner is visited, comforted, and included as part of the communal minyan. This approach gradually dissipates the sense of isolation.

VII.
MOURNING CUSTOMS

BLACK GARMENTS

Mourners of the talmudic era customarily wore black garments (*Shabbat* 114a). In modes of attire, Jews were generally greatly influenced by the customs of the non-Jewish community. Jews of Morocco wear white mourning garments.

THE PLACING OF GRASS AND SOIL

It is customary to place grass and soil upon the grave prior to leaving the burial site. Thus each person symbolizes his participation in the mitzvah of burying the deceased (Avudrahim).

CONDOLENCE

It was customary for mourners of the talmudic era to stand at the exit of the cemetery as friends passed by and offered the traditional condolence: "May the Almighty comfort you." This custom was subsequently changed. The friends form a double row and offer their condolences as the mourners pass between them on their way from the grave.

THE WASHING OF HANDS

Upon leaving a cemetery, it is customary to wash one's hands before entering a home. This is done for sanitary reasons, but some medieval scholars regarded the ritual as a reinactment of the biblical rite performed by the elders of a community in whose vicinity a murdered body had been discovered. The elders washed their hands and pronounced: "Our hands did not shed this blood" (Deut. 21:7; Avudrahim).

In the Middle Ages, the washing of the hands was given great ritualistic significance. The washing was repeated three times, and each time the person recited *Veyehi Noam* (Ps. 90:17) and *Yoshev Beseser* (Ps. 91). In most communities, however, the same selections from Psalms are recited at the cemetery when the deceased is carried to the grave.

Custom prohibits the direct transfer of the container of water for washing from one person to another. Instead, one puts the container down and the next person picks it up. This is symbolic of the wish that the trauma of bereavement not be communicated from one individual to another.

THE SPILLING OF WATER

Containers of water were normally kept outside of medieval homes. When a death occurred in a home, it was customary for three adjoining homes on both sides of the bereaved family to empty their containers of water. Initially this custom was based on sanitary considerations, but in time it came to serve another purpose. There was a reluctance to be a bearer of sad news. In ancient Israel a blast of a shofar was used in some communities to summon people to a funeral. In the Middle Ages the emptying of the containers of water signaled an occurrence of death *(Kol Bo)*.

A MEMORIAL CANDLE

It is customary for a candle to be kept alit in the house of a mourner throughout the shivah period. A verse in Proverbs, "The soul of man is the lamp of the Lord" (20:27), lent symbolic significance to the flame of a candle as a reflection of the surviving soul.

COVERING OF MIRRORS

The custom of covering the mirrors in a mourner's home dates back to the Middle Ages. The custom is still widely observed although its rationale is obscure. Some attribute the practice to superstition, but there are other explanations which warrant the retention of this old custom. Mirrors are used for cosmetic purposes which are inappropriate in a mourner's house. Also, mirrors reflect artificial light and brighten the home, but a mourner's home has been darkened. Finally, mirrors distract a person's mind and interfere with proper mourning for the dead.

THE CONDOLENCE MEAL

Hard-boiled eggs are customarily served as part of the condolence meal provided by friends of the mourners (Rema, *Orach Chaim,* 552:4). The round shape of eggs is a symbol of nature's recurring cycle. The deceased will someday return in the time of the resurrection.

PROVIDING A MINYAN

The custom of providing a minyan to conduct services at a mourner's home began in the Middle Ages. The practice is an offshoot of an ancient custom prevalent in the talmudic era. When a person died without leaving any mourners, it was customary for ten people to come to his home to assume the role of mourners. They sat shivah and received condolences (*Shabbat* 152a).

KADDISH

Kaddish, the preeminent mourner's prayer for more than a thousand years, is not mentioned in the Talmud. Only its responsive verse, *Yehe shme rabba mevarach* ("may his great name be blessed") was well known to the ancients (*Berachot* 57a, *Shabbat* 119b), apparently as a congregational response to a reader's mention of the name of God. By expressing man's blessing of the name of God, this verse assumed the importance of the congregational *Barachu et hashem hamevorach* ("bless the Lord who is to be blessed").

This public blessing of the name of God was in no way associated with mourning rites and is not to be confused with *Baruch dayan emet* ("blessed is the true judge"), which was recited upon hearing a report of an occurrence of death. However, the great mystical power attributed by third-century rabbis to the phrase *Yehe shme rabba mevarach* probably contributed to the emergence of the mourner's *Kaddish.*

Rabbi Joshua b. Levi said: "He who responds, 'Amen, may his great name be blessed, his decreed sentence is torn up' " (*Shabbat* 119b). The "decreed sentence" mentioned by Rabbi Joshua b. Levi was broad enough to cover a sentence affecting man's fate in this world or in the hereafter. This point was made clear in another talmudic source. "If one answers 'May his great name be blessed," he may be assured that he has a share in the future world" (*Berachot* 57a). Thus the basis for a mourner's prayer was established.

A prayer by the name of *Kaddish* was mentioned in *Masechet Soferim* (chap. 16, published in the 8th cent.), but it was not a mourner's prayer. Furthermore, this version is erroneous: the text should read *kadosh*, which was previously mentioned in the same chapter. It refers to the prayer of sanctification before *Shema*. The same correction should also be made in chapter 10 of *Masechet Soferim*, where *Kaddish* is mentioned for the first time. Here too the text generally refers to "*barachu* or *kaddish*," obviously a reference to the sanctification prayer of *kadosh*, which comes after *barachu* (*Kadosh, kadosh, kadosh. . . .*).

The first definite connection between *Kaddish* and mourners appears in the nineteenth chapter of *Masechet Soferim*. "Since the destruction of the Temple it was ordained that grooms and mourners should come to the synagogue so that [the congregation] may render an act of kindness to the grooms by praising them and walking them to their homes; [with regard to the] mourners, after the reader completes the service he goes to the door of the synagogue, or the corners, and finds the mourners and their relatives and pronounces a blessing and then recites *Kaddish*." The "blessing" was probably the traditional formula of condolence. The *Kaddish* was recited by the reader, not by the mourners.

The same chapter also mentions a special phrase, *bealma deatid leitcha-data* ("in a world which he will renew"), which is inserted in the *Kaddish* "for a student and a preacher." According to this version, the special *Kaddish*, with its reference to the resurrection, is only recited for deceased scholars who are worthy of resurrection. According to another version, the special *Kaddish* is recited "for the Talmud and Aggadah" *(drash)*. Whenever ten men are present at the conclusion of a talmudic or aggadic lecture this *Kaddish* is recited.

Since the thirteenth century, when the mourner's *Kaddish* was introduced, a number of changes have come about. The *Kaddish* referring to the resurrection is recited upon the conclusion of the study of a talmudic tractate and at the cemetery after all burials. A *Kaddish* including a prayer for scholars is recited after a talmudic lecture and after the reading of a talmudic passage which is part of the service *(Kaddish derabbanan)*. In addition to the mourner's *Kaddish*, there is also a reader's "half-*Kaddish*" and "whole *Kaddish*."

The mourner's *Kaddish* was allegedly inspired by a post-talmudic legend which appeared in *Eliyahu Zuta* (chap. 17, published ca. 10th cent.). Rabbi Akiva is said to have succeeded in freeing a man from the tortures of hell by teaching his son Torah so that he was able to recite the *Kaddish*. The ritual of *Kaddish* began in the Ashkenazic communities of Central and Eastern Europe.

According to tradition, punishment in the hereafter is limited in most cases to twelve months (*Rosh HaShanah* 17a). For this reason, the *Kaddish* was initially recited for twelve months *(Kol Bo)*. Beginning with the sixteenth century the rite was limited to eleven months so as not to create the impression that the deceased had been condemned to suffer the full extent of the punishment (Rema, *Yoreh Deah* 376:4). The period was subsequently shortened by one more day to allow for an interval of thirty days between the end of *Kaddish* and the yahrzeit. Despite the popularity of the *Kaddish,* the rabbis declared that leading a congregational service in the year of mourning is an act of greater merit (ibid.).

With the passage of time the significance of the *Kaddish* increased as a means of bringing comfort to the soul of the deceased and as an emotional outlet for the living. Its importance has been attested by a popular paternal greeting of the birth of a male child with the words: "I now have a *Kaddish."* The obligation to recite *Kaddish* rests only upon sons. Rabbi Yair Chaim Bacharach (17th cent.) expressed the opinion that a *Kaddish* recited by a girl is also beneficial to the soul of a deceased. However, he ruled against permitting girls to recite *Kaddish* as a violation of ancient custom (*Chavot Yair* 222). That is still the policy of Orthodox congregations. Women recite *Kaddish* in Conservative and Reform congregations.

The importance of *Kaddish* gave rise to the practice of engaging pious Jews to perform the rite in the absence of sons or when the sons are unable to fulfill their obligation. Regardless of the question of the religious merit of such a practice, it became widespread because it soothed the grief of mourners.

YIZKOR

See the discussion of Yizkor in chapter 8.

YAHRZEIT

It is customary to observe the anniversary of the death of a parent according to date in the Hebrew religious calendar. The practice of fasting on the anniversary date of the death of a parent is mentioned in the Talmud (*Shavuot* 20a). The proper manner of observing a yahrzeit was established in the seventeenth century. It includes the following rites: fasting, a yahrzeit lamp, leading a congregational service, *Kaddish*, visiting the grave, the giving of charity, an aliyah to the Torah, and a memorial prayer.

A MONUMENT

The custom of erecting a monument over a grave dates back at least to the second century (*Shekalim* 2:5). The practice did not gain the immediate approval of all rabbis, as is reflected in the talmudic statement, "Righteous people are not in need of monuments. Their deeds memorialize them" (Jer. *Sheklim* 2). This reservation might have resulted from a reaction to the practice of some unworthy rich people to commission the erection of lavish, self-praising monuments. The medieval scholars explained the objections of the Talmud as an expression of displeasure with expensive mausoleums. Markers on graves to warn kohanim to keep away were always considered essential (*Moed Katan* 2a).

Ancient monuments were erected soon after shivah, or even after the grave was filled (*Ketubot* 4b; Tosafot, *Ad sheyitam hagolel*). The modern practice, however, is to wait until twelve months after the death, when the memory of the deceased has begun to fade. The occasion of the unveiling is also planned to coincide with the official conclusion of the traditional mourning period.

The custom of eulogizing the deceased on the occasion of an unveiling dates back to the sixteenth century. The same is true of the practice of reciting prayers and the *Kaddish* at that time. It was also customary in some communities to mark the fulfillment of the obligation of erecting a monument with an appropriate meal. The American practice of serving refreshments in the cemetery is contrary to Jewish tradition, which regards eating in a cemetery as a violation of its sacredness (*Ach Letzarah*, p. 137).

2

Daily Traditional Practices

I.
ABLUTION AND IMMERSION

THE FIRST TRADITIONAL morning practice is the washing of hands in preparation for Shacharit (morning prayers). The ablution is a ritual act which is followed by the recitation of a benediction ("Blessed art thou . . . who commanded us to wash the hands").

The Talmud based this custom on a verse in Psalms: "I shall wash my hands in innocency and I will march around the altar, O God" (26:6). The juxtaposition of ablution and the altar inspired the following rabbinic comment: "If one attends to his physical needs [and washes his hands] and puts on tefillin and recites the *Shema* and the prayers, Scripture considers him as if he had built an altar and sacrificed upon it" (*Berachot* 15a).

Ritual ablution was a prominent feature of biblical religious ceremonialism. Aaron and his sons were instructed to wash their hands preliminary to their induction into the priesthood (Exod. 29:4). Officiating kohanim had to wash their hands and feet prior to entering the Sanctuary (Exod. 30:21).

Ablution was also on occasion an ethical ritual, not related to a religious function. When a murder victim was discovered in a field, and the assailant remained unknown, the elders of the nearest town were enjoined to offer a heifer in expiation, wash their hands, and pronounce: "Our hands have not shed this blood" (Deut. 21:6–7). The ablution was a symbolic declaration of innocence.

Purification from contamination required total immersion in water. This was confined to contaminations resulting from bodily discharges, leprosy, and defilement by contact with dead bodies. Ezra (5th cent.

61

B.C.E.) decreed immersion for men defiled by nocturnal ejaculation (Jer. *Berachot* 3:4).

A SYMBOL OF CONSECRATION

From a theological point of view, immersion was the supreme symbol of consecration. By complete submergence under water one severs all contact with his visible surroundings. Upon reemergence he begins life anew, like a newborn babe (*Yevamot* 22a). The high priest immersed himself five times in the course of Yom Kippur in a repeated gesture of consecration to the service of God. Converts to Judaism are similarly required to precede their initiation into the new faith with immersion as a symbol of consecration (*Yevamot* 46b).

The Essenes, according to Josephus (*Wars* 2:8), practiced daily immersion in cold water before entering the dining room for their midday meal. The meal was preceded and followed by a religious service. The immersion was apparently a ritual of consecration in which all members had to participate.

The Qumran sect prescribed ritual immersion for defiled persons who were in need of purification. In this respect they appear to have followed the rabbinic tradition of a mikveh (*Zadokite Document* X). However, they did not adopt immersion as a ritual of consecration. There was no provision for immersion by novices joining their ranks (*Manual of Discipline* I–II). In an apparent criticism of priestly immersions, they declared: "He [the priest] cannot be cleared by mere ceremonies of atonement, nor cleansed by any water of ablution, nor sanctified by immersion in lakes or rivers, nor purified by any bath" (ibid. II–III). They further stated: "No one is to go in any water in order to attain the purity of holy men. For men cannot be purified except they repent their evil" (ibid. V).

In traditional Judaism water is used for bodily cleanliness as well as spiritual cleansing. To attain the latter, conscious intent is required. The level of sanctity attained through immersion depends upon the expressed goal of the immersing individual (*Chagigah* 18b).

The need for consecration in priestly rituals and in conversion is self-evident. Judaism envisions a need for consecration even in the performance of routine functions of life. Sexual passion can be invested with a degree of sacredness if it is dedicated to procreation and the maintenance of harmonious domestic relationships. On the other hand, the sex drive can be prostituted and may become destructive of the family structure.

A woman ready to resume her sex life upon the termination of her menstrual cycle is required to undergo immersion. The purpose of this immersion is not hygienic cleanliness. Indeed, she must be thoroughly washed and cleaned prior to the immersion. The immersion is in fact a ritual of consecration to Judaic ideals of sex. As a ceremony of consecration, the woman's immersion is subject to many religious regulations. The recitation of a benediction is part of the ritual.

To a lesser degree, the ritual of ablution before a meal also reflects a need for consecration. The injunction "Sanctify yourself" (Lev. 11:44) refers, according to the Talmud (*Berachot* 53b), to the ritual of ablution before a meal. The rabbis revealed a deep insight into the significance of the dinner-table in the home. It can promote family unity, be a platform for meaningful dialogue, set a norm for the taming of one's appetite, teach gratitude for one's bounty, and instill concern for the hungry. The rabbinic analogy between the dinner-table and the altar (*Berachot* 55a) reflects Judaism at its best. On the other hand, the dinner-table can also stimulate voraciousness, waste, discord, and selfishness.

Rabbinic Judaism did not lose sight of the need for hygienic cleanliness. When that is the sole motivation of a given practice, no benediction is required. However, when an element of consecration enters into the performance of a practice, one gives expression to its presence through the recitation of a benediction.

HYGIENIC MOTIVATIONS

In the morning ablution in preparation for praying, the elements of consecration and cleanliness are equally present. To meet the ends of consecration, a benediction is required (*Berachot* 60b). To meet the needs of cleanliness, no restrictive regulations were attached to the ritual. If no water is available, one is permitted to rub his hands in the earth and thus clean them.

There are many occasions when cleanliness is the sole purpose of ablution. *Kol Bo* (ca. 14th cent.) listed the following: a visit to a bathhouse, the cutting of nails, the removing of shoes, the touching of one's bare feet, the scrubbing of one's head, and the use of a lavatory. The *Shulchan Aruch* added to this list visits to a cemetery and sexual intercourse (*Orach Chaim* 4:18). The code also mentions the need to wash one's mouth in the morning (ibid. 4:17).

In view of the hygienic objectives of the preceding ablutions, no benedictions were associated with those rituals. The sole exception is the ablution after the use of a lavatory, in which case one recites the following benediction: "Blessed art thou . . . who formed man in wisdom and created in him many orifices and vessels. . . . if but one of them be opened, or one of them be closed, it would be impossible to exist . . ." (*Berachot* 60b). Intake of food and elimination of waste are the two most vital bodily functions. Man should always express his admiration for the marvels of God's creation and his gratitude for the blessing of good health.

The ancient custom of bathing in preparation for Sabbaths and festivals is esthetically motivated. Kabbalists have added the custom of immersion before the Sabbath as a manifestation of a spiritual consecration for the holy day. Since this practice is of post-talmudic origin no benediction was attached to it.

ABLUTION BEFORE A MEAL

Ablution before a meal was initially a hygienic measure. The rabbis added an element of consecration. Rabbi Elazar b. Arak (1st–2nd cent.) based the custom on a biblical verse (Lev. 15:11; *Chulin* 106a). Rabbi Elazar flourished in the period following the destruction of the Temple. Ritual ablution was a prominent feature of the Temple service. With the end of the Temple, Rabbi Elazar shifted this ritual to a prominent place in the religious practices of the home.

The elevation of ablution before the meal to a sacred ritual subjected it to complex legal regulations. The washing cup must be in perfect condition, without holes or cracks. The water must be clean and have no foul odor. A lavish flow of water must spill over the top of the cup onto the hands. Spouts of cups are regarded as separate receptacles which do not meet the technical qualification of a ritual cup. The cup therefore must be spoutless. Water must be poured over both hands up to the wrists. Obstructions, such as rings, must be removed. The flow of the water must be manually manipulated, as is the case when one inclines the cup.

Manual propulsion of the water involves an individual's conscious participation in the process of washing. This assures awareness of the religious motivation of the ablution. One holds the cup in one hand and pours the water over the other. The cup is then transferred to the other hand and the process is reversed. Each hand is washed three times. An unwashed hand must not contact its washed mate because it is still in a state of contamination. This restriction led to the development of a traditional washing cup with two ears to facilitate the transfer of the cup from one hand to the other.

A benediction is recited after the hands have been washed and are in the process of being dried. The phrase *Al netilat yadayim* ("the washing of the hands") is derived, according to medieval scholars, from the Aramaic *natla,* a talmudic word for "ladle" (*Gittin* 69a; *Targum Jonathan,* Exod. 40:31). Due to the religious motivation of the ablution before a meal, even handicapped persons who have to be fed and do not touch the food are required to comply with the ritual. They, too, are in need of a sense of consecration.

MAYIM ACHARONIM

Upon the conclusion of the meal one pours water over his fingers before the recitation of Grace (*Chulin* 105a). This ablution, known as *mayim acharonim* ("last water"), was introduced in the third century for hygienic reasons. No benediction was prescribed for this ritual.

IMMERSION OF VESSELS

New glass or metal vessels which have been acquired from non-Jews must be immersed in a mikveh before they are put to use (*Avodah Zarah* 75b). According to the Jerusalem Talmud (*Avodah Zarah* 5:15), the immersion symbolizes a dedication of the vessels to usages sanctified by Jewish tradition. Due to the consecration element of this ritual, a special benediction (*Al tevilat kelim*) has been prescribed by tradition.

Initially, only used non-Jewish vessels required immersion, in keeping with the kashrut laws pertaining to such practices. In the third century, the law of immersion of vessels was extended to include new vessels.

II.
THE SYNAGOGUE

The institution of the synagogue emerged sometime after the destruction of the First Temple. However, long before that event people had offered prayers in the Temple in conjunction with the sacrificial rites. King Solomon anticipated this practice in his dedicatory oration, in which he asked God to heed "the supplication of thy servant and of thy people Israel when they should pray in this place" (I Kings 8:30).

He also supplemented his plea with an ecumenical note: "And the stranger who is not of thy people Israel, when he shall come out of a far country for thy name's sake . . . when he shall come and pray in this house . . . do according to all that the stranger calls to thee . . ." (ibid. 8:41–43).

Centuries later Isaiah predicted the fulfillment of Solomon's prayer: "Also the aliens, that join themselves to the Lord, to minister unto him . . . even them will I bring to my holy mountain and make them joyful in my house of prayer . . . for my house shall be called a house of prayer for all nations" (56:6–7). It is significant that as far back as the eighth century B. C. E. the prophet called the Temple a House of Prayer. The talmudic rabbis called the synagogue Bet HaKneset ("House of Assembly"), reflecting the multifaceted functions of the developing synagogue, beyond its principal character as a House of Prayer. In one respect, history fulfilled Isaiah's vision of the international scope of the Temple's functions by making the synagogue the model for church and mosque.

The earliest mention of the term Bet HaKneset appeared in its Aramaic rendition in *Targum Jonathan* (1st cent., Exod. 18:20). Rabbi Akiva (2nd cent.) was the first tanna to use this term (*Berachot* 49b). The early term for members of a congregation was *bnai kneset* (Tosefta, *Megillah* 2:2). Needless to say, synagogues had existed many centuries before Rabbi Akiva's time. The Talmud mentions the ancient synagogue of Shaf-Veyativ in Nahardea, Babylonia (*Megillah* 29a). According to a tradition recorded by Rav Sherira Gaon (10th cent.), the Nahardean shrine was built by Jews of the captivity of King Jeconiah (597 B.C.E.). The earliest synagogue discovered in Egypt by archaeologists dates from the reign of King Ptolemy III and Queen Berenice (246–221 B.C.E.).

Ancient synagogues were generally built on an elevation overlooking the town (*Tanchuma, Bechukotai* 3). The facade faced Jerusalem, in keeping with Jewish tradition (*Berachot* 30a). The congregants sat along three walls. A portable ark was placed in a niche in the fourth wall. The reader's lectern *(tevah)* was, in some instances, placed in a depressed area below the floor level, facing the ark. This arrangement conformed to the psalmist's exclamation: "Out of the depth have I called thee, O Lord" (130:1; *Berachot* 10b).

It is questionable whether a *bimah* (platform in the center for the reading of the Torah) was used in the early synagogue. The talmudic description of the basilica-synagogue in Alexandria mentions a wooden bimah (*Sukkot* 51b). The fact that this detail is included seems to indicate that the bimah was not a common fixture in other synagogues. The Alexandrian synagogue is said to have been extraordinarily large, compelling the use of a special attendant who was stationed on a bimah to signal the people when to say Amen. Most ancient synagogues were small. They probably positioned a platform, upon which the Torah was placed, close to the ark. When the size of synagogues increased, the platform was moved to the center of the structure for acoustical effect. In the early period, when arks were portable, the platform was also a portable fixture. When permanent arks were installed, the bimah undoubtedly became a permanent adjunct. The bimah was mentioned for the first time by a fourth-century Babylonian amora (*Megillah* 32b).

Large windows, essential to the decor of modern synagogues, were not favored in ancient times. They were discouraged for security reasons and because the outside scene might prove distracting to worshippers. However, Rabbi Yochanan (3rd cent.) decreed that synagogues must have some windows through which the heavens might be seen. The sight of heaven would induce a greater awareness of the divine presence (*Berachot* 34b).

The *ner tamid* ("perpetual light"), which commemorates the Temple menorah, was introduced into the synagogue in the post-talmudic era. Initially it was installed near the western wall, duplicating the location of the menorah in the Temple. Subsequently it was transferred to a place in front of the ark.

The location of the women's section in the early synagogue has not been definitely established. Some excavated synagogues show evidence of the existence of galleries, which might have been reserved for women. Such accommodations would parallel the rabbinical arrangements for the Temple celebrations of Simchat Bet HaShoavah (the festival of the drawing of the water) in the first century B.C.E. (*Sukkah* 51b).

A COMMUNAL RELIGIOUS CENTER

The development of the synagogue into a communal religious center began in the tannaic period. Elementary religious schools were attached to Jerusalem's synagogues in the first century (Jer. *Megillah* 3:1). Archaeologists have uncovered an inscription from a synagogue outside the walls of Jerusalem. The inscription gave the following description of the synagogue's functions: "The reading of the Torah, the learning of mitzvot, an inn and rooms and water vessels to accommodate the needs of strangers from afar." The synagogue dated from the Temple era. Inns were not normally adjuncts of the early synagogue. Jerusalem was an exception because of the large number of visiting pilgrims. The institution of an inn within the synagogue complex reappeared in medieval Europe in response to the prevailing conditions in that period.

Many communal aspects of the synagogue came to the fore in the post-Temple era. Congregations participated in a groom's celebration of the postnuptial week. At the other end of the emotional gamut, congregations offered condolences to newly bereaved mourners (*Yalkut*, I Kings 201). In another innovation, the rabbis decreed that finders of lost articles announce the find in the synagogue (*Baba Batra* 28b). This custom replaced the ancient practice of making similar announcements in Jerusalem on the occasion of the pilgrimages. The medieval synagogue adopted many customs for the social and economic welfare of the congregation. Jews who had grievances had the right to interrupt the service to get redress. Governmental decrees affecting the life of the community were announced on the Sabbath. Announcements were also made of new rabbinic decrees and a host of other matters of importance to the congregants.

THE BET HAMIDRASH

The first century B.C.E. witnessed the emergence of another vital institution, the Bet Hamidrash, an academy for advanced study of rabbinic law. Small, informal schools had undoubtedly existed since the days of Ezra (5th cent. B.C.E.). They were most likely adjuncts of the office of the high priest and Sanhedrin. Their main function was to teach the law rather than interpret it. With the rise of interpretive schools, rabbinic Judaism acquired its dynamism.

The earliest recorded Bet HaMidrash was established in Jerusalem by Shemaiah and Avtalion, heads of the Sanhedrin and the leading scholars of their age (*Yoma* 35b). With the proliferation of scholars in the succeeding generations, a network of academies was established in the land. The academies promoted the growth of the synagogue by stressing the merit of congregational services. However, judging from the puzzling attitude of a few third- and fourth-century scholars, there seems to have been a short interlude when relations between the two institutions were strained. Rabbis Ammi and Assi (3rd cent.) were the leading disciples of Rabbi Yochanan. Rabbi Ammi succeeded his teacher as president of the academy in Tiberias. Rabbi Yochanan was an enthusiastic promoter of the synagogue. That was not the case with his disciples. According to the Talmud, "Rabbi Ammi and Rabbi Assi, though there were thirteen synagogues in Tiberias, prayed only between the pillars [in the academy] where they used to study" (*Berachot* 8a). This practice seems particularly strange in view of their teacher's maxim: "A man must worship in a place which had been specifically set aside for prayer" (Jer. *Berachot* 5:1).

Rav Chisda (3rd cent.), the head of the Babylonian academy of Sura, also seems to have diminished the importance of the synagogue. He said: "The Lord loves the gates that are distinguished through halachah more than the synagogues" (*Berachot* 8a).

Rabbi Ulla, a Palestinian amora (3rd–4th cent.), similarly expressed a preference for the academy. He was quoted as follows: "From the day that the Temple was destroyed, the Holy One, blessed be he, has nothing in this world but the four cubits of halachah" (*Berachot* 8a). Rav Ulla, too, was at one time a student of Rabbi Yochanan.

Abaye, the celebrated Babylonian amora and head of the academy of Pumpedita (4th cent.), was strongly influenced by Rabbi Ulla's statement. He admitted that "at first [before he had heard Rabbi Ulla's opinion] I used to study in my home and pray in the synagogue, but [now] I pray only in the place where I study" (*Berachot* 8a).

It would be a grave error to assume that the attitude of the preceding rabbis was motivated by indifference to the fate of the synagogue. In reality their behavior reflected an effort to promote a high standard of scholarship and to attract more students to the academy.

Rabbis Ammi and Assi had a frustrating experience when they could not find the needed number of qualified teachers for elementary religious schools (Jer. *Chagigah* 1:7). Rabbi Chisda was totally immersed in the realm of scholarship and devoted his entire time to study. Even when his health was failing, he rejected his daughter's plea that he take a brief nap (*Eruvin* 65a). As for Abaye, the attendance at his academy had dwindled (*Ketubot* 106a), and he responded to the needs of the occasion by advertising the merit of academies. Incidentally, the disinclination to join communal congregations is still evident in modern yeshiva circles.

With the exception of the previously mentioned rabbis, the sages of the Talmud did their utmost to promote the growth of the synagogue. Rabbi Abba Benjamin (2nd cent.) said: "A man's prayer is heard only in the synagogue" (*Berachot* 6a). Rabbi Simon b. Yochai (2nd cent.) said: "When is the time acceptable [for prayer]? When the congregation prays" (ibid.). Rabbi Nathan (2nd cent.) said: "If a man occupies himself with the study of the Torah and with works of charity and prays with the congregation, [God] accounts it as he had redeemed me" (ibid.).

PROBLEMS OF THE EARLY SYNAGOGUE

The fledgling synagogue needed rabbinic support to create an atmosphere in which it could thrive. There were many impediments to overcome. Working people had little time for daily services. Tradition prohibited the publication of prayerbooks, and few people were able to commit the prayers to memory. The uneducated, whose ignorance would expose them to embarrassment, reacted with a disrespectful attitude toward the congregation. Their attitude reflected itself in their disparaging reference to the ark as a chest and to the synagogue as a "people's club" (*bet am; Shabbat* 32a).

Rabban Gamliel (1st–2nd cent.), the outstanding leader of the early post-Temple era, applied his practical wisdom and skill to the problem of the young synagogue, as he had done in other areas of Jewish life (Bloch, *Biblical and Historical Background of the Jewish Holy Days*, pp. 17, 137). He ruled that a worshipper who listens to the reader's recitation of the prayers fulfills the mitzvah of praying, even though he does not articulate the words (*Rosh HaShanah* 34b). This was a controversial ruling from which many rabbis dissented, but it brought the masses into the synagogue. The prohibition against the writing down of prayers, such as the *Amidah* (*Shabbat* 115b), was quietly lifted in the eighth century. This step was a further aid in boosting congregational attendance.

The early synagogue was also beset by ideological problems. The Sadducees had succeeded in capturing the high priesthood (Jer. *Yoma* 1:5) and also attempted to infiltrate their opinions into the Temple liturgy. This forced the rabbis to amend the phraseology of some prayers (*Berachot* 54a). These amendments were also introduced into the liturgy of the synagogue.

A special invocation for God's protection against the intrigues of the Sadducees was added to the *Amidah* (the twelfth benediction) by order of Rabban Gamliel, who named the prayer *Birkat HaTzadukim* ("the benediction of the Sadducees"; *Berachot* 28b). Rabbi Levi, who flourished more than a century after Rabban Gamliel, still referred to the prayer by that name (ibid.). The Sadducees were active in Rabban Gamliel's time (*Sanhedrin* 90b) but had all but vanished by the time of Rabbi Levi.

The disappearance of the Sadducees did not render the added prayer superfluous. Other Jewish sectarians replaced them on the list of enemies. The spread and belligerence of the Judeo-Christians was a source of serious concern to the rabbinic leadership, for the synagogue was undoubtedly a prime target of this sect. When Saul of Tarsus visited Damascus, he went to the synagogue to preach the new gospel (Acts 9:20). Similar incursions were undoubtedly experienced by Palestinian congregations.

It is very likely that the original text of the added benediction opened with the phrase *VelaTzadukim al tehi tikvah* ("and for the Sadducees let there be no hope"). There was no need to change the prayer; only the name of the enemy had to be altered. The new term was *meshumadim* ("converts"), an epithet fitting the Judeo-Christians. The term *meshumadim* appears in the version of the prayer in the *Siddur Rav Saadiah Gaon* (9th cent.). Due to the objections of Christian censors, *meshumadim* was eventually eliminated and *malshinim* ("informers") substituted.

There are other allusions in the Talmud to the synagogue's encounter with Judeo-Christians. Rabbi Joshua b. Levi, a Palestinian amora of the third century, said: "It is forbidden to pass behind a synagogue when the congregation is at services" (*Berachot* 8b). Rav Huna, a Babylonian amora of the same century, framed the prohibition in more forceful language: "He who prays behind a synagogue is wicked [*rasha*]" (*Berachot* 6b). Why should a man praying behind a synagogue be branded a *rasha*? Obviously the target of this condemnation was a sectarian, most likely a Judeo-Christian.

Hebrew Christians of the third century were no longer considered Jews. They could not join the synagogue under the pretext of being Jewish. To demonstrate contempt for rabbinic Judaism, some sectarians prayed on the outside, with their backs to the synagogue, a most provocative gesture. The rabbis branded such a demonstrator a *rasha*, a code name for a Judeo-Christian (Bloch, *Biblical and Historical Background of the Jewish Holy Days*, p. 159).

With the triumph of Christianity in the fourth century, the new faith ceased to be an internal Jewish problem. Abaye put the prohibition against praying behind a synagogue in its proper perspective. "This [the prohibition] applies only when he does not turn his face toward the synagogue" (*Berachot* 6b). He further narrowed the scope of the prohibition. "This applies only when there is no other door . . . when there is no other synagogue . . . when he does not carry a load and does not wear tefillin" (*Berachot* 8b).

The synagogue solved most of its problems and substantially increased its strength and influence by attaching a Bet HaMidrash as an auxiliary. Miniature academies thus became adjuncts of most synagogues. Adult and juvenile religious education has remained to this day a prominent feature of congregational programming.

Modern synagogues have lost some of their influence as a result of the diminished role of religion in the life of the community. Only the most traditional congregations have escaped the effect of the erosion.

THE LITURGY

The urge to pray was an innate and spontaneous instinct of primitive man. In its crudest stage, prayer took the form of flattery and appeasement of the deities. In Judaism prayer early reflected a submission to the will of God, an expression of contrition, and a recognition of the justice of the ways of God. To avoid any semblance of adulation, the rabbis recommended that adoration be expressed in phraseology formulated in the Scriptures or by the Men of the Great Assembly (*Berachot* 33b). In common with all creeds, Judaism also employs prayer for the purpose of interceding for God's salvation.

Prayer was always an informal adjunct of sacrificial rites. After the destruction of the First Temple, prayer was promoted to a position of primacy in the Babylonian diaspora. The weeping by the rivers of Babylon was, of course, a service of prayer and lamentation (Ps. 137:1).

THE AMIDAH AND SHEMA

Upon the restoration of the Temple (6th cent. B.C.E.), prayer retained its prime position in the religious life of the community. According to one tradition, the *Amidah* (eighteen benedictions) was formulated by Ezra (5th cent. B.C.E.). The Talmud credited the arrangement of the eighteen benedictions to the elders, among them some prophets. The final editing, however, was done at Yavneh in the first century C.E., under the leadership of Rabban Gamliel II (*Megillah* 17b). After the destruction of the Second Temple, prayer became the sole means of communing with God. In the words of Rabbi Elazar (2nd cent.): "Prayer is more efficacious than offerings" (*Berachot* 32b).

The *Amidah*, referred to in the Talmud as the *tefillah* ("prayer"), was the prime prayer of the early post-Temple era. Another important prayer of the period was the *Shema*, which consists of three sections: Deut. 6:4–9 (the unity of God); Deut. 11:13–22 (mezuzot); Num.

15:37–41 (fringes). A second-century ordinance required parents to train their children in the recitation of the *Shema* as soon as they were able to articulate words (*Sukkah* 42a). Adults recited the *Shema* at sunrise (*Yoma* 37b). Individuals who were not conversant with Hebrew were permitted to use the vernacular (*Berachot* 13a). Rabbi Levi (3rd cent.) attributed the importance of the *Shema* to its allusion to the principles of the Decalogue (Jer. *Berachot* 1:8).

The *Shema* was made part of the synagogue Shacharit service so that the *Amidah* could be recited after the reading of its scriptural portions (Jer. *Berachot* 1:1). The reading of the *Shema* was considered a fulfillment of the religious obligation of studying Torah (*Menachot* 99b). In time it became customary to read the *Shema* also at sunset. Its first section was read again upon retirement for the night (*Berachot* 60b). Since Maariv was not a regularly scheduled service in the tannaic period and some people skipped the evening *Shema*, the practice of reading it at night came into vogue.

This seems to be the custom described by Josephus (1st cent.; *Antiq.* 4:8): "Let everyone commemorate before God the benefits which he bestowed upon them at their deliverance out of Egypt [the *Shema*], and thus twice every day, when the day begins and when the hour of sleep comes on." Incidentally, the "benefits" of which Josephus speaks are mentioned in the second section of the *Shema*. In the rabbinic tradition only the first section of the *Shema* is read at bedtime.

According to Rabbi Joseph, (3rd cent.), the *Shema* keeps harmful intruders away (Jer. *Berachot* 1:1). The belief in the protective qualities of *Shema* is of long standing. It is said that the military chaplain who accompanied the ancient Hebrew army in battle used to read the *Shema* to them (*Sotah* 42a). Hence the widespread custom of reading the *Shema* in times of danger. Rabbi Akiva (2nd cent.) read the *Shema* in the agony of his martyrdom (*Berachot* 61a). His example served as a precedent for martyrs of all generations. According to the Zohar (*Terumah* 141), the *Shema* is part of a deathbed prayer.

The *Amidah* and *Shema* were the principal prayers of the Temple era and the early centuries following it. Other prayers were added from time to time, but they acquired a lesser importance. When people were pressed for time they confined themselves to the two main prayers. An abbreviated version of these prayers was formulated for people in places of danger (*Berachot* 28b). A special prayer, known as *Tefillat haderech* ("a prayer for the road"; *Berachot* 29b), was also composed for travelers.

The Temple Shacharit service included the Decalogue and the

Priestly Benediction (*Yevarechacha; Tamid* 5:1). A suggestion that the Decalogue remain part of the liturgy in the post-Temple era was rejected by the rabbis because of sectarian allegations that the Old Testament, with the exception of the Decalogue, had been superseded by the New Testament (*Berachot* 12a).

DAILY SERVICES

The three daily services were established after the destruction of the Temple. The Talmud attributed them to the patriarchs, thus giving this ritual the stamp of antiquity (*Berachot* 26a). The schedule of the services was fixed to approximate the time of the offering of the public sacrifice (*tamid*) in the Temple. Shacharit and Minchah substituted for the morning and afternoon Tamid (ibid.). On days when an additional offering (*musaf*) had been sacrificed in the Temple, such as Sabbaths and festivals, an additional service, Musaf, was appended to Shacharit (ibid.).

There was no Temple offering at night. The Maariv service was therefore a post-Temple innovation. Rabbi Joshua (1st–2nd cent.) considered the Maariv *Amidah* an optional prayer (*Berachot* 27b). His contemporary, Rabban Gamliel, differed with him, but Rava (4th cent.) ruled in favor of Rabbi Joshua (ibid.). In the geonic period, the evening *Amidah* was omitted and the prayer *Baruch hashem leolam* ("blessed be God forever") was substituted. God's name appears in that prayer eighteen times, paralleling the eighteen benedictions.

The rabbis of the post-geonic period considered Maariv an obligatory service. The *Amidah* was therefore restored, except that the leader does not repeat it. With the restoration of the *Amidah*, there was no longer any need for the substituted prayer instituted by the geonim, so it was eliminated by the Palestinian community and by Sephardim in the diaspora. However, Ashkenazim of the diaspora retained it, except for Sabbaths and festivals.

The nineteenth benediction of the *Amidah* comes in two versions, a long text (*Sim shalom*) and a short one (*Shalom rav*). The long text, containing elements of the Priestly Benediction, is read only in the mornings when the Priestly Benediction was offered at the Temple. The shorter version is read in the afternoon and evening.

RABBINIC GUIDELINES

The rabbis promulgated various rules to guide the conduct of worshippers and shape the development of the liturgy. The following rules date from the second century.

Worshippers must cultivate a reverential mood (*Berachot* 30b).

It was the custom of pious men of previous generations to meditate for an hour before praying as an aid to concentration. Such practice is recommended (ibid.).

One should not recite the *Amidah* in the midst of sorrow, idleness, laughter, chatter, frivolity, or idle talk, but only when rejoicing in the performance of a mitzvah (*Berachot* 31a).

Recitation of a prayer by rote is devoid of sincerity (*Berachot* 28b).

Individuals who are invited to act as readers should consider themselves unworthy of the honor and not accept it, but they must not refuse if the invitation is repeated three times (*Berachot* 34a).

The convenience of the congregation *(torach hatzibbur)* must be taken into consideration in determining the length of a service (*Berachot* 31a).

One should recite the morning prayers before indulging in food or drink (*Berachot* 10b).

The following rules were promulgated in the third century.

One should not pray for his personal needs in the first three benedictions and in the last three benedictions of the *Amidah* (*Berachot* 34a). This important guideline established the format of all prayers. The opening and concluding benedictions of the *Amidah* are prayers of thanksgiving and adoration. The supplicatory prayers come in-between. All individual prayers must follow the same format. This moral perception was recognized in the pre-talmudic era, as is evident in the prayers of Tobit and Sara (Tobit, chap. 3).

One should not raise his voice in prayer (*Berachot* 24b).

God helps those who pray for the welfare of others (*Baba Kama* 92a). Due to this guideline, most liturgical supplications are couched in the plural.

RABBINIC CUSTOMS

It is customary to place one's hand over the eyes when the opening sentence of *Shema* is read. This prevents distraction and aids concentration (*kavannah; Berachot* 13b).

The second sentence of *Shema* (*baruch shem*) is recited in a soft voice. According to an ancient tradition, Jacob was the author of this verse. However, since Moses did not include it in the Scriptures, it is read silently (*Pesachim* 56a).

It is customary to emphasize the enunciation of *echad* ("one"), the concluding word of the verse of *Shema*. According to the Talmud, whoever prolongs the *echad* (unity of God) has his days and years prolonged (*Berachot* 13b).

One must carefully enunciate the letter *zayin* in *tizkeru* and *uzechartem*. If the letter is slurred it may sound like an *S*, distorting the meaning of the words (Jer. *Berachot* 2:4).

It is customary to place one's feet close together when reciting the *Amidah*. Such a posture is a sign of respect (*Berachot* 10b).

When reading the *Amidah*, it is customary to bow one's head when the word *baruch* is pronounced and to return to an upright position when God's name is mentioned (*Berachot* 12a). This is done at the beginning and end of the first benediction and at the beginning and end of the eighteenth benediction (*Berachot* 34a).

Upon concluding the *Amidah*, it is customary to take three steps backward and then to recite the supplementary prayer for peace *(Oseh shalom)*. Thus one takes leave of God without turning his back on him (*Yoma* 53a).

When the reader repeats the *Amidah* and bows his head upon the recitation of *Modim*, the congregation rises and does the same (Jer. *Berachot* 1:8). The special prayer which it recites at that time is known as *Modim deRabbanan* (*Sotah* 40a).

POST-TALMUDIC CUSTOMS

The prayer of *Vehu rachum (Tachanun)* was composed in the geonic period. It is read on Monday and Thursday mornings, days considered propitious for supplication. The meritorious character of these days is attributed to the tradition that Moses ascended Mount Sinai on a Thursday and came down on a Monday, bearing a message of forgiveness. A shorter *Tachanun* prayer is read at the Shacharit and Minchah services of other weekdays.

It is customary to sit and repose one's head on an arm when the passage of *Vayomer David* is recited. This prayerful posture is assumed only if a Torah is present in the room.

It is customary to recite the first section of *Shema* aloud to remind one of the need for concentration.

THE MINYAN

The requirement for a minimal presence of ten men to form a congregational quorum is basic in Judaism. The source of this law is a mishnah in *Megillah* (23b). The literal meaning of *minyan* is a numerical entity or "the counted ones." The word per se is not related to the number 10, but it has been equated with the number 10 on the basis of a talmudic legal discussion. According to a mishnah, "The benedictions of bridegrooms require the presence of ten, the bridegroom is included in the counting [*min haminyan*]." By the process of association, the word *minyan* has become a synonym for a religious quorum.

The Mishnah lists several religious functions which require a minyan. In all instances they are occasions when congregational functions are performed. The minimal number of ten is arrived at by a rabbinic interpretation of the Hebrew word for "community," *edah* (*Megillah* 23b). Another source bases the need for ten men at a marriage ceremony on a verse in the Book of Ruth: "And he took ten men of the elders of the city" (4:2; *Ketubot* 7b).

The requirement of ten men for a congregational quorum may appear to be a mere technicality. In fact, however, this law had a far-reaching effect on the organization of Jewish communal life. The stress on congregational services in Judaism forced the establishment of communities with a minimum of ten families (not counting children). This prevented the scattering of Jews in isolated areas, where they would have fallen easy prey to assimilation. So soon as ten families were settled in one location, rabbinic law mandated the maintenance of a synagogue.

Even though the minimal number of ten needed for a minyan was first mentioned in a second-century mishnah, the practice antedated it by many centuries. A rule of the Qumran sect provided as follows: "In any place where there are ten, a priest versed in the Book of Study is not to be absent" (*Zadokite Document* XII). It further stated: "The people who follow these rules must consist of a minimum of ten." It is clear that the requirement of ten men was a firmly established rule long before the Qumran code was written.

The requirement of a quorum of ten has been dispensed with in the Reform movement. In the Conservative movement, a quorum is still required but women may be counted as part of the minyan.

III.
TALLIT, TEFILLIN, MEZUZAH

The mitzvot of tallit, tefillin, and mezuzah have a common characteristic—each of them is a commemorative ritual. The tallit was assigned the mission of reminding Jews of their obligation to perform the mitzvot of the Torah (Num. 15:39). Tefillin serve as a reminder of God's intervention in Egypt and of the need to be versed in the Torah. The mezuzah reminds every Jew of his obligation to abide by the mitzvot of the Torah and to transmit its sacred traditions to succeeding generations (Deut. 11:13, 19–20).

The Talmud linked the three mitzvot into a single tripartite unit, which became the insignia of a practicing Jew. "Whosover has the tefillin on his head, the tefillin on his arm, the tzitzit on his garment, and the mezuzah on his doorpost is secure against the commission of sin" (*Menachot* 43b). The unit of these three mitzvot was also regarded as a symbol of God's love for Israel. "Beloved is Israel, for the Holy One, blessed be he, surrounded it with mitzvot. Tefillin on the head, tefillin on the arm, tzitzit on the garment, and mezuzot on the doorposts" (ibid.).

The survival of Judaism is contingent upon Jewish consciousness (tefillin), a Jewish home (mezuzah), and Jewish distinctiveness (tzitzit). The link between the three mitzvot was impressed upon ancient Jewry by the three sections of the *Shema*, the day's first prayer.

The following Torah selections are inscribed on four parchments, which are inserted in the four compartments of the tefillah of the head: (1) Exodus 13:1–10; (2) Exodus 13:11–16; (3) Deuteronomy 6:4–9; (4) Deuteronomy 11:13–21 (*Menachot* 34b). The tefillah of the arm contains the same selections, except that they are written on a single parchment.

Despite the symbolic significance of tefillin as an insignia of monotheism, this ritual was somewhat neglected in various periods of Jewish history. Rabbi Simon b. Eliezer (2nd cent.) noted: "Every mitzvah which Israel performed at the time of the royal interdiction [Hadrian], such as the denial of idolatry and circumcision, they still rigorously abide by it. The mitzvot for which they did not risk their lives at the time of the royal interdiction, such as tefillin, they are still weak in its observance" (*Shabbat* 130a). More than eleven hundred years later, Rabbi Moses of Coucy (13th cent.) reported a widespread neglect of tefillin by the Jews of Spain (*Semag* 3). *Kol Bo* (14th cent.) objected to the custom of placing ashes on the forehead of a groom, on the place where the tefillah of the head normally rests. "One cannot assume," he said, "that tefillin will ever be put on that place" (*Hilchot Tisha B'Av* 62).

Various factors might have contributed to the neglect of tefillin. Many Jews wore their tefillin all day. Such an open declaration of their Jewishness might subject them to attacks by hostile elements. The high cost of tefillin was probably also a deterrent. To counteract the prevailing laxity, the rabbis engaged in an active campaign to promote the mitzvah of tefillin. Parents were urged to train their children in the practice of tefillin at an early age. "A minor who knows how to take care of tefillin, his father should buy him a set" (*Sukkah* 24a).

To offset the fear of non-Jews, the rabbis reassured the people that, on the contrary, the tefillin would inspire respect for the Jewish people. "How do you know that the tefillin are a strength to Israel? For it is written: 'And all the peoples of the earth shall see that the name of the Lord is called upon thee, and they shall be afraid of thee' [Deut. 28:10]. And it has been taught: 'Rabbi Eliezer the Great [1st cent.] says: 'This refers to the tefillah of the head' '' (*Berachot* 6a).

Resh Lakish (3rd cent.) held out the promise of long life to those who observe the mitzvah of tefillin (*Menachot* 44a). This statement of an anticipated divine reward was probably misconstrued by some ignorant people as an attribution of magical protective powers to tefillin. The same notion is reflected in "phylacteries," the translation of tefillin in the Greek text of the New Testament (Matt. 23:5). *Phylacteries* is the Greek word for "amulets" (*Encyclopedia Judaica*, vol. 15, col. 899).

The Talmud also stressed the importance of physically attractive tefillin. In this respect, tefillin were put in the same category as the lulav, sukkah, shofar, and tzitzit (Jer. *Peah* 1). The emphasis on the esthetic aspect of these mitzvot was intended to increase their popular appeal. This laudable effort was distorted by the author of Matthew. "They [the rabbis] broaden the phylacteries that they wear as safeguards [amulets], and enlarge the fringes of their garments for reasons of ostentation" (23:5). The beautifying of these rituals was attributed to motivation of ostentation. In fact, the rabbinic campaign was addressed to the masses, not to the leadership.

In ancient times, the wearing of tefillin all day long was considered an act of great piety. Rabban Yochanan b. Zaccai (1st cent.) kept his tefillin on all day (*Sukkah* 28a). Many sages followed his example. Rema (16th cent.) mentioned that it was the custom in his time to put on the tallit and tefillin at home and thus walk to the synagogue (*Orach Chaim* 25:2).

There was a consensus among the ancient authorities with regard to the four biblical selections which were inserted in the tefillin. They differed, however, as to the exact length of some of the selections which were to be inscribed on the parchment. In the tefillin of the Qumran sect, the third selection (Deut., chap. 6) began with verse 1. In the traditional tefillin it begins with the fourth verse ("Hear, O Israel"). It is obvious that the declaration of the unity of God was paramount to the rabbis of the second century, in view of the duality inherent in the belief of the Hebrew Christians. The verse of *Shema* was therefore given special prominence.

The Qumran tefillin also included the Decalogue. There is no evidence that the Decalogue was ever part of the traditional tefillin. It surely would have been excluded in the post-Temple era for the same reason that dictated its exclusion from the liturgy (*Berachot* 12a), the need to refute the Hebrew Christian assertion that the Decalogue was the only part of the Old Testament that was not superseded by the New Testament. The rabbinic sensitivity on this subject was expressed by Rabbi Chinena (4th cent.), who prohibited the use of tefillin written by a sectarian or a converted Jew (*Menachot* 42b).

TEFILLIN CUSTOMS

The tefillah of the arm is put on first. When the noose of the strap is tightened around the arm, one recites the benediction *lehaniach tefillin* ("to put on the tefillin"). The tefillah of the head is put on next and the benediction *al mitzvat tefillin* ("concerning the commandment of tefillin") is then recited. The text of the benedictions was published in the third century by Rabbi Yochanan (*Menachot* 36a).

When removing the tefillin the process is reversed. The tefillah of the head is taken off first (*Mechilta* 111).

The tefillah of the arm is placed just above the forearm (*Menachot* 36b). A left-handed individual wears the tefillah on his right arm (*Menachot* 37a). The tefillah of the head is placed at the hairline at the center of the forehead. The two straps hang over the shoulders, with the black sides outward.

The position of the parchments in the tefillah of the head follows, according to Rashi (11th cent.), the sequence in which they appear in the Bible. According to Rashi's grandson, Rabbenu Tam, the fourth selection precedes the third. Such tefillin are known as "tefillin deRabbenu Tam."

As a result of the difference in opinion between the two great talmudic giants, some medieval scholars instituted the custom of simultaneously wearing two tefillin on the head, one of Rashi and one of Rabbenu Tam. This custom was changed in the sixteenth century. The Rashi tefillin were worn until after the *Amidah*. They were then replaced by tefillin of Rabbenu Tam, which were worn until the conclusion of the service.

Tefillin are not worn on Sabbaths and festivals (*Menachot* 36b). Two customs prevail with regard to Chol HaMoed (intermediary days of a festival). Those who abstain from work do not wear tefillin. Others wear them only during Shacharit (*Orach Chaim* 25:13). The latter custom prevails on Rosh Chodesh.

TALLIT CUSTOMS

The mitzvah of tzitzit assumed great importance because, like tefillin, they proclaimed to the general community the wearer's Jewishness. By the same token they served as a reminder of one's religious commitments and acted as deterrents against violations of religious laws (*Menachot* 43b).

The Talmud emphasized the great merit of the mitzvah of tzitzit. "The mitzvah of tzitzit is equivalent to all the mitzvot of the Torah" (*Nedarim* 25a). "God demonstrated his love for Israel by surrounding them with the mitzvah of tzitzit in their garments" (ibid.).

The tallit of the talmudic era was a rectangular garment, the usual male outfit, worn in the daytime. The garment had no religious significance. However, since it had four corners, fringes had to be attached to them, in accordance with biblical law (Num. 15:38).

Medieval Jews adopted the garment styles of their non-Jewish neighbors. Since those garments were not rectangular, the biblical law of fringes did not apply to them. In order to comply with the law of tzitzit, the prayer tallit came into vogue. Not all Jews possessed these prayer shawls and the rabbis urged them to buy a tallit (Tosafot, *Shabbat* 32b). This tallit was worn only in the congregation for morning services. Eventually, the *tallit katan,* which is worn under the garments, came into use in the medieval period. The mitzvah of tzitzit is thus performed all day.

When the tallit is wrapped around the head, the benediction *lehitatef batzitzit* ("to wrap oneself with a tallit") is recited. The tallit is then moved back to the shoulders, with two corners suspended from each shoulder.

A minor who is old enough to wear tzitzit is obligated to do so (*Sukkah* 42a). This provision emphasized the educational importance of this mitzvah.

A tallit was traditionally worn by married men exclusively. It was customary for a bride to give a tallit to the groom as a wedding gift. In modern congregations, including some Orthodox, boys wear a small tallit beginning with their Bar Mitzvah Sabbath.

In the talmudic and geonic periods, when many Jews wore their tefillin throughout the day, it was customary to put on the tefillin first and then the tallit. The reverse practice was adopted in the post-geonic period, when the wearing of tefillin was mainly confined to the congregational service.

It is customary to sew a silk strip to the top of the tallit so a worshipper may easily distinguish between its top and bottom. This strip, called the *atarah* ("crown"), was introduced in the sixteenth century. To make the tallit more attractive, the *atarah* is often embroidered with silver trimming.

It is customary to gather the four fringes into the right hand upon the reading of the verse "And bring us together from the four corners of the earth" (in the prayer preceding the *Shema*).

It is customary to kiss the fringes when the word *tzitzit* in the *Shema* is pronounced. This practice apparently derived from an older custom mentioned by Rema (16th cent.). According to Rema, one looks at the fringes and kisses them when he recites the verse in *Shema: Ureitem otam* ("and you shall see them"; *Orach Chaim* 24:4).

TECHELET

The Bible prescribes the use of a "thread of blue" *(techelet)* among the fringes of the garment (Num. 15:38). The blue dye was obtained from one of the snail species, known in the Talmud as *chilazon* (*Menachot* 44a). This particular species was hard to get and the dye commanded a high price. There were undoubtedly many who could not afford the high cost of the dye, and some resorted to deception by misrepresenting the true nature of their blue fringe. Rava (4th cent.) strongly condemned such misrepresentation (*Baba Metzia* 61b).

The use of *techelet* was eventually discontinued as the source of the dye dried up. There was a short interlude in the 1880s when the head of the Chasidim of Radzin, Rabbi Gershom Leiner, claimed to have rediscovered the biblical *chilazon*. His followers reintroduced the *techelet* and financed the production of the dye. However, this experiment was ultimately abandoned.

MEZUZAH CUSTOMS

Mezuzah is the Hebrew for "doorpost." The religious parchment and case which are attached to the doorpost have assumed the same name.

The etymological root of mezuzah is *zv*, which means "tall, erect or prominent" (Fuerst, *Concordance*). The doorpost is a prominent place because it is visible to all who pass or enter the home.

The Talmud seems to have associated the word *mezuzah* with the root zz, which means "movement" (*Deut. Rabbah* 7). The human traffic into and out of the home passes the doorpost.

The doorpost played an important part in several rituals. The blood of the paschal lamb was smeared on both doorposts (Exod. 12:7). The ear of a Hebrew slave who continued in servitude beyond seven years was pierced at the doorpost (Exod. 21:6). The doorpost was an appropriate spot from which to declare the unity of God (Deut. 6:4–9) and to proclaim the parental obligation to instruct children in the lessons of the Torah (Deut. 11:13–21). Before the introduction of parchments and cases, the foregoing two passages were most likely written directly on the doorposts.

Josephus' description of the mezuzah is couched in biblical terminology: "They are also to include the principal blessings they have received from God upon their doors." By making the mezuzah a thanksgiving testimonial, Josephus overlooked the principal function of the mezuzah.

Josephus makes no mention of a parchment or a case. The use of a case is mentioned in the Talmud (*Baba Metzia* 102a).

A GUARDIAN OF THE HOME

The notion that a mezuzah is endowed with protective powers gained early credence. The belief probably stemmed from the biblical account of the smearing of the blood of the paschal lamb on the doorposts of Jewish homes, which granted Jews immunity from the tenth plague. "He will not suffer the destroyer to come in unto your houses" (Exod. 12:23). A tanna concluded that the mezuzah is much more effective in keeping out the destroyer (*Mechilta,* Exod. 12:23).

The protective power of the mezuzah is alluded to in several talmudic sources (Jer. *Peah* 1; *Avodah Zarah* 11a). The Zohar introduced the custom of inscribing *Shadai* (the name of God) on the blank side of the mezuzah parchment (*Voetchanan*). According to *Zohar Chadash* (*Ruth* 84), a destroyer will not come into the home if the name of God is visible.

The practice of inscribing God's name on the outside of the mezuzah became standard in the Middle Ages. Maimonides approved of this custom but criticized those who treat the mezuzah as an amulet (*Hilchot Tefillin* 5:4).

It was the practice of medieval Jews to affix a mezuzah only at the door leading to the street. However, according to rabbinic decision, all doors within the house require mezuzot (Rema, *Yoreh Deah* 287:2).

The mezuzah is affixed to the right-hand post as one enters the home (Rava, *Yoma* 11b).

The proper place for a mezuzah is the upper one-third of the post (Samuel, *Menachot* 33a).

According to Rashi (11th cent.), a mezuzah should be affixed in a vertical position (Rashi, *Avida kesikta, Menachot* 33a). According to Rabbenu Tam, it should be affixed in a horizontal position (*Ha deavida*, ibid.). The prevailing custom of affixing it in a diagonal position accommodates both opinions. The top of the mezuzah is placed in the direction of the house (Rema, *Yoreh Deah* 289:6).

Prior to the affixing of the mezuzah one recites the benediction, "Blessed . . . who commanded us to affix a mezuzah."

The mitzvah of mezuzah is limited to residences. Synagogues were therefore exempt from the requirement. However, if travelers sleep and board in a synagogue, a mezuzah is required (*Yoma* 11b).

It is customary to place one's hand on the mezuzah upon entering and leaving the home (*Avodah Zarah* 11a).

One should not remove mezuzot when moving out of a home (*Baba Metzia* 102a). The Jewish character of a home should not be erased. However, if non-Jews rent or buy the home, the mezuzot should be removed so that they will not be treated with disrespect (ibid.).

Mezuzot should be inspected at least twice every seven years (*Yoma* 11a).

IV.
BENEDICTIONS

Prayers which open or close with the traditional phraseology of a blessing, *Baruch ata HaShem* ("Blessed art thou, God"), are classified as "benedictions."

The form of ancient benedictions began with "Blessed be God" (Gen. 14:20, 24:27). The later form, "Blessed art thou, God," appears in Psalms (119:12). In I Chronicles (29:10), the phrase was used in the context of a benediction. This early benediction invokes the name of God and includes his attribute of fatherhood. The attribute of kingship is mentioned elsewhere in the Bible, not within the framework of a benediction (Exod. 15:18, Ps. 10:16, Isa. 24:23, Zech. 14:9, Mal. 2:14).

According to Rav (3rd cent.), no prayer may be classified as a benediction unless it invokes the name of God. Rabbi Yochanan (3rd cent.) required additionally the inclusion of God's attribute of kingship (*Berachot* 40b). Generally, individual benedictions outside the liturgy include the attribution of kingship. These have retained their form even when subsequently integrated into the daily service. Benedictions which form an integral part of the liturgy, such as the benedictions preceding and following the *Shema,* the *Amidah,* and Grace, omit this attribute.

The Talmud attributed the formulation of the benedictions to the Men of the Great Assembly (5th cent. b.c.e.; *Berachot* 33a). According to Rabbi Meir (2nd cent.), every Jew must daily recite a minimum of one hundred benedictions (*Menachot* 43b).

The rabbis recognized the importance of benedictions as a medium for expressing one's awareness of God's intervention in the momentous experiences of daily existence. Such occasions may arise at any time of day or night and may bring either happiness or sadness in their wake.

RABBINIC GUIDELINES

"It is forbidden to enjoy anything in this world without a benediction" (*Berachot* 35a).

The rabbis envisioned the concept of enjoyment in its broadest connotation, including pleasures derived from man's physical senses as well as from intellectual perceptions. Sensations, such as inspiration, admiration, surprise, and joy resulting from the performance of mitzvot, come within the broad definition of enjoyment.

"A man must bless God [recite a benediction] for evil as he blesses him for good" (*Berachot* 54a). Upon hearing good tidings, one recites: "Blessed art thou . . . who art good and bestowest good." In the event of sad tidings, one recites: "Blessed art thou . . . who art the true judge."

The benediction upon hearing ill tidings, which was formulated in the second century, had a twofold purpose. It denied the pagan belief in two independent divine sources of good and evil. It also precluded an instinctive rebellious reaction to tragedy by proclaiming the justice of God's decrees, which are motivated by truth and not by vindictiveness. Multiplying tragedies of the Palestinian Jewish community in the second century inspired the formulation of this benediction.

"One who alters the text of a benediction [and recites it] has not fulfilled his obligation" (*Berachot* 40b).

The author of this guideline was Rabbi Jose (2nd cent.). The number of benedictions had greatly increased by the second century. The frequent recitation of benedictions had stimulated extemporaneous prayers, and this entailed the risk of infiltration by sectarian interpolations. For practical reasons, the texts of the established benedictions were very concise. This enabled most people to commit them to memory. Children were trained to memorize the most common benedictions. Adults who were not familiar with the less common ones were advised to consult a rabbi (*Berachot* 35a).

The Talmud strictly prohibited the writing down of benedictions (*Shabbat* 116b). Since sectarian texts could easily gain wide circulation, the rabbis preferred that individuals receive oral instructions from authorized sources.

"Four classes of people should offer [a benediction of] thanksgiving. Those who crossed the sea, those who have traveled the wilderness, a patient who has recovered from illness, and a person who has been set free" (*Berachot* 54b).

The Babylonian amora Rav (3rd cent.) was the author of this ordinance. The occasions calling for thanksgiving were normally fraught with much danger. They occurred frequently and were part of the regular routine of life in ancient Babylonia. These dangers could not be avoided, and the exposed individuals were not accountable for them. Imprisonment, likewise, was mainly the result of religious and political persecution rather than criminal activity. The prayer therefore expressed gratitude rather than penitence.

Rav's ordinance developed into *Birkat HaGomel* (benediction of deliverance), which is recited by an individual after the second benediction of an aliyah to the Torah.

"Whoever recites a benediction when none is required violates the injunction of 'Thou shalt not take [God's name in vain]' " (*Berachot* 33a).

Resh Lakish (3rd cent.) was the author of this guideline, which marked the final stage in the formulation of benedictions. No additional benedictions were permitted beyond those officially fixed by the rabbis. No benedictions are recited for the performance of acts instituted in the post-talmudic era.

PARTIAL LIST OF BENEDICTIONS

The following is a partial list of occasions, other than daily services, when the recitation of a benediction is required:

On eating bread, other starches, proteins, vegetables, or fruit, and the drinking of wine and other beverages.

On smelling fragrant leaves, plants, fruits, spices, and oils.

On seeing lightning, meteors, high mountains, giants, dwarfs, the ocean, exquisite plants and animals, the rainbow, the blossoming of trees, a distinguished talmudist, a renowned scholar, a king, or a site where ancient miracles had occurred.

On hearing thunder, good tidings, or ill tidings.

On the performance of mitzvot, such as the affixing of a mezuzah, immersion of new vessels, etc.

BERACHAH ACHARONAH

A *berachah acharonah* (concluding benediction) is recited following the drinking of wine, the eating of any of five species of fruit (grapes, figs, olives, pomegranates, and dates), and the eating of food (other than bread) baked from any of the five species of grain (wheat, barley, rye, oats, and spelt).

PRE-MEAL AND POST-MEAL BENEDICTIONS

A pre-meal prayer, recited by the prophet, is mentioned in the Bible: ". . . for the people will not eat until he [Samuel] comes because he blesses the sacrifice and afterwards they eat . . ." (I Sam. 9:13). This ritual was not necessarily a general pre-meal practice. The occasion in I Samuel was a feast following a sacrificial offering on an altar. Evolving tradition made it a common practice to offer a pre-meal prayer on all occasions, private and public.

Pre-meal prayers were regularly offered by the Qumran sect. The *Manual of Discipline* (VI) provided as follows: "When they set the table for a meal or prepare wine to drink, the priest is first to put forth his hand to invoke a blessing on the first portion of the bread or wine."

Priests enjoyed a preeminent role in Temple rites. The Qumran sect retained the preeminence of its priests in most religious functions outside the Temple. Rabbinic Judaism also extended many honors to the kohen, but he was given no special privileges in the synagogue ritual, except for the Priestly Benediction. Piety and knowledge were the only requisites for the position of reader at a congregational service. There was no need for a reader to lead the pre-meal prayer. The benediction *(HaMotzi)* was brief and known to everyone.

The post-meal prayer is based on a biblical injunction: "And thou shalt eat and be satisfied and bless the Lord, thy God, for the good land which he has given you" (Deut. 8:10). This verse, according to Rav Yehudah (3rd cent.), mandates the prayer of Grace (*Berachot* 21a).

The Essenes, according to Josephus, recited Grace after the meal (*Wars* II, 8:5). A similar practice undoubtedly prevailed among other Jews, except that the priest had no leading role in it.

Rabbi Nachman (3rd–4th cent.) attributed the first section of Grace (gratitude for food) to Moses, the second (land) to Joshua, the third (Jerusalem) to David and Solomon, and the fourth (*Hatov vehametiv*— "the kind who does kindness") to the Sanhedrin of Yavneh. The latter ostensibly composed this section in 135, when the Roman authorities granted permission to bury the fallen defenders of Betar (*Berachot* 48b).

Rabbi Nachman's homiletical statement reflects two talmudic traditions. The ritual of Grace is very ancient. Its gradual development stretched over a long period, from antiquity to the second century.

The Talmud recorded a request of King Jannai (2nd–1st cent. B.C.E.) for a person to recite Grace after the royal meals (*Berachot* 48a). The recitation of Grace was obviously widely practiced at the time. The incident also reveals that readers who were familiar with the prayer led the service. This practice continued into the post-Temple era.

CUSTOMS ASSOCIATED WITH GRACE

It is customary to wash one's fingers before the recitation of Grace (see above, "Ablution and Immersion").

It is customary to fill a cup of wine before Grace and to recite the benediction and drink the wine after Grace (*Berachot* 51a).

When three men partake of a meal, it is customary for one to invite the others to join him in the recitation of Grace (*zimmun*; *Berachot* 45a). He must, however, first obtain the permission of the host and guests (*Bireshut baal habayit umaranan*). He then declares: "Let us bless him [if ten men are present, "let us bless the Lord"] of whose bounty we have partaken." The others respond: "Blessed be he of whose bounty we have partaken and through whose goodness we live." The response is repeated by the leader (*Berachot* 50a). A supplementary declaration, "Blessed be he and blessed be his name," was added in the twelfth century.

The custom of *zimmun* dates back to the time when most people were not familiar with the prayer of Grace and a reader recited it for them, as was done with the congregational service in the synagogue. The guests were invited by the reader to pay attention to his recitation and to respond Amen when such response was called for.

V.
KASHRUT

The field of kashrut encompasses religious laws which define permitted and prohibited foods. Strangely, the term *kosher*, which is a byword in every Jewish home and has even infiltrated the English language, is never mentioned in the Bible in connection with the dietary laws. The biblical designation of permitted and prohibited animals is "clean" (*tahor*) and "unclean" (*tame*; Deut. 14:19).

The biblical label of "unclean" has led to the assumption that sanitary considerations motivated the laws of kashrut. This assumption appears to be further supported by the biblical description of nonkosher food as "an abominated thing" (*toevah*; Deut. 14:4). However, this explanation is only partially true. The goal of sanctification, present in many religious precepts, is also a motivating factor in kashrut.

Holiness may be equated with religious distinctiveness. Kashrut has influenced Jewish social distinctiveness, an important deterrent to assimilation. The element of holiness in kashrut is emphatically stressed in several places in the Bible (Exod. 22:30, Lev. 11:44–45, Deut. 14:2).

There are areas of kashrut in which hygienic considerations are of no moment. The consumption of blood is strictly prohibited (Lev. 3:17). This prohibition was not based on sanitary but on ethical grounds (Deut. 12:23). Animal fat, known as *chelev*, is also strictly prohibited (Lev. 3:17). This prohibition likewise was not based on considerations of cleanliness. In fact, the fat of sacrificial animals was burned on the altar (Lev. 3:14). Furthermore, the fat of a deer is kosher. Obviously, fat per se was not regarded as unclean.

Maimonides' comment on the seventy types of injuries which render an animal unfit for consumption also illustrates the absence of a hygienic rationalization in some areas of kashrut. The rabbinic list of injuries, according to Maimonides, may not be enlarged "even though it should be discovered [in the future] by medical science that there are additional injuries which are dangerous to the life of the animal" (*Mishneh Torah, Hilchot Shechitah* 10:12).

On the other hand, some foods were prohibited solely for reasons of health. According to a mishnah, "an animal which has eaten poison, or has been bitten by a snake, although it is not forbidden on the ground that it has become terefah, it is forbidden as a danger to life" (*Chullin* 58b). Similar hazards to health motivated the talmudic prohibition of water, wine, or milk which has been left uncovered in a vessel. The rabbis were concerned that a snake might have injected its poison into the liquid (*Terumot* 8:4). The law was abolished by medieval rabbis because the danger of snake poison had been eliminated (Rema, *Yoreh Deah* 60:2).

BIBLICAL DIETARY LAWS

The Bible lists ten kosher animals (Deut. 14:4–5). All others are forbidden. There is also a list of twenty-one prohibited birds (Deut. 14:12–18). The identity of these species is obscure. The Talmud consequently permitted only such birds as have a long-standing tradition of kashrut (*Chullin* 63b).

The need for ritual slaughtering *(shechitah)* is based on a verse in Deuteronomy: ". . . thou mayest eat meat, after all the desires of thy heart . . . then thou shalt slaughter of thy herd and of thy flock . . ." (12:20–21). An animal which dies a natural death *(nevelah)* or is torn by beasts *(terefah)* may not be eaten (Deut. 14:21, Exod. 22:30). The biblical term *terefah* applies only to animals which have been fractured or torn by beasts; it took on a more comprehensive connotation in the Talmud, which included under that label all injuries fatal to an animal (*Chullin* 56a). An animal which was prohibited for reasons other than injuries was called *assur* ("forbidden"; *Chullin* 62b).

Post-talmudic usage broadened the designation *terefah* to include other varieties of prohibited food. *Kol Bo* (14th cent.) grouped all nonkosher animals under the heading "The Laws of Terefah" (10). A similar system was adopted by the author of the *Shulchan Aruch*. Maimonides (12th cent.), on the other hand, listed nonkosher animals under the heading *Maachalot Assurot* ("forbidden foods"). In modern parlance, the labels "kosher" and "terefah" have been used indiscriminately to designate all permitted and prohibited foods.

In addition to the prohibited animals, the Bible also prohibited some parts of the kosher animals. The sciatic nerve of a slaughtered animal must be removed (Gen. 32:33). Mention has already been made of the prohibition of blood and *chelev*.

The prohibition of flesh taken from a living animal, a common practice among primitive nations, is based on Deuteronomy 12:23 (*Chullin* 101b). An animal and its young may not be slaughtered on the same day (Lev. 22:28). This rule was based on the general principle of compassion for all creatures (*Baba Metzia* 32a).

The Bible prohibits the seething of a kid in its mother's milk. This injunction is repeated three times (Exod. 23:19, 34:26; Deut. 24:21). Such practices were part of pagan fertility rites. Within the narrow context of this verse, the prohibition constitutes a condemnation of the pagan character of the rite and its debasing cruelty. Tradition, however, based upon this verse a complex set of laws which rigidly separate meat from dairy products and require the use of distinct dishes and utensils.

The tokens of kosher fish are listed in Leviticus: "Whatsoever has fins and scales" (11:9). The Bible also lists four species of kosher locusts (Lev. 11:22). Their identity is obscure.

Wine used in libation rituals on pagan altars (*yayin nesech*) is forbidden. No benefit may be derived from it (Deut. 32:38; *Avodah Zarah* 29b). We will discuss later the rabbinic amplification of this law.

KASHRUT IN RABBINIC JUDAISM

The dietary laws were widely observed by the Jews of the postbiblical era. The swine became a popular symbol of all that is detestable and repugnant. The eating of swine was tantamount to a rejection of Judaism. King Antiochus demanded two symbolic acts as proof of conversion to paganism, the eating of nonkosher food and a sacrificial offering of a swine (I Macc., chap 1). One talmudic source attributed the destruction of the Temple to an incident in which two pigs were sent to the priests when Jerusalem was under siege (Jer. *Taanit* 4). In another version of this account, the rabbis followed up the incident with a proclamation prohibiting the raising of swine (*Baba Kama* 82b). The swine became a code-name for the oppressive government of Rome (*Lev. Rabbah* 13).

Even Jews who had been forced into baptism made every effort to adhere to the dietary laws. They were particularly loath to eat pork. This particular aversion was pathetically expressed in the year 654, by forcefully converted Jews of Toledo, in a memorandum to King Recceswinth: ". . . Moreover, all ceremonies enjoined by the Christian religion . . . we will truly and exactly observe. . . . with regard to flesh of animals which we consider unclean, if we should be unable to eat the same on account of ancient prejudices, nevertheless when it is cooked with other food, we promise to partake of it with no manifestation of disgust and horror."

The deep attachment to the dietary laws rendered the people receptive to extensive rabbinical elaborations. The rabbinic addenda were not motivated by a leaning toward stringency, for the rabbis were generally responding to the challenge posed by the political and social conditions of their time. The talmudic dietary laws fall into three categories; clarification of biblical laws, extension of biblical prohibitions, and new restrictions.

SHECHITAH

The Bible mandates the slaughtering of animals, but since it does not spell out the method of slaughtering or the qualifications of slaughterers, the rabbis had to fill in the necessary information. This area of rabbinic legislation falls into the category of a clarification of biblical law.

There were no professional slaughterers in the talmudic era. Butchers who were versed in the law of shechitah performed their own ritual slaughtering (*Chullin* 9a) or engaged other people to do it for them. Any adult Jewish man or woman was qualified to perform shechitah (*Zevachim* 31b). Due to the tension of the work, slaughterers were subject to fainting spells (*Chullin* 3a). Such incidents occurred much more often in the case of female slaughterers. The number of women engaged in this work was always small, and ever since the fifteenth century women have been disqualified from performing shechitah (Rema, *Yoreh Deah* 1:1).

The liberal standard for qualifying as a slaughterer left many loopholes for fraud, and there was a need to tighten the rules. This process began in the tannaic period and was accelerated in the amoraic era. Rabban Gamliel (1st–2nd cent.) outlawed Samaritan slaughterers, even though their labor was obviously in great demand. The restriction was at first disregarded (ibid.). A later reinactment of the same restriction by Rabbis Ammi and Assi (3rd cent.) was more effective (*Chullin* 6a).

The qualifications of ritual slaughterers were markedly raised in the third century. Most of the new regulations originated in the Babylonian Jewish community. Unlike the compact Palestinian community, Babylonian Jewry was dispersed over a larger area and as a result was not amenable to careful supervision by the religious authorities. Conditions changed in the third century. As the institution of the exilarchate consolidated its power, the exilarch was able to impose greater discipline. At the same time, the spectacular rise of Babylonian rabbinic scholarship improved the supervisory capacity of the community.

The following are some of the new regulations enacted in the third century:

A butcher who was not versed in the laws of shechitah was disqualified from performing a ritual slaughter (*Chullin* 9a).

Post-slaughter examination of the throat of the animal was instituted as a regular procedure (ibid.).

A slaughterer has to submit his knife to a scholar for examination before the shechitah (*Chullin* 18a). In Palestine this rule was regarded as a mere formality performed as a sign of respect for the local scholar (*Chullin* 17b).

Butchers were ordered to acquire three knives, one for the shechitah, one for cutting up the meat, and one for the removal of the forbidden fat (*Chullin* 8a).

Scholars were urged to acquire the skill of shechitah to enhance their competence for supervision, and if need be, to perform the ritual act (*Chullin* 69a).

A fourth-century ordinance disqualified minors from performing shechitah, even when supervised by a competent adult (*Chullin* 12b).

As a result of the foregoing regulations, the potential for fraud and error was practically eliminated. This gave rise to a new legal assumption: Whoever engages in slaughtering is assumed to possess the required expertise (*Chullin* 3b).

The professional slaughterer, known as a shochet, first emerged in the fifteenth century. One of the early sources to mention a shochet is the popular Passover hymn *Chad Gadya*, which was composed approximately in the fifteenth century. The emergence of the new profession made it possible for the German-Jewish community to introduce a system of official certification, known as *kabbalah*. A certified shochet required no further examination of his qualifications or inspection of his performance (Rema, *Yoreh Deah* 1:2). No kabbalah was granted to individuals under eighteen (ibid. 1:4).

THE SHECHITAH KNIFE

The Bible does not specify the area of the animal where the shechitah incision is to be made, nor the type of instrument to be used in the making of an incision. Prevention of cruelty to animals is a basic consideration of all biblical laws pertaining to the treatment of animals. This guiding rule mandated a method of killing which would end the animal's life in as swift and painless a manner as possible.

Pentateuchal law makes it clear that the death of the animal must result from a loss of blood (Lev. 17:13). This requires the cutting of a vein rather than a blow or a shock to the brain. The Talmud derived from etymological implications that it is the animal's throat that has to be cut (*Chullin* 27a). Due to the antiquity of the method of slaughtering, it was widely assumed that the details of the ritual had been transmitted to Moses (*Chullin* 28a).

Prior to the introduction of metal knives, people used sharpened flints and reeds. These remained in common use long after the advent of the iron age. Joshua used flint knives in the mass circumcision of the Jews (Josh. 5:2). Similar knives were used in the slaughter of animals. Flint implements gradually disappeared and were no longer in use in the period of the Mishnah (1st and 2nd cent.). The metal knife was known in the time of the Mishnah as *sakin* (*Avodah Zarah* 75b, *Chullin* 8a).

Despite the disappearance of the flint knife, the Mishnah reflected its ancient existence in a statement of law: "If he slaughtered with a hand-sickle or with a flint or a reed, what he slaughters is valid" (*Chullin* 15b). The use of glass implements was similarly approved (ibid.).

The major guidelines for a valid shechitah are listed in the Mishnah. The need for a swift and painless death mandated the use of a sharp, smooth knife to prevent the ripping of the animal's throat (*Chullin* 18a). The incision must result from a forward and backward stroke (*Chullin* 30b). A pause in the course of the slaughter invalidates the shechitah (*Chullin* 32a).

Laws pertaining to the *challaf* (shechitah knife) were extensively discussed by the tannaim. The amoraim continued the discussion and added some details. The principal regulations of a proper shechitah were summed up in the third century: (1) no pause in the course of the shechitah; (2) no pressure on the throat; (3) no insertion of the knife between the gullet and windpipe; (4) no cutting beyond the designated area of the throat; (5) the shechitah must not result in the ripping out of the gullet and windpipe from their normal position (*Chullin* 9a).

RABBINICALLY PROHIBITED FOODS

The biblical list of prohibited foods was expanded in the Talmud. Some of the added restrictions constituted extensions of biblical laws. There were also some restrictions which were not derivatives of biblical laws but new enactments in response to the exigencies of prevailing conditions.

The Mishnah lists eighteen symptoms of terefah resulting from a physical injury to an animal (*Chullin* 42a). These prohibitions were based on the assumption that the enumerated injuries were fatal to the animal and hence come under the biblical category of terefah. According to tradition, the list of injuries did not originate with the rabbis but was part of the oral instructions transmitted to Moses (ibid.).

The prohibition of a dying animal *(mesukenet)*, even when its condition is not attributable to a physical injury, was another rabbinic extension of the biblical prohibition of *nevelah* (natural death; *Chullin* 37a).

The law which requires the soaking and salting of meat prior to cooking is an extension of the biblical prohibition of the consumption of blood (*Chullin* 113a). Post-talmudic regulations provided the details of the process of koshering meat. It must be soaked for half an hour, salted for an hour, and then rinsed off to remove the brine. The salt should be neither fine (it melts) nor coarse (it falls off). The salting must be done on an inclined or perforated board so the blood may flow off.

There is a heavy concentration of blood in the liver. Since koshering will not drain the blood, liver must be incised and then broiled (*Chullin* 101a).

For proper drainage of blood from the heart, it must be incised prior to salting (*Keritut* 22a).

The blood in meat congeals after three days from the time of shechitah. Congealed blood cannot be drained by the normal process of koshering. To prevent congealment, the meat must be rinsed *(hadachah)* prior to the expiration of the three-day period. The fluidity of the blood is then retained for another three days. If the period expires without a rinsing, the meat may only be broiled (post-talmudic ordinance). Koshered meat requires no further rinsing and may be kept indefinitely.

Kosher fish requires no salting. However, red fish fluid, accumulated in a vessel, should not be consumed because it has the appearance of blood (*Keritut* 21b). Interestingly, the Qumran sect appears to have regarded the blood of fish in the same light as the blood of animals. According to a provision in the *Zadokite Document* (XII): "Fish are not to be eaten unless they are ripped open while still alive and their blood poured out."

MEAT AND DAIRY

The talmudic laws which prohibit the mixing of meat and dairy products are extensions of the biblical injunction against the seething of a kid in its mother's milk (Exod. 23:19). The biblical prohibition pertains only to mixed cooking or broiling (*Chullin* 115a), but the rabbis extended the prohibition even when no cooking is involved. As a precaution against a possible violation of these rules, the Talmud prohibited the placing of cheese on the table when meat is being served (*Chullin* 103b; 2nd cent.). In a further extension of this law, a third-century rule prohibited the eating of dairy food after a meat meal.

The time period which must elapse after the eating of meat before one may eat dairy was not initially spelled out. One rabbi waited twenty-four hours. Another rabbi waited the normal interval between meals (*Chullin* 105a). This vague specification was interpreted by post-talmudic rabbis to equal six hours. However, different customs developed in the course of time. In the German-Jewish community the interval was limited to three hours.

One may eat meat after dairy but he must first rinse his mouth and eat some bread (*Chullin* 105a; 3rd cent.).

Meat cooked in a dairy pot, and vice versa, may render the pot and the food nonkosher (*Chullin* 108a). Pots and utensils made of wood, metal, stone, or bone may be koshered (*Orach Chaim* 451–452).

The custom of acquiring multiple cutlery emerged in medieval Jewish communities. A family had to have a minimum of three knives, one to cut meat, one to cut dairy, and one to cut bread.

According to one opinion in the Talmud, fowl and clean beasts (deer) do not come within the biblical definition of "meat." Rabbi Akiva (2nd cent.) stated that the prohibition of mixing fowl or venison with milk is of rabbinic origin (*Chullin* 113a).

The biblical prohibition of *chelev* (fat on the intestines and kidneys) was extended by the rabbis to all internal fat which can be peeled off (*Chullin* 49b; 2nd cent.).

The biblical prohibition of wine used for idolatrous purposes (*yayin nesech*) was extended in the second century to all wines produced or handled by non-Jews (*setam yenam*). The added restriction was based on the assumption that it is the intent of a heathen to put the wine to pagan uses (*Avodah Zarah* 29b). The prohibition was also motivated by a rabbinic policy of preventing convivial interfaith gatherings and social intimacy which may lead to intermarriage (*Avodah Zarah* 36b). The use of sex as a weapon against the integrity of Judaism is illustrated in the Bible (Num. 25:1–2). Conditions in the diaspora increased the dimensions of this problem.

Jewish boiled wine *(yayin mevushal)* is not rendered unfit when handled by non-Jews. The relaxation of the general prohibition was promulgated in the third century on the ground that boiled wine is never used in pagan rituals *(Avodah Zarah* 30a).

Non-Jewish hard cheeses were prohibited by the rabbis because they are curdled with the rennet of a carcass *(Avodah Zarah* 29b; 2nd cent.).

NEW RABBINICAL PROHIBITIONS

Eighteen new decrees were promulgated in the chambers of Chananiah b. Hezekiah. Among these was a prohibition of non-Jewish milk, bread, and oil *(Shabbat* 13b). The prohibition of milk was based on the assumption that the source of the milk might be an unclean animal. It may therefore be classified as an extension of a biblical injunction. The prohibition of bread and oil came within the policy of preventing social intimacy.

The circumstances surrounding the session in Chananiah's chambers need to be clarified. According to the talmudic account, members of the Schools of Shammai and Hillel held a joint session. What was the occasion of this joint session? Why was it held in Chananiah's chambers? Why were the Hillelites outnumbered? With the help of some imaginative speculation, we may be able to reconstruct the conditions which led to this unusual session.

Chananiah lived in the first century. The Talmud attributed to him "and his companions" the editorship of *Megillat Taanit,* a compendium of Jewish festivals, which is assumed to have been composed shortly after the destruction of the Temple. Chananiah apparently headed a small academy, which was independent of the two major academies of Shammai and Hillel. His disciples or colleagues were identified in the Talmud as "his companions."

The grave events of the first century posed a serious threat to the Jewish state and also to the Jewish religion. There was ample reason to fear a mass defection of the youth to the assimilationist pro-Roman element of the population. The presence of large numbers of Roman military and civilian personnel, as well as indigenous non-Jews, raised the specter of intermarriage.

The School of Shammai favored the enactment of stringent restrictions to minimize interfaith social contacts. The cooperation of the Hillelites would lend the new enactments greater authority. The latter were normally opposed to a strategy of stringency. However, pressed by the Shammaites, they reached a compromise. An equal number of delegates of each school would meet in the neutral academy of Chananiah. The votes of Chananiah's colleagues would be decisive.

The news of the joint session had to be kept secret from the Roman authorities, who might suspect that the agenda was political rather than legal in character. Rumors were therefore spread that Rabbi Chananiah was ill. The visits of the scholars were disguised as sick-calls. This strategy is reflected in the mishnaic phrase *alu levakro* ("they went up to pay a visit"), an expression usually associated with a sick-call.

Chananiah and his companions joined forces with the Shammaites. In the words of the Mishnah: "They took a count and the School of Shammai outnumbered the School of Hillel, and on that day they enacted eighteen measures" (*Shabbat* 39b).

The prohibition of non-Jewish oil met with strong resistance and was finally lifted in the third century by Rabbi Judah Nesiah (*Avodah Zarah* 36a). Oil was an essential staple of the Palestinian economy. Much of it came from non-Jewish sources. Rabbi Judah Nesiah was also requested to lift the ban on non-Jewish bread. He refused for fear of earning a reputation as a "permitter" (*Avodah Zarah* 37a). Such a reputation would have undermined his authority in extremist circles.

Medieval scholars eased the ban on non-Jewish bread. They permitted the purchase of bread from non-Jewish commercial bakeries because such contacts do not involve social intimacy (Rema, *Yoreh Deah* 112:2).

The ban on non-Jewish milk was partially relaxed in the second century. The first exception was made in cases where the Jew witnessed the milking of the cow. This was further liberalized by omitting the requirement for witnessing the milking. Mere presence in the immediate vicinity was deemed sufficient (*Avodah Zarah* 39b).

With the emergence of large commercial milk companies it was no longer necessary to have a Jewish presence, in the opinion of many modern rabbis. This conclusion was based on the fact that government regulations prohibit the adulteration of milk. Furthermore, milk of unclean animals is more expensive than cow's milk. However, *chalav yisrael* is still widely sold in large Orthodox Jewish communities.

GLATT KOSHER

The designation *glatt kosher* is of recent origin, introduced into the

United States by the Zelimer Chasidim. The certification of glatt kosher means that the lungs of the animal were free of lesions or other symptoms of lung disease. Disorder of the lungs is the prime cause of terefah animals. There is no glatt kosher fowl.

Glatt kosher meat is koshered within the three-day period from shechitah. This eliminates the need for *hadachah* ("rinsing").

There is much confusion as to the real significance of the label *glatt kosher*. It is the belief of many people that it is a codeword for absolute kashrut. In this respect it has replaced the label in vogue a generation ago, *Kosher lamehadrin min hamehadrin* ("kosher even for those who are extra careful"). There are many organic disorders which may render an animal terefah. These have to be processed in the normal manner. There is also the question of proper deveining, which is done at the retail market.

HASHGACHAH AND HECHSHER

The great variety of modern food products and the increasing number of chemicals used in the processing and preservation of food has made the certification of kashrut an essential adjunct of the kosher trade. The need for supervision *(hashgachah)* existed on occasion in the talmudic era. Thus any person was initially qualified to perform schechitah if an expert supervised his performance. The presence of the expert constituted an oral certification *(hechsher)* of the kashrut of the animal.

Prior to the establishment of large commercial food-production plants, products were sold on the local market where the reputation of the seller or producer was well known to the community. Modern food products, however, are marketed on a global scale. Under such conditions, a consumer must depend upon a written certification. The onus of establishing the reliability of the certification is shifted to the buyer. To remedy this situation, rabbinical associations and religious lay organizations have undertaken the task of providing certification.

VI.
MITZVOT PERFORMED IN THE HOME

SEPARATION OF CHALAH

Home baking, especially for the Sabbath, was a common practice of Jewish housewives. Prior to the putting of the dough into the oven, a small portion, known as *chalah*, had to be separated and given to the kohen (Num. 15:20). The biblical mitzvah of chalah was mandatory only in Palestine from the time of Joshua's conquest of the land until the Babylonian exile (*Ketubot* 25a). According to Ravina (4th cent.), the rabbis retained the practice even in the diaspora so that the law of chalah would not be forgotten (*Berachot* 27a). The following benediction is recited prior to the separation of the chalah: "Blessed art thou . . . who commanded us to separate the chalah."

Palestinian agricultural laws have not been extended by the rabbis to the diaspora. Obligations arising from those laws were contingent upon Jewish ownership of the land. Removal from the land automatically canceled the obligations. Rabbinic retention of the agricultural laws in the diaspora would have amounted to a transfer of the sanctity of the soil of Israel to other countries. Chalah, on the other hand, is a personal obligation which may properly be performed in the diaspora as a reminder of the time when Jews lived in their own land.

The chalah is no longer turned over to a kohen, as was the practice in biblical times. Chalah is sacred food which a kohen may not eat unless he is purified from contamination, in the manner prescribed by biblical law. Furthermore, the genealogical descent of kohanim is in doubt. To circumvent this problem, the custom of setting aside two portions of chalah was practiced in some countries. The one which was assumed to be the sanctified chalah was burned in the fire. The other was given to a kohen in a reinactment of the ancient practice. This custom, however, is no longer followed. The single portion of dough which is separated as chalah is cast into the fire and burned (Rema, *Orach Chaim* 457:2).

(For a further discussion of the mitzvah of chalah, see below, chap. 3, "Preparations for the Sabbath.")

TZEDAKAH

Charity is not intrinsically a home mitzvah, but the presence of charity boxes in many Jewish homes warrants our classification of charity as a domestic practice.

Charity is indelibly associated in the Jewish lexicon with the Hebrew word *tzedakah*. That was not the word's biblical connotation. Its ancient Semitic root described a person who was standing upright or erect. The Bible used the word in its moral context, a person who leads an upright or righteous life *(tzadik)*. The term *tzedakah* was frequently hyphenated with justice *(mishpat*, II Sam. 8:15, I Kings 10:9, Ps. 33:5, Jer. 22:15,

Ezek. 18:5, I Chron. 18:14). Occasionally, it was also hyphenated with truth (*emet,* I Kings 3:6, Zech. 8:8).

Tzedakah is mentioned for the first time in Genesis: "And he [Abraham] believed in God, and he [God] counted it to him for righteousness" (*tzedakah;* 15:6). Abraham's faith was considered an attribute of tzedakah, i.e. moral rectitude. Only in one instance does the pentateuchal tzedakah reflect a remote association with an act of kindness for the poor. A night garment, taken in pledge for a loan to a poor individual, must be returned to him in the evening. A display of such compassion "shall be a righteousness [*tzedakah*] unto thee before the Lord, thy God" (Deut. 24:13).

According to Maimonides, there are seven biblical commandments addressed to the subject of charity. However, the word *tzedakah* does not appear in any of them.

The following are the seven commandments: peah (Lev. 19:9), gleanings (ibid.), forgotten sheaf (Deut. 24:19), defective grape-clusters (Lev. 19:10), grape gleanings (ibid.), poor man's tithe (Deut. 14:28), and loans (Exod. 22:24; *Sefer HaMitzvot* 120–124, 130, 197). We may also add the warning against withholding loans from the poor on the approach of the sabbatical year (Deut. 15:8), the obligation of people who make a pilgrimage to Jerusalem to provide for the poor (Deut. 16:11), and the provision for leaving the produce of the soil in a sabbatical year for the poor (Exod. 23:11).

In the ancient Hebrew agricultural society, contributions of food were the main form of charity. Financial assistance was involved only in the making of loans, which was deemed a charitable transaction. The charging of interest was therefore strictly forbidden.

The merit of charity was greatly extolled in the Scriptures. A righteous king is defined as one who "will have pity on the poor and needy" (Ps. 27:13). A woman of valor, among other virtues, "stretched out her hand to the poor" (Prov. 31:20). The pious man who "has given to the needy, his righteousness endures forever" (Ps. 112:9). In this verse, the term *tzidkato* ("his righteousness") is associated with the giving of alms.

A closer identification of tzedakah with charity is reflected in the following verse in Proverbs: "Treasures of wickedness profit nothing, but righteousness [tzedakah] delivers from death" (10:2). The same message is repeated in another verse: "Riches profit not in the day of wrath, but righteousness [tzedakah] delivers from death" (11:4). There appears to be a juxtaposition of hoarded wealth and money distributed for charity. However, the term *tzedakah* in these verses still retains the biblical connotation of "righteousness."

The earliest indication of the evolution of *tzedakah* into a synonym for "charity" appears in the apocryphal Tobit (ca. 3rd cent. B.C.E.). The author borrowed the phrase "delivers from death" from Proverbs and explicitly linked it to charity. "Alms deliver from death and suffer not to come into darkness" (4:10). "It is better to give alms than to lay up gold, for alms deliver from death" (12:8–9). Subsequently, the Talmud adopted the same interpretation of the word *tzedakah* in Proverbs: "Charity delivers from death" (*Baba Batra* 10a).

The new interpretation of tzedakah was firmly established in the talmudic era. This interpretation reflects the intuitive insight of Judaism that charity is an obligation based on justice rather than an optional act based on compassion. Rabbinic courts were empowered to levy special taxes for charitable purposes.

The rabbis continued to emphasize the importance of charity. "Charity and deeds of kindness are as important as all the mitzvot combined" (Jer. *Peah* 1:1). "Prayer, charity, and penitence annul a harsh decree" (*Rosh HaShanah* 16b). "Anyone who shuts his eye against charity is like one who worships idols" (*Ketubot* 68a). Dozens of similar maxims elevated charity to a position of paramount importance in Jewish religious life.

Among the early charitable institutions were *tamchuy* (daily free meals for those who had no food in the house), *kuppah* (funds to provide for Sabbath expenses), clothing funds, and burial funds (*Baba Batra* 8a). Special assistance was also extended to the poor to procure Passover provisions (*Pesachim* 99b, Jer. *Peah* 1:6) and the Purim seudah (*Baba Metzia* 78b). Raising and marrying off orphans was considered one of the worthiest charities (*Ketubot* 50a). The ransoming of Jewish captives was another must charity (*Baba Batra* 8b).

The ancient charitable institutions were expanded and diversified in the Middle Ages. The needs of itinerant indigents, refugees from mob violence, were met by the establishment of communal hostelries and inns. Special societies were set up for the care of the aged and the sick. The Chevrah Kadisha (burial society) attracted many volunteers. Societies for the provision of dowries and apparel for poor brides assumed great importance. Population growth was of vital importance to the Jewish community in view of the frequent massacres which regularly decreased the Jewish census. Funds for the ransoming of Jewish captives had a particular claim upon Jewish resources. Pidyon

Shevuyim (ransom of captives) was the medieval equivalent of the modern UJA. Special charity for Palestinian institutions was another prominent feature of medieval tzedakah.

The mitzvah of tzedakah is incumbent upon all Jews, including those who are recipients of charity (*Gittin* 7b; Tobit, chap. 4). Charity boxes were introduced in synagogues for the convenience of worshippers who wish to associate prayer with charity. In time, charity boxes were also introduced into private homes by various charitable institutions. At the beginning of the nineteenth century, the fund of Rabbi Meir *Baal Hanes* ("the miracle-maker"), which distributed money in Palestine, was among the first to place charity boxes in the home. Charity boxes for yeshivot and the Jewish National Fund were popular in the twentieth century.

It is customary to drop money in the charity box prior to the lighting of Sabbath candles.

HONOR OF PARENTS

The biblical commandment of parental honor is not centered exclusively on the home. However, most filial acts which flow from that mitzvah are performed in the home. A mishnah lists five filial obligations: "To feed him, give him drink, to clothe him, put on his shoes, and lead him" (*Edduyot* 2:9). Of these five obligations, four are domestic chores.

A beraita defines reverence of parents as follows: "He shall not stand in his place [where he is accustomed to stand], not sit in his place, not contradict him, and not openly voice agreement with a scholarly opinion with which his father disagrees" (*Kiddushin* 31b).

The apocryphal Tobit included parents-in-law in the same category as parents: "Honor thy father and thy mother in-law, which are now thy parents" (chap. 10). A similar opinion was expressed fifteen hundred years later by Rabbi Jacob Asheri in the *Tur* code (*Yoreh Deah* 240).

Tradition prohibits children from calling parents by their first names (*Yoreh Deah* 240:2). It also prohibits them from calling other people by their first names, in the presence of their parents, if their names are similar. This prohibition is one of the reasons behind the Ashkenazic tradition of not naming a child for a living parent. It would be improper for a sibling to call the child by name in the presence of his or her parents.

COVERING THE HEAD

Rav Huna b. Rabbi Joshua, a 4th century Amora, felt that he was entitled to a special heavenly reward because he never walked bareheaded a distance of 4 cubits (Shabbat 118b). His practice was motivated by a strong consciousness of the presence of God above his head (Kiddushin 31a). Apparently, he considered it unseemly to expose the nakedness of his head in the presence of God. However, Rav Huna did not suggest that his personal practice become the norm of an average individual.

Rav Nachman (4th cent.) was cautioned by his mother in his youth to cover his head to induce the fear of God in him (Shabbat 156b). It is obvious that this was not the standard custom of that time.

The idea that people in motion must at times abide by stricter religious regulations than sedentary individuals originated in Palestine in the 3rd century. The centralized seat of religion, embodied in the Temple and later in the Sanhedrin, was replaced by Isaiah's slogan of decentralized divine omnipresence: "The whole earth is filled with his glory" (6:3). The glory of God is more obvious in the great outdoors. Rabbi Joshua b. Levi (3rd cent.) said: "It is forbidden to walk a distance of 4 cubits with erect (proud or arrogant) stature because the whole earth is full of God's glory" (Kiddushin 31a).

Rabbi Joshua's perception was popularized by the Babylonian Amoraim of the 3rd and 4th centuries. Hence Rav Huna's practice to cover his head when he walked about. Rabbi Sheshet (3rd cent.) never walked about without his tefillin on him. Rav Nachman (4th cent.) never walked about without wearing tzitzit (Shabbat 118b).

What was the significance of walking? A moving person must direct his attention outward. He has to be aware of his environment. The sight of heaven should inspire him with an awareness of god's presence. A sedentary person, on the other hand, withdraws into his inner shell of existence and loses touch with the outside world.

There are times, however, when even a sedentary person's attention is forcefully drawn to an awareness of God. Such is the case of an individual engaged in prayer at home and in the synagogue. By the time of the publication of Masechet Soferim (8th cent.), the law requiring worshippers to wear hats was well established. "A person who wears tattered clothes, revealing his legs or body, or one whose head is uncovered is not permitted to mention God's name . . . he may not read from the Torah (for the congregation), he may not lead the service, nor pronounce the priestly benediction" (ch. 14). Bareheadedness was obviously considered a "nakedness" as objectionable as the exposure of other parts of the body which are normally covered.

Maimonides (12th cent.) similarly regarded bareheadedness a breach of modesty. "Scholars are accustomed to conduct themselves with great modesty to avoid being embarrassed by the uncovering of their heads or bodies" (Hilchot Deot 5:6). He drew no distinction between people in motion or in sedentary positions because modesty is equally compelling for both. However, he, too, imposed such high standards of modesty only upon scholars.

By the 16th century, rabbinic opposition to bareheadedness was backed by a consensus of most Jews. Rabbi Solomon Luria (Maharshal), an independent scholar who traced the talmudic sources of religious customs, asserted that he could find no basis in the Talmud for the blanket prohibition of uncovering one's head. However, he alleged that public opinion in this matter was so strong that one must defer to it even in the privacy of his home (Reponsum 72).

Rabbis of later generations offered an additional reason for the prohibition of bareheadedness. It is a non-Jewish practice and Jews were enjoined in the Bible not to follow their customs (Lev. 18:3).

The law requiring women to cover their heads so as not to expose their hair dates back at least to the 2nd century. The Talmud derived this restriction from a biblical verse (Ketubot 72a). The objection to the exposure of female hair was based on considerations of moraliry rather than modesty. The sight of a woman's hair was considered sexually provocative (Berachot 24a). A wife who defied convention and walked in the street with her head uncovered was guilty of an act of immorality. Interestingly, virgins were excepted from this restriction (Bayit Chadash, Tur Even HaEzer 21. Lo yelechu). This concession was probably due to the need of girls to display their beauty in order to attract prospective husbands. Married women traditionally covered their heads with scarves, hats and, since the 19th century, with wigs *(sheitel)*.

In modern times the head cover became a mark of distinction between the different groupings of Judaism. Most Reform Jews worship with heads uncovered. Conservative Jews cover their heads at Services and whenever prayers are recited. Orthodox Jews cover their heads at all times.

The skull-cap *(yarmulke)* came into use in answer to the need for lightening the weight of the hat on the head and to satisfy at the same time the religious requirement of covering one's head. Initially, there were only black caps which covered the entire head and were tall enough to be visible from a distance. Modern skull-caps come in all sizes and colors and lie flat on the head. To some extent, the yarmulke has become a criterion of the wearer's degree of Orthodoxy and Zionist sympathies. Extreme tradirionalists wear a large black skull-cap under the hat. The hat is worn in the street and during Services. Modern Orthodox Jews, supporters of religious Zionism, wear a medium sized skull-cap at home and in the synagogue. Activist youth groups, most of whom are products of religious day-schools, wear bright skull-caps of diminutive sizes which satisfy a need for symbolism rather than strict theology.

3

The Sabbath and Its Customs

INTRODUCTION

THE SURVIVAL OF the Jewish people, without territorial roots or a common language, is regarded by many historians as an enigma. If they are puzzled by the phenomenon of Jewish durability, it is because they fail to take into account the dynamics of Judaism and its customs. The crucial role of the Sabbath, for instance, in the preservation of Jewish identity is recognized only by those who observe it.

The element which immunized Jews against assimilation was their religious distinctiveness. Judaism, with its stress of pure monotheism, cannot be reconciled with any other faith known to man. However, abstract religious doctrines and philosophic differences alone would not be able to cope with the inevitable erosion by alien influences. Only physical and highly visible differences can form a shield against external forces and guarantee national and religious integrity.

Judaism has a complex code of laws and customs which regulates every aspect of life. Not all of them are distinctively Judaic in character. Prayer is common to all people. Justice and ethics are the avowed goals of all creeds. But there are a few areas, peculiar to Judaism, which have cast the Jew into a distinctive mold. The dietary laws have created a specific Jewish image which has hindered free social intercourse with people of other faiths. The rite of circumcision falls within the same category. Yet these rites could never have countered on their own the effect of the blandishments which were offered to the weak and the persecutions which were designed to crush the strong. Only the Sabbath, with its compensatory therapeutic features, could provide the essential preservative ingredients.

107

SABBATH AND CIRCUMCISION

The rites of circumcision and the Sabbath are equally basic to Judaism. Both laws are memorials to a special covenant between God and the children of Israel. "He that is born in thy house . . . must be circumcised and my covenant shall be on your flesh for an everlasting covenant" (Gen. 17:13). "Wherefore the children of Israel shall keep the Sabbath to observe the Sabbath throughout the generations for a perpetual covenant" (Exod. 31:16). Both laws precede the Sinaitic revelation.

The Sabbath and circumcision are rites which Jews have traditionally defended with their lives. Such commitment was regarded by the rabbis as a guarantee that these commandments shall never totally disappear (*Mechilta*, Exod. 31:17).

The primacy of circumcision and the Sabbath in Judaism gave rise to an allegorical discussion as to which of the two is more important. The question came up in an alleged debate between them. "The Sabbath asserted: 'I am greater than you because the Almighty rested on the seventh day.' " To which circumcision retorted: "I am greater than you. If not for me, God would never have created the world." This contention was based on a verse in Jeremiah (33:25). The argument was finally resolved in favor of circumcision. This conclusion was supported by the fact that circumcisions may be performed even on the Sabbath, proving the precedence of the former over the latter (*Yalkut*, Jeremiah 321).

Regardless of the relative theological importance of each of these rites, the sociological value of the Sabbath ranks it as the foremost tool in the struggle for Jewish survival in the diaspora. While the pentateuchal stress was upon the Jewish preservation of the Sabbath, the rabbinic stress, to borrow a phrase from Achad HaAm, was the preservation of the Jewish people by the Sabbath. Circumcision set the Jew apart from the non-Jew, but its impact on the Jewish psyche and outlook was minimal. The Sabbath, on the other hand, generated an abundance of therapeutic qualities. By providing a weekly opportunity for the renewal of faith and hope, it became the cornerstone of developing Judaism. Rabbi Judah HaNasi (2nd cent.) justifiably proclaimed: "The mitzvah of Sabbath is equal in importance to all other mitzvot combined" (Jer. *Berachot* 1:5). He based his statement on Nehemiah 9:14. A similar statement was subsequently expressed in *Shemot Rabbah* (25).

The frequent bracketing of circumcision and the Sabbath in the

Talmud reflects a period in Jewish history when the Sabbath began to gain the adherence of many non-Jews. The initial vile reaction of Greek and Roman historians to the Sabbath gradually gave way to a more tolerant view, as the Jewish diaspora spread and intimate contacts between the people of different communities were established. The idea of a weekly day of rest, a Jewish innovation, undoubtedly appealed to many individuals, both in the aristocracy and the lower classes. The growing circle of Sabbath-observers included pagans and also Christians who celebrated the Sabbath on Saturdays. It was not until the Council of Laodicea outlawed this practice in the second half of the fourth century that the number of Christian Sabbath-observers was drastically reduced.

A pagan Sabbath and a Christian Sabbath posed a threat to the Jewish Sabbath. The rabbis viewed with disfavor the spread of the Sabbath among non-Jews. They interpreted the biblical verse "See that the Lord has given you the Sabbath" (Exod. 16:29) as exclusionary in its intent. "It was given to you [the Jews] and not to the nations of the world" (*Shemot Rabbah* 25). The rabbis were particularly disturbed by Christian attempts to persuade the Jews to shift their Sabbath to Sunday. These efforts are reflected in the alleged question of the "nations of the world": "Why are you celebrating the Sabbath on this day [Saturday]?" Jews were advised to respond to this question by pointing to the manna, which had fallen in the desert every day of the week except for Saturdays. This established the fact that God had ordained Saturday as the Sabbath (*Shemot Rabbah* 25).

To give greater emphasis to their objection to non-Jewish Sabbath-observers, the rabbis declared: "The nations of the world who observe the Sabbath are not entitled to any reward. On the contrary, they are guilty of a capital offense" (ibid.). The expression "capital offense" was a figure of speech, reflecting the seriousness of an objectionable act. A Sabbath-observer who did not practice the rite of circumcision was not a Jew and his Sabbath did not convey a commitment to the Old Testament. Hence the statement of Rabbi Jose b. Rabbi Chanina (3rd cent.): "A Kusi [non-Jew] who observes the Sabbath prior to his acceptance of the rite of circumcision is guilty of a capital offense" (*Yalkut* 391). Isaiah's welcome to aliens who keep the Sabbath was limited to those who "joined the Lord" (56:6).

The rabbis established the Sabbath as the mainstay of Judaism. Before we discuss the impact of the rabbinic Sabbath upon the Jewish people, we have to trace the development of this unique institution from its inception in the Pentateuch.

THE BIBLICAL SABBATH

The first reference to the special character of the seventh day (Saturday) appears in Genesis (2:3). "And God blessed the seventh day and hallowed it" *(vayekadesh oto)*. The chief attribute of the Sabbath, "holiness," is repeatedly noted in the Bible (Exod. 16:23, 20:10, 14:15; Lev. 23:3; Deut. 5:12). The term "holiness" eludes a precise definition. In common parlance it is an exemplary state of virtue, such as piety, humility, charity, and other admirable traits that exceed the normal standard of human behavior. In other words, a holy person is one who is set apart from the rest of humanity by the quality of his life. A holy day is one which is set apart, or above, the other days of the year. A kohen is a holy person (Exod. 29:1) because he was set apart to minister to God. The nazirite is holy (Num. 6:5) because he abstains from some human pleasures in his dedication to God. The Jews are a holy people (Lev. 19:2) because they are set apart by their observance of the Torah.

The holiness of the Sabbath may be attributed to several reasons. As a social holiday which entitles the servant and beasts of burden to rest, it is distinct from other days by its ethical quality and is therefore a holy day (Exod. 20:8–11, 23:12). As a memorial to God's creation of the world and his resting on the seventh day, it is a holy day because it gives man an opportunity to imitate the ways of God.

The initial reference to the Sabbath in Genesis links God's cessation of work with the holiness of the day (Gen. 2:2–3). Therefore the holiness of the Sabbath is repeatedly linked in the Pentateuch with the cessation of labor (Exod. 20:10–11, 31:15; Lev. 23:3; Deut. 5:12–13). The Talmud similarly highlights the cessation of work as the factor which lent holiness to the biblical Sabbath. " 'Sanctify it' by cessation from work" *(Rosh HaShanah* 32a). The stress on holiness stemming from a commitment to God inevitably produced an aura of solemnity and austerity in the observance of the Sabbath.

The Sabbath, unlike other festivals, did not require a proclamation by a high priest or Sanhedrin since its date was always fixed in the religious calendar. Nevertheless, it did require a proclamation or sanctification by each individual Jew. This, too, was in imitation of God's sanctification *(kiddush)* of the first Sabbath. This is the implication of the scriptural text: "Six days shall work be done but on the seventh day is a Sabbath of rest, a proclamation of holiness [*mikra kodesh*]" (Lev. 23:3). We will discuss later the precise meaning of *mikra kodesh*. The rabbinic interpretation of the commandment "Remember the Sabbath day to keep it holy" (Exod. 20:8) is "remember it by a sanctification [*kiddush*]" *(Pesachim* 106a).

We have no definite information on the ancient kiddush. Fortunately, there is a record in the Talmud of the official proclamation or sanctification of Rosh Chodesh. "The Sanhedrin proclaim: 'It is sanctified; and the people who are present repeat: 'It is sanctified, it is sanctified' " (*Rosh HaShanah* 24a). As for the Sabbath, it is the people who proclaim that the Sabbath is sanctified (ibid.). The ancient kiddush, it appears, was a single word, *mekudash*.

The absence of any reference in the Pentateuch to feasting or rejoicing on the Sabbath leads us to the conclusion that the emphasis was on spiritual exultation rather than physical joy. Josephus (1st cent.) left a description of the ancient Sabbath. It probably represented a traditional concept of what the pentateuchal Sabbath was like. He mentioned no feasting or celebrations, only the fact that Jews set aside periods of study on that day. Moses issued a decree "permitting Jews to leave off their employment and to assemble together for the hearing of the law" (*Against Apion* 2:18). The same tradition is implied in the talmudic assertion which attributes to Moses the decree of reading portions of the Pentateuch in public on the Sabbath (Jer. *Megillah* 4).

Philo, the Alexandrian Jewish philosopher (1st cent.), mentioned a tradition that some ancient Jews used to assemble on the Sabbath for prayers. In his *Life of Moses* he comments on the wood-gatherer who violated the first Sabbath (Num. 15:32). The wood-gatherer, he says, was discovered by "some persons who had gone forth out of the gates to some quiet spot that they might pray in some retired and peaceful place" (3:19).

Philo conveys the impression that the Sabbath was exclusively a day of prayer and study. "When the body is laboring the soul may be at rest, and when the body is enjoying relaxation the soul may be laboring" (*On the Festivals* 3:270). He made no mention at all of any festive aspect of the Sabbath in the days of Moses or even of the Sabbath in his own time. This is surprising in view of the fact that the rabbinic sages Hillel and Shammai, who were his contemporaries, were already deeply involved in the process of transforming the Sabbath into a day of joy as well as a day of spiritual enrichment. Curiously, Philo's statement about the alternate periods when the body and mind are engaged in work was echoed in a late midrash (edited in the 9th century): " 'The Sabbath was given for pleasure', that refers to scholars who study hard all week long and on the Sabbath they relax and enjoy themselves. 'It was given for study,' that refers to laborers who work physically all week long and on the Sabbath they study the Torah" (*Pesikta Rabbati* 23).

We must caution against any conclusion that the pentateuchal Sabbath was completely devoid of physical joys. The chapter which deals with the "festivals" *(moadei)* opens with the Sabbath (Lev. 23:2). This seems to indicate that the Sabbath is a festival in substance, even if not in name. It is only natural to assume that the ancient farmer, who rested once a week from his chores, dressed and ate differently on that day. Surely the servant and the beast of burden relished their bodily relaxation on the day of rest. However, the Pentateuch emphasizes the holiness of the Sabbath and seems to regard any festive aspect as merely incidental to its objective.

MIKRA KODESH

What is the significance of the term *mikra kodesh*, which the Bible links to all festivals as well as the Sabbath (Lev. 23:3)? Nachmanides and Soforno, two outstanding exegetists, render *mikra kodesh* as "holy assemblies." Nachmanides relates the word *mikra* to the term *kruei haedah*, which he translates as "the assembled people of the congregation" (Num. 1:16). Soforno relates *mikra* to the implication of that word in Isaiah, *Chodesh veshabbat kro mikra* (1:13), which he renders "New moon and Sabbath, the holding of assemblies." This rendition of *mikra kodesh* has been adopted by most Jewish translators of the Bible into English.

The translation of *mikra kodesh* as "holy assembly" carries the implication of a biblical command that Jews hold assemblies on the Sabbath. Nachmanides elaborates upon the nature of such assemblies. "The reason for the holy convocation is that they [the Jews] should all be assembled on that day to sanctify that day because it is meritorious for all Jews to be assembled in one place on the festival, to sanctify the day in public with prayer and songs of praise, dressed in clean clothes, in a manner befitting a day of feasting" (Lev. 23:2). It is not clear whether his remarks are confined to festivals only. The same *mikra kodesh* upon which he centers his comments is also associated in the next verse with the Sabbath.

With all due deference to the opinions of such eminent exegetists, there appears little evidence to support their views. The *kruei haedah* cited by Nachmanides does not mean the "assembled people of the congregation" but more likely, "those who were called out (or elected) by the congregation." There might have been a Sabbath assembly in the days of Moses, who, according to tradition, ordained the reading of the Torah in public. Such assemblies were feasible in the encampment in the desert. There is no evidence of Sabbath assemblies after Moses, with the possible exception of the Temple era in Jerusalem, where informal crowds might have gathered to witness the Sabbath sacrificial rites.

Nachmanides cited the Aramaic translation of Onkelos, who rendered *mikra kodesh* as "when a holy day occurs" (Lev. 23:3). *Mikra,* according to Onkelos, is related to a Hebrew word which means "occurrence." Nachmanides obviously disagrees with this translation, and it has not been adopted by any other translator.

I believe that the most accurate rendition of *mikra kodesh* is indicated in the Talmud. "These are the festivals of the Lord which you must proclaim [*asher tikreu*]" (*Rosh HaShanah* 34a). *Torah Temimah* explains this passage as follows: "It seems that the Talmud interprets the word *tikreu* to mean 'you shall proclaim' or 'publicize.' *Tikreu* is related and used in the same sense as *ukaratem deror* 'and you shall proclaim liberty' [Lev. 23:3]" Following this rendition, we arrive at a translation of the text which is in accord with the talmudic interpretation: "Speak unto the children of Israel, and say unto them: The appointed seasons of the Lord, which you shall proclaim with a proclamation of holiness [*mikra kodesh*]" (Lev. 22:2). The Talmud assumes this to be a reference to kiddush.

THE POST-PENTATEUCHAL SABBATH

There was no substantial change in the character of the Sabbath in the period of the Judges and the Monarchy. The religious leadership continued to be engaged in a running battle with pervasive paganism and its orgies. There was very little incentive to diminish the solemnity of the Sabbath. God-fearing people attended Sabbath lectures given by the prophets (II Kings 4:23). There were special ceremonies connected with the Sabbath service in the Temple, which very likely attracted substantial crowds. There was an additional sacrificial offering *(karban musaf).* The loaves of the shewbread, exhibited for a week, were replaced on the Sabbath by fresh loaves. There was a change of the weekly watch of the priests on the Sabbath. The king's guards, too, were changed on Saturdays. Generally, in the atmosphere of religious laxity prevailing through most of the period, the Sabbath was as much neglected as most of the other precepts of the Torah.

Some historians believe that the Sabbath was transformed into a festival of joy in the period of the prophets. They base this opinion on a text in Hosea (8th cent. B.C.E.) in which the prophet denounced the iniquities of his time and warned the people in the name of the Lord: "I will cause all the mirth to cease; her feasts, her new moons, and her Sabbaths and all her appointed seasons" (2:13). It is assumed that the "mirth" is associated with all the enumerated occasions, including the Sabbath. Even if that is true, the Hebrew word for "mirth" used by the prophet is ambivalent. *Mesos* is more frequently applied to intellectual and emotional ecstasy than to sensual pleasures. Thus the prophet's exclamation: "I will greatly rejoice [*sos asis*] in the Lord, my soul shall be joyful in my God" (Isa. 61:10). Hosea might have referred to the festivity of the holidays and the ecstasy of the Sabbath.

The first clear indication of a conceptual change in the character of the Sabbath is found in Isaiah (8th cent. B.C.E.). "Call the Sabbath a delight [*oneg*] . . . and thou shalt honor it . . ." (58:13). What kind of "delight" did Isaiah have in mind—spiritual, physical, or both? The theme of the chapter is criticism of the insincerity of some Jews who follow the form of the law but not its substance. They fast on Yom Kippur and abide by the restrictions of the Sabbath, but their minds are preoccupied with mundane matters. The prophet appealed to them to regain the spirit of the holiness of the Sabbath.

Isaiah's appeal to the Jews to call the Sabbath a delight appears in the last third of the book, which addresses itself to the exilic period. The forty-fourth chapter specifically deals with King Cyrus and the rebuilding of Jerusalem. This raises the question whether we are to associate the *oneg* mentioned in the fifty-eighth chapter with the eighth century B.C.E. or the Babylonian period, when many changes took place.

The talmudic sages were not concerned with the timing of Isaiah's proclamation. What was important to them was that the word *oneg*, associated with the Sabbath, appears in the Bible, and that offered a biblical basis for their introduction of a new dimension to the concept of the Sabbath. The expression Oneg Shabbat, based on Isaiah, has become a household word in many modern Jewish homes and institutions. The new concept had its inception after the exile and took many centuries for its full fruition.

The Babylonian diaspora renewed its commitment to the Torah. The Sabbath and festivals were strictly observed. There is little evidence, however, of an early transformation of the Sabbath into a day of joy. The prophet Ezekiel (6th cent. B.C.E.), the religious leader of the diaspora, bent all his efforts upon the restoration of the solemnity and holiness of the pentateuchal Sabbath. Reminding the people that it was the desecration of the Sabbath, among other things, which had led to their exile (20:24), and reiterating the pentateuchal rationale of the Sabbath as a sign that God had sanctified them (20:12), he urged the people to sanctify the Sabbath (44:24). In his vision of the reconstructed Temple, he highlighted the renewal of the sacrificial rites of the Sabbath (46:4). He also spoke of the people who would come to bow down (or worship) at the door of the gate before the Lord on the Sabbaths and the new moons (46:3). That may reflect the first Babylonian innovation, public assemblies for worship on the Sabbath.

The Jews who returned to Palestine in 538 B.C.E. soon fell victim to assimilation and intermarriage. Nehemiah was appointed governor of Judea in 433 B.C.E. He left a report of his shock upon discovering a market day in Jerusalem on the Sabbath. "In those days, I saw in Judea some treading wine-presses on the Sabbath, and bringing heaps of corn . . . which they brought into Jerusalem on the Sabbath day" (13:15). Nehemiah reminded the Jewish leaders that it was the profanation of the Sabbath which had caused the destruction of Jerusalem by the Babylonians. He thereupon ordered the closing of the gates of the city on the eve of the Sabbath, and the market day was discontinued. We may assume that as a result of Nehemiah's drastic moves the number of Sabbath-observers greatly increased.

THE RABBINICAL SABBATH

The rabbis added many restrictions, or "fences," to the Sabbath to keep it from being violated. However, they also transformed the Sabbath into a day of delight and physical pleasure as well as spiritual expansion. The Sabbath was molded to promote holiness, religious ecstasy, happiness, tranquility, domestic harmony, relaxation of tensions, and intellectual stimulation. In addition to its effect on individuals, it also produced congregational solidarity and a tightening of communal ties and structure.

The earliest rabbinical enactments, designed to enhance the atmosphere of the Sabbath, date back to the beginning of the rabbinical era. Ezra (5th cent. B.C.E.) is said to have decreed that the family laundry be done on Thursdays, instead of Fridays, to make sure that clean clothes were ready for the Sabbath and that the housewife would have enough time on Friday to make all the elaborate Sabbath preparations (*Baba Kama* 82a).

The custom of providing clean clothes for the Sabbath obviously predated Ezra. It is also clear that the preparations for the Sabbath were already complex enough to take up the entire day of Friday. The cleaning of the house, purchasing of food, and cooking and baking were among the chores performed on Fridays. The insistance that Jews wear clean clothes on the Sabbath was widely publicized because it reflected respect for the holiness of the Sabbath and put the wearer in a festive frame of mind.

Doing the laundry has remained a prominent feature of the preparations for the Sabbath, from the days of Ezra and on. The time of doing it, however, varied from place to place and from time to time. Rabbi Simon b. Gamliel (2nd cent. c.e.) reported that it was the practice in his father's home to deliver the weekly wash to a Gentile launderer three days before the Sabbath (*Shabbat* 18a).

The *Zadokite Document* of the Essenes similarly stresses the importance of wearing clean clothes on the Sabbath. "No one is to wear soiled clothes or clothes that have been put in storage unless they first be laundered" (X. 14).

Another ordinance credited to Ezra was the provision for the reading of the Torah at Sabbath Minchah services and on Monday and Thursday mornings (*Baba Kama* 82a). The synagogue, as we know it today, did not exist at that time. People assembled at various places to hear the Torah read. Congregations thus emerged even prior to the establishment of synagogues. The return of the congregation to a place of worship for Minchah services presented another opportunity for lectures and study.

We hear of no more innovations until the Hasmonean period (2nd cent. b.c.e.). Syrian efforts to impose paganism on the Judeans triggered sporadic resistance by pious Jews even prior to the outbreak of the Hasmonean rebellion. The Syrians soon discovered that there was little resistence on the Sabbath because fighting was considered a serious violation of the holy day. The enemy exploited the piety of the fighters to their own advantage, bringing death to those who accepted martyrdom rather than defend their lives by desecrating the Sabbath. The Hasmonean court, however, ruled that human life takes precedence over the Sabbath (I Macc. 2). Out of this ruling emerged the fundamental rabbinical principle of *pikuach nefesh* (the saving of life; *Ketubot* 15b), which mandates the suspension of all Sabbath laws when a human life is at stake.

The pious resisters who had upheld the sacredness of the Sabbath, even at the cost of life, must have had a convincing argument in support of their view. A soldier who serves a king owes him complete obedience, including his life. Should one give less in the service of the

King of Kings? The Hasmonean liberalization reflects a basic Judaic concept that the value of a single life is equivalent to that of collective mankind. The Torah was designed to humanize life, to ennoble it, and to give it a godly quality, but not to make man forfeit it (*Yoma* 85b). With reference to the Sabbath, Rabbi Simon b. Menasya (2nd cent.) put it this way: "The Sabbath was turned over to you, but you were not turned over to the Sabbath" (*Mechilta, Ki Tisa* 2).

Rabbi Simon's maxim was well known long before his time. It is quoted in the Gospels (Mark 2:27). However, the rabbinical liberalization was confined only to cases where life was in danger. In that event all restrictions were removed, even if the life was that of a one-day-old infant (*Shabbat* 151b). The Hebrew Christians, on the other hand, sought to broaden the liberalization to permit the violation of the Sabbath even if it is only for the sake of convenience, such as appeasement of hunger.

At the other end of the spectrum, there were apparently some fundamentalist, non-rabbinic Jewish sects who refused to adopt the liberal maxim of *pikuach nefesh*. The *Zadokite Document* contains the following passage: "If a human being falls into a place of water . . . let no man bring him up by a ladder or a rope or any other implement [on the Sabbath]." Some scholars, startled by this conflict with a universally accepted Jewish principle, amended the text to read: "If a human being falls into a place of water . . . one is to bring him up by a ladder, etc." (Gaster, *Dead Sea Scriptures*, p. 104, note 54). This emendation is based on the assumption that the principle of *pikuach nefesh* was accepted by all Jews. That is questionable. The underlying theme of the Dead Sea Scrolls is that man's noblest and exclusive function is to serve God. His life may not be worth saving if God's command is thereby violated.

The pronouncement of the Hasmonean court that the Sabbath must preserve Jewish life was the forerunner of the subsequent talmudic concept of one of the basic functions of the Sabbath. It must not only preserve Jewish life but also Jewish identity. That concept was the seed from which the rabbinical Sabbath grew.

THE RITUAL USE OF WINE FOR KIDDUSH

The next step in the development of the Sabbath was the introduction of the use of ritual wine for its sanctification (*kiddush*). The need for a verbal proclamation to that effect is inherent in the command "to remember" the Sabbath and in the biblical term *mikra kodesh*, as was previously pointed out. The use of wine for Kiddush is of rabbinical origin (Maimonides, *Hilchot Shabbat* 29:6). It was most likely introduced in the first century B.C.E. (Bloch, *Biblical and Historical Background of the Jewish Holy Days*, p. 129).

Wine was not normally served on the ordinary days of the year. Its early appearance on the dinner table was timed with days of special significance, such as Sabbaths and festivals. A connection was thus established between the wine and the special nature of the day. The rabbis therefore suggested that the wine be used in conjunction with the Kiddush as an explanation that the wine is served in honor of the Sabbath. This is the significance of the rabbinical dictum: "Remember the Sabbath day to keep it holy, remember it over wine" (*Pesachim* 106a).

SABBATH LIGHTS

The custom of lighting Sabbath candles seems to have similarly emerged in the first century B.C.E. The mishnah which discusses the question "Wherewith may we kindle?" (*Shabbat* 20b) treats candle-lighting as a well-known and long-established custom. One of the sages mentioned in that mishnah is Nahum the Mede, a survivor of the destruction of Jerusalem. This appears to support our view of the antiquity of Sabbath candles. The use of lights for festive effect emerged in the first century B.C.E. Such was the case of the lighting of candelabra on Simchat Bet HaShoavah (libation of the altar; *Sukkah* 51a) and the lighting of Chanukah candles (*Shabbat* 21b). The Sabbath lights, like the other lights, were intended to heighten the festive character of the day. The Talmud discusses the legal aspects of these three occasions on which the kindling of lights was incidental to the celebration (*Shabbat* 21a). That too seems to indicate a common historical origin.

As a spontaneous custom which did not originate by rabbinical decree, it lacked preciseness of detail. The number of candles to be used was not definitely determined. Thus it paralleled the development of the custom of Chanukah lights. Initially, most people used only one candle on each of the Chanukah nights (*Shabbat* 21b). This was most likely also true of the Sabbath light. However, at the very outset there were some people who lit multiple candles on Chanukah (ibid.), and there were also people who used multiple candles on Friday eve (*Shabbat* 23b). A minimum number of two candles was ordained in the fourteenth century, corresponding to the two Sabbath injunctions, "remember" and "observe" (*Tur, Hilchot Shabbat* 263).

Unlike the Chanukah candles, which originated in Palestine, there is a possibility that the custom of Sabbath candles may have emerged first in the diaspora. In view of the early resistance to the celebration of Chanukah in some parts of the Jewish diaspora, it is conceivable that the Jews of those countries might have initiated the Sabbath lights in place of the Chanukah lights, which they felt compelled to reject for political reasons. Regardless of the place of origin of the Sabbath lights, the custom was widespread throughout the diaspora. Rabbi Yochanan b. Nuri (first half of the 2nd cent.) mentioned the prevailing candle-lighting customs of the Babylonian, Modean, Alexandrian, and Cappadocian Jews (*Shabbat* 26a).

Despite the popularity of the custom, candle-lighting was apparently neglected for a long time in many homes. The cost of candles was excessive for the poor. Thus the Talmud considered the situation of some people who were forced to make a choice between Chanukah and Sabbath candles when the two holidays coincided (*Shabbat* 23b). There were also women who were still too preoccupied with house chores when candle-lighting time arrived and were consequently in no position to comply with the custom.

To counteract this negligence, the rabbis publicized the punishment which results from failing to light candles and the reward of those who comply with the custom. "For three sins women die in childbirth, because they are not careful in the observance of the laws of niddah, chalah, and the kindling of lights" (*Shabbat* 31a). On the other hand, "The reward for regular Sabbath lighting is the promise of scholarly children" (*Shabbat* 23b). Again, "If you observe the lights of Sabbath, I will grant you the privilege of seeing the lights of Zion" (*Yalkut, Behaalotcha* 719). The custom eventually became universal as a result of persistent rabbinical efforts to enhance the glamour and joy of the Sabbath. Generations later, the sages based the custom of Sabbath candles on the verse in Isaiah "and thou shalt call the Sabbath a delight" (58:13). In the words of the rabbis: "There can be no delight if one dwells in darkness" (*Tanchuma, Noah* 1).

The lighting of candles was never classified as a mitzvah. Rav (3rd cent.) pronounced it a *chovah* [obligation] (*Shabbat* 25b; Maimonides, des, *Hilchot Shabbat* 5:1). Because it was only an obligation, no benediction for this ritual was ever indicated in the Talmud. Rav Ahai Gaon (8th cent.) was the first authority to refer to a benediction (*HaManhig, Hilchot Shabbat* 17).

Husbands were requested to remind their wives of the obligation to light candles (*Shabbat* 34a). They were cautioned, however, to use a calm, conversational tone. Intimidation might cause some women, who were delayed by work, to light candles after dark. A pleasant disposition was also essential to the maintenance of domestic harmony on the Sabbath.

IN THE FIRST CENTURY C.E.

A concerted effort to enhance the impact of the Sabbath was begun in the first century. By stressing the preparations for the Sabbath the joy of anticipation is increased. Hillel, we are told, used to scrub his head on Fridays (*Shabbat* 31a). His colleague, Shammai, emphasized the importance of a tasty Sabbath meal. "If he found a well-flavored animal, he said: 'Let it be for the Sabbath.' If he subsequently found a better-flavored animal, he put aside the second for the Sabbath and ate the first" (*Betzah* 16a).

Shammai was also mindful of the need to prevent sadness and sorrow from disturbing the serenity of the Sabbath. He therefore prohibited visits to the sick and the offering of condolences on the Sabbath (*Shabbat* 12a). Although these restrictions were liberalized later, his effort to preserve the peacefulness of the Sabbath continued to motivate rabbinical legislation. Thus we were told that "we do not recite the eighteen benedictions on the Sabbath because if one has a sick member of the family at home, he will be saddened by the benediction which is addressed to God 'who is the healer of the sick of his people Israel,' and he will be distressed. The Sabbath was given to Israel for sanctity, delight, and rest, not for sorrow" (*Tanchuma, Vayera* 1).

SHOFAR SIGNALS

The practice of announcing the coming of the Sabbath with blasts of the shofar most likely originated in the first century C.E. "Six blasts were blown on the eve of the Sabbath. The first for farmers to cease work in the field; the second, for the city shops to close; the third, for the Sabbath candles to be lit" (*Shabbat* 35b). After a short interval, there were three more blasts "and the Sabbath was commenced." Rabban Simon b. Gamliel (2nd cent.) commented on a slight difference in the custom of the Babylonian Jews and added that it was inadvisable to interfere with their practice "because they retain their fathers' custom," i.e., it is an old and well established tradition. We may therefore assume that the practice had already been in vogue in the first century.

In a society where the position of the sun was the only means of gauging the time of day, there was a real need for informing the people when to return home for the Sabbath. The shofar was a convenient medium for transmitting public announcements, although its range was obviously limited. The practice of using the shofar for Sabbath signals was not carried over into other countries of the diaspora. In place of the shofar, medieval Jewish communities adopted the custom of having the shamash knock on doors to summon the people to Sabbath services. However, the use of the shofar was retained in some Italian ghettos (Roth, *History of the Jews in Venice*, p. 148). It was also renewed in many settlements of the Yishuv in Palestine.

IN THE SECOND CENTURY

The transformation of the Sabbath into a day of joy and festivity continued at an accelerated pace in the second century. The stressing of the preparations for the Sabbath heightened the eagerness with which Jews began to anticipate its coming. "This was the practice of Rabbi Judah b. Ilai. On the eve of the Sabbath, a basin filled with hot water was brought to him. He washed his face, hands, and feet and wrapped himself and sat in fringed linen robes, and was like an angel of the Lord" (*Shabbat* 25a).

The spiritual fragrance of the Sabbath was symbolized by fragrant herbs. When Rabbi Simon b. Yochai and his son Eleazar emerged from their hideout at the end of the Hadrianic persecution, they were thrilled by the sight of an old man, with two bundles of myrtles in his hands, rushing to get home in time for the Sabbath. "What are these for?" the sages asked. "They are in honor of the Sabbath," the old man replied. The custom persisted for many centuries. The Essenes attached great importance to the fragrance of the Sabbath. Their regulations provided that Sabbath clothes must be rubbed with frankincense (*Zadokite Document* X–XI). The Ari (16th cent.) renewed the custom of myrtles for the Sabbath.

Another custom introduced in the second century was the practice of eating at least three meals (*shalosh seudot*) on the Sabbath, instead of the two meals normally eaten on weekdays (*Shabbat* 117b). Rabbi Chidka held out for four meals (ibid.). This practice acquired great importance in later generations (*Shabbat* 118a).

The new trend of emphasizing the feasting aspects of the Sabbath is reflected in the pseudepigraphic Book of Jubilees (ca. 2nd cent.). "The

Sabbath was given to Jews to observe it, to eat and drink and to praise the Lord" (2:21). However, in contrast to the rabbinical approval of conjugal relations on the Sabbath as a meritorious act, the author of Jubilees prohibits it.

The centrality of the dinner table in the Sabbath home was given great prominence in the second century. "Rabbi Eleazar said: 'One should always set the table on the eve of the Sabbath' " (*Shabbat* 119b). The famous legend of the two angels was created to stimulate the effort to beautify the Sabbath home. "Two ministering angles accompany man on the eve of the Sabbath from the synagogue to his home. One is a good angel and the other an evil one. When a Jew arrives home and finds the lamp burning, the table set, and the bed covered with a spread, the good angel exclaims: 'May it be thus on another Sabbath,' and the evil angel unwillingly responds 'Amen' " (*Shabbat* 119b).

To make sure that the peace and serenity of the Sabbath are not disturbed by the anxieties and worries common to daily existence, the rabbis prohibited even thinking about business problems (*Shabbat* 150b). The weekday world was thus totally expunged from the Jew's Sabbath mind.

The transformation of the Sabbath entailed an investment of considerable expenditures for food and light. In periods of persecution and impoverishment, the added weekly expense constituted an undue burden for the poor. Despite the assurance of the rabbis that the extra expenses for the Sabbath would be repaid by heaven (*Betzah* 16a), the poor could not buy on credit. Rabbi Akiva (2nd cent.) responded to the critical situation in his time by declaring: "Make your Sabbath an ordinary day rather than resort to the assistance of other people" (*Shabbat* 118a). Most rabbis, however, felt that in times of stress the therapy of the Sabbath was needed more than ever. They therefore ordained that public help be extended to the poor so that they not be deprived of the joys of the Sabbath (ibid.). The custom of providing money and food for the Sabbath has persisted to our time.

Despite the emphasis on the esthetic and culinary aspects of the Sabbath, the rabbis did not overlook the opportunity for intellectual stimulation presented by a day of leisure. Rabbis delivered discourses to the public on Friday nights and Saturday afternoons (Jer. *Sotah* 1). The tragic end of two Jerusalemite families who used to schedule their meals at a time when lectures were delivered in the synagogue was noted in the Talmud (*Gittin* 58b). In addition to these lectures and study sessions, capacity crowds were present at Sabbath morning services to hear the interpretation in the vernacular of the weekly Torah selection.

IN THE THIRD CENTURY

The dimension of the Sabbath, as we know it today, was practically achieved in the third century, except for the significant innovations of the kabbalists in the sixteenth century. With the end of the cultural supremacy of Palestinian Jewry, the Babylonian sages assumed an active role in the shaping of the Sabbath.

Among the foremost Babylonian scholars was Rav (d. 247), founder of the academy of Sura. He declared the lighting of Sabbath candles an absolute obligation (*Shabbat* 25b). He said that "he who delights in the Sabbath is granted his heart's desires" (*Shabbat* 118b). He described the Sabbath menu which brings delight: "A dish of beets, a large fish, and heads of garlic" (ibid.). He instituted the custom of attending a bath-house prior to the Sabbath (*Berachot* 27b). The importance of the bath-house in preparing for the Sabbath was confirmed by a Palestinian scholar in the fourth century (*Shabbat* 25b). This practice became a significant hygienic factor in the life of medieval Jewry. Some municipal administrative bodies recognized the ritualistic need of the Jewish population for the bath-house. Thus, in the fourteenth century, the government of Arles, Provence, which had prohibited Jews from attending the public baths, excepted Fridays from the ban.

To further impress upon Jews the crucial role of the Sabbath, Rav declared that "had Israel kept the first Sabbath no nation or tongue could have dominated them" (*Shabbat* 118b). He undoubtedly referred to cultural and religious domination by other nations.

At the same time that Rav was promoting the role of the Sabbath, new metaphors came into being. Rabbi Chanina called the Sabbath a "queen." Rabbi Yannai called the Sabbath a "bride." This introduced an element of majesty and romanticism to the Sabbath image, which the sixteenth-century kabbalists were to embroider with much skill and flourish. Rav's contemporary, the famous Samuel, suggested that scholars should perform their conjugal relations on Friday eve (*Ketubot* 62b). This suggestion fitted in with the romantic aura of the Sabbath.

The emphasis on domestic peace as an essential element of the relaxed atmosphere of the Sabbath gained increased recognition with time. Thus the *Tikunei Zohar* stated: "An individual must please his wife on the Sabbath with endearing words" (86). A medieval maxim declared it more succinctly: "A meal of greens with love is better than a stuffed ox with hate" *(Sefer HaChasidim)*.

The Palestinian contemporaries of Rav and Samuel also contributed to the enhancement of the Sabbath. Rabbi Yochanan stressed the importance of wearing special garments on the Sabbath and called his own Sabbath outfit "my honorers [of the Sabbath]" *(Shabbat* 113a). He also declared that he who observes the Sabbath according to the law, even if he practiced idolatry, he will be forgiven" *(Shabbat* 118b).

Rabbi Yochanan's colleague, Simon b. Lakish, introduced a far-reaching term into the Sabbath lexicon, *neshamah yeteirah* ("additional soul"), which transforms every Jew on the Sabbath *(Betzah* 16a). This concept affected the subjective feeling and reaction of most Jews to the Sabbath.

Personal involvement in the preparations for the Sabbath was actively recommended by the sages of the third and fourth centuries. Men were advised to assist their wives, even if but symbolically. The Talmud lists the names of many rabbis who set the example of personal participation. Rabbi Abahu fanned the fire. Rabbi Anan helped with the cooking. Rabbi Safra singed the head of the animal. Rav Chuna lit the lamps. Rav Papa plaited the wicks. Rav Chisda cut up the beet roots. Rabba and Rav Joseph chopped the wood. Rav Zera kindled the fire *(Shabbat* 119b).

To add to the physical relaxation provided by the Sabbath, the rabbis coined the slogan "A nap on the Sabbath is a delight" *(Yalkut Reuveni, Vaetchanan)*. It is indeed the pause that refreshes.

The development of the rabbinical Sabbath did not meet with unanimous approval. Thus Rabbi Chiya bar Aba contended that the purpose of the Sabbath and festivals is to further the goal of knowledge by giving Jews an opportunity to study Torah (Jer. *Shabbat* 15:3). The rabbinic consensus, however, preferred to mingle the holiness of the Sabbath with its delights.

It was left to Rav Nachman bar Yitzchak (4th cent.) to sum up the effect of the Sabbath on the Jew. The Sabbath, he said, saves the Jew from the servitude of the diaspora *(Shabbat* 118b). He thus expressed the opinion that the objective of the rabbinical Sabbath is to act as an antidote to the degradation and dehumanization of the dark periods in the diaspora and to save the soul as well as the dignity of the Jew.

What were the historical factors which initiated the development of the rabbinical Sabbath in the first century, and what accelerated the process in the next three centuries? It seems to me that the original incentive of the rabbis was a desire to counteract the influence of the Sadducees, who had gained much power in the first century. As fundamentalists, who interpreted the scriptural text literally, the Sadducees retained an aura of austerity and great solemnity in their Sabbath. By introducing the element of "delight," the rabbis enabled the people to realize that rabbinical Judaism was a realistic creed which addressed itself to their welfare and dignity.

The threat posed by the Sadducees disappeared with the destruction of Jerusalem in the year 70. However, a new threat, much more ominous, replaced it. The question of Jewish physical and cultural survival took on serious proportions. With the passage of time, the problem became more acute. Roman oppression in Palestine was severe from the outset. The tolerable condition of the Jews of Babylonia drastically deteriorated in the third century, beginning with the Neo-Persian period. The rabbinic leadership quickly seized upon the therapeutic qualities of the Sabbath and appointed it a guardian angel of the Jewish people.

PREPARATIONS FOR THE SABBATH

Many of the customs listed below have been discussed in this chapter in conjunction with the study of their background and development. Only new material, which has not been part of that study, will be discussed in the section dealing with customs.

MARKETING FOR FOOD

It is customary to buy ample food for the Sabbath meals. The purchase of food, the cooking, and the baking were usually done on Fridays to make sure that the food would not spoil and would retain its freshness on the Sabbath. The invention of efficient refrigeration makes it possible for the modern housewife to buy the food in honor of the Sabbath throughout the week.

CLEAN CLOTHES

One should wear clean clothes on the Sabbath. Custom prescribed the washing of laundry once a week in preparation for the Sabbath. This practice was probably based on a text in Exodus which describes the preparation of the people for the Sinaitic revelation, which was to take place on the Sabbath (*Shabbat* 86b). "And Moses went down from the mount unto the people, and sanctified the people; and they washed their garments" (19:14).

Initially, the washing was done on Fridays. Ezra ordained that it be done on Thursdays. In time, however, the custom of setting aside a specific day for the laundry was relaxed.

HOME-BAKED BREAD

It is customary to have home-baked bread for the Sabbath because it is considered meritorious to eat bread baked by Jews for the Sabbath.

The custom of baking bread on Fridays is alluded to in the Talmud (*Taanit* 24b). It seems that this was already the practice of Jewish housewives in the first century. The custom was discontinued in post-talmudic times and was not mentioned by the major codes. However, Rabbi Moses Isserles (16th cent.) renewed the custom in his annotations to the code (Rema, *Orah Chaim* 242).

The task of baking bread fell to the woman as part of her house-keeping obligations. It was therefore logical to assign to her the biblical mitzvah of setting aside the first portion of the dough (chalah) which used to be given to the kohen (Num. 15:18–21). This obligation survived the destruction of Jerusalem and remains in force by rabbinic decree (*Ketubot* 25a, *Bechorot* 27a).

Rabbi Joshua (1st cent.) offered a homiletical reason for the assignment of the mitzvah of chalah to women (*Yalkut, Bereishit* 23).

The kabbalists suggested that twelve loaves of bread be baked for the Sabbath in commemoration of the twelve loaves of shewbread in the Temple, which were replaced on the Sabbath.

The Sabbath bread was not designated by any special name and was referred to as *lachamim* (Rema). Subsequently, however, the Sabbath bread was called chalah as a reminder to women of their obligation to set aside the biblical portion of dough (chalah). In modern times all white bread came to be known as chalah.

The neglect of the mitzvah of chalah was alleged by the Talmud to be responsible for the death of women in childbirth (*Shabbat* 31b). The same punishment is said to result from the neglect of Sabbath candles and the menstrual purity laws. The three laws are related to the Sabbath. Chalahs are baked for the Sabbath, the candles are lit for the Sabbath, and Sabbath eve was the time for conjugal relations (*Ketubot* 62b). The rabbis may have perceived a moral link between neglect of the only three obligations which devolve upon women and childbirth, the main female physiological function.

FISH FOR SABBATH

One should procure meat, fish, tasty side dishes, and wine for the Sabbath meal.

Meat and wine were considered important sources of human pleasures and joy (*Pesachim* 109a). The tradition of fish on the Sabbath menu most likely antedates the Talmud.

Nehemiah (5th cent. B.C.E.) mentions the presence of fishermen from Tyre who used to come to Jerusalem to sell fish on the Sabbath (13:16). While this may reflect an ancient custom of eating fish on the Sabbath, we cannot attribute to the Jews who violated the Sabbath a desire to honor it by including fish on their menu.

Fish acquired a place of distinction in the tradition of the Sabbath because it was an important source of protein, cheaper than meat, and within the reach of most poor people. Rav's published menu for the Sabbath included fish but not meat (*Shabbat* 118b). In time, the fish took on a mystic rationale of its own. Jacob's blessing of his grandchildren was concluded with the phrase "May they multiply like fish in the midst of the land" (Gen. 48:16). The fertility symbolism of the fish fitted in with the reward of scholarly children promised to women who light Sabbath candles (*Shabbat* 23b) and the suggestion that Sabbath night was the proper time for scholars to have conjugal relations (*Ketubot* 62b).

The Jewish demand for fish for the Sabbath was frequently exploited by unconscionable fish merchants who rigged the price on the eve of Sabbaths and festivals. This practice was counteracted by some rabbis in the nineteenth century by a temporary ban on fish (*Baer Heitev, Orach Chaim* 242). The ban was frequently invoked in the twentieth century.

ANTICIPATING THE SABBATH

It is customary to refrain from working on Friday afternoons (*Pesachim* 50b). This talmudic restriction was taken to apply only to regular work which one performs all week. It does not apply to any work done in the preparation for the Sabbath.

One should not impair his appetite for the Sabbath meal by eating substantial food on late Friday afternoons. This restriction dates back to the first century (*Gittin* 38b).

On Friday afternoon it is customary to read the weekly Torah portion twice in Hebrew and once in Aramaic (Onkelos). This custom was instituted by Rav Ammi (3rd cent.; *Berachot* 8a). The purpose of this custom was to familiarize Jews with the Hebrew text of the Pentateuch. The reading of the Aramaic text was ordained for the benefit of the people of that time who were conversant in Aramaic. In the opinion of some rabbis, a vernacular translation may be substituted for the Aramaic.

It is customary to read the Song of Songs on Friday afternoon. This custom was introduced by kabbalists who cited the talmudic statement that all the Scriptures are holy but the Song of Songs is the holy of holies. (*Yodayim* 3:5). Another reason was the talmudic metaphor of the Sabbath as a bride. The Song of Songs was interpreted as an expression of God's relation to Israel in the romantic terminology of human love.

It is customary to bathe on Fridays in warm water, to wash one's head, and to pare one's nails. The custom of bathing goes back to the first century, and most likely long before that. The custom of paring one's nails dates from the thirteenth century and probably originated in Germany. The Talmud suggests extreme care in the disposal of cut nails (*Niddah* 17a). As a result, odd customs emerged prescribing the days on which to cut nails and the sequence of cutting them (*Orach Chaim* 260). These were not generally accepted.

Pious Jews have adopted the custom of immersing in a ritual bath (mikvah) after the warm bath. The hot bath is intended for physical cleanliness. The ritual immersion is designed to achieve spiritual purification in anticipation of the Sabbath. This practice was particularly endorsed by kabbalist and Chasidic sects.

ATTIRE AND APPEARANCE

It is customary to put on clean Sabbath clothes before the Sabbath sets in. One should not wear weekday clothes on the Sabbath, even if they are clean. In this manner, one pays special honor to the Sabbath, in keeping with Isaiah's admonition: "And thou shalt honor it" (58:13; *Shabbat* 113a).

It is customary to examine one's pockets prior to leaving the house on Friday eve, in order to make sure that they are empty. In this manner one will prevent a violation of the Sabbath by carrying an object into the street (*Shabbat* 12a).

It has been the custom since talmudic times to place cooked food in a heated oven on Friday so as to have a warm dish on the Sabbath (*Shabbat* 35b). Rabbi Zerachya Halevi, a famous twelfth-century codifier, is said to have alleged that the piety of anyone who neglects this custom is suspect.

Out of this custom emerged the distinctive Sabbath dish known as "cholent," a compound of meat, potatoes, beans, and other ingredients.

It is customary to place a white tablecloth and the chalot on the table prior to the kindling of the candles.

The white tablecloth is placed in honor of the Sabbath (*Shabbat* 119b). The chalot are placed on the table prior to the lighting of the candles to prevent the extension of the law of *muktzeh* ("untouchable") to the table. Without the chalot, the table would be considered merely a tray for the candles and consequently, like the candle sticks, become muktzeh.

THE CHALOT

It is customary to have two chalot at each Sabbath meal. This custom, dating from talmudic times, is based on the biblical expression of *Lechem mishneh* ("double bread"; *Berachot* 39b).

It is customary to cover the chalot with a cloth. This practice is of medieval origin and is based on both an ethical and a legal reason.

The ethical reason takes into consideration the fact that it is proper to make Kiddush over chalot when wine is not available. Since the chalot might be "insulted" by our failure to use them ritually for the Kiddush, we hide them when Kiddush is made (*Tur, Hilchot Shabbat* 271). This practice illustrates the regard that Judaism has even for inanimate objects which serve a religious purpose.

The legal reason is more prosaic. The chalot are covered to prevent an erroneous conclusion that they may never be used for Kiddush. No such conclusion will be drawn if the presence of the chalot is not noticed.

In modern times, the chalah coverlet has become an object of elaborate embroidery and design. This added another religious article as a medium for imaginative artistic expression.

SABBATH CANDLES

It is customary to light the Sabbath candles at least eighteen minutes before sunset. The extra time added to the Sabbath, at the outset and after its expiration, is known as *tosefet Shabbat* (*Yoma* 81b, *Bereishit Rabbah* 9:16).

The obligation to light candles was assigned to the housewife. Maimonides attributes this to the fact that women are usually at home at the time of candle-lighting (*Hilchot Shabbat* 5:3). The Talmud offers a homiletical reason for the practice.

Although men are qualified to light candles, the rabbis admonished husbands against depriving their wives of this privilege. Rabbi Jacob Emden (18th cent.) ruled that an offending husband must make financial reparations to his wife (*Sidur Bet Yaakov*).

It is customary for women to cover their eyes with their hands when they recite the benediction over the candles. There is a legal reason for this practice. Benedictions must precede the performance of an act. This is impossible in the case of Sabbath candles. if the woman were to recite the benediction prior to the lighting, she would no longer be permitted to light the candles because her Sabbath would begin immediately upon the conclusion of the benediction. She must of necessity light the candles first and then pronounce the benediction. By screening her eyes from seeing the light, she symbolically retains the sequence of benediction and performance.

SABBATH EVE CUSTOMS

Sabbath Eve services are held earlier than weekday evening services in order to introduce the Sabbath sooner.

The kabbalists of the sixteenth century introduced many innovations into the evening service. Chiefly among these is Kabbalat Shabbat, consisting of six psalms (95–99, omitted by Sephardim, and 29), corresponding to the six days of the week. This is followed by the famous liturgical poem *Lecha Dodi,* which was composed by Solomon Alkabetz in 1540. This hymn is followed by a seventh psalm (92), dedicated to the Sabbath.

The addition of these prayers, introduced by the kabbalists, quickly spread to many parts of the world, giving the Sabbath Eve service its special and unique distinctiveness.

When the last stanza of the hymn of *Lecha Dodi* is chanted, it is customary for the congregation to rise and face west. Thus we face the Sabbath bride and welcome her as she enters through the door. The kabbalists also noted the fact that the Shechinah (the spirit of God) is always present in the west (*Shemot Rabbah* 2:2).

It is customary at the Sabbath Eve service to recite an entire chapter of a mishnah (*Bame madlikin, Shabbat* 2). The earliest prayerbook, *Seder Rav Amram Gaon* (9th cent.), included that chapter. It is said that it was included to permit latecomers to catch up with the congregation so that they would not have to go home by themselves in the dark.

The reason for the selection of this particular chapter is obviously the fact that it deals with the laws of Sabbath candles. It was intended either as a reminder to those who had forgotten to light candles or as a demonstration against the Karaites, who had prohibited the use of light on the Sabbath.

Kiddush is chanted in the synagogue prior to the conclusion of the service. Kiddush should normally be recited in the room where the meal is served (*Pesachim* 101a). However, the Babylonian sages of the third century introduced the custom of Kiddush in the synagogue for the sake of transients who used the synagogue quarters as a hostel (ibid.). Subsequently, Jews instituted a *hachnosat orchim*, an inn for transients, but the Kiddush in the synagogue was never discontinued.

IN THE HOME

It is customary to sing *Sholom Aleichem* upon entering the home after services. This custom was also introduced by the kabbalists in the sixteenth century. The song is based on the talmudic legend of the two angels who accompany every Jew from the synagogue to his home (*Shabbat* 119a).

Another custom introduced by the kabbalists is the blessing of the children by the head of the family, following the singing of *Sholom Aleichem*. This practice promotes the solidarity and cohesiveness of the family unit and gives the Sabbath eve its distinctive character of being a family night.

A third custom introduced by the kabbalists is the recitation by the husband of the thirty-first chapter of Proverbs: "A woman of valor who can find . . ." (10–31). Although the kabbalists read into this chapter a description of the relation between man and God, it nevertheless constituted, in the minds of most men, a tribute to the wife whose arduous labors had created the beautiful atmosphere of the Sabbath. This was in keeping with the talmudic effort to enhance the joy of the Sabbath by promoting domestic peace and affection.

RITUAL WINE

It is customary to use ritual wine for the chanting of the Kiddush. The use of wine was introduced in the first century B.C.E..

The Kiddush is opened with the recitation of the passage in Genesis "And the heaven and earth were finished . . ." (2:1–3). This passage is also part of the Friday Eve service but is repeated at home for the sake of women and children who did not attend services (*Pesachim* 106a; *Tosafot, zochrenu*).

The benediction for the wine is preceded by an Aramaic exclamation, *saveri moranon*. It is a request to the assembled to join the host so that their obligation to chant the Kiddush will be fulfilled by the Kiddush chanted by him.

It is customary to make a mark with the knife on the chalah, prior to the benediction of *Hamotzi*, to indicate the part of the loaf which will be cut. Normally, bread should be eaten immediately following the benediction. For that reason one makes an incision in the bread prior to the making of the *Motzi* benediction and completes the cutting thereafter. No preliminary incision is made on the Sabbath due to the requirement of two whole chalot. Therefore one merely makes a mark and after the benediction cuts where the loaf was marked.

Even though there are two loaves on the table, one should cut and break off some pieces from one bread so as not to appear gluttonous.

ZEMIROT

Zemirot, or Sabbath table songs, are sung at Sabbath meals. A late rabbinic midrash stresses the importance of Sabbath songs. "When the Sabbath arrives we receive it with songs and chants, as it is said: 'A Psalm of song for the Sabbath day' " (*Shochar Tov,* Psalms 92). No *zemirot* were composed for the Sabbath prior to the tenth century.

THE LATE FRIDAY NIGHT SERVICE

The late Friday night service was introduced in the twentieth century by the Reform movement. It consisted of an abridged service and a sermon. Torah reading was added in time, and Bar and Bat Mitzvah ceremonies were conducted on Friday nights.

The Conservative movement was next to adopt the late service, which consisted of an abridged service, songs, and a sermon, followed by refreshments. A traditional Friday Eve service was held at sunset.

The Orthodox adopted a late Friday Oneg Shabbat, which featured songs, followed by a sermon and refreshments.

A FAMILY NIGHT

The Talmud designated Friday nights as a proper time for scholars to have conjugal relations (*Ketubot* 62b). According to Maimonides, this custom falls within the category of Oneg Shabbat (*Hilchot Shabbat* 30:14).

SABBATH DAY CUSTOMS

The outline of the Sabbath morning service was fixed after the destruction of the Temple. The reading of the Torah, according to the Talmud, was ordained by Moses. Prayers were added to the order of services throughout the centuries. Not all of them were accepted, giving rise to many variations in the prayers of different communities.

Nine psalms were added to the Sabbath liturgy in the early part of the service (*Lamenatzeach*, etc.). They are songs of praise which were deemed appropriate for Sabbaths and festivals. They were omitted on weekdays so as not to prolong the service.

The hymn *Nishmat* dates back to the talmudic period (*Shabbat* 118a; *Tosafot,* Rabbi Yochanan). It seems to have been originally composed for the Passover celebration.

The hymn *El Adon* was probably composed in the ninth century. The versions in the prayerbooks of Rav Amram Gaon (9th cent.) and Rav Saadiah Gaon (10th cent.) contain significant variations.

The eighteen benedictions which are recited on weekdays are reduced to seven on the Sabbath. The Talmud prohibited petitions for help on the Sabbath so as not to disturb the serenity of the day (*Tanchuma, Vayera* 1).

After the reading of the Torah, the service resumes with the prayers of *Yekum Purkan.* The first paragraph (a prayer for scholars) was composed in Babylonia after the third century. The second paragraph, a prayer for all people who are active in communal life, dates from the geonic period (6th–11th cent.) The third paragraph, a prayer for the congregation, was originally composed to be recited by the reader only. The prayer for the government, based on a talmudic prescription (*Avot* 3), is of medieval origin.

The hymn *Ein Keloheinu* dates from the ninth century. The Song of Adoration *(Olenu)* was, according to tradition, composed by the Babylonian sage Rav (3rd cent.) for the Rosh HaShanah service (Jer. *Rosh HaShanah* 1:5). Since the fourteenth century it has become the

closing prayer of all services. The closing hymn *Adon Olam* is said to
have been composed by the renowned poet Solomon ibn Gabirol (11th
cent.).

THE TORAH AND HAFTARAH

It is customary to have three persons present near the Scroll when it is
rolled open for public reading. This practice is said to have arisen
because of the biblical admonition: "I call heaven and earth to witness
against you today" (Deut. 30:19). The entire Torah is in the nature of a
warning to the Jewish people. All warnings must be given in the
presence of two witnesses.

Initially, the Torah was read on the Sabbath or special occasions by
the king, a prophet, or a kohen. In time, distinguished people were
called to read portions of the Torah. The Torah was on a platform to
which the reader ascended, hence the Hebrew term *aliyah* ("going
up"). Eventually, the rabbis ordained that a professional reader do the
reading to avoid embarrassing those who were unable to read the
Torah script (*Shabbat* 11a).

There are seven aliyot on a Sabbath (*Megillah* 21a). *Bet Yoseph* quotes
a geonic source in explanation of this number (*Ein Pochasim, Tur,
Hilchot Shabbat* 282). In the event that someone missed an entire week's
services and as a result had not responded to the reader's daily
invocation of *Borachu*, he may make up for it by responding to the
Borachu of the seven blessings of the aliyot.

A more acceptable reason is the midrashic explanation for the seven
benedictions on the Sabbath (in place of the eighteen). The seven
benedictions correspond to the seven voices of God *(kol)* mentioned in
the Twenty-ninth Psalm and again in connection with the giving of the
Torah (beginning with Exod. 19:16, *Midrash Yelamdenu*). This explanation is equally applicable to the seven aliyot.

The first aliyah is assigned to a kohen and the second to a levi. This
order was ordained to avoid public competition for the honor of being
first (*Gittin* 59b).

Babylonian Jewry completed the reading of the Torah within one
year. Palestinian Jewry adopted a triennial cycle (*Megillah* 29b).

The reading of a selection from the Prophets originated in the time of
the Mishnah (*Megillah* 24a). This practice probably began after the
canonization of the Bible and the ensuing effort to highlight the
Prophets.

SABBATH AFTERNOON

It is customary to make Kiddush over wine after the completion of the Sabbath morning services (*Pesachim* 106a).

It is customary to have two chalot at the second meal of the Sabbath, in keeping with the biblical phrase *lechem mishneh* (Exod. 16:22).

A nap on Sabbath afternoons is in the spirit of Oneg Shabbat (*Yalkut Reuveni, Voetchanan*).

It is customary to set aside a period for study on Saturday afternoons, or to attend a religious discourse. The practice of reading *Pirke Avot* at the Minchah service, which dates back to the ninth century, may have been instituted to provide an opportunity for the study of rabbinic literature on the Sabbath.

THE MINCHAH SERVICE

The custom of reading the Torah at Minchah services was instituted, according to tradition, by Ezra (*Baba Kama* 82a).

It is customary to honor the Sabbath by eating a third meal (*shalosh seudot*) on that day (*Shabbat* 117b).

POST-SABBATH CUSTOMS

The official end of the Sabbath is proclaimed after the evening service by the ritual of Havdalah (the separation of the Sabbath from the weekday).

Havdalah, like Kiddush, is recited over wine. Rabbi Yochanan (3rd cent.) alleged that he who recites Havdalah over wine will be rewarded with male children (*Shevuot* 18b). He based his statement on Leviticus 11:47, which calls for the drawing of a distinction between that which is clean and the unclean (*lehavdil*). The application of the principle of "separation" in life's numerous transactions and the quality of living was thus impressed upon the men as they were to resume their weekday tasks. The man's duty to proclaim the end of the Sabbath with the Havdalah light paralleled the woman's duty to announce the beginning of the Sabbath with the Sabbath lights. Her promised reward was greater than that of her husband. Scrupulous care of the Sabbath candles would bring her, she was told, scholarly children (*Shabbat* 23b), an appropriate reward for those who bring holiness into the home.

The later rabbis further emphasized the merit of making Havdalah over wine. "He who does not recite the Havdalah over wine at the end of the Sabbath will never enjoy a blessing in his life" (*Piskei deRabbi Eleazar* 20).

According to Rabbi Yochanan, the ritual of Havdalah was instituted by the Men of the Great Assembly (in the post-Ezra era). Initially, the ritual of Havdalah was fulfilled by reciting an added passage in the course of the eighteen benedictions *(Ata chonantanu)*. Subsequently, the use of ritual wine was introduced (*Berachot* 33a). It is probable that the Havdalah wine was introduced at the same time as the Kiddush wine, in the first century B.C.E.

In addition to the wine, the Havdalah ritual calls for the use of a candle and spices, over which special benedictions are recited (*Berachot* 52a). The reason for the candle is to mark the creation of light, which God ordained at the beginning of the week (*Bereishit Rabbah* 11:2). The practice of using a candle and spices most likely emerged in the first century C.E. The schools of Shammai and Hillel were still in disagreement on the proper sequence of the Havdalah benedictions (*Berachot* 51b). This indicates that the custom was of recent origin and not yet clearly defined. Rava (4th cent.) ordained that one use a torch, a candle with several wicks (*avukah*; *Pesachim* 8a).

The lighting of the candle signals the end of the Sabbath. It is customary to cup one's hand and to observe the shade formed by the folded fingers. The borderline between the light and the shade conforms to the phrase which refers to God as the one "Who separates the light from the darkness." This custom is mentioned in *Pirkei deRabbi Eleazar* (9th cent.), where the author offers a different reason for the practice of looking at the nails after the recitation of the benediction.

The ritual of the spices, which also dates back to the first century (*Berachot* 52a), is said to have been introduced in order to refresh the spirit, which is weakened by the departure of the additional Sabbath soul.

The passage of *HaMavdil*, which we recite at the conclusion of Havdalah, was composed (or adopted) by Rabbi Judah HaNasi (2nd cent.; *Pesachim* 103b).

It is customary to sing the hymn *Eliyahu HaNavi* after the Havdalah, expressing one's hope for the speedy coming of the prophet Elijah. The reason for this song on the expiration of the Sabbath is the talmudic statement that Elijah will not come on a Friday (so as not to interfere with the preparations for the Sabbath) or on a Saturday (so as not to disturb the Sabbath peace; *Eruvin* 43b). With the expiration of the

Sabbath, Elijah's arrival is once again anticipated. The kabbalists also point to the numerical value of *vayavdel,* which equals that of *Eliyahu.*

MELAVEH MALKAH

Just as we anticipate the Sabbath with elaborate preparations for its arrival, so must we remember, upon its conclusion, to escort the Sabbath with pomp and ceremony. This practice dates back to the third century, when Rabbi Chanina decreed that a table be set and refreshments served on Saturday nights. According to the code (*Orach Chaim* 300) a table should be set (and a tablecloth spread, *Magen David*) even if one serves only limited refreshments. The code explains this custom with the need for escorting the Sabbath (*lelavot et haShabbat*). This figure of speech was based on an expression by Rashi, *lelavot biyetziato* ("to see it off as it departs"; *Shabbat* 119b; *bemotzoei Shabbat*). Hence the name *Melaveh Malkah* ("escorting the queen") which appears in the *Kitzur Shulchan Aruch* (96:13). According to the Ari, the *neshamah yeteirah* (additional soul) lingers on until after this meal, which the kabbalists named "the fourth meal."

Another name used by the kabbalists for the Saturday night repast is *Seudah deDavid Malkah* ("the feast of King David"). David is said to have known that he would die on a Sabbath (*Shabbat* 30a). He celebrated his survival every Saturday night with a festive meal. The kabbalists composed special songs and prayers for the occasion.

The Melavah Malkah has been used in modern times for the purpose of fund-raising for Orthodox religious institutions. Traditional refreshments are served and appeals for funds conclude the festivity.

ERUV CHATZEROT

Biblical law prohibits the transporting of objects on a Sabbath from a private domain into a public domain, and vice versa. Rabbinic law prohibited the transporting of objects from one private domain into another or into a court owned in partnership with other homeowners.

When several homes face a common courtyard, which is fenced in at least on three sides, carrying to and fro may be permitted by means of a legal procedure known as *eruv chatzerot* ("commingling of domains"). This creates a symbolic merger of the proprietary rights vested in each homeowner.

An *eruv chatzerot* is established by setting aside a loaf of bread in a home on Friday and granting a share in the bread to each neighbor. This symbolic joint meal for all the homeowners creates the effect of a joint ownership of the entire property.

The Talmud attributed the authorship of the ordinance of *eruv* to King Solomon (*Shabbat* 14b), indicating a belief in the law's great antiquity. From all indications, it dates at least from the period of the Second Commonwealth. Apparently, the increasing urbanization of the Jewish community in that period resulted in growing social intercourse and the building of multiple homes within a single courtyard.

Whoever sets up the *eruv* must recite the benediction, *al mitzvat eruv* (". . . who commanded us concerning the *eruv*"). He then must make a declaration that by virtue of this *eruv* it will be permissible to bring and take out objects from house to house and from house to yard, etc.

An *eruv* may also be established to cover a city, or part of it, including the public streets of the area. The borders of the section concerned must be "fenced" with overhead wires, and symbolic "gates" must be set up at stated intervals. The "gates" are formed by two posts, each forty inches high. The posts are "connected" by planks or wires directly over them. They do not touch the posts. Telephone wires strung above ground create the fence and the gates. When an *eruv* is city-wide, the loaf is placed in a synagogue.

The major cities in Israel are covered by an *eruv*. A similar *eruv* in New York's borough of Manhattan became the subject of a controversy regarding its validity and has fallen into disuse. Some local areas in other boroughs and on the outskirts of New York have set up their own *eruv* to serve a small community.

SPECIAL SABBATHS

Shabbat HaGadol. See chapter 5.

Shabbat Chol HaMoed. When the Sabbath occurs on an intermediary day of Passover or Sukkot, it is called Shabbat Chol HaMoed.

Two Scrolls are removed from the ark for the reading of the Torah during the Shabbat Chol HaMoed morning service. The selection in the first Scroll for Passover and Sukkot is from the Book of Exodus (32:12–34:26). The portion is divided into seven aliyot. The Passover maftir selection is from the Book of Numbers (28:19–25). The Sukkot maftir selection is also from the Book of Numbers (29:17–34). This portion deals with the order of the Sukkot sacrificial offerings.

The offerings of each day of Sukkot varied in number. The maftir portions of Sukkot have been selected to accord with the number of the day on which it is read. Shabbat Chol HaMoed Sukkot could occur on the third, fifth, or sixth day of the holiday. When it occurs on the third day, the paragraphs dealing with the offerings of the second and third days are read. This reflects the uncertainty in the ancient diaspora of the exact day of Rosh Chodesh. The third day of the diasporic Sukkot could actually have been the second day of the biblical Sukkot. To meet this doubt, the paragraphs dealing with the offerings of both days were read.

When Chol HaMoed Sukkot occurs on the fifth day, the paragraphs of the fourth and fifth days are read. When it occurs on the sixth day, the paragraphs of the fifth and sixth days are read.

The complete *Hallel* is chanted on Shabbat Chol HaMoed Sukkot and the partial *Hallel* on Passover. The reason for the partial *Hallel* is discussed in the chapter on Passover.

Shabbat Chazon. See chapter 12.

Shabbat Nachamu. See chapter 12.

Shabbat Shuvah. The Sabbath between Rosh HaShanah and Yom Kippur is called Shabbat Shuvah (The Sabbath of Return). It derives its name from the Haftarah *Shuvah Yisrael* (Hosea 14:2) which is read on that day.

East European rabbis of the sixteenth century instituted the custom of delivering a major sermon on Shabbat Shuvah to stimulate a mood of penitence.

Shabbat Parashat Shekalim. See chapter 10.

Shabbat Parashat Zachor. See chapter 10.

Shabbat Parashat Parah. Shabbat Parashat Parah derives its name from the maftir selection in the second Scroll, which deals with the subject of the red heifer *(parah adumah)*, the ritual of purifying contaminated people (Num. 19:1–22).

Contaminated people who remained impure by Passover were barred from offering the paschal lamb. It was therefore important to inform the people of the need for purification.

The portion of *Parah* is always read on the Sabbath preceding Shabbat Parashat HaChodesh (see below).

Shabbat Parashat HaChodesh. Shabbat Parashat HaChodesh derives its name from the maftir selection in the second Scroll, *Hachodesh haze lachem* (Exod. 12:1–20). This portion deals with the ritual preparations for the paschal offering. This portion is read on the Sabbath preceding

Rosh Chodesh Nisan or on Rosh Chodesh Nisan if it occurs on a Sabbath.

The entire series of four parashiyot—Shekalim, Zachor, Parah, and Chodesh—dates from the Temple era (*Megillah* 29a).

4

Customs of Rosh HaShanah and the Days of Penitence

I.
INTRODUCTION

A DAY OF BLOWING

THE DEVELOPMENT OF the "day of blowing" (*yom teruah*; Num. 29:1) into the second most solemn day of the Jewish religious calendar is discussed in my book *The Biblical and Historical Background of the Jewish Holy Days* (chap. 2).

The object of this chapter is to trace the evolution of numerous customs which have enhanced the significance of the period of judgment. The outstanding Rosh HaShanah ritual, the blowing of the shofar, is central to the very essence of the holiday and is featured in its biblical name. As late as the first century C.E., Philo the Alexandrian identified Rosh HaShanah by the name "The Festival of the Shofar." A midrashic text, dating from the second century, similarly calls this holiday "The Festival of the Shofar" (*Midrash Tadshe* 6).

Considering the importance of the shofar, one may wonder why the text does not explicitly name the instrument which is used on Rosh HaShanah. The first reference to the blowing of an instrument on Rosh HaShanah (*teruah*) is found in Leviticus: "In the seventh month shall be a day of rest unto you, a memorial blast [*zichron teruah*], a holy proclamation" (23:24). In the second reference to the holiday, the designation reads "a day of blowing" (*yom teruah*; Num. 29:1). The

141

crucial word in both references is *teruah,* a series of staccato sounds on a musical instrument. The specific nature of the instrument is not indicated.

A teruah may be produced on a horn (Lev. 25:9), trumpet (Num. 10:5), or cymbal (Ps. 105:5). The teruah of the Rosh HaShanah text is therefore ambiguous and it fails to provide a clue as to the identity of the instrument.

The term *zichron* ("memorial" or "remembrance"), which is linked to the teruah in Leviticus (23:24), likewise fails to shed light on the particular instrument which is ritually acceptable. The significance of *zichron* is inherent in its definition, a sound which will arouse God's remembrance (or judgment) of his people. The Talmud points to the historical association between the shofar and the ram which replaced Isaac at the time of the Akedah (*Rosh HaShanah* 16a). God will recall the loyalty of Abraham and Isaac and temper justice with mercy. In light of this tradition, *zichron* is associated with the horn of a ram. However, the association is not implicit in the word itself. Indeed, *zikaron* is also linked to the blowing of trumpets (Num. 10:9–10).

THE TRUMPET IN ANCIENT RITUALS

To the average Jewish layman of the Temple era, the trumpet had greater religious significance than the shofar. Trumpets were much more visible because they were used in conjunction with many sacrificial rites. Their sacredness was emphasized by the fact that only kohanim were qualified to blow them. This restriction was scrupulously observed. In the procession led by Nehemiah on the occasion of the dedication of the rebuilt walls of Jerusalem (5th cent. B.C.E.), a special contingent of kohanim blew the trumpets (Neh. 12:35).

The trumpet gained a position of great prominence in the Second Temple. A large band of instrumentalists was introduced in the Second Temple to provide a musical background for the Levite chorus. Temple regulations permitted the employment of 120 trumpeters (*Mishneh Torah, Hilchot Kelei HaMikdash* 3:4).

In addition to their ritual functions in the Tabernacle, trumpets were also used for administrative purposes. Moses summoned and dispatched the tribal encampments with blasts of the trumpets. Trumpets were likewise used in time of war to invoke God's blessing (Num. 10:8–10). According to a rabbinic tradition, Moses concealed the silver trumpets before his death. They were not used again until the reign of David (*Bamidbar Rabbah* 15:12). Thereafter they were placed on display in the Temple. The high regard for the trumpets was evidenced by their use on occasions of public joy and celebration, such as coronations (II Kings 11:14).

In the course of time, the trumpets assumed a symbolic identification with the Temple. The left-hand bas-relief of the Arch of Titus portrays the destruction of the Temple by depicting the removal of the essential holy vessels. the golden table, the menorah, and the silver trumpets. When Bar Kochba, the leader of the rebellion against Rome (132–135), sought to publicize his plan to rebuild the Temple, he engraved his coins with an image of the trumpets.

THE FUNCTIONS OF THE SHOFAR

Despite the veneration of the trumpet, the Torah singled out one history-making occasion which was highlighted by the sounds of the shofar. "And it came to pass on the third day, when it was morning, that there were thunders and lightnings and a thick cloud upon the mount and the sound of the shofar, exceedingly loud" (Exod. 19:16). "And the sound of the shofar waxed louder and louder" (ibid. 19:19).

The shofar was also used to announce the commencement of the Jubilee Year. "Then shalt thou make proclamation with a blast of the shofar . . . throughout all your land" (Lev. 25:9). Why was the shofar given preference on these two occasions?

The shofar was a mass-produced instrument, relatively cheap, a common household article in the homes of farmers, shepherds, and many urbanites. It was used as a means of communication in everyday life. The shofar was a less sophisticated instrument than the trumpet, and its use required little skill. Temple rituals and military strategy required only two trumpeters. However, when an occasion called for mass participation of wind instrumentalists, it was imperative to use the shofar. That was the reason for Joshua's use of shoferot prior to the fall of Jericho (Josh. 6:4). Even if Moses' trumpets had not been concealed, Joshua needed seven instruments, and that many trumpets were not available. The same was true of Gideon's army, which used three hundred shoferot (Judg. 7:16).

The need for a readily available instrument may explain the use of the shofar on Mount Sinai and on the occasion of the pronouncement of the Jubilee Year. The revelation on Mount Sinai was one of the most decisive experiences of the Jewish people. Like the exodus from Egypt, it must forever be recalled by the Jewish people in order to reinforce the faith. "You have seen what I did unto the Egyptians. . . . Now therefore, if you will hearken unto my voice, and you will keep the covenant, you shall be my chosen . . ." (Exod. 19:45). The celebration of Passover was to be an annual reminder of the exodus. The ritual blast of the shofar would similarly recall by association the revelation on Mount Sinai.

Ancient Jews, long before the establishment of the synagogue, engaged in prayer. Many of them accompanied their prayers with song and music. The psalmist urged the people to "praise him with the blast of the shofar" (150:5). One of the traditional purposes of the shofar on Rosh HaShanah is to recall the memory of Mount Sinai. The obligation to blow an instrument on that day devolved upon each individual Jew (*Rosh HaShanah* 33a). As a mass-participation mitzvah, the instrument, for practical reasons, had to be a shofar. It seems obvious that the shofar was used on Mount Sinai so that subsequent generations of Jews would readily recall the experience whenever they blew the shofar.

The injunction to proclaim a Jubilee Year was similarly addressed to all the Jews throughout the land. It was important that even those residing in the most remote parts of the country be immediately informed of the advent of the Jubilee (*Sifra, Behar* 16). This was accomplished by means of blasts of wind instruments. In view of the required mass participation in the blowing of the instrument, the text specifically indicated that the shofar was to be used for this purpose.

TALMUDIC INTERPRETATION

The talmudic conclusion that a shofar is to be blown on Rosh HaShanah is based on a derivation from the use of the shofar in a Jubilee Year. "How do we know that the same [the shofar on the Jubilee] applies to Rosh HaShanah? The text reads: 'And you shall make a proclamation with the blast of the shofar on the tenth day of the seventh month, on Yom Kippur.' The phrase 'of the seventh month' is superfluous [because the date of Yom Kippur is well known]. The reason for the insertion of this phrase is to indicate that the blast of the 'seventh' [Rosh HaShanah] is governed by the same law as this one [Jubilee]. Just as this one requires a shofar, so does the blast of Rosh HaShannah" (*sifra, Behar* 15). This halachic deduction is in accord with our conclusion based on historical grounds.

One may still wonder why the Rosh HaShanah text failed to mention the shofar as was done in the texts on the revelation and the Jubilee. The answer may be found in the Rosh HaShanah text itself, which differs in one respect from all the other holiday texts. The norm in all the other texts is to cite the name of the holiday and follow it up with its basic function. Thus, "On the seventh day is the Sabbath . . . no manner of work shall be done" (Lev. 23:3). "On the fifteeth day of the month is the Feast of Matzot . . . seven days you shall eat unleavened bread" (Lev. 23:6). "You shall number fifty days, and you shall present a meal-offering to God (Lev. 3:16). "On the tenth day of the seventh month is Yom HaKippurim . . . you shall afflict your souls" (Lev. 23:27). "On the fifteenth day of the seventh month is the Feast of Sukkot. . . . You shall dwell in sukkot seven days" (Lev. 23:34, 42). However, in the case of Rosh HaShanah, the text describes it as a day of "a memorial blast" (Lev. 23:24) and does not follow with an injunction mandating the blowing of the instrument, as was done in the Jubilee text (Lev. 25:9).

Names of holidays reflect in general terms the character of the occasion but do not include specific details of its rituals. The outstanding characteristic of Rosh HaShanah is the blowing of an instrument. That is reflected in the biblical name *yom teruah*, a "day of blowing." A description of the type of instrument should not be incorporated in the name of the holiday. That detail properly belongs in a follow-up injunction which mandates the performance of a function. As we have already mentioned, there is no such mandatory sentence in the case of Rosh HaShanah. This still leaves us with an unresolved question. Why was such a sentence omitted from the Rosh HaShanah text?

Halachists may suggest an answer to the question by pointing to a legal issue which was in contention among the principal medieval rabbinic scholars. Is one obligated to listen to the sounds of a shofar, or must he blow it? According to Maimonides, the former is correct. The benediction should read: ". . . who commanded us to listen to the sounds of the shofar." Rabbenu Tam, however, disagreed. The obligation is to blow the shofar and the benediction should be amended to read: ". . . who commanded us to blow the shofar" (Zevin, *Moadim BaHalachah*, p. 41). It may be argued that if the Rosh HaShanah text had included an injunction "to blow the shofar," it would have been misinterpreted as an obligation to blow rather than to listen to the shofar.

THE SHOFAR THROUGH THE AGES

The shofar was not overly venerated as a religious instrument in the early period of Jewish history. Despite the biblical injunction, it is unlikely that the shofar was blown on Rosh HaShanah outside of the Temple (Bloch, *Biblical and Historical Background of the Jewish Holy Days*, p. 15). The common use of the shofar in daily communications divested it of any claim to sacredness. However, a gradually developing perception of the shofar as an instrument for communing with God had the effect of endowing it with mystical qualities.

The Bible reflects the progressive nuances of the symbolism of the shofar through the period of the Judges and the Monarchy. Except for its ritual use on Rosh HaShanah and at the outset of the Jubilee Year, the shofar was primarily a noisemaker. The principal musical instrument was the trumpet, which was used in conjunction with the sacrificial rites, on occasions of religious celebration (I Chron. 13:8, 15:24), and at the dedication of the Temple (II Chron. 5:12).

While the trumpet retained its primacy, the shofar was gradually introduced on special occasions to add volume to the sounds of the trumpets. King David (9th cent. B.C.E.) used trumpets and shoferot when he celebrated the return of the Ark (II Samuel 6:15). A psalmist urged the people to praise God with trumpets and the sounds of the shofar (98:6). As the importance of the shofar grew, another psalmist omitted the trumpet and urged that God be praised with blasts of the shofar (106:3).

A new dimension was added to the significance of the shofar in the eighth century B.C.E., when its sounds were used to invoke penitence and a return to God, a concept which was to have a profound impact on the rabbinical development of Rosh HaShanah. Thus in the religious reformation under King Asa, the proclamation of a new covenant "to seek the Lord, the God of their fathers, with all their heart and all their soul" (II Chron. 15:12) was confirmed by an oath and "with trumpets and shoferot" (II Chron. 15:14). The prophet Joel (8th cent. B.C.E.) also called for blasts of the shofar in Zion to signal the need for penitence (2:15).

The prophets of the seventh and sixth centuries B.C.E. used the metaphor of the shofar as a call to attention in anticipation of news of impending war and destruction (Isa. 58:1, Zeph. 1:16, Jer. 4:5, Ezek. 33:3). Zechariah (6th cent. B.C.E.) introduced a new meaning to the sounds of the shofar, a promise of salvation (9:14). All of these nuances added significantly to the solemnity as well as the hopefulness engendered by the shofar on Rosh HaShanah.

Upon the return of the Babylonian diaspora to Jerusalem, the trumpets were restored to the Temple and their use was mainly confined to the Sanctuary. The chronicler of the Hasmonean period (2nd cent. B.C.E.) described the general desolation of the country ravaged by Syrian forces. "The sounds of the flute and harp were no longer heard in the land" (*Chashmonaim* 8:45). The trumpet was apparently not in vogue as a secular musical instrument. On the other hand, when Judah made ready to fight Gorgias, he ordered the warriors to blow shoferot, not to frighten the enemy, as in the case of Gideon, but to invoke God's assistance (ibid. 8:54).

The establishment, in the first century, of many synagogues in Jerusalem, and the introduction of the shofar at congregational Rosh HaShanah services, gave the shofar prominent visibility as a religious article of great solemnity. Henceforth it was used for strictly religious purposes on solemn occasions and no longer for enhancing the din of hilarity and joy. Thus the dances and rejoicing on the occasion of Simchat Bet HaShoavah (the libation of the altar) was done to the tunes of the flute (*chalil*) rather than the shofar (*Sukkah* 50a). However, the ceremonies conducted within the Temple grounds were paced by two trumpets. These were accompanied by orchestral music which also included trumpets (*Sukkah* 51b).

The use of the shofar on Rosh HaShanah became widespread throughout the diaspora in the second century. Yet even as late as the third century there were still some ignorant Jews who did not know whether the Rosh HaShanah ritual called for trumpets or shoferot (*Shabbat* 36a, Rashi, *l'shofar shel Rosh HaShanah*).

VARIOUS FUNCTIONS OF THE SHOFAR

In addition to its principal function on Rosh HaShanah, the shofar was also used in rituals ordained for public welfare, the administration of justice, and sundry religious occasions.

In the public welfare ordinances, the shofar was blown when a communal fast was declared by the rabbis in the event of drought, failure of crops, a plague, the collapse of a building, a threat of mildew or locust or cricket or wild beasts, the siege of a city, and a ship in danger of sinking (*Taanit* 19a–22b).

The custom of fasting in times of stress dates back to biblical times. The blowing of a shofar in conjunction with the fast, in order to inspire penitence, was introduced in the second century, when the shofar had reached a state of eminence as a religious instrument. The talmudic sages who discussed the shofar ritual on fast days were all of the second century. On the other hand, two recorded fasts on occasions of drought in the first century (*Taanit* 19a, 20a) do not mention the use of a shofar.

Rabbinic courts ordered the blowing of a shofar when a person was placed under a ban (*Moed Katan* 16a, 3rd cent.) and when a ruling was handed down regarding food whose kashrut had been questioned (*Avodah Zara* 40a, 4th cent.). The purpose of the shofar was to publicize the court's decision.

It was customary in some localities to blow the shofar to announce a death in the community and to summon the citizens to attend the funeral (*Moed Katan* 27b, 3rd cent.).

The shofar was also blown on festive occasions. It was used to signal the coming of the Sabbath (*Shabbat* 35b, 1st cent.). It was also used in conjunction with the proclamation of Rosh Chodesh (*Niddah* 38a, Rashi, *Shipura*), at the morning service of Rosh Chodesh Elul (*Pirke de Rabbi Eliezer* 46; subsequently extended to the entire month of Elul), and after the *aravot* were placed upon the altar on Sukkot (*Sukkah* 45a). It is blown at the end of the Neilah service on Yom Kippur (*Machzor Vitry*, 12 cent.).

II.
PRE-ROSH HASHANAH CUSTOMS

THE SHOFAR IN THE MONTH OF ELUL

It is customary to blow three blasts on the shofar (tekiah, shevarim, teruah) beginning with the Shacharit service on the first of Elul.

The *Tur* code (*Hilchot Rosh HaShanah* 581) traces this custom to the midrashic *Pirke deRabbi Eliezer* (published in the 9th cent.). The practice was allegedly based on a tradition that a blast of the shofar on the first of Elul informed the Jews that Moses was about to ascend Mount Sinai for the third time (see Rashi, Exod. 33:11). It was felt that an annual commemoration of this event on the first of Elul would stimulate a mood of penitence.

Initially, the custom of blowing the shofar in the month of Elul was limited to Rosh Chodesh. Ashkenazic communities in the Middle Ages extended the custom to the entire month (except for the last day). The new practice was firmly established by the time of the *Tur* (13th cent.).

PSALM 27

The twenty-seventh chapter of Psalms ("The Lord is my light") is recited daily after Shacharit and Maariv services from the beginning of Elul until Shemini Atzeret. This custom is based on a passage in *Midrash Shochar Tov*, according to which the twenty-seventh chapter contains references to Rosh HaShanah, Yom Kippur, and Shemini Atzeret. The practice of reciting this chapter, beginning with Elul, became widespread among Ashkenazim in the eighteenth century.

EXPRESSING GOOD WISHES FOR THE NEW YEAR

Medieval German Jewry instituted the custom of expressing special greetings and good wishes when leaving the synagogue on Rosh HaShanah night. The following was the traditional verbal greeting: "May you be inscribed for a good year" (*Tur, Orach Chaim* 582). This practice was extended in the fifteenth century to the entire month of Elul. Letters and messages written in that month generally included an expression of good wishes for the new year. Out of this practice emerged the modern custom of mailing special New Year cards prior to Rosh HaShanah.

VISITATION OF GRAVES

It is customary to visit ancestral graves in the month of Elul. This practice was instituted by medieval Ashkenazic communities. It was first mentioned by Maharil (14th–15th cent.), the noted author of a book of customs. Originally, it was the practice to visit cemeteries on the eve of Rosh HaShanah to pray at the graveside of pious and scholarly Jews. Rema (16th cent.) included this custom in his annotations to the code (*Orach Chaim* 581). Due to the influence of Rema, the practice of visiting graves spread to all Ashkenazic communities. Eventually, the custom was extended to the entire month of Elul and greater emphasis was given to the visiting of ancestral graves.

Prayers at gravesides were common in the period of the Talmud. Rabbi Joshua (1st cent.) prayed at the graves of Bet Shammai (*Chagigah* 22b). Rabbi Mani (4th cent.) prayed at his father's grave (*Taanit* 23b). The phrase *kever avot*, which in modern parlance designates parental graves, was applied in the talmudic lexicon to the graves of the patriarchs (*Sotah* 34b).

In addition to the month of Elul, it is also customary to visit a parental grave on the day of the yahrzeit (see *Yevamot* 122b, Rashi, *Telata rigli*). It was also customary in some communities to visit parental graves after the conclusion of Shacharit on Tisha B'Av (Rabbi Jacob Emden, *Bet Yaakov*, 17th cent.).

SELICHOT

Selichot (penitential prayers) are recited during the week of Rosh HaShanah, beginning with Sunday morning or on the preceding Saturday night, after midnight. According to tradition, there must be a minimum of four consecutive Selichot services prior to Rosh HaShanah. In the event that Rosh HaShanah commences on a Monday or a Tuesday (it cannot commence on a Wednesday), leaving fewer than four days between Sunday and the holiday Selichot services begin on Sunday of the preceding week (Rema, *Orach Chaim* 581).

Levush (16th cent.) offered the following explanation for the required number of Selichot services. It was the custom of pious Jews to observe ten fasts in the course of the judgment period. These fasts coincided with the ten days when Selichot were recited. In the period between Rosh HaShanah and Yom Kippur, only six fasts are permissible (the two days of Rosh HaShanah, Shabbat Shuvah, and Yom Kippur are not included). It was therefore necessary to add at least four more Selichot days on which four more fasts could be observed. The validity of his explanation is questionable in view of the fact that the tradition of ten fasts was never mentioned in older sources.

The custom of reciting Selichot originated in the geonic period. The first to mention the practice is Rav Hai Gaon (10th–11th cent.), quoted in *Tur, Orach Chaim* 581. Initially, Selichot were recited only between Rosh HaShanah and Yom Kippur. Such was the practice in the Babylonian academies. However, several communities of the period instituted Selichot services beginning with Rosh Chodesh Elul. Medieval Ashkenazic Jews adopted the extended period of Selichot services. Rabbi Joseph Caro, author of the *Shulchan Aruch*, endorsed this practice. It was Rema (16th cent.) whose opinion was decisive in fixing the date of Selichot as it is practiced today (*Orach Chaim* 581).

ABSOLUTION OF VOWS

On the day before Rosh HaShanah, it is customary in some communities to ask a rabbinic court to absolve one from vows of the preceding year which might have been forgotten or inadvertently violated (*hatarat nedarim*). Absolution is limited to vows by which one assumes self-restrictions or personal religious obligations and which do not involve transactions with a second party. An individual may designate any three laymen to constitute a religious court (*Kitzur Shulchan Aruch* 128:16).

Annulment of future vows of a personal nature is valid without rabbinic action. Our version of *Kol Nidre,* which is recited on Yom Kippur night, deals with future vows. The custom of *hatarat nedarim* appears to have originated in Palestine. The Babylonian geonim never heard of the practice. The earliest authority to mention it is Shelah (16th–17th cent.).

PERSONAL CLEANLINESS AND APPEARANCE

It is customary to bathe, cut one's hair, pare one's nails, and dress in Sabbath clothes, as is generally done on Fridays. Despite its solemnity, Rosh HaShanah is considered a joyous holiday (Neh. 8:10). The festive appearance reflects one's confidence that the Almighty will temper justice with mercy (Jer. *Rosh HaShanah* 1:3). Pious men also immerse in a mikveh in order to be ritually clean for the holidays.

ERUV TAVSHILIN

It is forbidden to cook on a festival for the Sabbath. However, if one performs the ritual of *eruv tavshilin* on the day before the holiday, the prohibition is lifted. It is customary to set aside on a plate some bread and cooked or roasted food, thus demonstrating the fact that the cooking for the Sabbath had begun prior to the holiday. A statement to that effect, which is printed in most prayer books, is recited when the ritual is performed. The phrase *eruv tavshilin* means "a combination of dishes."

III.
ROSH HASHANAH CUSTOMS

LIGHTING OF CANDLES

The laws of Sabbath candles are equally applicable to holiday candles. They undoubtedly originated at the same time in the first century B.C.E. The benediction of the holiday candles is concluded with the words *ner shel yom tov* ("candles of the festival"). Rosh HaShanah is technically a *yom tov* because it is included in the list of holidays which are listed under the caption *moade HaShem* (Lev. 23:4, 24). Furthermore the term *yom tov* (Esther 8:17, 9:19, 22), which was originally associated with feasting and gladness (*mishteh vesimchah*), was broadened by talmudic interpretation to cover all holidays on which work was prohibited (*Megillah* 5b). This definition also includes Rosh HaShanah. By the ninth century, when candle benedictions were first introduced, the name Rosh HaShanah had already been in use for about a thousand years. However, the name Rosh HaShanah was omitted from the candle benediction because it was not the biblical designation of the holiday. It was impractical to use the biblical names *yom teruah* or *yom hazikaron* because most women were not familiar with them. The only choice left was to use the general well-known designation, *yom tov*.

An additional benediction, *Shehecheyanu*, is also recited when the holiday candles are lit.

WHITE PAROCHET

It is customary to cover the ark and the lectern with a white cover and cloth in the period between Rosh HaShanah and Yom Kippur. White, a symbol of forgiveness (Isa. 1:18), is appropriate at this time. The Talmud also mentions a custom of wearing white garments on Rosh HaShanah as a symbol of forgiveness and continuity of life (Jer. *Rosh HaShanah* 1:3).

KIDDUSH

The phrase *moadim l'simchah* ("festivals for gladness"), inserted in the Kiddush of other festivals, is omitted on Rosh HaShanah because the term *moadim* only applies to the three pilgrimage festivals.

Unlike the candle-lighting benediction, the Kiddush identifies the holiday by its biblical name, *yom hazikaron*.

It is customary to put a new seasonal fruit on the table on the second night of Rosh HaShanah prior to the chanting of Kiddush. This is done to meet a legal objection to the benediction of *Shehecheyanu*, which is part of the Kiddush. *Shehecheyanu* is normally recited only on the occurrence of an event which is a "first" in that year. Since both days of Rosh HaShanah are legally considered one long day, the recitation of *Shehecheyanu* on the second night in honor of the occurrence of the holiday may be inappropriate. By placing a new fruit on the table, one addresses the *Shehecheyanu* to the fruit, which is a "first," rather than the holiday.

APPLE AND HONEY

It is customary to dip a slice of apple into honey and to recite a special prayer: "May it be thy will to renew unto us a good and sweet year."

As a special encouragement to Jews during the fateful days of judgment, the talmudic rabbis favored the introduction of customs which serve as symbolic omens of a happy year to come. Thus was the custom of wearing white garments which we previously mentioned. Abaye (4th cent.) listed several food items which he recommended for Rosh HaShanah because their names (in Aramaic) connote a continuity of good fortune and an end of misfortune (*Horyot* 12a). It was customary in some medieval Franco-Jewish communities to eat white grapes and figs. The head of a sheep was another traditional item because it serves as a reminder of the Akedah (the binding of Isaac). Fish, too, was a proper Rosh HaShanah dish in many countries because of its symbolism of fertility. The custom of eating sweets on Rosh HaShanah was alluded to in the order of Nehemiah to the assembly: "Go your way, eat the fat and drink the sweet . . ." (Neh. 8:10).

THE RITUAL OF THE SHOFAR

The principal ritual of Rosh HaShanah is the blowing of the shofar. It is customary to use a curved ram's horn. The ram invokes memories of the binding of Isaac and the substitution of a ram which took his place on the altar. The curvature of the horn reflects man's obligation to bend his will before the Almighty in penitence and contrition (*Rosh HaShanah* 26b).

The Bible refers to two distinct musical sounds, tekiah (glissando; Lev. 25:9) and teruah (staccato; Num. 10:6). By rabbinic interpretation, each teruah must be preceded and followed by a tekiah (*Rosh HaShanah* 34a).

The basic mitzvah of blowing a shofar was originally fulfilled by nine blasts, three at each section of the Rosh HaShanah service (*Malchiyot, Zichronot,* and *Shoferot*). Each group of three consisted of tekiah, teruah, tekiah. In time there developed a doubt as to the exact nature of the sound which is designated as teruah. Does it consist of nine uninterrupted tremulous notes or six interrupted staccato notes? The latter is known as shevarim ("broken notes"). To resolve this doubt, Rabbi Abbahu of Caesarea (3rd–4th cent.) instituted a new order of blasts: tekiah, shevarim, teruah, tekiah (*Rosh HaShanah* 34a).

Rabbi Abbahu's ordinance did not lay the issue of the form and sequence of shofar blasts to rest. The question was still hotly debated by Rabbis Avira and Ravina (4th–5th cent.). Following an eventual clarification, Rabbi Abbahu's ordinance was interpreted to require a sequence which takes all doubts into account. This was accomplished by adopting three groupings of various combinations: tekiah, shevarim-teruah, tekiah; tekiah shevarim, tekiah; tekiah, teruah, tekiah (*Mishneh Torah, Hilchot Shofar* 3:3). This order was repeated three times, once for each section of the service, making a total of thirty blasts. In congregational services the entire order was repeated once more when the reader chanted the three sections of the liturgy (*Rosh HaShanah* 32a), bringing the total number of shofar blasts to sixty.

A second question arose regarding the repeated series of shofar blasts. Should they be sounded in the course of the reader's rendition of the *Amidah*, as he chants each section of the service, or only upon his completion of the last section (*Shoferot*)? For want of a clear decision it was resolved to continue the custom of blowing the shofar in the course of the reader's chanting of the service and then once again repeat the entire series of thirty blasts upon his completion of the service. This practice brought the total number of blasts to ninety. In many communities the number of blasts was increased to one hundred to match the one hundred letters in the lamentation of Sisera's mother when he failed to return from the war (Judg. 5:28–29). We thus pray that the wailing of the shofar should end in our triumph. (See Zevin, *Moadim BaHalachah*, p. 44; Kitov, *Sefer HaToadah*, p. 18). The link between the blasts of the shofar and the lamentation of Sisera's mother was mentioned by Rabbi Abraham b. Nathan HaYarchi (12th–13th cents.) in *HaManhig, Hilchot Rosh Hashanah*.

THE PRAYERS

The three sections of Musaf are named *Malchiyot* (Kingship), *Zichronot* (Remembrances), and *Shoferot* (Ram's Horns). God appears in the period of judgment in the role of king and ruler. It is therefore proper to refer to the Almighty at that time as "The King." For that reason one substitutes for the titles "The Holy God" and "The God of Judgment" (in the *Amidah*) the special titles "The Holy King" and "The King of Judgment."

The stirring petition entitled *Avinu Malkenu* is commonly attributed to Rabbi Akiva (2nd cent.). The Talmud relates the story of a public fast for rain which had been decreed by Rabbi Eliezer (2nd cent.). His prayers were unanswered. Rabbi Akiva followed him with a special prayer which he had composed for the occasion: "Our father our king, we have no other king beside thee. Our father our king, for your sake have mercy on us." This prayer was answered (*Taanit* 25b). According to Rashi, "When they saw that this prayer was answered, they added to it from time to time [new verses] and they decreed that it be read on days of penitence" (*Siddur Rashi* 180).

The three divisions of Musaf were widely discussed by the talmudic sages of the second century, by which time this arrangement had been well established. The first division proclaims God's kingship over the universe. The second division proclaims Rosh HaShanah a time of heavenly remembrance, when the deeds of mankind, past and present, are recalled by God and man's destiny is determined. The third division lists great historical events which were highlighted by the sounds of the shofar. The final format of the three divisions was edited in the Babylonian academy of Rav (3rd cent.). The text of these prayers was thereafter referred to as the *Tekita deRav* (*Tanchuma*, *Haazinu* 4).

The stirring service of the High Holidays inspired liturgical poets to contribute soulful compositions which appealed to the mood of the average penitent worshipper. These compositions significantly heightened the emotional effect of the service. Among the most prolific poets were Eleazar Kalir (8th–10th cent.), Meshullam b. Kalonymos (10th cent.), Rabbi Simon b. Isaac of Mainz (10th cent.). Some of the other prominent poets were Rabbenu Gershom b. Judah (10th cent.), Solomon ibn Gabirol (11th cent.), Solomon b. Judah HaBavli (11th cent.), and Amittai b. Shephatiah (11th cent.).

The ark is frequently opened in the course of the High Holiday services. When the ark is opened and the Scrolls are revealed, it is customary for the congregation to rise and to remain standing until the closing of the ark.

The opening of the ark symbolizes the opening of the heavenly gates of prayer. When the ark is opened, it is traditional to recite a silent prayer: "Our father, our king, open the gates of heaven to our prayers."

It is customary for the congregation to recite with the reader the sentence from *Alenu* "and we bend our knees and prostrate ourselves." As the sentence is recited, one bends his knees and prostrates himself.

The rite of the Priestly Benediction is practiced on both days of Rosh HaShanah. The background and development of this ritual is discussed in chapter 8.

The need for an additional day of Rosh HaShanah and its time of origin is discussed in my *Biblical and Historical Background of the Jewish Holy Days*, p. 196.

TASHLICH

After the Minchah service of the first day of Rosh HaShanah, one goes to a running stream to cast away his sins. The inspiration for this symbolic ceremony, as well as the name of the ritual, is derived from a verse in Micah: "He will again have compassion upon us, he will subdue our iniquities and you will cast [*tashlich*] all their sins into the depth of the sea" (7:19). The "casting away" is graphically symbolized by shaking out one's pocket as the special Tashlich prayer is recited. If the first day of Rosh HaShanah occurs on a Saturday, the ritual is performed on the second day in order to avoid an inadvertent desecration of the Sabbath by the carrying of prayerbooks to the river.

The earliest source of the ritual of Tashlich is Maharil (15th cent.). He linked it to the midrashic allegorical account of Satan's effort to prevent Abraham from sacrificing Isaac by converting himself into a river and thus blocking the road to Mount Moriah. According to his interpretation, the purpose of Tashlich is to recall the incident of the Akedah.

The Tashlich ceremony won the immediate acclaim of kabbalists. As a result of the warm endorsement of Rabbi Isaac Luria (16th cent.), the practice, which had originated in Germany, was also adopted by the Sephardim.

IV.
THE DAYS OF PENITENCE

The Ten Days of Penitence comprise the period beginning with Rosh HaShanah and ending with Yom Kippur. The dictum of Rabbi Yochanan (3rd cent.) that the fate of the average individual, who is neither perfect nor wicked, is reviewed beginning with Rosh HaShanah and determined on Yom Kippur (*Rosh HaShanah* 16b) has converted the entire period between the two holy days into a season of continuous judgment.

One of the early rabbinic statements pointing to the special character of the "ten days" was made by Rabbah bar Avuha (3rd cent.).

Commenting on the verse in Isaiah: "Seek you the Lord while he may be found, call you upon him while he is near" (55:6), he remarked that "the reference is to the ten days between Rosh HaShanah and Yom Kippur" (*Rosh HaShanah* 18a). His comment implied that God is most accessible to man's overtures and most attentive to his prayers during these ten days.

Isaiah did not spell out the manner of "seeking" (*dirshu*) the Lord. A similar expression in Psalms, "I sought [*darashti*] the Lord and he answered me" (34:5), means that he prayed to the Lord and his prayers were accepted. Nachmanides translated the phrase *vatelech liderosh* (Gen. 25:22) as "and she [Rebecca] went to pray to the Lord." Isaiah's "seeking the Lord" is undoubtedly synonymous with "praying to the Lord." Surely the second half of his verse, in which he urges the people "call you upon him," suggests prayer. However, Isaiah had more than just prayers in his mind. He also recommended penitence. In the succeeding sentence (55:7) he proclaimed: "Let the wicked forsake his way . . . and let him return [*veyashav*] to the Lord and he will have compassion upon him."

The sages of the early part of the third century had not yet determined the relative merits of prayer and penitence and which of them was more effective in attaining forgiveness. The original formulation of the three principal keys to salvation listed prayer first, charity second, and penitence last (Jer. *Taanit* 2:1). Rabbah bar Avuha therefore did not designate the period between Rosh HaShanah and Yom Kippur as the "Ten Days of Penitence" but merely as the "Ten Days."

Penitence gradually gained preeminence in the talmudic literature. Rabbi Levi (3rd cent.) said: "Penitence is important because it reaches the throne of glory" (*Yoma* 86a). Rabbi Jonathan (3rd cent.) said: "Yom Kippur cannot atone without penitence" (Jer. *Yoma* 8:7).

The interval between Rosh HaShanah and Yom Kippur continued to be designated "The Ten Days," but the term was increasingly used in conjunction with the theme of penitence. Rabbi Samuel bar Nachman (3rd cent.) said: "God waited for him [Nabal; I Sam. 25:38] ten days, like the ten days between Rosh HaShanah and Yom Kippur so that he may repent" (Jer. *Bikkurim* 2:1).

The next step in the substantive development of the interval between the two holy days was the appending of penitence to the name of the period. It appears that by the end of the third century, the name "The Ten Days of Penitence" became commonplace (*Pesikta Rabbati* 41; *Tanchuma, Haazinu* 4; *Yalkut, Isaiah* 389). The text of Rabbah bar Avuha's statement, which was quoted above, also appears in the

Jerusalem Talmud (Jer. *Rosh HaShanah* 1:3). It is apparently a later version. Unlike the Babylonia text, it specifically mentions the new name, "The Ten Days of Penitence."

THE FAST OF GEDALIAH

The Fast of Gedaliah is observed on the third day of Tishri. The background and customs of this fast are discussed in chapter 13.

PENITENTIAL PRAYERS

It is customary to recite Selichot during the days of penitence. This practice was instituted in the Babylonian academies of the geonic period (Rosh, end of *Rosh HaShanah*, 4). Medieval Ashkenazic communities adopted the custom of reciting daily the prayer of *Avinu Malkenu*.

JEWISH BREAD

It is customary to purchase the bread eaten during the days of penitence from Jewish bakeries. This practice was introduced by Ashkenazim in the Middle Ages to make sure that the bread had not been contaminated by contact with an object which would render it impure.

The Jerusalem Talmud cites an admonition of Rabbi Chiya (3rd cent.) to eat uncontaminated food at least for seven days in the year (Jer. *Shabbat* 1:1). Rosh (13th–14th cent.) assumed that the seven-day period referred to the interval between the holy days (Rosh, conclusion of the last chapter of *Rosh HaShanah*).

PAYMENT OF DEBTS

It is customary to pay all outstanding debts prior to Yom Kippur so that one may enter the awesome day free of claims (Agnon, *Days of Awe*, bk. 2).

VISITATION OF GRAVES

It is customary to pray at the graveside of pious people during the week prior to Yom Kippur (Maharil, 14th cent.). A similar custom prevails prior to Rosh HaShanah.

ETROG AND LULAV

It is customary to buy an etrog and lulav prior to Yom Kippur so as to perform an additional mitzvah and appear more meritorious on the holy day (Agnon, *Days of Awe*, bk. 2, quoting from Mateh Efraim, 18th–19th cent.).

RECONCILIATION

It is customary to seek reconciliation and forgiveness from all persons whom one might have offended in the preceding year. This practice, adopted by the Ashkenazim of the Middle Ages, was based on a precedent mentioned in the Talmud. Rav (3rd cent.) had a disagreement with Rabbi Chanina. Although he did not consider himself guilty of an impropriety, he visited the home of his colleague on the eve of Yom Kippur to seek reconciliation (*Yoma* 87b).

KAPPAROT

One of the most controversial pre–Yom Kippur customs is the ritual of Kapparot (forgiveness). One circles a white fowl around his head as he recites: "This is my substitute . . . this fowl will die and I will enter upon a good and long life . . ." The fowl is slaughtered and its cost is given to charity. The innards of the fowl are fed to birds in a spirit of compassion for all living creatures.

The custom of Kapparot dates back at least to the ninth century. The geonim were not sure of its rationale and assumed that the custom reflected a symbolic transfer of fate from the individual to an animal. A twelfth-century scholar conjectured that the ritual of Kapparot was designed as a reinactment of the biblical rite of Azazel (Lev. 16:8; *Machzor Vitry* 373).

An ancient custom similar to Kapparot existed in the talmudic era. Abaye (3rd–4th cent.) discussed Sabbath laws relating to a *parpisa* (a perforated pot) which is deposited on the ground and in which greenery is growing (*Shabbat* 81b). Rashi quotes a geonic responsum which explains the use of the *parpisa*. It was customary to plant beans or other vegetables in a palm basket filled with earth and manure. The planting was done about three weeks before Rosh HaShanah, one basket for each minor in the family. On the eve of Rosh HaShanah, each member took his own basket, circled it around his head seven times, and recited: "This is my substitute, this is my exchange, this will replace me." The basket was then thrown into the river. This custom appears to have been an ancient progenitor of two current customs, Tashlich and Kapparot.

The Yom Kippur Eve practice of throwing the innards of a fowl to the birds to feed on is mentioned in the Talmud (*Chulin* 95b). There is no indication, however, that the custom was associated with the ritual of Kapparot.

The propriety of Kapparot has been seriously questioned. Nachmanides denounced the custom for its smell of heathenism *(Orchot Chaim, Hilchot Erev Yom Kippurim)*. Rabbi Solomon Adret (13th–14th cent.) prohibited the ritual in Barcelona (Responsum 392). Rabbi Joseph Caro (16th cent.) also opposed it *(Orach Chaim* 605). Rema, however, approved it. It has increasingly become the custom in modern times to use money instead of a fowl and to contribute the money to charity.

IMMERSION

It is customary to immerse oneself in a mikveh prior to Minchah services. This practice, first mentioned by Rav Amram Gaon (9th cent.), was most likely inspired by the immersion of the high priest on Yom Kippur (*Yoma* 19b). In addition to the ritual significance of immersion, bodily cleanliness was an important factor in the proper observance of the holy day.

LASHES

Pious Jews submit to symbolic lashes to atone for sins which were punishable by lashes in the days when rabbinic courts had the jurisdiction to impose corporal punishment. This practice was introduced by medieval Ashkenazic communities. In some localities the lashes were administered after the immersion in the mikveh.

CONFESSION OF SINS

It is customary to confess one's sins *(al chet)* after the conclusion of the Minchah *Amidah*. This practice was most likely introduced in the second century. However, the final details were not determined until the third century (*Yoma* 87b).

Despite the fact that the *Al Chet* is recited on the night of Yom Kippur, the rabbis instituted an additional confessional in the afternoon, for fear that some people might neglect the evening prayers due to overindulgence in food and drinks in preparation for the fast (ibid.). The importance attributed to confession is based on the prominence of the confessional prayer in the Yom Kippur ritual performed by the high priest (Lev. 16:21).

The prayer of *Al Chet* was mentioned for the first time by Rav Achai Gaon (8th cent.). It consisted of a few lines which did not follow an alphabetical arrangement. The *Al Chet* was subsequently rewritten several times and considerably expanded. Maimonides' text of the *Al Chet* is close to our modern version, except that it has no dual lines for each letter in the alphabet. That format was adopted by Ashkenazim.

Al Chet is known as the Major Confession. The passage commencing with *Ashamnu*, which also follows an alphabetical arrangement, is called the Minor Confession.

THE CONCLUDING MEAL

The concluding meal *(seudah hamafseket)* is an essential part of the preparations for the fast. Some rabbis regarded this meal as a medical imperative to provide the needed strength for fasting. Other rabbis considered the meal a contributing factor to the enhancement of the Yom Kippur "affliction." By conditioning the body to food, one's appetite is whetted, creating a sharper sensitivity to the pangs of hunger.

The importance of the concluding meal is stressed in the following talmudic statement: "He who eats and drinks on the ninth [of Tishri], the text [Lev. 23:32] regards it as if he fasts on the ninth and the tenth" *(Yoma* 81b). In other words, the merit of eating on the ninth in preparation for the fast is as great as that of the fast.

Regardless of the religious implications of the concluding meal, Jews throughout history tended to consume a lavish dinner in the hope of easing the stress of the fast. As we noted before, the rabbis instituted a confessional prayer at Minchah because many people overindulged in food and were unable to recite the evening prayers.

Medieval traditions established guidelines to help select a proper menu for the concluding meal. One should eat easily digestible food to prevent satiation when Yom Kippur begins. One should not eat dairy or spicy food. One should also avoid eating the kind of food which stimulates sexual desires.

A tradition of more recent vintage prescribes the serving of dumplings (kreplach) filled with meat. Two more festive occasions, Purim and Hoshana Rabba, have a similar gastronomical tradition. Various explanations have been offered for this custom but none meets the test of common sense. We can merely note a few facts which may be of help to those who are inclined to probe deeper into the origin of this dish. The dumpling is tricornered, a possible allusion to the three festive occasions. All of them may be categorized as judgment days. Purim follows a day of fasting and praying, Hoshana Rabba is traditionally a judgment day, and, of course, so is Yom Kippur.

YOM KIPPUR LIGHTS

The function of light on Sabbaths and festivals is to enhance the holiday atmosphere and promote conjugal harmony. Some rabbinic authorities, feeling that this rationale was not in keeping with the spirit of solemnity on Yom Kippur, questioned the propriety of lighting Yom Kippur candles. It was particularly felt that placing candles on the dining table would be incompatible with a fast. However, the custom of spreading a white cloth on the table and placing candles on it took hold. Initially, the usual candle-lighting benediction was omitted. However, in the seventeenth century the custom of reciting a benediction was introduced.

MEMORIAL LIGHTS

It is customary to light a candle in memory of deceased parents for the atonement of their souls. This practice was instituted by Ashkenazic communities in the Middle Ages. In some localities the memorial candle was lit in the synagogue. However, most Jews light it at home.

It is customary to bless one's children before one leaves the home for the evening services. The text of the blessing is printed in most prayerbooks.

A KITTLE

It is customary to wear a *kittle* (white robe) on Yom Kippur because white is a symbol of forgiveness. The kittle also reminds one of shrouds and therefore stimulates penitence.

One puts a talit over the kittle and keeps it on throughout the evening service.

5

Yom Kippur Customs

I.
INTRODUCTION

YOM KIPPUR IS the most solemn day in the Jewish religious calendar. The solemnity is inherent in the theological significance of a day of atonement. There is little room for relaxed composure in the tense atmosphere of Yom Kippur, when one's fate is in the balance. The gravity of the occasion is reflected in the biblical command: "And you shall afflict your souls" (Lev. 23:27). A state of affliction is a prerequisite to confession, contrition, and penitence. All of these are calculated to induce a mood of serious introspective meditation.

Despite the awesomeness of Yom Kippur, this holy day did not generate an undue number of customs, as one would normally expect of the most solemn day in the year. The Temple rituals were indeed impressive and rich in pageantry. However, for the majority of Jews, who were not in Jerusalem on Yom Kippur, the spirit of the fast expressed itself mainly through abstention. One had to abstain from food and pleasure. Prior to the establishment of synagogues, there were few set prayers to be recited outside the Temple. There were practically no customs or rituals which one had to perform.

With the widespread establishment of synagogues in the first century, prayer became the basic Yom Kippur ritual of world Jewry. The Bible, particularly the Book of Psalms, provided a rich source of prayers. Sectarians, like the Essenes, who wished to stress their uniqueness, composed their own psalmic literature. At any rate, there were enough prayers available to keep the people engaged in prayer throughout the day. Philo (1st cent.), speaking of the Jews of Egypt, mentioned that they were busy praying "from morning until evening" (*Treatise on the Festivals*, The Ninth Festival). Most of the Yom Kippur customs that were adopted in the course of time are related to the ritual of worship.

163

The Bible indicates the distinctiveness of Yom Kippur by designating it *Shabbat shabbaton* ("a sabbath of sabbaths"; Lev. 16:31, 23:32). The same designation was given to the weekly Sabbath (Exod. 31:15, Lev. 23:3). Most Jewish biblical scholars have translated *shabbat shabbaton* as "a day of solemn rest." This rendition is in my opinion incorrect. It is erroneous to describe the weekly Sabbath as "a day of solemn rest." Furthermore, the term *shabbaton* is also linked in the Bible to the festival of Sukkot (Lev. 23:39). One would hardly associate solemnity with Sukkot. We must also question the assumption that there is a connotation of solemnity in the Hebrew *shabbaton*. If *shabbat* is devoid of solemnity, what is there in the structure of the word *shabbaton* that makes it take on a nuance of solemnity: A more precise definition of *shabbaton* may prove helpful.

DEFINITION OF SHABBAT AND SHABBAT SHABBATON

Is *shabbat* the name of a day, a proper noun like Saturday, or is it a common noun, defining the category of the day as a time of rest? If it is a proper noun, then we must assume that it is the name of a specific day of the week, Saturday. If it is a common noun, it may designate any day in the year which is categorized as a day of rest. That would include all holidays on which the performance of work is prohibited.

An analysis of the biblical sources raises a number of questions in addition to the question of the definition of *shabbat*. What is the significance of the phrase *yom hashabbat*? What is the implication of *shabbat shabbaton*? Why was the sequence of these two words reversed in the scriptural sentence which introduced for the first time the term *shabbat* (*shabbaton shabbat kodesh*; Exod. 16:23)? What is the definition of *shabbaton* when it is not hyphenated with *shabbat*? Why were Rosh HaShanah and Sukkot designated a *shabbaton*, but not Passover and Shevuot? Why was the word *shabbaton* never used in the post-pentateuchal biblical literature?

For the sake of clarity we will sum up our conclusions and then analyze the sources upon which our conclusions are based.

1. *Shabbat* and *shabbaton* are not proper nouns and therefore may apply to any day of rest, unless otherwise indicated in the text.
2. The phrase *bayom hashabbat* ("on the day of the Sabbath") refers to the weekly Sabbath exclusively.
3. Where the phrase *bayom hashabbat* appears in a passage to indicate a

reference to the weekly Sabbath, all subsequent mentions of the Sabbath in the same passage omit the *bayom*.

4. *Shabbatot*, the plural form of *shabbat*, always refers to the weekly Sabbaths.
5. *Shabbaton* means a recurring period of rest.
6. *Shabbat shabbaton* is best translated as "a day of complete rest."
7. The aforementioned pentateuchal guidelines are followed by some of the texts of the Scriptures and Prophets and are ignored in others. The gradual change reflects an emerging trend to convert *shabbat* into a proper noun. The trend culminated in the Talmud and the nonrabbinic literature of the talmundic period, where *shabbat* is used exclusively as a proper noun.

We will now discuss the sources upon which our conclusions are based. The Bible identifies specific days by their numerical sequence in the week (Gen. 1). Saturday was initially identified as "the seventh day" (Gen. 2:2–3). This identification was retained even after the name *shabbat* was introduced into the Bible (Exod. 16:26, 20:10–11; 31:15, 17; 35:2; Deut. 5:14). Thus it is evident that the *shabbat* in these texts cannot be construed as the name of a specific day in view of the retention in the same text of the old name, "the seventh day." We must therefore conclude that *shabbat* is a common noun which categorized the seventh day as a day of rest (first conclusion).

The noun *shabbat*, a time of rest, is elastic in its duration. Thus the entire sabbatical year *(shemitah)* is called *shabbat* (Lev. 25:4). When *shabbat* is preceded by *bayom* ("in the day") the duration of this time of rest is narrowed to one day. The only Sabbath which comes regularly once a week is Saturday. "The day of the Sabbath" is therefore synonymous with Saturday (second conclusion).

When the specific identification of the *shabbat* has been made clear in the text, the qualifying *bayom* may be dropped. Thus the *shabbat* in the incident of the manna dispensed with the *bayom* because its identification was indicated by the designations "tomorrow" (Exod. 16:23), "today" (16:25), and the "seventh day" (16:26). The same is true of the injunction "and you shall observe the sabbath" (Exod. 31:14). Its precise definition is clarified by the subsequent reference to "the seventh day" (Exod. 31:15; third conclusion).

Significantly, the *shabbat* mentioned in connection with the ritual of the Omer (Lev. 23:11) is not qualified by hyphenation with *bayom* or by any other identifying term. Consequently one must interpret this *shabbat* as a day of rest which refers to the previously mentioned festival of Passover (Lev. 23:6).

The definition of the *shabbat* in the passage of the Omer was in contention between the Sadducees and the rabbinic sages (*Menachot* 95b). The Sadducees erroneously assumed that *shabbat* was a proper noun, synonymous with Saturday. This is disproved by our first conclusion. Furthermore, the broad definition of *shabbat* is evidenced by the biblical description of the festivals of Rosh HaShanah and Sukkot as *shabbaton,* another form of *shabbat* (Lev. 23:34, 39).

Shabbatot (plural) always refers to the weekly Sabbaths. Thus "My Sabbaths you shall observe" (Exod. 31:13). Its reference to the weekly Sabbath is made clear by the indicated motivation: "Because it is a sign between me and you throughout the generations." Only the weekly Sabbath has been declared such a "sign" (Exod. 31:17). To make sure that the *shabbatot* of verse 13 is not misunderstood, Onkelos and Yonathan b. Uziel interpolated in their Aramaic translation the word *yome* ("the days of my Sabbaths") to indicate its reference to the weekly Sabbath.

The plural of *shabbat* also appears in Leviticus (19:3, 30; 23:38). All of these were interpreted to refer exclusively to the weekly Sabbath (*Yevamot* 5b, 6a; *Torat Kohanim*). Common sense supports this assumption. There are more than fifty weekly Sabbaths in a year. When one speaks of Sabbaths it is logical to assume that the reference is to the many Sabbaths which regularly occur during the year (fourth conclusion).

We have discussed the definitions of *shabbat* and *shabbatot*. What about *shabbaton?* It appears to me that *shabbaton* is similar in structure to *Yomam* (a modified form of *yom*). *Yoman* means "in the day" or "daily." *Shabbaton* similarly means "on the Sabbath" or "a recurring period of rest" (weekly or annually). Its construction reflects great antiquity, as is evidenced by the Aramic masculine *nun* suffix. *Yomam,* a more recent word, has the Hebrew *mem* suffix.

Curiously, the first time the Sabbath appears in the Bible it is designated by the name *shabbaton* ("a weekly day of rest"; Exod. 16:23). According to a rabbinic tradition, Moses had persuaded Pharaoh to permit the Hebrew slaves to rest on Saturdays (*Shemot Rabbah* 1:19). According to Avudrahim's version of this Midrash, Moses had felt that Pharaoh would oppose any other rest day. The Egyptians considered Saturday, the day of Saturn, an unlucky day, and whatever was produced on that day would also turn out to be unlucky.

The attribution of a Roman superstition to the Egyptians (not included in *Shemot Rabbah)* reflects some of the legendary aspects of this tradition. However, most legends emanate from historical facts. The Egyptians rested on the first and fifteenth of each month. The first of the month, coinciding with the appearance of the stricken moon (in the lunar calendar), was considered an unlucky day. The fifteenth of the month, when the moon was at its zenith, was a festive day. It is conceivable that the Hebrew slaves rested on both of those days, or at least on the first of the month. The bi-weekly or monthly rest day might have been called *shabbaton.* After the manna incident, Moses informed the Jews that their *shabbaton* (periodic day of rest) has become "a holy Sabbath unto the Lord" (Exod. 16:23).

The term *shabbaton* embraces the Sabbath and also festivals (an annual period of rest). The Bible designates the holidays of Rosh HaShanah, Yom Kippur, and Sukkot a *shabbaton* to indicate the recurring cycle of these festivals which must be observed every year. There was no need for attaching the label *shabbaton* to Passover, the only festival which marks the anniversary of a historical event. Like a birthday, it must of necessity be observed every year. Furthermore, the annual celebration of Passover was clearly spelled out in Exodus: "Thou shalt therefore keep this ordinance in its season from year to year" (13:10). There was similarly no need for designating Shavuot a *shabbaton* because Shavuot is an appendage of Passover and, like it, must be observed every year (fifth conclusion).

The term *shabbaton* gradually fell into disuse. As a relic of ancient Aramaic it was considered archaic by the biblical post-pentateuchal authors. Whenever it was necessary to convey a sense of recurrence, the temporal index was repeated: *Miyamim yamimah* ("from year to year," Exod. 13:10), *chodesh bechodesh* ("every month," I Chron. 27:1), *Shabbat beshabbato* ("every Sabbath"; Isa. 66:23). The term *yomam,* however, gained popularity and was used extensively in the post-pentateuchal literature.

The phrase *shabbat shabbaton* is analogous to *kodesh hakadashim* in its construction and implication (Exod. 26:33). The latter is translated "the holiest of the holy" or the "most holy." The former should be translated "the most restful of the recurring days of rest" or more concisely, "the Sabbath of the most complete rest" (sixth conclusion).

The Sabbath and Yom Kippur are the only holy days which have been designated in the Bible as *shabbat shabbaton* (Exod. 35:2, Lev. 16:31). Unlike other festivals, when some categories of work are permissible, no manner of work is permitted on these two holy days.

The sabbatical year *(shemitah)* was also designated *shabbat shabbaton*

(Lev. 25:4). The implication of this designation is the same as in the case of the Sabbath and Yom Kippur. There are partial planting restrictions (*kilayim*) every year, but the restrictions of the sabbatical year are complete.

A modification of the previously mentioned guidelines relating to the definition of *shabbat* emerges in some of the hagiographic and prophetic texts. The hyphenated *yom hashabbat* is frequently used by Jeremiah (6th cent. B.C.E.). Ezekiel (6th cent. B.C.E.), Nehemiah (5th cent. B.C.E.), and in the Book of Psalms. It does not appear in Isaiah (8th cent. B.C.E.) and Amos (8th cent. B.C.E.). According to tradition, the prophecy of Isaiah was put into writing in the sixth century B.C.E. (*Baba Batra* 15a). At that time the phrase *yom hashabbat* was still in common use.

The books in which the *yom* was dropped are Kings and Chronicles. According to tradition, Kings was written by Jeremiah (*Baba Batra* 15a). Jeremiah frequently used the expression *yom hashabbat* in the book bearing his name. There is no apparent reason why the style was changed in Kings, unless we assume that the final redaction took place much later.

As for Chronicles, historical evidence points to the fact that it could not have been written prior to 350 B.C.E. One may detect a deliberate effort on the part of the author of Chronicles to delete the *yom*. Thus the arrangement of the shewbread is described in Leviticus as follows: *Bayom hashabbat yaarchenu* ("every Sabbath day he shall set it in order"; 24:8). The same arrangement is described in Chronicles in the following manner: *umin bene hakehati . . . al lechem hamaarechet behachin shabbat shabbat* ("and the sons of the Kohatites . . . were on the shewbread to prepare it Sabbath after Sabbath" (9:32). It is obvious that by the time the Chronicles had been edited, the term *shabbat* had become a proper noun (seventh conclusion).

AFFLICTION

The biblical source from which all Yom Kippur restrictions are derived is found in Leviticus: "And it shall be a statute forever for you, in the seventh month, on the tenth day of the month, you shall afflict your souls, and shall do no manner of work . . ." (16:29). The list of prohibited acts, in addition to cessation from work, includes the following: eating, drinking, washing, anointing, wearing of leather shoes, and sexual intercourse (*Yoma* 73b).

The verb *veinitem* ("you shall afflict") is rather vague. The Talmud provides some guidelines and definitions. "Affliction" is not to be construed as a condition resulting from the performance of painful and distressing acts. It is a feeling of discomfort resulting from natural causes, which are not relieved because one abstains from taking preventative measures (such as eating and drinking).

The two basic prohibitions, in addition to cessation from work, are eating and drinking. Two rationales are offered for the opinion that abstinence from food constitutes a state of affliction. One links the term "affliction" to the punishment prescribed for violators of the laws of Yom Kippur: ". . . that soul will I destroy from among his people" (Lev. 23:30). This rationale assumes that the affliction must be of the kind which would ultimately destroy life, if permitted to continue indefinitely (*Yoma* 74b). Of all the enumerated prohibited acts, only fasting suspends life-sustaining functions. The proponent of this view obviously interprets fasting as a symbolic ritual of self-sacrifice. This fits in with the tradition that Yom Kippur falls on the anniversary of the binding of Isaac (*Pirke deRabbi Eliezer, Akedat Yitzchak, Asara Maamarot* 3).

The second explanation is that of the school of Rabbi Ishmael, which equates affliction with fasting because of an explicit link between the two in a deuteronomic text: "and he afflicted you and suffered you to hunger" (8:3). The text seems to offer a different rationale for the ritual of fasting. "And you shall remember all the ways in which the Lord thy God has led thee these forty years in the wilderness, that he might afflict thee, to test thee, to know what was in your heart, whether you would keep his commandments or not" (8:2). According to this text, fasting is a test of one's sincerity and loyalty to God.

The restrictions of washing, anointing, wearing of leather shoes, and sexual intercourse are not based on pentateuchal texts. These prohibitions obviously derived from very ancient traditions, and the Talmud looked for texts in the Hagiographa and Prophets which placed these prohibited acts within the context of affliction (*Yoma* 76b–77a). Most medieval rabbinic scholars considered these prohibitions to be of rabbinic origin (*Bet Yoseph, Tur, Orach Chaim* 611). The view that affliction mainly results from fasting is confirmed by the psalmist: "I afflicted my soul with fasting" (35:13).

The prohibition of wearing shoes is limited to leather shoes only. According to Maimonides, leather cushions the feet from the discomfort of walking on rocky and uneven ground (*Mishneh Torah, Hilchot Shevitat Asor* 3:5). A later rabbi offered a highly moralist explanation. It is not proper to wear a garment for which it was necessary to kill a living animal (Agnon, *Days of Awe*, 3:276). Attractive as this explanation may appear, it does not fit within the context of affliction. Furthermore, fur hats and coats should equally have fallen under the same ban.

A DAY OF SPIRITUAL EXALTATION

Technically, Yom Kippur may not be designated a *yom tov* because such a designation is incompatible with fasting. Broadly speaking, however, Yom Kippur is a day of spiritual ecstasy and joy. Thus Rabbi Simon b. Gamliel said: "There never were in Israel greater days of joy [*yomim tovim*] than the fifteenth of Av and Yom HaKippurim" (*Taanit* 26b). Another rabbinic passage states that "the Day of Atonement for Israel is an occasion of great joy for the Almighty" (*Seder Eliyahu Rabbah* 1). The spiritual joy of a penitent derives from the knowledge that he has attained a state of purity and a cleansing from sin in anticipation of God's forgiveness.

Grief and mourning are not among the emotional ingredients which motivated the restrictive laws of Yom Kippur. This is true even though the principal prohibitions of Yom Kippur are identical with the prohibitions of the mournful day of Tisha B'Av. Four of the restrictions are also part of the rituals observed by a mourner in the week of shivah.

The purpose of a fast is to incline one to penitence (*Mishneh Torah, Hilchot Taaniyot* 1:2; *Chinuch*, mitzvah 313). The denial of other pleasurable acts on Yom Kippur was similarly designed to induce total dedication to the pursuit of moral perfection rather than bodily comforts. The avoidance of pleasure is merely a means to an end. On the other hand, for a mourner the avoidance of pleasure is an end in itself. In effect, a mourner withdraws from the society of the living and its joys to seek total communion with the departed through a profound sense of bereavement. The biblical sources upon which the mourning restrictions are based are entirely different than those from which the Yom Kippur prohibitions derive.

Due to the radical distinction between the motivations of the Yom Kippur and mourning prohibitions, many of the customs relating to Tisha B'Av do not apply to Yom Kippur. Thus it was an ancient custom for mourners to wear black garments. On Yom Kippur, however, one wears white. A mourner does not exchange greetings with visitors. On Yom Kippur, one is urged to extend greetings and good wishes to his neighbor. The study of Torah provides spiritual pleasure to a student and is therefore prohibited on Tisha B'Av and in the period of shivah.

There is no such restriction on Yom Kippur. On Tisha B'Av one sits on the ground and a mourner sits on a low stool. On Yom Kippur one sits on a chair or a bench. A mourner withdraws from society. On Yom Kippur one joins the community in a sense of brotherhood and common prayer.

II.
YOM KIPPUR EVE CUSTOMS

PRELIMINARY PRAYERS

Due to the centrality of worship in the Yom Kippur ritual, Jews have been receptive to new liturgical compositions which have been integrated into the regular order of congregational prayers. Several additional prayers, which have received widespread acceptance, have been adopted as preliminary invocations to be recited individually prior to the commencement of the congregational service. Among these are the prayer of Rav Saadiah Gaon (10th cent., printed for the first time in Mantua, Italy, in 1575), the confession of Rabbenu Nissin (11th cent.), and *Tefilah Zakkah* (a prayer for purification), printed for the first time in 1810 (*Chaye Adam* 143:20).

KOL NIDRE

The solemnity of Yom Kippur has always acted as a spiritual magnet, attracting Jews from all walks of life. Among them were men who might have incurred the censure of the rabbis and the community. There might even be some who had been banned from the synagogue. No Jew, however, was to be denied admission to the synagogue on Yom Kippur or barred from attending the most emotional part of the service, the chanting of *Kol Nidre*. His mere presence attested to a desire to make amends.

The admission of offenders requires a judicial declaration of forgiveness. It is customary to open the ark and remove two Scrolls, which are held by two individuals on the right and on the left of the reader. The three men constitute a judicial court and proclaim the formula which permits the offenders to join the congregation in prayer. "By authority of the court on high, and by the authority of the court on earth; with the knowledge of the Almighty, and with the knowledge of the congregation, we declare it now lawful to offer prayers in the company of the transgressors [*avaryanim*]."

Who were the "transgressors"? It is popularly believed that the declaration was aimed at the Marranos, who had at one time embraced Christianity and now wished to be readmitted to Judaism. This seems unlikely. The readmission of apostates to Judaism requires a more formal procedure than the mere recitation of a general formula in which the convert did not participate. Furthermore the declaration of the admission of the transgressors predates the period of the emergence of a large body of Marranos in Spain.

The declaration was instituted by Rabbi Meir of Rothenburg (d. 1293). The situation of German Jewry in the thirteenth century had gravely deteriorated in the wake of the Crusades and widespread anti-Jewish riots. Repressions undoubtedly led to an increase in the number of Jewish apostates and to a general decline in the cultural level of German and French Jewries. This unquestionably led to a lessening of religious observances among the common people. Organized communities might have sought to defend the faith by barring the transgressors from the synagogue. No services were conducted if a violator was in attendance. Yom Kippur presented a problem because of the considerable number of such violators present in the synagogue and the impossibility of postponing the services because *Kol Nidre* has to be recited before sunset. Furthermore, one has to take into account the Yom Kippur spirit of reconciliation. Hence the declaration of admission.

After the admission of the transgressors, the reader chants the *Kol Nidre*, which is a declaration of annulment of vows of a personal nature that may be made in the course of the coming year.

We have previously mentioned the custom of absolution of vows on the day before Rosh HaShanah. That custom was rooted in an ancient tradition, which timed the annulment of vows with Rosh HaShanah. According to a talmudic statement: "He who desires to have his vows which he may make all year nullified, let him announce on Rosh HaShanah: 'All pledges which I will make are void' " (*Nedarim* 23b). However, the talmudic passage deals with the annulment of future vows and not with absolution of past vows.

Absolution of past vows (*hatarat nedarim*) can only be declared by a rabbinical court which inquires into the circumstances and intent of the vow. No absolution may be granted on a Sabbath or festival. It was for this reason that the early medieval custom of *hatarat nedarim* was set for the day prior to Rosh HaShanah.

The custom of *Kol Nidre* on the eve of Yom Kippur dates from the geonic period. The original version of *Kol Nidre* was that of an absolution of vows which had been taken in the past, thus duplicating the pre–Rosh HaShanah ritual. A rabbinical decree of absolution is repeated three times, hence the three recitations of *Kol Nidre*. Since absolutions may not be granted on a holiday, *Kol Nidre* has to be recited before sunset.

The institution of *hatarat nedarim* and *Kol Nidre* was contemporaneous. There were undoubtedly many people who could not remain long enough to participate in the individualized and time-consuming procedure of *hatarat nedarim*. Such individuals could avail themselves of *Kol Nidre*, which covered the entire congregation.

From a legal point of view, the early version of *Kol Nidre* left much to be desired. One cannot annual past vows without a properly conducted judicial proceeding. In addition to the legal objection, there was also opposition to *Kol Nidre* on the ground that some people might misconstrue its effect and treat all religious vows with disrespect.

The earliest source to mention *Kol Nidre* was Rav Natronai Gaon (9th cent.). He was highly critical of it and said: "It is not the custom in the two academies [of Babylonia] or in other localities to absolve vows, neither on Rosh HaShanah nor on Yom Kippur. We heard that such a custom prevails in other lands. . . . We have already expressed our view that *Kol Nidre* should not be recited" *(Kol Bo)*.

Rav Natronai's disciple, Rav Amram Gaon (9th cent.) quoted a Hebrew version of *Kol Nidre*, without commenting on its legality or propriety. Rav Hai Gaon b. Rav Nachshon Gaon (9th cent.) criticized *Kol Nidre* and concluded that it has no validity. When he was asked whether *Kol Nidre* would be acceptable if it addressed itself to future vows, he refused to comment or give his approval. Rav Saadiah Gaon (10th cent.) limited the scope of *Kol Nidre* to pledges assumed by an entire congregation. Maimonides (12th cent.) made no mention of *Kol Nidre* in his code.

Despite the discouragement of the early sages, the custom of reciting *Kol Nidre* spread to many countries. Rabbenu Tam (12th cent.) took note of it and decided to meet the legal objection by changing the time reference of the old version, which read "from last Yom Kippur to this Yom Kippur," to "from this Yom Kippur until next Yom Kippur." He also changed the past tense of the Aramaic text to the future tense.

The prestigious codifier Rabbenu Asher (Rosh, 13th–14th cent.) favored the retention of the early text, which granted absolution for past vows. His decision was not based on legal grounds but on a deep reluctance to tamper with old traditions. His son, Rabbenu Jacob, retained the early version in his code (*Tur, Orach Chaim* 619). However,

Rabbi Isaac bar Sheshet (14th cent.), a popular author of responsa, continued the opposition to *Kol Nidre* and stated that it was not recited in Catalonia.

Despite the approval of the *Tur* code, the amendment of Rabbenu Tam eventually became the accepted version. Rabbi Joseph Caro, the author of the *Shulchan Aruch,* mentioned *Kol Nidre* in the code but did not comment on its form or content. By that time the version of Rabbenu Tam had become the norm. Yet Rabbi Jacob Emden (18th cent.) felt that the original version should not be ignored, out of respect for tradition. He therefore suggested that *Kol Nidre* should include a reference to future vows as well as past vows *(Siddur Bet Yaakov, Leil Yom Kippur).* His suggestion gained no support.

Why does *Kol Nidre* have such a strong and almost mystical appeal? Its emotional hold may be partly attributed to its stirring melody, which sets the solemn tone of the holy day. The fact that it is the opening ritual of Yom Kippur, and as such is identified with the holiday itself, was another factor in attributing to it a significance which is not warranted by the contents of the passage.

The spell of *Kol Nidre* has remained unbroken even in modern times. When a Reconstructionist congregation attempted a few years ago to eliminate *Kol Nidre,* there ensued a near-riot and the custom had to be restored. Many Reform congregations which have omitted *Kol Nidre* have made a concession to its nostalgic and emotional appeal by retaining the melody. Despite all attempts to modify or eliminate *Kol Nidre,* and despite spurious anti-Semitic charges that it puts the validity of Jewish pledges in doubt, the strong position of *Kol Nidre* in the Yom Kippur ritual remains unchanged.

CONFESSION

Penitence, prayer, and charity are the three principal keys to salvation. Confession is an essential prerequisite to penitence. In the words of Maimonides: "How does one confess? One must say, 'O Lord, I have sinned, I have strayed, I have transgressed. I have done such and such. I repent and I am ashamed of my deeds and I will never do it again' " *(Mishneh Torah, Hilchot Teshuvah* 1:1).

The Bible stresses the paramount role of confession as a preliminary to atonement. "When a man or a woman shall commit any sin . . . they shall confess their sin which they have done . . . besides the ram of atonement whereby atonement shall be made for him" (Num. 5:6–8). According to rabbinic interpretation, confession is an independent rite, mandatory even when there are no longer any sacrificial offerings (Zevin, *Moadim BaHalachah,* p. 63).

Confession was a prominent feature of the high priest's performance of the Yom Kippur ritual (Lev. 16:21). He confessed three times: once for himself and his family, a second time for himself, his family, and all the kohanim, and a third time for the entire household of Israel (*Yoma* 35b, 41b, 66a).

In the course of the Yom Kippur service worshippers confess ten times: once at the Minchah service prior to Yom Kippur, twice each during Maariv, Shacharit, Musaf, and Minchah, and once more at Neilah (*Ashamnu*). Some commentators attribute the number ten to a symbolic atonement for the transgression of the Ten Commandments. According to another explanation, the ten confessions correspond to the number of times the high priest pronounced the ineffable name of God on Yom Kippur (*Orach Chaim* 670).

A NIGHT OF WAKEFULNESS

Pious Jews of all generations have made it a practice to stay awake in the synagogue throughout the night to pray or to read religious books on the subjects of piety and ethics. This ancient custom was inspired by the practice of the high priest to stay awake the entire night of Yom Kippur. According to the Talmud, this custom was commemorated by pious Jews in the diaspora even after the destruction of the Temple (*Yoma* 19b).

Rabbi Isaiah Horowitz (Shelah, 16th–17th cent.) applauded the good intentions of those who stay awake on Yom Kippur night. However, he expressed his misgivings that such a practice might be injurious to health and detrimental to the proper observance of the next day's rituals. He therefore cautioned all people who are not in vigorous health to refrain from following this custom.

III.
YOM KIPPUR DAY CUSTOMS

THE READING OF THE TORAH

Six persons are called to the Torah for the Yom Kippur Shacharit reading. When the holy day falls on a Sabbath, the number of aliyot is increased to seven. It has been suggested that the number of aliyot serves as a symbolic atonement for the people of the world, which was created in six days.

YIZKOR

It is customary to recite a memorial prayer for the departed on the last day of each holiday. The most important occasion for Yizkor is Yom Kippur because it is a day of atonement for the living as well as the dead, who are also in need of atonement (*Orach Chaim, Hilchot Yom HaKippurim* 621:6; for a discussion of the custom of Yizkor, see below chap. 8).

PROSTRATION

It is customary for the reader to prostrate himself during the recitation of the prayer of *Alenu* when he chants the following sentence: "We bend the knee and prostrate ourselves and offer thanks to the supreme king of kings, the holy one, blessed be he." It is customary for the congregation to join the reader in the ritual of prostration. This ritual is repeated several times in the course of the recitation of the *Avodah*.

THE AVODAH

The recitation of the entire order of the *Avodah* (sacrificial rites) in the Temple is an important part of the Musaf service. Thus we reinact verbally the Yom Kippur pageantry of the Temple.

It was customary for the high priest and the congregation to prostrate themselves ten times on Yom Kippur, every time the name of God was mentioned. After the destruction of the Temple, the number of prostrations in the synagogue, during the *Avodah*, was reduced to three, corresponding to the number of confessions of the high priest on Yom Kippur (Kitov, *Sefer HaTeudah* 58).

After each prostration, the congregation exclaims: *Baruch shem kavod malchuto l'olam vaed* ("Blessed is the name of the glory of his kingdom forever and ever"). This custom was practiced in the Temple and has survived to our day.

SELICHOT

A series of penitential prayers (*selichot*) comprises the third part of Musaf. One of the most striking of these prayers is an elegy, *Eleh Ezkerah* ("These I recall"), based on a Midrash by the same name. The elegy recalls the tragic episode of the Ten Martyrs (for the historical background of this episode, see below, chap. 12).

A similar elegy, named *Arze HaLavanon* ("The cedars of Lebanon"), is recited on Tisha B'Av. Its inclusion in the Tisha B'Av liturgy was intended as a reminder of the calamities that followed the destruction of the Temple. The recitation of the tragedy enhances the general atmosphere of mourning and lamentation.

Unlike Tisha B'Av, Yom Kippur is not a day of mourning. The elegy was included in the Yom Kippur liturgy as an incentive to penitence. It proclaims that theological doctrine that most heavenly decrees may be averted through penitence and prayer, though some decrees are irrevocable.

THE PRIESTLY BLESSING

The Priestly Blessing is pronounced at the conclusion of Musaf. For the background of this custom, see chapter 8.

MINCHAH

The Minchah service opens with the reading of the Torah. Psalm 145 (*Ashre*), which precedes every Minchah service throughout the year, is omitted on Yom Kippur. It is recited as the opening prayer of the Neilah service. This practice was instituted by Ashkenazim in the Middle Ages. The Sephardim, however, do not follow this custom.

Three men are called to the Torah; the third person reads the Haftarah, the Book of Jonah.

The Torah selection for the Minchah service is the eighteenth chapter of Leviticus, which lists the laws of forbidden sexual relationships. According to *Kol Bo*, the purpose of this selection is to remind people who are guilty of sexual transgressions to repent. One may justifiably question the basis of this explanation. In the period of the Talmud it was the laws regulating financial transactions which were most frequently subject to infraction (*Baba Batra* 165a). It may be said that similar conditions still prevail today. This subject would offer a much wider field for penitence.

The Torah selection for Minchah is, in effect, a continuation of the Shacharit selection (Lev., chap. 16). The seventeenth chapter is irrelevant to the theme of Yom Kippur and was therefore omitted. Chapter 16 concludes with a promise of "atonement for the children of Israel because of all their sins, once in the year" (34). Chapter 18 is an important reminder that forgiveness is not an unconditional promise. It is contingent upon a rejection of the abominations of the Egyptians and the Canaanites. Sexual perversions were prominent among their abominations (3).

Siddur Otzar HaTefilot (neilah) offers another, highly plausible, explanation. The author refers to the talmudic account of public dances by the girls of Jerusalem to pursue matrimonial alliances. The dances were held on the fifteenth of Av and on the expiration of Yom Kippur (*Taanit* 26b). It was therefore timely to publicize the laws of prohibited sex relationships.

The entire Book of Jonah is read for the Minchah Haftarah. The book conveys two messages relevant to Yom Kippur: one cannot escape the judgment of God, and the Almighty welcomes penitence, even of the most wicked of sinners (*Kol Bo*).

NEILAH

In the Mishnah the concluding service of Yom Kippur was named *neilat shearim* ("the closing of the gates"; *Taanit* 26a). The name was shortened in the Tosefta (also in *Yoma* 87b, and *Taanit* 26b) to Neilah. In the days of the Talmud, Neilah was not exclusively a Yom Kippur service. It was conducted on all public fast days (Rashi, *Neilat Shearim, Taanit* 26a).

The talmudic name Neilat Shearim is vague because there is no indication as to the nature of the gates which it refers to. This is a substantive question because it affects the time when the service is to be conducted.

According to Rav (3rd cent.), the reference is to the closing of the gates of heaven, a euphemism for the setting of the sun. According to Rabbi Yochanan (3rd cent.), the name of the service refers to the time of the closing of the gates of the Temple (Jer. *Berachot* 4). The Temple gates were closed while there was still daylight. The prevailing custom is to begin Neilah "when the sun is over the treetops" and to complete it when the stars emerge (*Tur, Orach Chaim* 623; *Taz, Orach Chaim* 623).

It is customary to keep the ark open during the entire Neilah service. It is concluded with the recitation of *Avinu Malkenu,* even when Yom Kippur falls on a Sabbath. Man's fate is decreed and sealed by the end of the day, and for that reason the word *chatmenu* ("seal us") is substituted for *katvenu* ("inscribe us").

THE CONCLUSION

After the recitation of *Avinu Malkenu,* it is customary to pronounce the

Shema once. This single proclamation reflects the unity of God. Another medieval custom is to proclaim three times *Baruch shem kevod . . .* , corresponding to the number of times that benediction is repeated in the course of the *Avodah*. The verse "The Lord is God" is then proclaimed seven times, corresponding to the seven spheres of heaven which praise God (Tosafot, *Berachot* 34a, *Amar pesuka*).

A BLAST OF THE SHOFAR

It is customary to signal the end of Yom Kippur with a blast of the shofar. The earliest source for this custom is Rav Amram Gaon (9th cent.), who mentioned four blasts: tekiah, shevarim-teruah, tekiah. Rav Hai Gaon (10th–11th cent.) did not consider the blowing of the shofar at the conclusion of Yom Kippur a mandatory practice. He suggested that it was an optional practice in commemoration of the blowing of the shofar on Yom Kippur of a Jubilee Year. Several later scholars rejected this opinion. It appears that the most likely reason for the blowing of the shofar after Neilah is to inform the congregation that Yom Kippur has come to an end.

It was the practice of the Ashkenazim of the Middle Ages to blow the shofar at the expiration of Yom Kippur only once (tekiah). That is still the prevailing custom.

NEXT YEAR IN JERUSALEM

The slogan "Next year in Jerusalem" is exclaimed twice a year, at the end of the Seder service and at the conclusion of Yom Kippur. The same rationale motivated both practices. On Passover one pleads for a complete redemption from the diasporic bondage. That can be attained only with the rebuilding of Jerusalem. On Yom Kippur we pray that God's forgiveness of Israel be wholehearted and complete. Such forgiveness will be indicated only when Jerusalem is rebuilt.

MAARIV AND HAVDALAH

Neilah is followed by Maariv and Havdalah. The benediction of *besamim* ("spices") is omitted (on weekdays) because the soul is euphoric at the end of Yom Kippur and is in no need of stimulants to cheer it up.

It is customary to bless the new moon at the end of the fast in order to begin the new season with a mitzvah. It is also customary, for the same reason, to begin the construction of a sukkah after one breaks the fast (Maharil, 14th–15th cent.).

YOM KIPPUR NIGHT DANCES

Rabbi Simon b. Gamliel said: "There were no happier days in Israel than the fifteenth of Av and Yom Kippur, when the daughters of Jerusalem used to go out dressed in white . . . and dance in the vineyards" (*Taanit* 26b). The reference to dancing is omitted from a quotation of the same passage in *Baba Batra* (121a). There surely was no dancing on the day of Yom Kippur, and Rabbi Simon must have been referring to the night after Yom Kippur. This custom is an ancient precedent for the modern youth festivities held in some congregations after the breaking of the fast.

6

Sukkot Customs

I.
A PILGRIMAGE FESTIVAL

THE PILGRIMAGE FESTIVAL in the month of Tishri has two biblical names, Chag HaAsif ("the Festival of the Ingathering"; Exod. 23:16) and Chag HaSukkot ("the Festival of Tabernacles"; Lev. 23:34). The two names identify two distinct holidays which coincide to form a single duo-faceted festival. Chag HaAsif is a harvest thanksgiving festival. Chag HaSukkot commemorates God's protection in the post-exodus period.

A blend of agricultural and historical themes is common to all the pilgrimage festivals. On Passover the historical element is dominant and the agricultural is incidental. On Shavuot it is the reverse. On Sukkot both aspects are equally prominent.

The dual character of Sukkot is clearly reflected in Leviticus (23:33–44). Chapter 23 lists all the holidays in the Jewish religious calendar. The chapter opens with an introductory sentence: "These are the appointed seasons of the Lord, holy proclamations which you shall proclaim in their appointed seasons" (23:4). Verse 34 lists the last holiday of the year, the festival of Sukkot. "On the fifteenth day of this seventh month is the Feast of Tabernacles, for seven days unto the Lord." This is followed by a provision for sacrificial rites and another provision for the termination of the holiday with an additional holy day of Atzeret. The passage ends with a repetition of the introductory sentence as a concluding summation: "These are the appointed seasons of the Lord which you shall proclaim with a holy proclamation" (23:37). Surprisingly, this verse does not end the subject of Sukkot.

Verse 39 is in effect the opening sentence of a lengthy postscript. Strangely enough, it repeats the date and duration of the festival of Sukkot, information which has already been provided in verse 34. Why the repetition?

181

The repetition and sequence of the portion becomes clear if we bear in mind the dual character of Sukkot. Verse 34 introduces the name Sukkot. The postscript was added to supply the background of the name and to point out that Sukkot does not supersede Asif but coexists with it. This is indicated by the restatement of the date. The fifteenth of Tishri, which is the date of Sukkot (Lev. 23:34), is also the date "when you have gathered in the fruits of the land" and therefore "you shall keep the feast of the Lord seven days" (23:39). In other words, there is a concurrent date for both holidays, the agricultural and the historical.

The postscript continues to list the rituals of each holiday. Asif is celebrated for seven days with lulav and etrog. Sukkot is celebrated for seven days by dwelling in booths. The link of Sukkot to the exodus is explained in verse 43: "That your generations may know that I made the children of Israel to dwell in booths, when I brought them out of the land of Egypt . . ."

While the harvest festival of Asif and the exodus festival of Sukkot have separate identities, they are linked to each other in substance as well as in time. Just as Passover must always occur in the spring season, so Sukkot must always occur in the harvest season (Deut. 16:13). God's pre-exodus message to the children of Israel held out a double promise: freedom from slavery, and a land flowing with milk and honey (Exod. 13:3, 5). The fulfillment of both promises was stressed in the Shavuot ritual of bikkurim (Deut. 26:8–9) and in the dual rituals of the sukkah and lulav on Sukkot.

The link between the exodus and the ingathering of the harvest accounts for the timing of the festival of Sukkot. According to tradition, the Jews arrived in Sukkot on the fifteenth of Nisan (Rashi, Exod. 12:37). It was in Sukkot that God provided them with shelter for protection against the sun (*Targum Yonatan b. Uziel*, Exod. 13:20). If Sukkot had commemorated this event exclusively, it should have been observed in the month of Nisan. However, it was the need for linking a commemoration of the exodus with the celebration of the ingathering of the harvest that was decisive in the establishment of the date of Sukkot. (For a full discussion of the timing of Sukkot, see Bloch, *Biblical and Historical Background of the Jewish Holy Days,* p. 40.)

Of the three pilgrimage festivals, Sukkot attracted the largest number of pilgrims. King Solomon may have timed the dedication of the Temple to coincide with Sukkot because of the anticipated large attendance (I Kings 8:2, II Chron. 7:8). In his description of the assembly of Jews in Jerusalem in the days of Ezra (5th cent. B.C.E.), Josephus wrote: "Now when they kept the feast of Sukkot, almost all the people came together to it" (*Antiq.* 9:4). The large attendance on Sukkot probably accounts for the fact that the public reading of the Torah by the king of Israel took place on Sukkot (Deut. 31:10). There was a practical reason for the larger attendance on Sukkot, despite the possibility that rainfall might hamper the pilgrims' return to their homes. Passover and Shavuot interrupted a farmer's busy season. Most agricultural chores, however, are completed by the time of the ingathering of the harvest.

THE PASSOVER PILGRIMAGE

The pilgrimage festival of Passover, like that of Sukkot, is also identified by two names. It is known as Chag HaMatzot (Exod. 23:15) and Chag HaPesach ("the festival of the paschal lamb"; Exod. 34:25). Unlike Sukkot, both Passover names derive from the historical aspects of the holiday. Chag HaPesach commemorates the events from the fourteenth of Nisan up to the exodus; Chag HaMatzot is a memorial to the events following the exodus.

The seasonal element of Passover is indicated through its calendrical link to spring (Exod. 23:15, 34:18; Deut. 16:1). It is also reflected in the ritual offering of the Omer on the second day of Passover to mark the opening of the season of new cereal crops (Lev. 23:10).

THE SHAVUOT PILGRIMAGE

The pilgrimage festival of Shavuot also has two names: Chag HaKatzir ("the festival of the harvest"; Exod. 23:15) and Chag HaShavuot ("the feast of weeks"; Exod. 34:22). The first name is distinctly agricultural. The second name falls into the same category. Shavuot commences at the end of a "seven-week period" which begins "from the day which you brought the sheaf of the waving" (Lev. 23:15). In other words, Shavuot is not linked directly to Passover but to the Omer, an agricultural ritual. In another text, the same interval of weeks is described as beginning "from the time the sickle is first put to the standing corn" (Deut. 16:9). The intervening time is a factor in the ripening of the grain.

The principal rituals of Shavuot are also agricultural in character. The first mandatory ritual was the offering of "two wave loaves," baked from the flour of new wheat (Lev. 23:17). Another ritual usually performed on Shavuot was the presentation of "the first of all the fruits of the ground" (*bikkurim*; Deut. 26:2). In my opinion, Shavuot was in fact the seventh day of the celebration of the grain harvest, which began on the second day of Passover (see Bloch, *Biblical and Historical Background of the Jewish Holy Days,* p. 180).

Yet the historical theme of the exodus, common to the other pilgrimage festivals, was not overlooked on Shavuot. This is inherent in the biblical admonition relating to the celebration of this holiday. "And you shall remember that you were a slave in Egypt" (Deut. 16:12). The ritual of bikkurim also included a declaration in which one proclaimed: "and the Lord brought us forth out of Egypt with a mighty hand . . ." (Deut. 26:8).

THE NEED FOR PILGRIMAGE

Pilgrimages to the Sanctuary were essential to the survival of Judaism. In the absence of synagogues, schools, and influential local religious leaders, it was important to maintain physical contact between the people and the ecclesiastic leadership of the Temple. Jerusalem was not only the religious and cultural capital of the nation but also its political center. The pilgrimages to Jerusalem helped keep ancient traditions alive and also enhanced national solidarity.

While the purpose of pilgrimages is self-understood, one may still wonder what was the reason for three annual pilgrimages and why they were timed with the three festivals. From a purely theological point of view, a visit to Jerusalem in time for Yom Kippur would have better served the ends of a religious national commitment.

The answer to this question must be sought in the context of the unremitting struggle of monotheism against pervasive paganism. The celebration of Passover was central to that contest. The paschal lamb was an annual reminder of an ancient decisive triumph over idolatry (Exod. 12:12). The reinactment of the Passover pageantry also served as a reaffirmation of the ancient covenant which God had concluded with the exodus generation (Lev. 26:45). The paschal lamb, like all sacrificial offerings, could not be slaughtered beyond the precincts of the Temple (Deut. 16:5). For that reason alone, it was necessary to proclaim Passover a pilgrimage festival.

The uprooting of pagan practices also motivated the selection of the other agricultural festivals for pilgrimages to Jerusalem. The seasons of the harvest and ingathering were occasions for folk celebrations in many parts of the ancient world. Most of them were characterized by excessive feasting, orgies, and pagan rites. There is an indirect allusion in the Bible to one of these repulsive customs. The proclamation of the pilgrimage festivals is followed by a commandment to bring the bikkurim to the Temple and the admonition "Thou shalt not seethe a kid in its mother's milk" (Exod. 23:19, 34:26). According to Maimonides, the admonition was motivated by the need to uproot the revolting pagan custom of serving kids boiled in their mother's milk at harvest feasts.

It was important to raise the moral tone of the agricultural folk festivals and to endow them with an uplifting religious and social significance. This was achieved by shifting the locale of the celebration to Jerusalem, where the spontaneous exuberance was kept within the bounds of religious propriety. The release of national joy was carefully channeled to support the maintenance of the Temple and to provide relief to the widow and orphan.

The utilization of the pilgrimage as an important weapon against paganism is reflected in the sequence of the twenty-third chapter of Exodus. The portion which proclaims the three pilgrimage festivals is concluded with the warning: "Thou shalt make no covenant with them [the native heathens], nor with their idols" (32).

The initial establishment of the pilgrimage festivals was based only on a socio-ethical motif. The twenty-third chapter of Exodus is highly instructive in this regard. The chapter begins with a warning against slander, the bearing of false testimony, the perversion of justice, and the oppression of strangers. This is followed by a reminder that dumb animals are entitled to our compassion. The produce of the sabbatical year must be turned over to the poor, and whatever is left should be given to the beasts. The Sabbath is a day of rest for the master, the slaves, and the beast of burden. These social laws are followed by an injunction mandating the pilgrimages to Jerusalem. Obviously, these too were to serve the humane purposes of the chapter's social laws by making it possible for the needy to celebrate the festivals in Jerusalem and by permitting them to share in the wealth of the nation.

The socio-ethical motif of the agricultural pilgrimage festivals is restated in Deuteronomy. "And thou shalt keep the Feast of Weeks unto the Lord . . . and thou shalt rejoice before the Lord, thy God, thou . . . thy man servant and the Levite, and the stranger, and the fatherless and the widow . . ." (16:10–11). "Thou shalt keep the Feast of Sukkot . . . and thou shalt rejoice . . . and thy man servant . . . and the Levite, and the stranger, and the fatherless and the widow . . ." (16:13–14).

The pilgrimage festivals are mentioned for the first time in the twenty-third chapter of Exodus and are restated in the thirty-fourth chapter. There was a change, however, in the indicated motif. The new motif appears to be theological rather than socio-ethical. "Behold I make a covenant, before all thy people I will do marvels. . . . Take heed lest thou make a covenant with the inhabitants of the land whither thou goest . . . but you shall break down their altars . . . for thou shalt bow down to no other god . . . Thou shalt make thee no molten god. The Feast of Matzot shalt thou keep . . . and thou shalt observe the Feast of Weeks . . . and the Feast of Ingathering . . ." (Exod. 10–22). The sequence of this passage plainly suggests that the purpose of the pilgrimage festivals is to reinforce the faith and reaffirm the covenant with God.

The reason for the added motif is indicated in the very first verse of the thirty-fourth chapter: "And God said unto Moses: 'Hew thee two tablets of stone, like unto the first' . . ." The transgression of the golden calf had intervened between the time of the original institution of the pilgrimage festivals in chapter 23 and the restatement in chapter 34. The tragic incident of a relapse into idolatry reflected an urgent need to revitalize the faith. An important step in that direction was the conversion of the Sabbath and festivals into educational tools to serve religious ends. As with the festivals, the Sabbath, too, was assigned a theological goal in addition to its original socio-ethical motivation (see Bloch, *Biblical and Historical Background of the Jewish Holy Days*, p. 4).

II.
SUKKOT CUSTOMS

INTRODUCTION

The major rituals of Sukkot—the dwelling in a sukkah and the waving of a lulav—are clearly spelled out in the Bible (Lev. 23:40, 42). To this day they are still the major features of the holiday. Unlike Passover and Shavuot, the traditional manner of observing Sukkot was not substantially affected by the destruction of the Temple, as far as the two rituals are concerned.

The only immediate change, resulting from the destruction of the Temple, was introduced by an ordinance of Rabbi Yochanan b. Zakkai (1st cent.), which provided for the observance of the ritual of the lulav throughout the seven days of the holiday (*Sukkah* 41a). Previously, this practice prevailed only in the Temple; everywhere else it was limited to the first day only. Another change was the suspension of the lulav ritual on the Sabbath. There was no such suspension in the Temple if the first day of Sukkot occurred on a Sabbath (*Sukkah* 41b).

Despite the fact that the two ancient traditions were preserved intact, rabbinical interpretations had a profound impact upon their form and motivation. The conciseness of the biblical texts left much room for speculation and debate. What are the minimal and maximal dimensions of a sukkah? What constitutes a qualified covering (*sechach*)? What functions must one perform in a sukkah which would constitute compliance with the command to "dwell" in it? What is the definition of "taking" a lulav? These and a host of other questions claimed the attention of the talmudic sages. It is reasonable to assume that diversified customs prevailed until the rules were finally promulgated in the rabbinical academies from the first to the fourth century.

PRAYERS FOR WATER

The first substantive change in the character of Sukkot was a new rabbinical perception of the holiday as a period of judgment when the availability of water in the coming year is decided (*Rosh HaShanah* 16a). This perception predated the destruction of the Temple by many centuries and was a point of contention between the rabbis and the Sadducees.

The coincidence of Sukkot with the beginning of the rainy season was the reason for the prominence given in the course of the Festival of the Ingathering to rituals invoking God to provide an ample supply of water. This was in keeping with the biblical promise: "And I will provide rain for your land in its proper time . . . and you will gather your corn and grapes . . ." (Deut. 11:14). The only hint in the biblical text of a link between Sukkot and the promise of water is the inclusion of willow branches among the four species which make up the lulav set. These branches (*aravot*) are termed in the Bible "willows of the brook" (Lev. 23:40). The promise of rain is implicit in the reference to brooks, for which it is the principle source of water. We will discuss this point at great length in conjunction with an analysis of the four species of the lulav ritual.

A popular ritual, the pouring of water on the alter (*nisuch hamayim*) on Sukkot mornings, when the offering of the Tamid was sacrificed, was attributed to an oral tradition handed down by Moses (*Taanit* 3a). The libation of the altar was in fact a symbolic prayer for rain. The

Talmud explained this practice as follows: "The Almighty said: 'Pour the water [on the altar] on the holiday so that the rains of the year may be blessed' " (*Rosh HaShanah* 16a).

The Sadducees denied the validity of the oral tradition mandating a libation of the altar. When the rabbis triumphed over the Sadducees in the first century B.C.E., they publicized their victory by giving the ritual of libation great prominence. The rejoicing lasted through the night. There were torch lights, parades, bands of music, dancing, and singing. The nightly festivities were given the name of Simchat Bet HaShoavah ("the rejoicing of the drawing of the water"; *Sukkah* 51a). The daily Sukkot rituals of placing aravot on the altar and of the defoliation of the aravot on Hoshana Rabba (*Sukkot* 45a) were also symbolic prayers for water.

The daily prayer for rain, *mashiv haruach umorid hageshem* ("He makes the wind blow and brings down the rain"), is recited in the winter season, beginning with Shemini Atzeret. This prayer is attributed to the Men of the Great Assembly (5th cent. B.C.E.). Tradition thus established the antiquity of prayers for rain. However, many centuries were to elapse before the practice became fixed. As late as the second century C.E., Rabbis Eliezer and Joshua still debated whether the prayer is begun on the first or the last day of Sukkot (*Taanit* 2a).

The crucial need for water influenced some rabbinical interpretation of the lulav ritual. "Said Rabbi Eliezer [2nd cent.]: 'Seeing that these four species [lulav, etrog, hadas, aravah] are intended only for intercession for water, therefore as these cannot [grow] without water, so the world cannot exist without water' " (*Taanit* 2b).

Ben Azai (2nd cent.) associated the etrog with water. Thus was his interpretation of the biblical phrase *peri etz hadar* ("the fruit of a beautiful tree"). "Do not read *hadar* but *idur*. The Greek word for 'water' is *idur*. Which is the fruit which grows near water? It is the etrog" (*Sukkah* 35a). He was obviously referring to the sea or ocean climate essential to the cultivation of the citrus fruit. *Midrash Rabbah* attributes the previous statement to Akilas the Proselyte (*Emor* 30).

THE RABBINICAL PERCEPTION OF THE SUKKAH

Most rabbinical laws which define the qualification of the sukkah date from the second century. The amoraim of the third and forth centuries, who researched the sources upon which the tannaim had based their laws, resorted to technical rules of derivation, such as analogies, spellings, and so forth, the normal procedure in the development of rabbinical law. Few of the regulatory laws relating to the sukkah are reflected in the literal interpretation of the text. However, in addition to the technical rules, the amoraim enunciated some broad principles which take into account the historical origin of the sukkah and its objectives. The following are some of these principles.

A PROVIDER OF SHADE

The sukkah is a memorial to the shelter which God provided in the desert to protect the Jews from the heat of the sun. Only a people which had experienced the broiling desert sun and the debilitation of a tropical climate can appreciate the life-saving qualities of shade. It is not surprising that in biblical phraseology "shadow" or "shade" is synonymous with protection. Lot spoke of his guests who came "under the shadow of my roof" (Gen. 19:8). Joshua and Caleb described the panicky inhabitants of Canaan as people whose "shadow has been removed from them" (Num. 14:9). The Psalm of David in the wilderness of Judea expresses his confidence and gratitude because "in the shadow of thy wings I rejoice" (Ps. 63:8).

The covering of the sukkah, which provides the shade is the most important part of the sukkah. Hence it is regulated by a greater number of qualifying restrictions than the walls (*Sukkah* 2a). The shade provided by the covering must exceed the sunshine. The occupant of a sukkah must have the covering within the normal range of his vision so that he will be constantly conscious of the fact that he is dwelling in a sukkah. If the covering is higher than twenty yards (*amot*) above the ground, an occupant loses sight of it. Furthermore, the shade comes from the walls rather than the covering and the sukkah is therefore disqualified.

THE SUKKAH AS A HOME

The sukkah must become one's "home" for the duration of the holiday. All functions normally performed in a home, such as eating and sleeping, must take place in the sukkah. To give a sukkah the appearance and atmosphere of a home, one should move fine furnishings and dishes into it. Beautifying the sukkah with fruits is a custom which dates back to talmudic times.

A TEMPORARY ABODE

The sukkah, a memorial to the movable sukkot in the desert, must not take on the appearance of a permanent home. A solid ceiling disqualifies a sukkah. The covering is designed to screen out the sun but it must not block the visibility of the stars. Despite the temporary nature of the sukkah, it must be sturdy enough to withstand ordinary winds and to last at least for seven days.

ENJOYING THE SUKKAH

If one suffers physical or mental discomfort in a sukkah, he is exempt from the obligation of dwelling in it (*Sukkah* 25b). The sukkah, a memorial to God's protection, is designed to enhance the joy of the festival. If the element of joy is missing, the mitzvah of dwelling in a sukkah is suspended. The exemption is extended to sick people and also to a bridegroom in the first week of his marriage. Rain is similarly a cause for exemption.

The broad formula of exemptions was invoked by the Jews who settled in European countries, where weather conditions were too inclement to permit sleeping in the sukkah (Rema, *Orach Chaim, Hilchot Sukkah* 639:2). Talmudic law had been very stringent with regard to the obligation to sleep in a sukkah.

The ritual of the sukkah created practical problems for people whose tasks made it impossible for them to comply with the biblical obligations. This included watchmen, traveling salesmen, and public emissaries. For practical reasons, the rabbis were very lenient in their broad application of the law of exemption to all these men.

The congregational public sukkah is a medieval innovation which was introduced for the benefit of travelers. However, worshippers soon adopted the custom of making Kiddush in the public sukkah before repairing to their own sukkah for the festival meal. The new custom met with some opposition from contemporary rabbis. The opposition had little success in face of the persistence of this practice.

POPULARITY OF THE SUKKAH

Dwelling in a sukkah had always been a popular ritual. To avoid obstructing narrow streets, ancient Jews used to build their sukkot on the flat roofs of their homes (Neh. 9:16; *Sukkah* 26b). This provided good ventilation and exposure to cooling breezes. The combination of gourmet menus, lavish decorations, and the fragrance of woods and streams created a sense of exhilaration, intimately bound up with the sukkah. There was a similar custom to chant the *Hallel* on Passover night on the roofs of the homes (*Pesachim* 86a).

The popularity of the sukkah is reflected in the talmudic account of the pilgrimage of Queen Helena of Adiabene. Helena had embraced Judaism in 30 c.e. and thereafter visited Jerusalem on several occasions to bring gifts to the Temple and to provide food for the needy in years of drought. On one of her visits she received important guests in a magnificent sukkah constructed for her for the festival of Sukkot. As a woman, she was exempt from the obligation of dwelling in a sukkah. Nevertheless, she insisted on having her own royal sukkah as an obvious gesture of conformity with a highly popular and widespread custom (*Sukkah* 2b).

The ritual of the lulav and etrog was similarly popular and widely observed. Like tefillin, which many pious Jews wore all day, the lulav was a common sight in the hands of Jerusalemites as they walked about throughout the day performing their daily tasks, including visiting the sick and the bereaved (*Sukkah* 41b).

THE FOUR SPECIES

The identity of the four species was transmitted by oral tradition, dating back to the earliest period of Jewish history. The species are indigenous to the Holy Land and were readily obtainable for the performance of the ritual.

The biblical description of the species is vague, and the talmudic sages had to reconcile the oral tradition with the biblical terminology. The four species are described in the text as follows: "And you shall take on the first day the fruit of the tree of *hadar* ['pleasant'], branches of palm trees [*kapot temarim*], boughs of thick trees [*anaf etz avot*], and willows of the brook [*arve nachal*]" (Lev. 23:40).

One rabbi interpreted the biblical definition of the etrog in the following manner. "*Peri etz hadar* means that the fruit [*peri*] and the tree [*etz*] on which it grows are equally pleasant [*hadar*]. What fruit tastes like the tree? It is the etrog" (*Sukkah* 35a). Nachmanides, in his commentary on this verse, stated that the talmudic interpretation was merely supportive of an established tradition which is implied in the text. He pointed out that the name *etrog* is a literal Aramaic translation of the Hebrew *hadar*, both of which mean "pleasant." However, in view of the fact that there are many pleasant species of fruits, one had to rely on tradition or rabbinical interpretation to determine the specific fruit indicated in the text.

The phrase "boughs of thick trees" refers, according to the Talmud, to the myrtle (*hadas*), whose leaves cover the stem (*Sukkah* 32b). There is an apparent contradiction to this interpretation in Nehemiah (8:15), where myrtle branches (*ale hadas*) are listed separately from branches of thick trees (*ale etz avot*). The two are obviously not identical. The Talmud resolves this inconsistency with the explanation that there are several breeds of myrtles. One type, identified as "wild myrtles," was commonly used for covering a sukkah but may not be used as one of the four species of the lulav ritual.

THE RATIONALE OF THE FOUR SPECIES

A casual reading of the biblical text gives the unmistakable impression that the motif of the lulav ritual is a thanksgiving for the bounteous harvest. The four species are selected samples of the harvest, which one must hold in his hand and rejoice before the Lord (Lev. 23:40). The "rejoicing" was in due time affected by a later rabbinical perception of the festival of Sukkot as a period of judgment concerning water, thus adding an element of solemnity to the ritual of the lulav. This is reflected in the opinion of Rabbi Eliezer that the purpose of the four species is to intercede for water (*Taannit* 2b).

The ancient ritual of the waving (*naanuim*) of the four species, sideways, forward and backward, and up and down, was an outgrowth of the new rabbinical perception of the rationale of the lulav. Rabbi Jose b. Rabbi Chanina (3rd cent.) explained that the waving is demonstrative of one's prayer to God to keep out damaging winds from any direction and harmful deposits of dew (*Sukkot* 37b).

The ritual of waving was not exclusive to the lulav. There is a precedent in the Bible in the offering of the Omer on Passover and the two loaves of wheat on Shavuot (Lev. 23:11, 17). In both instances the waving is inherent in the terms *vehenif* and *tenufah* ("lift up"), which are traditionally interpreted to mean "and he shall wave" and a "waving." Rabbi Jose's statement that the waving is a prayer for protection against harmful winds was originally made in reference to the Omer and the two loaves of bread (*Menachot* 62a). It was subsequently applied to the waving of the lulav.

The term *tenufah* does not appear in the text of the lulav ritual. Instead, the text employs the term *ulekachtem* ("and you shall take"). It is obvious that the requirement to wave the lulav is not based on a textual implication but on an analogy of this agricultural rite with the other two agricultural rites of Omer and *lechem tenufah*. Thus the three agricultural seasons—Passover, Shavuot, and Sukkot—have similar prayers for protection against inclement weather elements which might be detrimental to farming. The waving of the Omer and the two breads was undoubtedly practiced in the First Temple. The introduction of waving on Sukkot most likely dates from a later period. According to the Talmud, the most important time for waving the lulav is when *Hallel* is chanted (*Sukkah* 37b). The public chanting of *Hallel* was first introduced early in the period of the Second Temple (5th cent. B.C.E.). It appears likely that the waving of the lulav dates from the same time.

The view that the ceremony of the lulav is intended as a prayer for proper climatic conditions seems to be inconsistent with the biblical intimation that it is an expression of joy. A statement in the Jerusalem Talmud apparently takes note of this contradiction. According to the statement, the joy mentioned in the Bible derives from the *shelamim* ("whole-offerings"; Lev. 24:37) which provided large quantities of meat, a source of physical joy. However, a dissenting opinion associated the joy with the waving of the lulav, thus assuming it to be a ritual of thanksgiving (Jer. *Sukkah* 3:11). According to Rashi, the latter view is the accepted opinion of the Babylonian Talmud (*Sukkah* 43b, Rashi, *Lulav havi*).

HOMILETICAL EXPLANATIONS FOR THE CHOICE OF SPECIES

The midrashic literature, for homiletical purposes, sought to stress the moral implications of the lulav ritual by attributing to it various rationales of social significance. The four species, it was alleged, reflect four categories of Jews. Scholars who perform good deeds are symbolized by the etrog, which has a good taste and an equally good aroma. Scholars without good deeds to their credit may be compared to the lulav, which is tasty but devoid of an aroma. Those who perform good deeds but lack scholarship are like the myrtle, which has an aroma but is tasteless. Men who are bare of scholarship and good deeds are like the willow, which has neither taste nor aroma. By joining all the categories together, one class atones for the other and helps to raise the prestige of all the components which comprise the unit (*Vayikra Rabbah* 30).

Another homiletist suggested that the four species represent four historical figures. The etrog is Abraham, the lulav is Isaac, the myrtle is

Jacob, and the willow is Joseph (ibid.). Thus in celebrating the bounty of the land one renews his ties to the history of the Jewish people, going back to the days of his heroic forefathers, whose remains are forever enshrined in the land which God gave them.

Still another homiletist looked at the shape of the species. The etrog is shaped like a heart to atone for the immoral thoughts of the heart. The leaf of the myrtle is shaped like an eye to atone for the lustful winking of the eye. The leaf of the willow is shaped like the lips to atone for sinful words. The lulav has one spine. It symbolizes Israel, united as one, in the service of the heavenly father (*Tanchuma, Emor*).

HISTORICAL RATIONALE OF THE SPECIES

No serious effort outside the purview of a homiletical framework was ever made to explain the choice of the four species. Considering the fact that the lulav and its companions symbolize the abundance of the ingathered harvest, it may appear as a surprise that the four species are hardly likely to be found in the harvest which the average farmer removes from the fields.

We have previously discussed the intimate link between the themes of the exodus and the abundance of the harvest. In the initial instruction to Moses, God revealed the two stages of the delivery of the Hebrews. "And I come down to deliver them out of the hand of the Egyptians, and to bring them up out of that land unto a good land, and a large one, unto a land flowing with milk and honey" (Exod. 3:8). Freedom from bondage and the acquisition of a fruitful land were the two components of the promise. The first part is marked by Passover and the second by Sukkot.

A common biblical code name for a fruitful land is "a land flowing with milk and honey." The Hebrew word for "honey," *devash,* has two definitions, the honey of bees and the sap or juice of dates. The term "flowing," which connotes abundance, can only be used in conjunction with fluids, such as milk, and not solids. We must therefore assume that the *devash* in this instance is date honey. The broad implication of the phrase "flowing with milk and honey" is a land rich in meat (cattle), dairy, produce of the soil, and fruit.

The most detailed description of the quality and fruitfulness of the Promised Land is found in Deuteronomy. "For the Lord, thy God, brings you into a good land, a land of brooks of water, and fountains and depths spring forth in valleys and hills. A land of wheat and barley, and vines and fig trees and pomegranates, a land of olive trees and honey" (8:7–8).

The highlights of this description are: brooks and springs of water in the valleys and in the hills, grain, vines, and fruit. The honey in this text is the honey of dates (*Sukkah* 6a). All the species mentioned in this verse were acceptable on Shavuot in the ritual of Bikkurim, which were offered in thanksgiving to God for bringing his people into "a land flowing with milk and honey" (Deut. 26:9).

The next occasion for thanksgiving, after the ritual of Bikkurim, is the Festival of Ingathering. The lulav ritual is a thanksgiving rite which reflects God's fulfillment of his promise of a "good land." The "willow of the brook" is a testimony to the country's brooks, which sustain the growth of the willows. The myrtle, which normally grows in the hills (Neh. 8:15), is a testimony to the "fountains . . . in valleys and hills." The lulav, a branch of the date palm tree, is a testimony to the "land of . . . honey."

The etrog is not included among the seven deuteronomic species which characterize the land (8:7–8). It may not be included in the basket of bikkurim. It is also kept apart from the other three species which make up the lulav set. As an exotic fruit, it is not produced in great quantities. It is not an "abundant" fruit and therefore not typical of the wealth of the nation's agricultural production.

Several factors might have motivated its selection for the Sukkot ritual. The name of the fruit is *hadar*, which means "pleasant" or "beautiful." Beauty is an important element in the enhancement of the ceremony. It is also possible that it was chosen for practical reasons. It is a hardy fruit which does not rot. There was a need for a fruit which could be preserved for at least seven days. There was also a need for a fruit which could be shipped to distant communities where it would serve as a reminder of the bounty of the Promised Land.

THE EVE OF SUKKOT

One must honor a holiday in the same manner as one honors the Sabbath. This includes attention to personal cleanliness, appearance, and attire. Similarly, one must abstain from eating a substantial meal late in the afternoon so that the festival meal may be eaten with relish.

A traditional holiday meal is even more lavish than a Sabbath meal. Sumptuous Sabbath meals are not implicit in the biblical Sabbath laws, except for the comprehensive rabbinical interpretation of the term *oneg*

(Isa. 58:13). However, a lavish holiday meal is part of the "rejoicing" mandated in the Bible (Lev. 23:40). Only with respect to the third meal (*shalosh seudot*) are the holidays less demanding than the Sabbath. The abundance of holiday food obviates the need for an officially instituted third meal.

THE CONSTRUCTION OF A SUKKAH

It is customary to begin the construction of a sukkah after the breaking of the Yom Kippur fast. One may also use a permanent sukkah and merely place a new covering on it.

The Babylonian Talmud mentioned a prevailing custom of reciting the benediction of *Shehecheyanu* upon the completion of the construction of a sukkah (*Sukkah* 46a). In addition to this benediction, it was customary in Palestine to recite a special benediction: "Blessed . . . who commanded us to make a sukkah." Both benedictions were discontinued by the tenth century. The eating of a meal in a sukkah came to be perceived as the principal fulfillment of the mitzvah of "dwelling" in a sukkah. All benedictions were therefore timed to precede the meal.

It is customary to light the holiday candles in the sukkah and to remove them into the home after they are lit. There are two candle-lighting benedictions, *l'hadlik ner shel yom tov* and *Shehecheyanu*.

SEVEN USHPIZIN

The belief that seven heavenly guests (*ushpizin*) visit the sukkah at mealtime was mentioned for the first time in the Zohar. "When Jews leave their homes to enter a sukkah, in accordance with the command of the Almighty, they are worthy of receiving the holy presence. The seven faithful shepherds come down from paradise and enter the sukkah as guests of the host." Abraham, Isaac, Jacob, Joseph, Moses, Aaron, and David are the honored guests. The leadership of the heavenly delegation changes from day to day. Abraham heads the group on the first day. Isaac is the leader on the second day, and so on successively until it is David's turn on the seventh day.

The tradition of ushpizin made little headway until the sixteenth century, when it was popularized by the kabbalists, who composed a formal declaration of welcome to be recited by the host in honor of the guests. The declaration names the visitors in the order of their appearance. Some Sephardim embellished the custom by placing a special chair in the sukkah, which they call the "chair of the ushpizin." They also send provisions to the poor for the holiday with a note which states that "This is the share of the ushpizin."

The Zohar's allegation of ushpizin was most likely inspired by the midrashic interpretation of the four species as symbolic of Abraham, Isaac, Jacob, and Joseph (*Lev. Rabbah* 30).

KIDDUSH

Kiddush on Sukkot comprises four benedictions: wine, sanctification, *leshev basukkah,* and *Shehecheyanu.* The latter is a prayer of thanksgiving which one expresses upon reaching an anniversary. In the case of Sukkot, one is thankful for two anniversaries: the anniversary of the holiday, and the anniversary of the sukkah. The *Shehecheyanu* covers both anniversaries and is therefore recited last to indicate that it refers to the preceding benedictions over the holiday and the sukkah. On the second night, however, the sukkah is no longer a new ritual and the *Shehecheyanu* refers only to the holiday. It therefore precedes the benediction of *leshev basukkah.*

The benediction of *leshev basukkah* is recited daily prior to each meal eaten in the sukkah (except for Shemini Atzeret). It is our custom to recite *leshev basukkah* after the benediction of *Hamotzi.* The reverse was true in some medieval Jewish communities.

THE LULAV SET

The lulav, hadas, and aravah are placed together in a case made of palm strips or tied together by two rings made of palm strips. Three myrtles are placed on the right of the spine of the lulav and two willows on the left. If any of the species are missing, the entire set is disqualified. Rings are also placed on the center and upper part of the lulav to keep its branches from breaking off during the waving ritual. The case which holds the set, as well as the ring, must be made of palm strips exclusively because no foreign material may intervene between the lulav and the species which adjoin it.

It is customary to fulfill the mitzvah of lulav in the sukkah at the earliest opportunity in the morning. One takes the lulav set in the right hand and the etrog in the left. They must be held in an upright position, in the manner in which they grow. The etrog must be held with its apex (*pitum*) at the top.

To make sure that the benediction precedes the performance of the mitzvah, it is customary to hold the etrog upside down pending the recitation of the benedictions. Upon the completion of the benedictions, the etrog is reversed to its proper position and the mitzvah is then fulfilled. This practice dates back to the thirteenth century.

Two benedictions are incidental to the mitzvah of lulav, *al netilat lulav* and *Shehecheyanu*. In the period of the Talmud, the benediction of *Shehecheyanu* was recited at the time of the "making" of the lulav, i.e., when the lulav was prepared and the other species joined with it in readiness for Sukkot. Eventually, it became the practice to buy ready-made sets and the recitation of *Shehecheyanu* was deferred to the time of the performance of the mitzvah. The change was welcomed by the majority of Jews in the diaspora who performed the mitzvah with a congregational lulav.

In the period of the Talmud, the *Shehecheyanu* was recited only once, when the lulav was "made" prior to the holiday. The ultimate deferment of the benediction to the morning of Sukkot raised the question whether it should be repeated on the second day. The geonim expressed conflicting opinions. The issue was resolved in the twelfth century, when the custom of reciting the benediction on both days was universally adopted.

As we mentioned before, the four species are mutually interdependent. The absence of one of the species disqualifies the entire set. Of the four, it was the etrog that was occasionally hard to obtain in the European diaspora. Wars frequently disrupted communications with the countries which produce citrus fruits. Communities are known to have spent enormous sums to procure at least one etrog for the entire congregation.

Even in Palestine, where the species are indigenous, war conditions made the procurement of some of the species difficult at times. Thus Jacob Berav recounts an incident which occurred in 1742, when the Jewish community of Tiberias was under siege by the forces of Suleiman Pasha. The myrtle was not available. The distress of the community was finally relieved on Hoshana Rabba, the last day for performing the mitzvah of lulav. An unexpected truce permitted the delivery of myrtles (Yaari, *Zichronot Eretz Yisrael*, vol. 1, p. 74).

To properly fulfill the mitzvah of lulav, one must own the set. However, one may accept it as a temporary gift, with the provision that it be returned after the performance of the ritual. Medieval communities introduced the custom of taxing each Jew for the purchase of the communal lulav. It was understood that every man would temporarily yield his share in the lulav so that the person performing the mitzvah would at that time own the complete set.

THE WAVING OF THE LULAV

The principal time for the waving of the lulav is during the chanting of the *Hallel* (*Sukkah* 37b). The association of the ritual of the lulav with *Hallel* (or psalms) is also mentioned in II Maccabees (ca. 1st cent. B.C.E.). The length of Chanukah was explained by the author with an analogy to Sukkot. The analogy was justified by the fact that the original Chanukah incorporated some Sukkot rituals which had not been observed at the proper time due to the war with Antiochus. The author described Judah's state of mind when he purified the Temple and restored the ancient rites. He could not but recall "that not long before, they had spent the feast of Tabernacles as they wandered in the mountains like beasts" (chap. 10). The author conveys the impression that Judah decided to celebrate a delayed Sukkot at the same time that he was establishing the festival of Chanukah. "Therefore they carried branches and fair boughs and palms also [the three species which were available] and sang psalms" (ibid.). The carrying of the lulav was thus associated with the singing of psalms.

The Talmud mentions the directions in which the lulav is to be waved. It does not specify, however, the order of the rotation of the waving or the number of times that the lulav is to be waved in each direction. As a result, various practices have emerged. There was an early consensus that the lulav should be waved three times in each direction. No universal custom regarding the order of rotation has ever developed. The most widespread practice is to begin by waving the lulav eastward and then continue clockwise in the other directions (south, west, north) and conclude by waving it up and down.

The waving is done in the verses of *hodu* and *ana* of *Hallel*. The verse of *hodu* has six words, excluding the name of God. As each word is slowly enunciated, the lulav is waved in one direction. The verse of *ana* has six syllables, excluding the name of God. Here again, as each syllable is enunciated, the lulav is waved in one direction. The ritual is repeated a third time in the verse of *hodu*, which appears once more in the concluding paragraph of *Hallel*.

HAKAFOT

The ritual of hakafot (a procession circling the bimah) is performed after the conclusion of the Musaf service. An individual stands on the bimah with a Torah in his arms. Every individual who owns a lulav joins a procession which marches once around the bimah. The entire congregation joins in the recitation of the prayer of *Hoshana* ("help us, please"). On the Sabbath of Chol HaMoed (intermediary days), the ark is opened and a prayer is recited. There is no hakafah because there is no lulav ritual on the Sabbath.

The custom of hakafot is based on an ancient Temple practice of circling the altar with a lulav in hand (*Sukkah* 45a). In addition to this procession, it was also customary to place a willow at the altar (ibid.). This ceremony, which was attributed to an oral tradition from Moses (Jer. *Sukkah* 4:1), was given great prominence. Three blasts of a shofar signaled the conclusion of the ritual. We will explore the significance of this custom in connection with the discussion of the origin of Hoshana Rabba.

SABBATH CHOL HAMOED

It is customary to read the Book of Kohelet (Ecclesiastes) prior to the reading of the Sabbath portion of the Torah. This custom was instituted by medieval Ashkenazim.

SIMCHAT BET HASHOAVAH

The elaborate and festive ceremony of *nisuch hamayim* ("the pouring of water" over the altar) was carried out with much pomp and publicity. There were torch parades, public dancing, and music as the water drawn from the spring of Shiloach was carried into the Temple and poured over the altar (*Sukkah* 51a).

This ceremony was conducted daily, beginning with the second night of Sukkot. The revelry, in which many of the famous sages participated, continued through the night and culminated with the pouring of the water on the altar when the Korban Tamid of the morning was sacrificed.

The elaborate ceremonialism was introduced in the first century B.C.E. to demonstrate the triumph of rabbinic Judaism over the Sadducees, who had opposed the ritual of *nisuch hamayim*. The significance of the rite, as an intercession for water on a festival when "judgment is passed in respect of water" (*Rosh HaShanah* 16a), lent the occasion great prominence.

The formalized festivities of Simchat Bet HaShoavah came to an end with the destruction of the Temple. However, the event has been commemorated by pious Jews with extraordinary celebrations held on one of the Chol HaMoed nights. Jacob Berav (19th cent.) records in his memoirs the staging of tumulteous parades in the streets of Tiberias, to the accompaniment of instrumental music.

HOSHANA RABBA

The last day of Chol HaMoed Sukkot acquired the name of Hoshana Rabba ("many Hoshanot") due to the multiple prayers of *hoshana* recited at the conclusion of the morning service. The name appears for the first time in *Midrash Shochar Tov* and was popularized in the geonic period. The mishnah which describes the ritual of the last day of Chol HaMoed does not designate it by a special name and merely refers to it as "on that day" (*Sukkah* 45a). The Jerusalem Talmud calls the day Aravah, a reflection of the prominent part played by the aravot in the morning ritual of Hoshana Rabba (Jer. *Rosh HaShanah* 4:8). Another name, dating at the latest from the first century, was "the day of the beating" (of aravot). This name reflected the ritual of striking the aravot on the ground and the defoliation which culminated the morning service (*Sukkah* 45a).

THE BEATING OF ARAVOT

The quaint Hoshana Rabba custom of beating a bundle of aravot on the ground has its source in a statement of Rabbi Yochanan b. Beroka (1st–2nd cent.): "They [the worshippers in the Temple] used to bring branches of palm trees and beat them on the ground, at the side of the altar. That day was called '[the day of] the beating of the branches' " (*Sukkah* 45a).

Rav Huna (3rd cent.) wondered why palm branches were used in this ceremony. "What was the reason of Rabbi Yochanan b. Beroka?" (*Sukkah* 45b). The wording of his question calls for an explanation. Rabbi Yochanan merely reported a quaint custom which had been in vogue in the Temple. Historians need not account for the reasons of ancient customs. If Rav Huna wished to explore the basis of the practice, he should have asked "What was the reason for the Temple custom?" It is obvious that Rav Huna assumed that Rabbi Yochanan's source of information did not supply the name of the branches which had been used in the ceremony and it was Rabbi Yochanan who filled in the gap by stating that they were palm branches. He therefore wondered what was the basis of Rabbi Yochanan's assumption.

Rav Huna concluded that Rabbi Yochanan based his opinion on the word *kapot* ("branches;" Lev. 23:40). This indicated that at least two palm branches were used on Sukkot, one for the lulav ritual and one for the beating on Hoshana Rabba. The rabbis disagreed with Rabbi Yochanan and contended that only one palm branch was used on Sukkot. However, they never denied the report of branch-beating on Hoshana Rabba, though they never mentioned the custom. We must therefore assume that according to the rabbanan, the branches which were used in the beating ceremony on Hoshana Rabba were aravot.

The significance of the beating of aravot, which the Bible called "willows of the brook" (Lev. 23:40), may be best understood if it is viewed in the context of a ritual intercession for water. As we have pointed out, the willow was included in the lulav set in thanksgiving for the waters of the brook. The additional willows, which were placed at the side of the altar every Sukkot morning, symbolized an ongoing prayer for a plentiful supply of water. The entire week of Sukkot was considered a period of judgment with regard to water. Hoshana Rabba, as the last day of the period, naturally assumed special importance. The altar was circled seven times, and a corresponding number of prayers were recited.

The final ritual was the beating of the aravot. The aravah, which uses up much water to sustain its life and growth, became a symbol of the abundance of water. However, it is essentially a useless plant which bears no fruit, a squanderer of water resources. The destruction of the aravot was a symbolic gesture of water preservation as one was about to pray for rain.

The practice of hakafot with the lulav and the custom of beating the aravot were not resumed immediately after the destruction of the Temple. The mishnah which recorded those Temple customs did not refer to a similar contemporary practice (*Sukkah* 45a). Rav Huna, a third-century amora, similarly did not draw attention to any custom of his period.

According to tradition, the ritual of aravot in the Sanctuary was ordained by Moses. The prophets were said to have extended it to the diaspora. However, hakafot were not included in the diasporic ritual. This is understandable in view of the intimate association between the hakafot and the altar. The original diasporic custom was apparently confined to the waving of the aravot, as was the case with the lulav.

After the destruction of the Temple, Rabban Yochanan b. Zakkai (1st cent.) ordained that the lulav ritual continue for seven days, as it had been practiced in the Temple. However, he did not mention the resumption of hakafot or the beating of aravot in the absence of the altar.

The altar was a visible symbol of God's forgiveness. In time, as prayers replaced the sacrifices, the Torah took on the symbolic significance of atonement. The table, where Jews dined and which was sanctified with words of Torah, assumed the image of an altar (*Pirke Avot* 3:4). The image of a table-altar was extended to the table, or lectern, upon which the Torah was placed in the synagogue. This development made possible the resumption of hakafot and the beating of the aravot in the geonic period.

A WAKEFUL NIGHT

Pious Jews stay awake on the night of Hoshana Rabba to read the Pentateuch and recite prayers. This practice, which originated in the Middle Ages, was based on an increasing perception of Hoshana Rabba as a day of judgment. A similar custom prevails on the night of Yom Kippur.

A FATEFUL OMEN

Some medieval Jews made it a custom to stand in the moonlight on Hoshana Rabba night to watch one's shadow. If the shadow of the head was invisible, it was considered an omen of an impending tragedy to a male relative. If the shadow of the left hand was invisible, a female relative would meet with tragedy.

Superstitions have a life of their own, and their credibility is seldom affected by the ridicule of sophisticated people. Yet it seems that even the contemporary sages were reluctant to suppress this superstition. The great Nachmanides, who did not hesitate to denounce the custom of Kapparot as a superstition (*Orchot Chaim, Hilchot Erev Yom Kippurim*), alluded to the omen of the shadow without a critical comment. He referred to this belief in his exegesis of Numbers 14:9: " 'Their shade is removed from over them,' this is possibly an allusion to the known belief that on the night of the sealing [Hoshana Rabba] if the shadow of one's head is not there, he will die in the same year" (Avudrahim, *Hoshana Rabba*).

The reluctance of the sages to denounce the superstition might have been due to the fact that it was based on a practice recorded in the Talmud. "If one is about to set out on a journey and he wants to know whether he will return [alive], let him stand in a half-dark house; if he sees a double shadow it is an omen that he will return to his house" (*Horayot* 12a).

Divination by shadows has been a common superstition among many nations. It is not at all surprising that some Jews were influenced by it. The Talmud compiled an anthological collection of superstitions as a valuable record of Jewish folk practices. The recording of a super-stition did not imply approval. In the case of the omen of the shadow, the Talmud admonished against the practice because it may lead to anxieties which are detrimental to health.

The omen of the shadow, mentioned in the Talmud, was not associated with Hoshana Rabba. One may wonder why the medieval offspring of the ancient superstition came to be linked to that specific day. The fact that Hoshana Rabba increasingly assumed the character of a concluding day of judgment was undoubtedly a contributing factor. Once the final decree had been set, there was a normal curiosity to find out what it was. Divination by one's shadow offered a peek into the future.

Another reason for linking the omen of the shadow to Sukkot may have been the fact that shadow plays an important part in the qualification of a sukkah. The latter is a testimonial to the protective shade provided by God in the desert. Since Hoshana Rabba is the last day when one must sit in the shadow of the sukkah, it may have been considered an appropriate time for testing the premonition of one's own shadow.

Rema (16th cent.) mentioned this custom in his annotations to the code (*Orach Chaim* 664) but cautioned against the practice.

SHACHARIT

The judgment aspect of Hoshana Rabba is reflected in the Shacharit rituals. The reader wears a kittle. The series of psalms, beginning with *Lamenatzeach*, normally recited on Sabbaths and festivals, is included in the service. The verse of *Shema*, prior to the reading of the Torah, is chanted in the solemn mood of the High Holiday melody.

BITING OFF THE PITUM

A curious custom of comparatively recent origin (ca. 18th cent.) is the practice of some women to bite off the apex of the etrog after its ritual use has been completed. It was rumored that this action was conducive to the bearing of a male child.

Contemporary sages who took note of the practice conjectured that its therapeutic qualities were based on the tradition that the fruit which Eve had proffered to Adam was an etrog. Eve had sinned by eating the etrog. Her pious daughters atone for her sin by biting off the pitum but refraining from tasting the fruit. They are thus entitled to a heavenly reward, particularly if they follow up the demonstration of their restraint with a generous contribution to charity.

The obligation of Jewish women to atone for the sin of Eve is mentioned in midrashic literature. Rashi quoted *Bereshit Rabbah* to the effect that the duty of lighting Sabbath candles devolved on women because they must atone for Eve, who by her transgression had extinguished the light of the world (*Shabbat* 32a, Rashi, *Iske Reshit*). Women who light candles are rewarded with scholarly children (*Shabbat* 23b). A similar reward was expected by women who atoned for Eve by biting off the pitum.

Another recent custom is the serving of dumplings (kreplach) on Hoshana Rabba. (For a discussion of this custom, see above, chap. 4, "The Concluding Meal.")

SHEMINI ATZERET

The Eighth Day of Assembly is, as its name indicates, the eighth day of the Sukkot period. Yet it is entirely distinct from the preceding seven days. The name Sukkot does not apply to it. It does not commemorate the exodus or mark the ingathering of the harvest. The word *chag* ("festival") is never appended to it. The text describes it as *yom* ("the day"), Shemini Atzeret (Num. 29:35), or just Atzeret (Lev. 23:26). The Talmud stresses the special character of the holiday by describing it a *regel bifne atzmo* ("a distinct holiday by itself," *Rosh HaShanah* 4b).

As we mentioned above, pilgrimage holidays were timed to coincide with agricultural folk-festivals. In each instance, the biblical text which lists the occasion for a pilgrimage to Jerusalem does not mention Shemini Atzeret. Thus we are told that the occasion for the pilgrimage of the fall season is the Festival of Ingathering (Exod. 23:16, 35:22) or the Festival of Sukkot (Deut. 16:16). The deuteronomic text clearly indicates the exclusion of Shemini Atzeret by the statement that the Festival of Sukkot is to be observed for seven days (16:13). In contrast to the preceding texts, the passages which do not mention pilgrimages and deal exclusively with the sacrificial rites of the holidays specifically mention Shemini Atzeret (Lev. 23:36, Num. 30:35).

The rationale of Shemini Atzeret is not spelled out in the Bible. The Talmud offers a homiletical explanation for one of the sacrificial rites of Shemini Atzeret. The total number of oxen sacrificed on the seven days of Sukkot is seventy, equivalent to the traditional number of the nations of the world. The rites thus constitute a symbolic prayer for the welfare of mankind. One additional ox is sacrificed on Shemini Atzeret, a day set aside for a prayer for the welfare of Israel (*Sukkot* 55b).

A substantive analysis seems to point to the fact that Shemini Atzeret falls into the category of two other single-day holidays, Rosh HaShanah and Yom Kippur (Shavuot is an appendage of Passover). Like them, it is neither a commemorative nor an agricultural festival. It has been pointed out that the sacrificial ritual of Shemini Atzeret is the same as the Musaf ritual of Rosh HaShanah and Yom Kippur, an ox, a ram, and seven sheep. The calendar of Jewish holidays is thus evenly divided between three socio-religious holidays (the pilgrimage festivals) and three theological holidays (Rosh HaShanah, Yom Kippur, and Shemini Atzeret). The beginning of the year is marked by a theological holiday and the series of festivals which follow it ends on the same note.

Two benedictions are recited when the Shemini Atzeret candles are lit, *lehadlik ner shel yom tov* and *shehecheyanu*. The latter is also recited on the first days of Sukkot but is nevertheless repeated on the last days because of the special character of Shemini Atzeret as a distinct holiday.

It is customary to make Kiddush in the sukkah. If the meal is eaten in the sukkah, the benediction of *leshev basukkah* is omitted.

The Men of the Great Assembly (5th cent. B.C.E.) ordained that the daily prayer for rain, *mashiv haruach umorid hageshem* ("he causes the wind to blow and the rain to come down"), be recited beginning with Shemini Atzeret. Due to the solemnity of the occasion, it is customary for the reader to wear a kittle when he leads the congregation in the chanting of special prayers for water.

The background of the ritual of Yizkor is discussed in chapter 4.

The Priestly Benediction is pronounced at the conclusion of Musaf. For the background of this custom, see chapter 4.

SIMCHAT TORAH EVE

The name Simchat Torah was introduced in the Middle Ages. Prior to that, the ninth day of Sukkot was called Shemini Atzeret. This day was set aside to celebrate the completion of the reading of the Torah at the congregational Sabbath services.

Many of the elaborate ceremonies connected with Simchat Torah were introduced in the sixteenth century. The most popular of these ceremonies is hakafot, seven marches around the bimah by Torah-bearing congregants. It is customary to remove all the Torah scrolls from the ark for this purpose.

The ritual of hakafot with Torah scrolls is an adaptation of the ancient Temple hakafot with lulavim. There were seven such hakafot on the morning of Hoshana Rabba. Sephardim also conduct hakafot with Torahs Scrolls on Shemini Atzaret night.

Among the popular customs, dating from the eighteenth century, is a procession of children who join the hakafot, bearing flags, tipped with apples and with candles inserted into the apples. The flags symbolize a marching army, and the lit candles, the light of the Torah. This custom, like the custom of Kal HaNearim (see below), reflected the effort of the community to involve children at a very early age in the rejoicing of the Torah.

It is customary to read the concluding portion of Deuteronomy in public after the completion of the hakafot on Simchat Torah night. Three men are called to the Torah for this occasion.

THE MORNING OF SIMCHAT TORAH

Hakafot are conducted once again on the morning of Simchat Torah. After the completion of the hakafot, all the Torah scrolls, except three, are returned to the ark. The first scroll is unrolled for the reading of the concluding portion of the Pentateuch. The portion is divided into two parts. The first part, from chapter 33:1 to 33:27, is reserved for aliyot for the general public. It is customary on Simchat Torah to honor all the worshippers in the congregation with aliyot. In order to expedite the procedure, the rabbis permitted collective aliyot (on Simchat Torah only). A group of people is honored with the same aliyah and they recite the benedictions in unison.

When most of the adults have been honored with aliyot, it is customary to call all the minors to the Torah, in the custody of an adult. A tallit is spread over the heads of the children and the adult prompts them in the recitation of the benedictions. After the second benediction, the boys are blessed with the words of Jacob's blessing of his grandchildren: "The angel who has redeemed me from all evil . . ." (Gen. 48:16). This ceremony is called Kal Hanearim ("all the boys"). It was customary for the women in the synagogue to throw fruit and dainties at the children on the bimah, but most rabbis opposed the practice to avoid undue levity.

The individual who is honored with an aliyah for the conclusion of the reading of the Torah is officially named Chatan Torah ("the groom of the Torah"). The concluding portion begins with verse 27 of the thirty-third chapter and continues to the end of the Scroll (34:12).

The next major honor is an aliyah for the reading in the second Scroll of the opening portion of Genesis (1:1–2:3). This honoree is officially named Chatan Bereshit ("the groom of Genesis"). The practice soon developed for both "grooms" to serve a lavish collation to the entire congregation in appreciation of the honor accorded to them.

The custom of reading Genesis after the completion of Deuteronomy dates from the geonic period. The purpose of this practice was to demonstrate the people's love of the Torah. As soon as the congregation finishes the reading of the Pentateuch it immediately commences to read it all over again.

The regular festival maftir portion (Num. 30:35) is read in the third Scroll. The original haftarah assigned by the Talmud for this day was from II Kings (8:22) "And Solomon stood before the altar . . ." This selection was motivated by the fact that Solomon's dedication of the Temple took place on Sukkot. However, as the theme of the completion of the Torah took on great significance, the haftarah was changed. Rav Amram Gaon (9th cent.) mentioned the first chapter of Joshua, which deals with events after the death of Moses, as the haftarah of the day. This is still our custom.

REJOICING WITHOUT HAKAFOT

The custom of rejoicing on Simchat Torah is inherent in the name of the festival. How did one rejoice in the thirteenth or fourteenth centuries when the new name was first unveiled? *Kol Bo* gives us a glimpse of that early period. "It is customary on the last day of the holiday, which is called Simchat Torah because all the people rejoice over the completion of (the reading of) the Torah, to have the entire congregation read in the Torah, including those who do not normally receive an aliyah during the year. . . . After that (the haftarah and recitation of Ashere) they stand on the platform with the Torot. It is also customary to remove all the Torot from the Ark. The elders stand on the platform with the Torot in their arms and they bewail the death of Moses . . .

and they pray for those who had contributed to the honor of the Torah, the living and the dead . . ." The "rejoicing" of the early Simchat Torah obviously had a strong flavor of Yizkor.

7

Passover Customs

I.
INTRODUCTION

PASSOVER IS THE most popular Jewish holiday. The rich Seder pageantry, with its appeal to young and old, the display of sparkling dishes, the traditional gourmet meals, the family reunions, and the general gay and festive atmosphere, all combine to create a charm and exuberance unparalleled on other occasions.

Nature, too, cooperates by exhibiting its radiant colors and exuding a heady fragrance after the bleak harshness of winter. In the lyrical words of the Scriptures: "For, lo, the winter is past and the rains are gone. The flowers appear on the earth. The time of singing is come . . ." (Song of Songs 2:11–12).

On the other hand, the preparations for Passover are the most exacting in terms of the effort and planning required by numerous complex religious regulations. Basic biblical laws, reinforced by rabbinical ordinances, attest to the unique and extraordinary status of this festival.

Passover is the only holiday whose principal ritual, the offering of a paschal lamb, is performed prior to the commencement of the festival (*Pesachim* 61a). The same is true of the prohibition of the consumption of chametz, which becomes effective at midday on the fourteenth of Nisan (*Pesachim* 5a, 28b). Chametz is the only prohibited food which may not be owned by Jews or stored in Jewish homes during the week of Passover (Exod. 12:15). The prohibition of chametz is so strict that it was spelled out in two separate injunctions: "No chametz shall be found in your homes" (*lo yimatze*; Exod. 12:19) and "No chametz shall be seen with you" (*lo yeraeh*; Exod. 13:7).

Chametz owned by a Jew in violation of the laws of Passover is forever unfit for consumption and enjoyment (*Pesachim* 29b). This

211

rabbinical penalty applies equally even if the chametz had been inadvertently overlooked.

An admixture of a grain of chametz, even when its proportion to the permissible food is less than one-sixtieth (the normal gauge in the laws of kashrut), renders the entire mixture unfit for consumption (*Pesachim* 29b).

The punishment for eating chametz on Passover is *karet* ("extirpation"; Exod. 12:19), unlike the usual punishment of lashes for violation of a negative injunction.

Biblical law requires merely the annulment (*bitul*) of chametz. The Talmud, however, added the requirement of a search (*bedikah*) and removal of the chametz (*biur*) in addition to the annulment (*bitul*; *Pesachim* 4b).

To paraphrase the well-known question of the Haggadah, why is the festival of Passover different from all other festivals? This question was discussed by many medieval scholars. With regard to annulment, it was said that a proper annulment is not easily effected because it is an intangible, mental act, which the average individual is not competent to perform. The rabbis therefore decreed that chametz should be physically removed and destroyed.

Another popular explanation for the numerous rabbinical restrictions is based on the need for precautionary measures with regard to Passover. Since chametz is eaten throughout the year, one may easily forget the temporary prohibition and accidentally violate the law.

The noted Avudrahim (14th cent.) rejected this explanation and pointed out that wine may remain in the house of a Nazirite, even though the restrictions of a Nazirite are also of a temporary nature. Avudrahim therefore accepted another popular explanation, namely that the rabbinical restrictions were influenced by the strictness of the biblical laws. The biblical strictness is evidenced by the prohibition of the possession of chametz as well as its consumption (*Seder Tefilot HaPesach*).

This explanation is undoubtedly well taken. However, we are still left wondering why the biblical law is so strict in the first place. Rabbenu Nissim Gerondi (Ran, 14th cent.) attributed the biblical strictness (such as the double injunctions) to the need for extreme caution in view of the permissibility of chametz throughout the year (on Alfasi, *Pesachim*, first mishnah). However, the practice of enacting preventive "fences" is common in the Talmud. One hardly expects to find them in the Bible.

The key to the biblical strictness with regard to Passover most likely lies in the historical background of this festival. The exodus marked the finalization of God's covenant with Abraham and its reaffirmation with the generation which left Egypt (Lev. 26:45). To impress posterity with the importance of the exodus, God commanded that the events of the historic fourteenth of Nisan be annually reinacted as a reminder of the ancient covenant (See Bloch, *Biblical and Historical Background of the Jewish Holy Days*, p. 102). In the same vein the Talmud interpreted the command "Then thou shalt keep this service in this month" (Exod. 13:5) to mean that most of the rules relating to the Egyptian Passover are also applicable to all subsequent Passovers (*Pesachim* 96a).

The basic Passover laws were issued on the first of Nisan (Exod. 12:2; *Menachot* 29a). This was done in anticipation of a sudden departure. The conditions which might prevail on the fourteenth of Nisan were taken into consideration. Hence the order to slaughter the lamb after midday, not to tarry over the feast, and to commemorate those events for all time (Exod. 12:6, 14). In further anticipation of events on the morning after the exodus, Jews were ordered to eat matzot on that day and to remove all chametz from their homes (Exod. 12:15). In view of the centrality of the paschal lamb in the observance of Passover, the matzot were to be eaten with the lamb. A subsequent injunction made it clear that there was to be no chametz in the home when the paschal lamb is offered (Exod. 34:25).

Due to the paramount role of the paschal lamb as a confirmation of God's covenant with Israel, one who violates the Passover laws denies the covenant and excludes himself from the founding charter of the Jewish people. Failure to offer the paschal lamb, or the eating of chametz on Passover, is punishable by *karet* (extirpation), symbolizing removal from the roots of one's people (Exod. 12:19; *Keritot* 2a).

By the time the paschal lamb was offered in Egypt, Jews no longer had any chametz in their possession, in keeping with the injunction to "put away [*tashbitu*] leaven from your home" (Exod. 12:15). Despite the talmudic interpretation of the term *tashbitu*, which merely called for annulment, without a physical removal of chametz (*Pesachim* 4b), it is a reasonable assumption that the Jews in Egypt had in fact thrown out whatever chametz they owned, in preparation for a sudden departure. The formula of annulment had not yet been promulgated at that time, and even if they had known of such a formula, it is ineffective insofar as visible chametz is concerned.

The emerging picture of the Jewish homes in Egypt at midday of the fourteenth of Nisan is one in which chametz was neither seen (in the open) nor found (stored away) nor owned. In the annual reinactment of the events of the fourteenth of Nisan, the Bible ordered a duplication of the conditions that had existed at that time. Accordingly, chametz must neither be seen nor found in a Jewish home on Passover. Even the minutest particle of chametz is out of place in the dramatization of that historic day.

PREPARATIONS FOR PASSOVER THIRTY DAYS BEFORE THE HOLIDAY

Due to the complexity of Passover laws, the rabbis recommended that people begin to inquire about them thirty days before the holiday. Rabban Simon b. Gamliel (2nd cent.) shortened the period to two weeks (*Pesachim* 6a). This ordinance did not institute a program of rabbinic lectures at a set time before the holidays but merely urged the public to seek information during that period. Thus the early version of the beraita in *Sanhedrin* (12b) and *Megillah* (29b) reads: "They [the people] inquire [*shoalin*] about the laws of Passover thirty days before Passover." However, it must have become apparent in time that it is important that the rabbis stimulate these inquiries by public discussions of the law. A beraita in *Pesachim* (6a), obviously a later version, reads as follows: "They [the people] inquire and they [the rabbis] lecture [*shoalin vedorshin*] on the laws of Passover thirty days before Passover." Rava's statement that "from Purim we begin to lecture on the laws of Passover" (*Sanhedrin* 12b) indicates that by the fourth century the practice of discussing Passover laws thirty days before the holiday was well established.

According to Rashi, rabbinic discussions of festival laws were the practice prior to all holidays (*Sanhedrin* 7b, *Shabbata de rigla*). There is no evidence of the existence of such customs, nor is there any need for a prolonged educational period, prior to festivals other than Passover.

In addition to the complexity of the Passover laws, there was a practical reason for making inquiries as early as thirty days before the holiday. The law provides that a person who leaves on a long journey within thirty days of Passover must perform the ritual of *bedikah* (search of chametz) prior to his leaving. Various questions might therefore arise in connection with that ritual thirty days before Passover. The baking of matzot normally began thirty days before Passover. That, too, may give rise to questions.

In the medieval Jewish community, halachic lectures were delivered by rabbis on Shabbat HaGadol (the Sabbath before Passover) and Shabbat Shuvah (the Sabbath before Yom Kippur). The lecture before

Passover discussed the laws of the holiday. The Shabbat Shuvah lecture dwelt on the subject of penitence and morality. Maharil (14th cent.) instituted the custom of discussing the laws of Sukkot on Shabbat Shuvah. This practice did not spread.

PREPARATIONS DURING THE MONTH OF NISAN

The entire month of Nisan has taken on a festive character due to its historical background. *Masechet Soferim* (edited ca. 8th cent.) prohibits fasting during the month of Nisan because Moses had set up the Tabernacle on the first of the month. For the following twelve days the heads of the tribes brought dedicatory offerings. To these festive days one must add the seven days of Passover. According to the *Tur* code (14th cent., *Orach Chaim* 429), the intent of this passage is to prohibit fasting and eulogizing the dead throughout the month of Nisan.

Megillat Taanit (edited in the 1st cent.) and the Talmud (*Taanit* 17b) looked to later historical events to account for the festive character of Nisan. The period between the first and the eighth of Nisan was declared a semi-festival because the rabbinical laws regarding the daily offering (Tamid) prevailed over the Sadducean custom. The period between the eighth of Nisan and the beginning of Passover was declared a semi-festival in commemoration of the rabbinical triumph over the Sadducees in the fixing of the date of Shavuot. Both victories date from the first century B.C.E., when the Sadduceans lost their power.

The explanation in *Megillat Taanit* offers no apparent reason for extending the festive commemorations in the month of Nisan beyond Passover. In fact, it appears from the text that there was no intention to extend the ban on fasting beyond the holiday. Furthermore, all the holidays listed in *Megillat Taanit*, with the exception of Chanukah and Purim, were abolished in the second half of the third century.

The explanation in *Masechet Soferim*, on the other hand, is based on biblical texts, assuring the commemorations a permanence in the religious calendar. There is an additional text which alludes to the festive character of the entire month of Nisan. This is implied in the command to "observe the month of Aviv" (Deut. 16:1).

SHABBAT HAGADOL

The origin of the name "Great Sabbath," by which the Sabbath preceding Passover is generally known, is obscure. It came into vogue in the early Middle Ages and various explanations have been offered since then.

1. The Sabbath preceding the exodus was dated Nisan 10. That was the day when the Jews prepared lambs for the paschal offering (Exod. 12:3), in defiance of Egyptian opposition. The unexpected restraint of the Egyptians, who refrained from attacking the Jews, was considered a miracle. That Sabbath was therefore called a "great" Sabbath. This far-fetched explanation gained wide circulation and was frequently quoted.

2. The Jewish people was initiated into the performance of mitzvot on Saturday, Nisan 10, when they prepared the lambs in accordance with God's command of Nisan 1. In honor of this distinction the Sabbath was named Shabbat HaGadol. This explanation seems to have as little basis as the first. If the origin of the name is to be found in biblical events, the name would have appeared much sooner than the Middle Ages. Furthermore, the very premise of the explanation is questionable. The plague of darkness took place, according to tradition, on Adar 18. It lasted for three days. Soon thereafter, God requested the Jews to borrow valuables from their Egyptian neighbors (Exod. 11:2). That was the first divine command, even though it was couched in the form of a request.

3. The name Shabbat HaGadol is based on a phrase in the Haftarah of that Sabbath, *yom hashem hagadol* ("the Lord's great day"; Mal. 3:23). Haftarah-based names are indeed common, such as Shabbat Chazon, Shabbat Nachamu, and Shabbat Shuvah.

4. The rabbis delivered lengthy discourses on the Sabbath preceding Passover, thus prolonging the service by several hours. As a result of this delay, the people named that Saturday the "long" Sabbath. This explanation seems to be the most realistic. It is unlikely, however, that the *gadol* alluded to the length of the service. The name Shabbat HaGadol came into being before the *derashah* of that day became a tradition. The *gadol* more likely alluded to the increased number of prayers (*piyutim*) which had been introduced into the service of that day.

Similar developments led to the hyphenation of *gadol* with several holidays. Yom Kippur, for instance, was referred to in the Jerusalem Talmud as Tzoma Rabba, "the great fast" (*Peah* 7:4). The name was not based on the length of the fast. Tisha B'Av is a longer fast. Yom Kippur, however, has many more prayers in its service. Philo (1st cent.) took note of the fact that Jews pray on Yom Kippur "from morning until evening" (*Treatise on the Festivals,* The Ninth Festival).

The talmudic passage which refers to Tzoma Rabba appears also in another Jerusalem tractate (*Baba Batra* 9:7). The adjective *rabba* is omitted from that text. It refers to Yom Kippur only as Tzoma. This is apparently an earlier version, before the introduction of numerous additional prayers gave Yom Kippur its special character.

The name Tzoma Rabba was probably coined in Palestine before the final editing of its Talmud was completed in the fourth century. The Babylonian Talmud was sealed a century and a half later, yet the name Tzoma Rabba does not appear in it. Apparently the name did not spread to the diaspora.

Another festival to which the adjective *rabba* was attached is Hoshana Rabba. This name does not appear in either Talmud, except once in one edition of *Midrash Shochar Tov*. This Midrash also originated in Palestine, and the name Hoshana Rabba was probably interpolated by a post-talmudic editor. Here, too, the *rabba* is based on the great number of *hoshanot* recited on that day.

The kabbalists similarly called the elaborate Sabbath morning Kiddush, *Kiddusha Rabba*. The many prayers and psalms which are collectively known as *Hallel HaGadol* are called the Great *Hallel* because of the great number of prayers which comprise this *Hallel* (the Talmud offers a homiletical explanation for this name, *Pesachim* 118a). The length of the prayer is also the reason for the name *Vidui HaGadol* ("the long confession") by Rabbi Nissim. The same is true of *Minchah Gedolah,* the early afternoon Minchah service (*Shabbat* 9b).

The Hebrew *gadol* was used in the tannaic period and the Aramaic *rabba* in the amoraic period. The early geonim continued to use the Aramaic names, and the same was true of the kabbalists. The name Shabbat HaGadol was probably coined in the later part of the geonic period.

RECITATION OF HAGGADAH PASSAGES

It is customary to recite a number of Haggadah passages (from *Avadim hayinu* to *lechaper al kal avonotenu*) at the conclusion of the Minchah service on Shabbat HaGadol This custom was popularized by Rema (16th cent, *Orach Chaim* 430). The purpose of the recitation is to familiarize the reader with the text of the Haggadah. One who is not familiar with the text may be tempted to move the candle closer to the Haggadah on the Seder night for better illumination. Such an act would constitute a violation of the Sabbath when a Seder is conducted on Friday night.

According to some scholars, there was no need for reading the balance of the Haggadah on Shabbat HaGadol because that part was familiar to most Jews. This may be true of *Hallel* and *Nishmat,* which are recited after the meal. However, no Jew will claim familiarity with the important remaining portion of the Haggadah which precedes the meal, particularly Rabban Gamliel's exposition of the meaning of *pesach, matzah,* and *maror.* It is probable that the reading of the Haggadah on Shabbat HaGadol stopped short of Rabban Gamliel's statement because of its intimate association with the Passover platter, which was available only on the Seder night.

MAOT CHITIN

The custom of assisting the poor with free provisions of food for Passover is very ancient. The Mishnah mandated a distribution of wine to the poor, for the obligatory four cups at the Seder, so that every person may proclaim the miracle of the exodus (*Pesachim* 99b). There was apparently no special distribution at that time of food for Passover, except for the daily *tamchuy,* a tray of food regularly given to the poor.

We learn from a source in the Jerusalem Talmud (*Baba Batra* 1:6) of a third-century Palestinian custom to give wheat to the poor for the baking of matzot. This custom was mentioned by Rabbi Jose b. Rabbi Bun (latter part of the 3rd cent.) in connection with a discussion of the time period required for the establishment of residence. Resident citizens were subject to a special Passover charity tax, and indigent residents were entitled to Passover assistance of free wheat. One gains the impression that the custom of distributing wheat was already well established by the time of Rabbi Jose. Only the question of residence remained to be settled.

Initially residence was established after one year. The required period of time was subsequently reduced to thirty days. Even that period was eventually whittled down for persons moving into a city with the intention of establishing a permanent residence. Such individuals were entitled to immediate assistance.

The original custom was known as *chite HaPesach* ("wheat for Passover"). The recipient of the wheat took it to the mill, obtained his own flour, and baked his own matzot. In the Middle Ages the custom was changed in many localities. The community took on the responsibility for the baking of matzot and their distribution to the poor. When commercial bakeries were established, the method of Passover assistance changed once again. It was more convenient to give money to the poor, who in turn bought wheat and baked their own matzot or had them baked in a commercial bakery. This form of assistance became known as *maot chitin* ("money for wheat"). Modern custom has adopted both practices, the distribution of money and of food packages.

MECHIRAT CHAMETZ

The following discussion of the subject of the sale of chametz is mainly based on the excellent treatise of Rabbi Sh. J. Zevin in his book *Moadim Bahalachah*, p. 245.

Up until the late Middle Ages, the quantity of accumulated chametz possessed by Jews was generally small. It was therefore easy to dispose of it before Passover, either by destroying it or by selling it to a non-Jew (*Pesachim* 21a). The sale was an outright transaction and the seller never reacquired his chametz.

Sales of chametz to non-Jews were a common expedient for Jewish passengers aboard ships. Long-distance travel took many weeks and even months. Passengers had to provide their own food, and most of it was chametz. The food had to last for the duration of the voyage. If one were to dump his chametz into the sea before Passover, he would surely starve after the holiday. There was no choice but to sell the chametz to a non-Jew before Passover and reacquire it afterwards (Tosefta, *Pesachim* 2).

The Tosefta came down in several versions. According to one version, there is a concluding verse which reads: "on condition that he should not use it as a subterfuge." Based on this admonition, Rav Amram Gaon (9th cent.) warned against those who make an annual habit of selling and repurchasing their chametz.

In the early stages of the custom of mechirat chametz, the chametz was removed from the home and turned over to the non-Jew. The sale was legal, even if both parties understood that a repurchase of the chametz after Passover was contemplated. Such sales, however, were discouraged unless there was no other choice, as in the case of ship passengers.

A change in the occupation and economic conditions of sixteenth-century East European Jewry had made the sale of chametz a necessity not only for seafarers but also for vast numbers of homebound Jews. A large segment of East European Jews derived a livelihood from innkeeping and the sale of liquor. The chametz could no longer be destroyed or removed to non-Jewish quarters. Rabbi Joel Sirkes (16th–17th cent.) permitted the sale of chametz, including the place of storage, to a non-Jew. He also ordered that the key to the storage be turned over to the purchaser.

To avoid the appearance of a legal fiction, particularly when the non-Jew was unable to make full payment, a written contract was eventually introduced to lend greater formality to the transaction. Model contracts were published for the use of laymen who did their own selling. This arrangement met with no opposition, and this method for the selling of chametz was used for about two and a half centuries.

It was to be expected, however, that the method would have to be eventually changed. The inevitable mistakes of laymen, ignorant of the complex laws of sales and contracts, put the legality of many sales of chametz in question. A new procedure was adopted in the nineteenth century. The rabbi was authorized by a written contract of agency, signed by all the sellers of chametz (*shtar harshaah*), to sell their chametz to a non-Jew. The rabbi then executed a sales contract (*shtar mechirah*) to effect the sale of the chametz.

This procedure was introduced for the first time in 1856. There was considerable initial opposition to the new arrangement. It was contended that an agent's signature on a sales contract is not binding upon a principal. This objection was overcome by the enclosure of the authorization contract with the sales contract and the delivery of both to the purchaser. The signatures of the sellers on the authorization contract validated the agent's signature of the sale's contract.

KASHERING OF DISHES

Pots, dishes, and utensils which are used throughout the year absorb chamtez and may not be used on Passover. The Talmud discusses the types of dishes which may be kashered, the deadline for kashering them, and the question of the use after Passover of chametz dishes which had not been kashered (*Pesachim* 30a). For a detailed discussion of this subject, we refer the reader to the code (*Orach Chaim* 451–452).

BEDIKAT CHAMETZ

As we mentioned in the introduction, biblical law merely requires annulment of chametz (*bitul; Pesachim* 4b). The concept of an annulment of a physical object does not exist in non-Jewish jurisprudence, where annulment is limited to the voiding of contractual obligations or status. In the Hebrew law, the annulment of an object constitutes a renunciation of ownership coupled with a declaration of the value-lessness of the object. In the case of chametz, the annulment prior to Passover deprives the owner of his ownership and divests the object of its legal definition of chametz because it is no longer considered an object of value.

The Talmud, for reasons which we have previously indicated, decreed that in addition to annulment one must also conduct a search of chametz *(bedikah)* and perform an act of destruction of the chametz *(biur),* preferably by burning. The ancient custom of *bedikah* is mentioned in the very first mishnah in *Pesachim.* The mishnah discusses the proper time for conducting the search. The practice itself was obviously well known already in the Temple era.

It is customary to search for chametz by candle light. It is easy to maneuver a candle and bring it close to the cracks and holes which have to be examined. The search is conducted on the evening of the thirteenth of Nisan, shortly after the emergence of the stars, while some daylight still lingers on.

One may continue to own and eat chametz after the search has been completed. It may therefore appear that it would be more appropriate to conduct the search on the next morning, when the deadline for owning chametz is reached. However, the rabbis preferred the prior evening because most people are at home at that time and candles are in use. To make sure that this important custom is not neglected, the rabbis ordained that no one is to engage in work, or even study, beginning with thirty minutes before the emergence of the stars.

Prior to the search one recites a benediction: "Blessed art thou . . . who commanded us to remove the chametz" *(Pesachim* 7b). Curiously, there is no reference in this benediction to the search of chametz. The reason for this omission is the fact that the search is merely incidental to the main objective of removing all chametz from the home *(Bet Yoseph, Orach Chaim* 432).

Upon the completion of the search, one recites the following formula of annulment: "All leaven food and grain fermentation which are in my possession, which I have not seen or removed, shall be null and considered as the dust of the earth." Despite the fact that the rabbis had ordered the removal and destruction of chametz, they also retained the practice of annulment. In the event that some chametz might have been overlooked and not removed, one avoids a violation of the law by having the overlooked chametz annulled *(Pesachim* 6b).

The annulment which is recited at night applies only to the chametz "which I have not seen" and consequently overlooked. The visible chametz is still legally in the home and may be enjoyed until the next morning.

It is customary to prepare some crumbs of chametz in a prominent place so that they may be gathered up at the end of the search. This is done to make sure that some chametz will be on hand for ultimate removal and destruction and thus the benediction will not have been in vain.

BAKING OF MATZOT

It was customary to bake matzot within thirty days of Passover. Shemurah matzot (see below) were baked on the afternoon of the fourteenth of Nisan so as to approximate the time when the paschal lamb was sacrificed.

Machine-baked matzot were introduced in the second half of the nineteenth century. There was much initial opposition to machine-baked matzot on religious and social grounds. The religious opposition was based on fears that leavened dough might remain on the rollers. The social objections were based on the same reasons for which modern organized labor objects to labor-saving machinery. Poor people used to secure seasonal employment in the production of hand-baked matzot. The machine triumphed in the end, but there are still some people who eat only hand-baked matzot.

SHEMURAH MATZOT

The biblical edict *ushemartem et hamatzot* ("you shall guard the matzot"; Exod. 12:17) was interpreted by the Talmud as an injunction to watch the flour to prevent leavening. It was also interpreted as an order to see to it that the kneading of the dough and the baking are done with the intent of producing matzot for Passover (*Pesachim* 38b). Hence the term *matzah shemurah* ("guarded matzah").

The extent of the required guarding is not spelled out in the Talmud. Ancient custom called for several levels of guarding. First, one harvested some wheat and earmarked it for matzot. Then one guarded the wheat until it was ground into flour. The next step was to watch the flour to keep it from getting wet. One also has to make sure that the flour is at least one day old when it is kneaded into dough. Fresh flour is susceptible to leavening. The stringency of the guarding was relaxed in the Middle Ages when the watching of the wheat began from the time when it reached the mill.

II.
THE FOURTEENTH OF NISAN

TAANIT BECHORIM

It is customary for firstborn Jews to fast on the fourteenth of Nisan in commemoration of the escape of the Jewish firstborn when the Egyptians perished in the tenth plague. If the firstborn is a minor, the duty of fasting devolves upon his father.

Firstborns who participate in a *siyum* (completion of the study of a talmudic tractate) are exempt from fasting and they may partake of the collation which is normally served on such occasions.

For a discussion of the background of this fast, see chapter 13.

DEADLINE FOR EATING CHAMETZ

The Talmud restricted the eating of chametz on the fourteenth of Nisan to the end of the fourth hour after the onset of daylight (*Pesachim* 11b). The rabbinical deadline is two hours ahead of the biblical deadline of six hours (*Pesachim* 28b). The restriction was instituted to prevent inadvertent violations of the prohibition of chametz.

The "hours" designated in the various Passover regulations are relative or seasonal hours. A seasonal hour is one twelfth part of the time between dawn and sunset. Its length will depend upon the date of Passover in the solar calendar. The fourteenth of Nisan could occur as early as the twenty-fifth of March, at which time the seasonal hour is considerably shorter than the absolute hour. On the other hand, it could also occur as late as the twenty-third of April, when the seasonal hour is considerably longer than the absolute hour.

PROHIBITION OF MATZOT

One must abstain from eating matzot on the fourteenth of Nisan so that he may enjoy and eat with relish the matzah which fulfills the mitzvah of matzot on the Seder night. The origin of this prohibition is a statement in the Jerusalem Talmud (*Pesachim* 10:1). In keeping with this restriction, it was customary to limit the diet on the afternoon of the fourteenth of Nisan to proteins, vegetables, and fruit. The diet was expanded in the Middle Ages to include egg matzot. The talmudic prohibition applied only to matzot which may be used at the Seder in fulfillment of the mitzvah of matzot. Egg matzot may not be used for that purpose.

The prohibition of matzot on the fourteenth of Nisan is effective from the beginning of the day and does not extend to the preceding evening (*Kitzur Shulchan Aruch, Maadane Shemuel* 5:12).

BIUR CHAMETZ

Whatever chametz is left in the house, including the chametz that was gathered in the course of the *bedikah* on the previous night, is removed and burned before the end of the fifth hour. Following the burning, the formula of annulment is repeated. At this time one annuls the chametz "which I have seen and have not seen." The chametz which was seen on the previous night, and which had been left to be eaten on the following morning, must now be annulled. There is also a possibility that some chametz might have fallen into a hole during the night and is now no longer seen. That, too, must be annulled. Hence the formula "which I have seen and not seen."

Rav Saadiah Gaon (10th cent.), in his Arabic commentary on the siddur, translated the text of the annulment into Arabic. The nullification of the chametz would be ineffective if the person who recites the legal formula is ignorant of the meaning of the phraseology and its intent. It is therefore preferable to recite it in the vernacular. However, since most Jews of his generation were conversant with Aramaic, the Gaon added that those who understand Aramaic should recite the formula in the original.

ERUV TAVSHILIN

If the second day of Passover falls on Friday, one must perform the ritual of Eruv Tavshilin prior to the holiday so that the cooking for the Sabbath may be done on Friday. (See above, chap. 4, "Eruv Tavshilin.")

ATTIRE AND APPEARANCE

The customs pertaining to personal appearance and attire on the Sabbath apply to all holidays. (See above, chap. 3.)

SATURDAY THE FOURTEENTH OF NISAN

When Passover commences on Saturday night, most of the rituals which are normally performed on the fourteenth of Nisan are advanced to earlier dates (*Pesachim* 13a).

The following is the altered schedule:

Taanit Bechorim (Fast of the firstborn). Since fasting is not permitted on Saturdays, and this fast is of neither biblical nor talmudic origin, it was the opinion of some medieval scholars that it should be omitted. However, the custom of anticipating the fast prevailed. Normally, fasts are not observed on Fridays, but there are some exceptions to this rule. When Taanit Bechorim falls on a Friday (when Friday is the fourteenth of Nisan), the fast is observed on that day. If the fast has to be advanced (when Saturday is the fourteenth of Nisan), it is observed on the preceding Thursday.

Bedikat Chametz. The search for chametz is conducted on Thursday night (the twelfth of Nisan).

Biur Chametz. The burning of the chametz is done before the end of the fifth hour on Friday, the thirteenth of Nisan. The formula of annulment, however, is not recited at that time because some chametz is left for the Saturday morning meal. The chametz is annulled after that meal.

One may use egg matzot for the third seudah of the Sabbath. It should be eaten prior to the tenth hour.

Those who begin to eat Passover food on Friday night may use two regular matzot for *lechem mishneh* at the evening Sabbath meal, but only egg matzot may be used for *lechem mishneh* on Saturday morning.

PREPARATIONS FOR THE SEDER

Due to the urgent need for the participation of children in the educational program of the Seder, it is necessary to make all possible preparations beforehand so that the Seder ceremony may begin promptly as night sets in. Chairs for all expected guests should be put in place before the holiday and the table set. It is customary to display beautiful tablewear and goblets. Haggadot, the Passover platter with its ritual dishes, matzot, and wine are also prepared in advance. A ceremonial Cup of Elijah is placed at the center of the table.

It is preferable to use red wine. Rabbi Chiyah (2nd–3rd cent.) was the first amora to stress the importance of the color of the wine. Rabbi Yirmeyah (4th cent.) amplified that it should be red wine (Jer. *Shekalim*

3:2). Both were natives of Babylonia who spent their mature years in Palestine, where the custom of red wine most likely originated. Rabbi Yirmeyah based the preference for red wine on a scriptural verse (Prov. 23:31). Taz (16th cent.) attributed the preference to a symbolic memorial to the blood of the Jewish infants killed by Pharaoh (*Orach Chaim* 472:10). Incidentally, there is a curious historical observation in his commentary: "Now people avoid the use of red wine because of the false charges" (blood ritual).

FOUR CUPS OF WINE

The four cups of wine reflect four expressions of redemption mentioned in the Bible: "And I will take you out"; "And I will deliver you"; "And I will redeem you"; "And I will take you" (Exod. 6:6–7; Jer. *Pesachim* 10:1). Other homiletical explanations of the significance of the four cups are also provided in the Talmud. A desire to enhance the joy of the Seder was undoubtedly an important factor in the introduction in the first century, shortly after the destruction of the Temple, of the multiple number of cups.

In the talmudic period, each individual had his own small table. The ceremonial objects were placed only on the table of the leader of the Seder. His table was brought to him after the chanting of the Kiddush (*Pesachim* 100b). When large tables came into use in the post-talmudic era, all the ceremonial objects were placed on the table prior to the Seder.

THE PASSOVER PLATTER

The Passover platter (*kaarah*) was formerly known as a *sal* ("basket"; Avudrahim, *Seder Hahaggadah*). When the ritual Seder dishes were placed in a basket, it was impossible to arrange them in a prescribed order. However, when platters or trays were introduced, various arrangements came into vogue. Thus Maharil (14th–15th cent.) placed the different items in the order of their ritual use. The dish that was used first was placed closest to the leader (Rema, *Orach Chaim* 473:4). Subsequent arrangements took the symbolic importance of each item into consideration.

It is our custom to arrange two triangles. The upper triangle has the shankbone on the right and the egg on the left. Both commemorate sacrificial offerings, the paschal lamb (symbolized by the shankbone) and the festival offering, the chaggigah (symbolized by the egg). The maror (bitters) is placed in the center on a lower line. This completes the first triangle. The second triangle, at the bottom half of the platter, has the charoset on the right, the karpas on the left, and the lettuce in the center below them. These are placed in the lower triangle because they are of rabbinical origin.

The shankbone (*zeroa*) and the egg (*bea*) are commemorative dishes that were introduced after the destruction of the Temple (*Pesachim* 114a). The original source of these items mentions "two dishes" without specifying their identity. The information was provided by the Jerusalem Talmud (quoted by *Kol Bo* but missing in our texts). According to this quotation, the choice of these dishes was motivated by the significance of their names. *Zeroa* ("arm") commemorates God's "outstretched arm." *Bea* ("desires," in Aramaic) commemorates God's desire to redeem his people.

The zeroa is roasted just as the paschal lamb had to be roasted. As a symbolic offering the zeroa may not be eaten because the consumption of the paschal lamb outside of Jerusalem was prohibited. Since we do not eat the zeroa, it must be roasted prior to the holiday. Only food which is prepared for eating on the holiday may be cooked on that day.

The egg stands for the additional festival offering, the chaggigah. Additional offerings were sacrificed in order to provide an ample supply of meat. The chaggigah did not have to be roasted, and the egg similarly may be either roasted or boiled.

Charoset is a compound of crushed nuts and grated apples which commemorates the clay from which the Hebrew slaves made the bricks. Cinnamon is added because of its residual shreds, which give an appearance of straw, a required component in the process of brick-making (Exod. 5:7; *Pesachim* 116a). Wine is added to moisten the compound so that the maror may be dipped into it. Charoset was introduced in the first century, prior to the destruction of the Temple (*Pesachim* 116a).

For karpas (first dipping) it is customary to use either parsley, celery, or boiled potatoes. Karpas, like charoset, was introduced in the first century, prior to the destruction of the Temple (*Pesachim* 114b). Early post-talmudic rabbis used to dip the karpas in the charoset. However, beginning with the twelfth century, the karpas was dipped only in salt water, in keeping with the widespread practice of dipping greenery either in vinegar or salt water.

For maror we use either horseradish or lettuce. The biblical injunction to eat maror was limited to the Temple era, when the bitter herbs were eaten together with the paschal lamb. However, by rabbinic decree, the ritual of maror was retained in the post-Temple era in commemoration of the ancient practice (*Pesachim* 120a).

HAGGADAH

The name Haggadah is based on the biblical injunction *vehigadeta lebincha* ("you shall instruct your son"; Exod. 13:5). Prior to the invention of printing, Haggadot were expensive, beyond the reach of many people. Medieval scholars introduced several topical indices to guide the leader in the proper sequence of the Seder service. *Machzor Vitry* (12th cent.) is the earliest source to include such an index, which was attributed to Rashi (*Hilchot Pesach* 65). This index, which was called Seder Pesach ("the order of Passover"), became standard in all Haggadot.

Medieval sages encouraged the leader to explain the Haggadah in the vernacular. Some rabbis read the entire text twice, once in the original and once in translation (*Kol Bo;* Rema, *Orach Chaim* 473:6). Comprehension of the text was considered vital to the educational objective of the Seder. The need for elaboration invited various interpolations and made the Haggadah receptive to additional liturgical poems. Rav Saadiah Gaon (10th cent.) preserved two poems which were recited in the course of Kiddush, but most of the liturgical poems were inserted in the concluding section of the Haggadah, after the completion of *Hallel* and the fourth cup of wine. In this manner the ancient form of the Haggadah was left intact.

The Holocaust, the Warsaw Ghetto uprising, the independence of Israel, and the struggle of Soviet Jewry have been commemorated in some modern Haggadot. The Holocaust is memorialized with a Pledge of Remembrance which is read before *shefoch chamatcha,* as the door is opened for the symbolic entrance of Elijah. A solemn vow pledges all Jews to eternal remembrance of the fate of the victims of the Holocaust and the resistance fighters who died with a song of faith on their lips. The independence of Israel is remembered with a song of praise for the achievement of total freedom in a Jewish state. A fourth matzah, the Matzah of Hope, is set aside together with the afikoman, with a declaration of solidarity with the prisoners of conscience who have been condemned to Soviet labor camps.

In addition to insertions relevant to the theme of the ongoing Jewish struggle against persecution and annihilation (*bechol dor vador omdim alenu lechalotenu*), attempts have been made to secularize the Haggadah by the introduction of the universal theme of social conflict and civil rights. Such innovations can only weaken the impact of the Haggadah as the classical Jewish manifesto of freedom.

Jews have been prominent among the framers of manifestos addressed to the protection of the rights of the proletariat and the dispossessed. Sadly, their concern for the underprivileged ends short of the continuing problem of anti-Semitism. Their solution for the Jewish problem calls for the assimilation and disappearance of the Jewish people, the very antithesis of the message of the Haggadah.

III.
PASSOVER EVE CUSTOMS

MAARIV

The evening service of Passover follows the order of all holiday Maariv services, with two significant exceptions. Many congregations chant *Hallel* as part of the service and the chanting of Kiddush is omitted.

The first two Maariv services of Passover are the only occasions when *Hallel* is recited at night. The *Hallel* at the Seder is divided into two parts. The first part is recited prior to the meal and the second part after the meal. Due to this division, the usual benediction, "Blessed art thou . . . who commanded us to read the *Hallel*," is omitted. However, the benediction is recited by those who chant the entire *Hallel* at the Maariv service. This is probably one of the reasons for the inclusion of *Hallel* in the evening service. This practice is mentioned in *Masechet Soferim* (chap. 20, edited 8th cent.).

The chanting of Kiddush is omitted in the congregation on Passover night because it is assumed that every transient worshipper present in the synagogue will be invited to a family Seder where the Kiddush will be chanted. An additional reason for omitting Kiddush is to avoid creating a wrong impression that the Kiddush cup is a fifth cup of wine, exceeding the limit of four cups.

THE SEDER
A WHITE ROBE

It is customary for the leader of the Seder to put on a white robe *(kittel)* in honor of the festive occasion. In Aramaic, the word *chor* ("free") is akin to *chavar* ("white").

HESEIBAH

In ancient times people sat on couches when their meals were served. In order to support one's back, it was customary to pile up pillows for reclining on the left side while the right hand was used to get the food to the mouth. Generally, this was the privilege of the master. Servants ate sitting on the ground or standing up. In the second century, when the Seder was transformed into an occasion of great joy, the rabbis introduced the custom of *heseibah* ("reclining") at the Seder as a gesture of freedom. With the spread of the Jewish diaspora into Europe and the elimination of the practice of reclining at the table, some medieval scholars felt that the custom of *heseibah* had lost its significance and should be discontinued. However, their opinion was ignored because of a reluctance to tamper with traditional practices. Additionally, *heseibah* is the subject of one of the child's four questions. Elimination of this practice would have necessitated an amendment of the text. *Heseibah* was therefore retained on a limited scope. One should recline when drinking the cups of wine and when eating the *korech* and *afikoman*. The ancient practice is commemorated by placing a pillow on the left arm of the leader's chair.

KIDDUSH

One rises for the chanting of the Kiddush but reclines when drinking the wine.

THE WASHING OF HANDS

Prior to the first dipping (greens in salt water), the leader washes his hands but does not pronounce the customary benediction. Talmudic law mandated the washing of hands before one dips food in liquid. This was done to avoid ritual contamination of the liquid by impure hands. The law was discontinued in post-talmudic times. The leader of the Seder is therefore under no religious obligation to wash his hands and hence must not recite the benediction. However, the practice of washing the hands at the Seder was continued to preserve an old custom and also to excite the curiosity of children and stimulate them to ask questions.

KARPAS

According to the Talmud, the dipping of greens in salt water was intended to stimulate children to ask questions (*Pesachim* 114b). It is for that reason that this ritual precedes the four questions. However, the intrinsic function of the dipping of greens is to commemorate the dipping of the hyssops in the blood of the paschal lamb (Exod. 12:7, *Daat Zekenim Baale Tosafot;* Abarbanel on Haggadah, *shete peamim*).

THE BREAKING OF THE MIDDLE MATZAH

The middle matzah is broken into two parts. The larger part is wrapped in a napkin and put away to be distributed at the end of the meal (afikoman).

The wrapping is done to dramatize the exodus of the Hebrews, who left their homes with "their kneading troughs wrapped in their clothes upon their shoulders" (Exod. 12:24).

This episode was commemorated in the course of time by various customs. In some localities it was the practice of the leader to place the afikoman on his shoulders, from which it was transferred to the shoulder of each participant. The last person to receive the afikoman declared: "This is how our ancestors left Egypt with their kneading troughs wrapped in their clothes upon their shoulders." He then took four steps. Whereupon the participants asked in unison: "Where do you come from?" To which he replied: "From Egypt." The dialogue continued with the question: "Where are you going?" and he would answer: "To Jerusalem." The dramatization was concluded with a choral exclamation: "Next year in Jerusalem" (Kitov, *Sefer HaTodaah*, vol. 2, p. 114).

STEALING THE AFIKOMAN

The origin of the well-known practice of children to "steal" the afikoman and return it later upon a promise of a payment of ransom is obscure. Some scholars traced this custom to a beraita in *Pesachim* (109a) which reads as follows: "Matzot are snatched [*chotefin*] on the night of Passover on account of children so that they should not fall asleep." According to one interpretation, the term *chotefin* means to "raise." The beraita urges the leader to call the attention of children to the matzot by raising them so that they may focus their vision on the matzot.

A second interpretation of *chotefin* is to "snatch," a euphemism for eating fast. The matzot (or the meal) should be consumed quickly before the children fall asleep.

A third interpretation of *chotefin* is to "take away." Children should be prevented from eating too many matzot. If they eat their fill they will fall asleep.

Maimonides' interpretation of the beraita is to get children to indulge in games of snatching matzot from one another in order to keep them awake (*Hilchot Chametz Umatzah* 7:3).

One commentator suggested that a misinterpretation of the "snatching" in the beraita led to the custom of "stealing" the afikoman (*Orach Chaim* 422:1, *Chok Yaakov, shemitzvah lemaher*).

Early medieval rabbinical sources do not mention the practice of "hiding" the afikoman. It is important, of course, to keep the afikoman apart from the rest of the matzot on the table so that it should be available at the end of the meal, when the biblical command to eat matzot is fulfilled. Most people had only three shemurah matzot at each Seder. Two and one-half matzot were eaten at the beginning of the meal. It was essential to preserve the remaining half for the afikoman.

To make sure that the afikoman would be available when needed, one was required to place it under the tablecloth. *Machzor Vitry* (completed in 1208) stated *venoten* ("and he places it") under the cloth. There is no implication of hiding it to prevent its being stolen. The place where the matzah was deposited was known to everyone. The same is true of *Siddur Rashi* (12th cent.), which stated *umaniach tachat hamapah* (284, "and he places it under the cloth").

There appears to be an intimation of the practice of "hiding" in *Machzor Vitry*'s index of the order of the Seder, in which the eating of the afikoman is listed under the heading of *tzafun* ("hidden"). However, *tzafun* may also mean "reserved" or "put away." Furthermore, the *tzafun* in *Machzor Vitry* was most likely interpolated at a later time. The same index was copied by Avudrahim (14th cent.) and the caption of *tzafun* does not appear there.

The origin of *tzafun* can be traced to Rokeach (12th–13th cent.), who mentioned the practice of some people to put aside the afikoman. He based this custom on a biblical verse: "Oh, how abundant is thy goodness which thou hast laid up [*tzafanta*] for them that fear you" (Ps. 31:20). He thus linked the afikoman to the term *tzafanta*, from which *tzafun* eventually derived. The Washington Haggadah (completed 1470) lists *tzafun* in its index.

The *Tur* code (14th cent.) stressed the need for guarding the afikoman. Thus he stated: "He [the leader] gives the half to one of the participants to watch it so it may be used for the afikoman . . ." (*Orach Chaim* 473). The next step in the development of the custom of hiding the afikoman appears in *Kol Bo* (ca. 13th–15th cent.): the afikoman is hidden to prevent children from eating it. It is quite apparent that it became the practice in the fourteenth or fifteenth century to hide the afikoman from the children. Out of this practice evolved the custom of having the children "steal" the afikoman and guard it in anticipation of a reward. This served a dual purpose. The afikoman was safe and the children remained awake.

HO LACHMO ANYO

After the breaking of the middle matzah, the leader explains the purpose of this custom by reading the passage of *Ho lachmo anyo*. The broken matzah symbolizes the "bread of affliction" which our forefathers ate in Egypt. The tone of the Seder is set in three brief sentences: (1) the Hebrews had been enslaved and afflicted in Egypt; (2) social consciousness and a sense of mutual responsibility have been the key to our survival; (3) the hope for eventual redemption is forever in our hearts.

Rav Saadiah Gaon's (10th cent.) version of this passage consists of only two sentences. "This year we are here [in Babylonia], next year in the land of Israel; this year we are slaves, next year free. Let all those who are hungry come and eat, let all those who are in need come and celebrate the Passover with us." The introductory sentence, "This is the bread of affliction . . . ," is not mentioned in his text.

It seems that in Rav Saadiah's time the matzah was broken at the beginning of the meal, prior to the *motzi*, rather than at the beginning of the Seder. In the absence of a broken matzah, a reference to "this bread of affliction" would have been incongruous.

The phrase *kol ditzrich yete veyifsach* was patterned after a similar phrase coined by Rav Huna (3rd cent.) According to the Talmud, whenever Rav Huna sat down to a meal he would open the door and declare: "Whosoever is in need let him come and eat" (*kol ditzrich yete veyechol, Taanit* 20b). Rav Huna had spent his early life in extreme poverty. When his fortunes improved he dedicated his means to the welfare of the poor.

With the reading of *Ho lachmo*, the leader concludes the preliminary section of the Haggadah. The child's interest has been aroused by the dipping of the greens, the breaking of the matzah, the filling of a second cup of wine, and the temporary removal of the Passover plate (it is restored after the four questions). He is now ready to proceed with his questions. The mitzvah of *vehigadeta* ("you shall instruct") is fulfilled by the father's answer, which begins with *Avadim hayinu* ("we were slaves").

MISHNAIC GUIDELINE FOR THE HAGGADAH

The father's answer must conform to the following guideline: "He begins [the answer] with shame [a shameful or distressing period in Jewish history] and concludes with praise [gratitude to God for the delivery from oppression]; and expounds from 'A wandering Aramean was my father' [Deut. 26:5]" (*Pesachim* 116a).

The concise phraseology of this framework requires some elucidation. The Mishnah defines the dual character of the Seder. It is a memorial to Jewish suffering and degradation and also a victory feast. There are two facets to the "shame" and "praise" mentioned in the Mishnah. The physical phase encompasses slavery and emancipation; the spiritual phase, idolatry and monotheism.

The Mishnah does not spell out the particular historical incidents which illustrate the "shame" and the "praise." The deuteronomic verse "A wandering Aramean was my father," upon which the father must elaborate, deals with the physical enslavement and ultimate liberation of the Jewish people. The initial part of the father's answer must therefore relate to the spiritual phase of the "shame" and "praise" ("In early times our ancestors were idol-worshippers . . .").

The amoraim discussed the meaning of "shame." "What is 'shame'? Rav said that the answer should open with the statement: *mitechilah ovde avodah zara . . .* ['our ancestors were idol worshippers'].'' The emphasis is thus placed upon the early spiritual degradation. However, Rava (4th cent.) stated that one should begin with *Avadim hayinu . . .* ("we were slaves"). He apparently felt that the faith of our primitive progenitors was not relevant to the theme of Passover. By opening the answer with the story of slavery, Jews of all generations, victimized by oppression, could immediately identify with the Hebrew slaves in Egypt.

Since there was no clear-cut decision as to which opinion prevailed, both were incorporated into the Haggadah. The major part of the Haggadah was completed by the end of the fourth century. The editors wisely selected the portion dealing with slavery for its opening statement.

THE SPILLING OF DROPS OF WINE

It is customary to spill drops of wine when the Haggadah verse *Dam vaesh vetimrot ashan* ("blood, fire, and pillars of smoke") is recited. The same is true for the recitation of the ten plagues and the mnemonic *detzach, adash beachav,* in all, sixteen drops of wine. This custom is of kabbalist origin. It was said that the Ari (16th cent.) recommended that the wine be spilled into a broken vessel (which symbolizes the *klippah,* or impure shell) and that one pray, as he spills the wine, that the Almighty spare him from the plagues which afflicted the Egyptians.

There is no reference in early Haggadot to the custom of spilling wine. The earliest mention of the practice appeared in eighteenth-century Haggadot. A parchment Haggadah completed in 1731 alludes to the mystical significance of the spilled wine drops. As the custom spread, commentators offered various rationales. One widespread explanation was based on the opinion that Egyptian power was diminished with each plague, a process reflected by the decrease of wine in the cup (which, however, has to be refilled). Another explanation has a moral rationale—our cup of joy is diminished even when our enemies suffer.

BOILED EGGS

It is customary to serve boiled eggs for the first course of the Seder meal. Boiled eggs are traditionally served to mourners for the first meal of the shivah period. It has been assumed by some rabbinic scholars that this mournful ritual was introduced at the Seder in memory of the destruction of the Temple.

In support, it has been pointed out that the first day of Passover, Tisha B'Av, and the seventeenth of Tammuz all occur on the same day of the week, but this explanation has little merit. Grief and mourning are out of place in the joyous atmosphere of a Seder, and for this reason most rabbis have rejected the notion that a white robe is worn by the leader of the Seder because it resembles shrouds. A more likely explanation is the statement in the Jerusalem Talmud (quoted by *Kol Bo*) that an egg is included on the Passover plate because of the significance of its Aramaic name, *bea,* which means "desires." It is an allusion to God's desire to save his people. The ritual egg of the Passover plate is generally left uneaten because it represents a sacrificial offering of chaggigah. Other eggs are therefore served to indicate God's desire to help Israel.

MOTZI-MATZAH-MAROR

Normally one pronounces a single benediction over bread. However, on the Seder night, when the eating of matzah is a biblical obligation, there is an additional benediction, *al achilat matzah*. It is customary to hold the two and one-half matzot in one's hand when the *motzi* is recited. The two whole matzot meet the requirement of *lechem mishneh*. The broken matzah is sandwiched between the two whole matzot and remains invisible.

After the *motzi*, the leader puts down the bottom matzah and retains in his hand the one and one-half matzot over which he pronounces the benediction of *achilat matzah*. He then breaks off a piece of the upper and middle matzot and eats them. All the participants do likewise.

The next ritual is the dipping of maror in charoset (second dipping) and the benediction of *achilat maror*. In the Temple era the mitzvah of eating matzah and maror was performed at the end of the meal, when the paschal lamb was served for the last course of the meal. However, after the destruction of the Temple and the elimination of the paschal lamb, the mitzvah of eating matzah, which is still a biblical injunction even in the absence of a paschal lamb, is performed at the outset of the meal. The mitzvah of eating maror, now only a rabbinical injunction, is also performed at the outset of the meal. Matzah and maror were always considered joint mitzvot.

Were matzah and maror eaten simultaneously in the Temple era, or consecutively? In Hillel's opinion the two should be eaten at the same time. It was therefore his practice to wrap the lettuce around the matzah and eat them together (*Pesachim* 115a). This procedure could no longer be followed in the post-Temple era, due to the basic rule that a mitzvah of biblical origin may not be combined with one of rabbinical origin. It is therefore our practice to eat matzah and maror separately and to pronounce a distinct benediction over each. However, having done that, we pay respect to the memory of Hillel by eating the two together (*korech*).

It is customary to use the bottom matzah in the performance of the ritual of *korech*, so that each of the three matzot may serve a religious purpose. This practice was instituted in the eleventh century. A secondary custom, deriving from this practice, is to place each matzah in a separate pocket of the matzah cover or to insert napkins between each matzah. Thus we indicate that each has a distinct religious function to fulfill.

AFIKOMAN

The broken matzah set aside at the beginning of the Seder is produced at the end of the meal and distributed to all the participants. No solid food may be eaten after that.

In the Temple era the paschal lamb was the dessert, or concluding course, of the meal (*Pesachim* 119b). After the destruction of the Temple, the matzah served as the dessert (*afikoman*, ibid.). The eating of the afikoman constitutes the principal fulfillment of the biblical injunction to eat matzah.

The identity of the afikoman with the paschal lamb was the basis for the opinion of some medieval sages that the laws which regulate the eating of the paschal lamb are equally applicable to the eating of the afikoman. It was therefore ruled that the afikoman, like the paschal lamb, may not be eaten after midnight.

THE CUP OF ELIJAH

After the drinking of the third cup of wine, upon the conclusion of *Birkat HaMazon*, one fills a special cup which had been empty until this time. This cup is known as the Cup of Elijah. When the cup is filled, the door is opened and the participants read the passage of *Shefoch chamatcha* ("pour out thy wrath . . ."; Ps. 79:6–7, 69:25; Lam 3:66). This impressive little ceremony, between the third and fourth cups, needs elucidation.

What is the purpose and origin of the Cup of Elijah? Is it linked to the prayer of *Shefoch chamatcha?* What is the significance of the opening of the door?

The popular explanation of the Cup of Elijah leaves much to be desired. The origin of this cup is commonly traced to a talmudic controversy regarding the number of cups which one should drink at the Seder. The talmudic text in our possession makes no mention of a fifth cup. However, Alfasi quotes an opinion by Rabbi Tarfon that one should drink a fifth cup (*Pesachim* chap. 10, gemara on the fifth mishnah). According to Rav Saadiah Gaon (10th cent), four cups are obligatory, the fifth is optional. Rav Hai Gaon (10th–11th cent.) opposed a fifth cup.

The controversy was never resolved. It is said that in an effort to comply with both opinions, it was decided to fill a fifth cup but not to drink it. The special cup was in time named the Cup of Elijah, a reference to a talmudic tradition that Elijah will appear someday to resolve all moot questions.

This contrived explanation is unsatisfactory for several reasons. If the Cup of Elijah constitutes a fifth cup, it should be filled after the fourth cup, not the third. Why does the passage of *Shefoch chamatcha* follow the filling of this cup?

The Cup of Elijah undoubtedly signifies the anticipated coming of the prophet for whom the cup is prepared. This anticipation is partly based on the traditional character of the Seder night as a *leil shimurim* ("a night of watching unto the Lord"; Exod. 12:42). According to the Talmud, Jews are under the constant protection of God on this night (*Rosh HaShanah* 11b). Elijah, the protector of Israel, has a special function to perform in the "night of watching."

There is an added tradition that the future deliverance of the Jewish people will take place in the month of Nisan (ibid.). In the talmudic lexicon, "future deliverance" refers to the coming of the Messiah and of Elijah, who is to precede him (Mal. 3:23). A liturgical poem entitled *Leil Shimurim*, written for the Passover evening service, expresses the hope that the footsteps of the messenger (Elijah) will once again be heard on the night of watching (*Machzor Vitry* 446).

The name Elijah's Cup does not appear in the medieval literature. However, the cup was symbolically filled for Elijah as an expression of faith in his coming. To demonstrate that faith, one opened the door when the cup was filled. It was truly an act of faith and courage for a medieval Jew to open his door on Passover night.

The illuminated Washington Haggadah (1470) is indeed very illuminating in this respect. On the page of *Shefoch chamatcha* there is a large drawing of Elijah riding a donkey. As he passes, a Jew stands in an open doorway, holding a cup of wine to welcome the prophet. The cup was actually filled for the heavenly guest, whose arrival was duly expected.

Why was the Cup of Elijah filled after the third cup? The third cup is drunk soon after *Birkat HaMazon*. According to an ancient tradition, Elijah will not appear on the Sabbath or a holiday because he does not wish to disrupt the preparations for the festival or the eating of the festival meal (*Eruvin* 43b). The earliest possible moment when Elijah might be expected on a Seder night was after *Birkat HaMazon*. Furthermore, its prayer "May the Merciful send unto us the Prophet

Elijah . . ." might have been another reason for the timing of the Cup of Elijah.

SHEFOCH CHAMATCHA

One of Elijah's functions in the future redemption is to punish the tormentors of Israel (see above, chap. 3). The recitation of *Shefoch chamatcha*, a stirring and pathetic outcry of a martyred people, was therefore timed to coincide with his anticipated arrival.

Shefoch chamatcha was included in *Machzor Vitry* (completed 1208). That version opens with the three verses of our modern texts (Ps. 79:6–7, 69:25). These are followed by six verses which have been omitted from subsequent texts (Ps. 69:26, 35:5–6, 28:4, 5:11; Hosea 9:14). The concluding verse is the same as ours (Lam. 3:66). *Machzor Vitry* instructs the reader to recite *Shefoch chamatcha* after *Birkat HaMazon*. However, it does not link this prayer to the Cup of Elijah.

One of the three extant manuscripts of *Seder Rav Amram Gaon* (in the British Museum) mentions *Shefoch chamatcha*. This would seem to advance the origin of the prayer to the ninth century. However, its omission in the other manuscripts and in the later *Siddur Rav Saadiah Gaon* (10th cent.) leads to the conclusion that its inclusion in the British Museum version was a later interpolation, leaving *Machzor Vitry* as the earliest source.

Shefoch chamatcha did not gain immediate acceptance. The early reluctance was probably due to a justifiable fear that the vehemence of *Machzor Vitry*'s long text might provoke a hostile Gentile reaction. One can only sympathize with the pent-up anger of the author of *Machzor Vitry*, a contemporary of the Crusades. The same is true of Rabbi Nissim Gerondi (Ran), a contemporary of Barcelona's Black Death massacres in 1348. He, too, strongly urged all Jews to recite the prayer of *Shefoch chamatcha* (quoted by Rema, *Orach Chaim* 480).

Early Haggadot limited *Shefoch chamatcha* to the first verse only (Washington Haggadah, 1470; *HaMachzor Roma Haggadah*, 1540; Venice Haggadah, 1609). However, Rema's approval of the prayer in his annotations to the code (*Orach Chaim* 480) gave it widespread popularity. Rema stated that the opening of the door was a demonstration of faith in the coming of the Messiah. God will reward such faith by sending the Messiah to pour out his wrath on the oppressors. The link between Elijah and *Shefoch chamatcha* was thus clearly established.

Seventeenth-century Haggadot condensed the original *Shefoch chamatcha* to four verses. The condensed version has been reprinted ever since. Curiously, a Bene Israel Haggadah, printed in 1846, contains only the first two verses in its text.

IV.
PASSOVER DAY CUSTOMS

HALLEL

One recites the complete *Hallel* (Pss. 113–118) at the morning service on the first two days of Passover. Beginning with the third day, to the end of the holiday, the paragraphs of *Lo lanu* (Ps. 115:1–11) and *Ahaveti* (Ps. 116:1–11) are omitted.

The traditional explanation for these deletions is based on the following talmudic statement: "The angels wanted to chant their hymns [when the Jews crossed the sea] but the Holy One, blessed be he, said: 'The work of my hands is being drowned, shall you chant hymns?' " (*Megillah* 10b). The rabbis conveyed a moral principle. Rejoicing is offensive when victory is attained at the cost of the enemy's life. The partial *Hallel* is commonly known as "half-*Hallel*."

The omission of parts of chapters 115 and 116 (the first eleven verses of each) was intended to reflect a diminishment of one's joy. However, there appears to be no reason for diminishing one's joy on Passover, prior to the seventh day, when the Egyptians drowned. Nevertheless the half-*Hallel* restriction was extended to Chol HaMoed in order to avoid creating the impression that Chol HaMoed is more sacred than the last days of Passover (Taz, *Orach Chaim* 490).

A third-century Palestinian list of holidays on which *Hallel* is recited is mentioned in the Talmud (*Taanit* 28b). It includes the first two days of Passover, Shavuot, Sukkot, and Chanukah. We may assume that *Hallel* was not recited at all at other festival services. The reason for the differentiation between Passover and Sukkot, with regard to *Hallel*, is explained by the fact that the sacrificial rituals of Passover were uniform on every day of the holiday. This gave Passover a single identity, calling for a single *Hallel* (*Arachin* 10b).

The Babylonian diaspora adopted at the same time the practice of reciting *Hallel* on every day of Passover and on Rosh Chodesh. To avoid a conflict with the Palestinian list, the custom of skipping (*dilug*) some parts of *Hallel* was instituted (*Taanit* 28b). The Talmud does not designate the parts which were skipped.

Rav Saadiah Gaon (10th cent.) mentioned the following omissions: *Lo lanu* (Ps. 115:1–11), *Ahaveti* (Ps. 116:1–11), and four verses of *Ma ashiv* (Ps. 116:14–17). The last omission was not accepted by medieval custom.

Rav Saadiah Gaon did not explain why these particular parts were selected for omission. An analysis of the content of these verses reveals it to be supplicatory rather than laudatory. Since *Hallel* was not considered obligatory on Chol HaMoed and Rosh Chodesh, the supplicatory verses were omitted because they did not conform to the festive spirit of the holiday.

The association of the half-*Hallel* with the drowning of the Egyptians was first mentioned in the thirteenth century (*Shibole HaLeket*). Sympathy for the Egyptian victims may be a reason for not rejoicing, but it hardly explains why the supplicatory parts of the psalms should be omitted.

THE PRAYER FOR DEW

Palestine's rainy season ends on Passover. Thereafter, rain is considered harmful. The seasonal prayer for rain (*mashiv haruach*) which is daily recited from Shemini Atzeret on, is discontinued on Passover. A prayer for summer dew (*tal*) is substituted.

The prayer for dew injects into the festive tone of the holiday liturgy a mood of solemnity, normally associated with a period of judgment. Passover, according to the Talmud, is the time when God blesses the crops (*Rosh HaShanah* 16a). In keeping with this spirit, it is customary for the chazan to don a white robe for the Musaf service of the first day of Passover.

THE PRIESTLY BENEDICTION

For a discussion of this ritual, see chapter 8.

THE COUNTING OF THE OMER

The Omer, a measure of the newly harvested barley, was brought to the Temple on the second day of Passover. On the evening of the same day, the countdown for Shavuot begins. Shavuot does not have a fixed calendrical date. Only the span of time between Passover and Shavuot is fixed. It was therefore important that every Jew count "from the morrow after the Sabbath . . . seven weeks" (Lev. 23:15).

According to the Sadducees, the Sabbath mentioned in Leviticus is synonymous with Saturday. It was therefore their practice to count the number of days which had elapsed from the Sunday of Passover. The rabbis, however, interpreted "the Sabbath" to mean "a day of rest," a designation applicable to the first day of Passover. They therefore counted the number of days which had elapsed since the Omer. (For a discussion of the term *shabbat,* see above, chap. 5).

In addition to the injunction in Leviticus (23:16) which mandates the counting of fifty days, there is a second injunction in Deuteronomy (16:9) which mandates the counting of seven weeks. One must therefore keep a count of the days as well as the weeks. Thus, upon reaching the seventh day, it is customary to mention that it is the seventh day, making one week of the Omer. The number of the *sefirah* ("counting") must be understood by every Jew. It was therefore customary in the days of Rav Saadiah Gaon (10th cent.) to count in Aramaic, the language in which most people were conversant. The counting is preceded by a benediction, *Baruch . . . al sefirat HaOmer.*

The counting of the Omer was mandatory only in the Temple era. However, the rabbis retained the custom in memory of the Temple.

V.
THE LAST DAY OF PASSOVER

YIZKOR

Yizkor services are conducted on the last day of Passover. (For a discussion of this ritual, see chap. 8.)

HAVDALAH

Havdalah is recited at the end of Maariv on the second and eighth days of Passover. The candle ritual, a prominent feature of Havdalah at the end of the Sabbath, is omitted on holidays. Lighting of candles is permitted on holidays and a Havdalah candle would not indicate the end of the holiday. The benediction of *besamim* ("spices") is also omitted. According to tradition, the soul is not weakened by the departure of the holiday, as it is on the Sabbath, and therefore does not require spices to restore its vigor.

POST-PASSOVER CHAMETZ

Chametz may not be acquired prior to the expiration of Passover. This law created a problem for some Jews in the Middle Ages. Friendly Gentiles made it a custom to deliver chametz to their Jewish neighbors late in the afternoon of the last day of Passover. A rejection of the gift would have insulted the Christians at a time when good relations had to be carefully cultivated. The rabbis ruled that the chametz could be accepted and put in a place where it would not be seen. There must be a mental proviso, however, not to acquire ownership of the chametz before the end of the holiday (Avudrahim).

8

Shavuot Customs

I.
INTRODUCTION

THE BIBLICAL FESTIVAL of Shavuot was an agricultural holiday marking the beginning of the harvest season of wheat and fruit. This motif was reflected in the two names by which the festival was identified: Chag HaKatzir ("the feast of harvest"; Exod. 23:16) and Yom HaBikkurim ("the day of the first fruit"; Num. 28:26). The name Shavuot ("Weeks"; Exod. 34:22) is a calendrical index, referring to the seven weeks which must elapse from the sixteenth of Nisan, the day when the Omer (a measure of barley) was brought to the Temple (Deut. 16:9).

Shavuot, like Passover and Sukkot, was declared a *mikra kodesh* ("a proclamation of holiness"; Lev. 23:4—the definition of this term is discussed in chap. 3). The three pilgrimage festivals have in common identical provisions for feasting and the same prohibitions of labor which are applicable to days of rest.

In one respect Shavuot differs from Passover and Sukkot. The latter have distinctive rituals which are not based on the Temple. The Seder and matzot, the sukkah and lulav are permanent mitzvot. On the other hand, the ritual ceremonies of Shavuot were exclusive to the Temple.

The primary ritual of Shavuot was a "new meal-offering" (*minchah chadashah*, Lev. 23:16), which consisted of two loaves of bread baked from flour of the new crop of wheat. The technical designation of this offering was *lechem tenufah* ("wave-loaves"; Lev. 23:17). This name paralleled the designation of the Omer, which was called *Omer-tenufah* ("the sheaf of waving"; Lev. 23:15). The waving of an offering was, according to the Talmud, a prayerful act, imploring God to contain harmful winds and bad weather conditions (*Menachot* 62a). The Shavuot wave-loaves invoked God's blessing of fruit (*Rosh HaShanah* 16a).

245

The second Shavuot ritual was an offering of bikkurim ("first fruits"; Deut. 26:1–11). The period in which bikkurim may be brought to the Temple was elastic, from Shavuot to Sukkot (*Bikkurim* 1:6). Fruit began to ripen in the Shavuot season and was available in time for Shavuot pilgrims. However, the number of Shavuot pilgrims was considerably smaller than the number of pilgrims on the other two festivals. Some Jews must have regarded the interval between Passover and Shavuot as too short to accommodate two pilgrimages. Furthermore, Shavuot was celebrated at the peak of a farmer's busy season, forcing many of them to stay home. This consideration might have been a factor in the extended bikkurim deadline, from Shavuot to Sukkot.

Both Shavuot rituals were suspended after the destruction of the Temple. The Sanhedrin of Usha (convened in 140) introduced a new historical Shavuot motif, the anniversary of the Sinaitic revelation (see Bloch, *Biblical and Historical Background of the Jewish Holy Days*, pp. 187, 188).

With the introduction of a new motif, the former agricultural facets of Shavuot were practically erased. In this respect, too, Shavuot differs from the other pilgrimage festivals, which have retained vestiges of their ancient agricultural character. Thus on Passover we still pray for *tal* ("dew") and on Sukkot for *geshem* ("rain"), climatic conditions which were vital to the farmers of Judea.

The reasons for these divergent developments lie in the transcendence of Torah in Jewish life. The traditional preoccupation with the Law was so pervasive that it became the sole focus of intellectual pursuit. In a celebration of the Sinaitic revelation there was little room for commemorations of historical aspects which are only of academic interest.

Yet the memory of the ancient Shavuot was by no means totally obliterated, even though it has been obscured. Thus there is a reminder of the Jewish agricultural society in the Torah portion which is read on the second day of Shavuot: "Seven weeks shalt thou number unto thee; from the time the sickle is first put to the standing corn" (Deut. 16:9). The Musaf *Amidah* includes the biblical text pertaining to the offering of bikkurim. The reading of the Book of Ruth and the flowers and plants which decorate the synagogues are reminders of bucolic scenes from the distant past.

In modern Israel, the original agricultural motif of Shavuot is once again given great prominence, albeit within a secularist framework. Many kibbutzim have introduced folk festivities with baskets of fruit and flowers for centerpieces.

PRE-SHAVUOT CUSTOMS

The mourning customs of the Sefirah period taper off beginning with Rosh Chodesh Sivan. Fasting is prohibited until the ninth of Sivan (in the Sephardic ritual until the thirteenth). *Tachanun* (a penitential prayer) is omitted from the daily service until the ninth of Sivan.

SHELOSHET YEMEI HAGBALAH

The three days preceding Shavuot (beginning with the third of Sivan) are known as Sheloshet Yemei Hagbalah ("three days of limitation"; Exod. 19:10–12). This period commemorates the anticipation of the Sinaitic revelation and the limitations imposed upon the Jews in Sinai, in preparation for the momentous occasion. They were restricted from climbing Mount Sinai and from having sexual intercourse. According to the Talmud, they were also ordered to bathe in order to be ritually clean (*Yevamot* 46b).

The Sheloshet Yemei Hagbalah took on semi-festival status in the post-talmudic era. The Sefirah prohibitions of hair-cutting and nuptial celebrations, introduced in the eleventh century, are relaxed beginning with the third of Sivan.

ATTIRE AND APPEARANCE

Customs pertaining to attire and appearance on the Sabbath are also observed on Shavuot. (See above, chap. 3.)

IMMERSION

Some rabbis have stressed the importance of immersion in preparation for Shavuot in commemoration of the immersion of the Jews prior to the Sinaitic revelation (*Baer Hetev, Orach Chaim* 494:7).

GREENERY

Before the use of wooden floors, it was customary to spread grass on the floors of the synagoguge and private homes. The synagogue was also decorated with plants and flowers. This custom was first mentioned by Maharil (14th–15th cent.) and popularized by Rema (16th cent.).

According to Rema, the custom of spreading greenery on Shavuot was introduced in commemoration of the pastoral scene in the vicinity of Mount Sinai, as evidenced by the biblical reference to the grazing of cattle near the mountain. This explanation is questionable. The desert of Sinai is not overly distinguished for its flora and vegetation. It is more likely that the custom was instituted in commemoration of the rural atmosphere of the biblical "Festival of Harvest."

In the period when Jews remained close to the soil, engaging in farming and the 'cultivation of vineyards, the flavor of the biblical Shavuot was to some degree retained in the diaspora. With the expulsion of Jews from the Western countries and the widespread restriction of the right of Jews to own land, they gradually lost touch with the soil. The narrow alleys of the ghetto were rarely embellished by colorful foliage. Changed conditions created a desire for an artificial reproduction of the atmosphere of the Festival of Harvest. This fact may account for the late emergence of the custom of greenery.

In addition to the use of grass and flowers for decorative purposes, tall plants were added in the eighteenth century to create the appearance of an arboretum. The Gaon of Vilna objected to this innovation as an imitation of Christian practices. Nevertheless, the custom persisted and leading rabbis found a basis for it in ancient Jewish tradition. Shavuot is a day of heavenly judgment of fruit (*Rosh HaShanah* 16a). The sight of plants will move the congregation to pray for God's blessing of the fruit (*Magen Avraham, Orach Chaim* 494:5).

Shelah (16th cent.) mentioned a Palestinian Sephardic practice to distribute myrtles to worshippers on Shavuot morning so that they may smell the aroma. This custom might have been inspired by a midrashic allusion to the aromatic air of the Jewish encampment at Mount Sinai (*Shir HaShirim Rabbah* on 1:12).

II.
SHAVUOT EVE CUSTOMS

MAARIV

The Shavuot night Maariv follows the order of all festival evening services. Shavuot is described in the *Amidah* and in Kiddush as *zeman matan Toratenu* ("the time of the giving of our Torah").

It is customary to delay the evening service until dark to make sure that the Kiddush will be chanted after the stars have emerged. Thus we fulfill the biblical command that "seven complete weeks" (Lev. 23:15) elapse from the sixteenth of Nisan.

A WAKEFUL NIGHT

The practice of staying awake through the first night of Shavuot was first mentioned in the Zohar (Lev. 98; published in the 13th cent.). The Zohar attributed this custom to *chasidei kadmai* ("early zealots"). However, there is no evidence to corroborate the existence of such a practice in ancient times.

Subsequent commentators have explained this custom by the need for being awake at the exact moment when the Sinaitic revelation took place. According to a midrashic tradition, the Jews had fallen asleep on the night preceding the revelation and Moses had to wake them after God had already appeared on the mountain (*Shir HaShirim Rabbah* on 1:12). The wakeful night is in the nature of an atonement for the oversight of our ancestors.

The practice of staying up on Shavuot night had a special appeal for the kabbalists. The Ari (16th cent.) said that he who participates in this custom may feel assured that no harm will befall him before the end of the year.

A special Shavuot night service, known as *Seder Tikkun Leil Shavuot*, was composed by Rabbis Solomon Alkabetz and Joseph Caro (16th cent.) and supplemented by Shelah (16th–17th cent.). It contains brief selections from each portion of the Pentateuch. This is followed by excerpts from Joshua, Judges, Samuel, Kings, Isaiah, Jeremiah, Ezekiel, Hosea, Habakkuk, all of Ruth, Psalms, Job, Proverbs, Ecclesiastes, Song of Songs, Lamentations, Daniel, Esther, Chronicles, and Ezra. In addition it includes selections from the six talmudic divisions, the kabbalist *Sefer Yetzirah*, the Zohar, and an enumeration of the 613 mitzvot (according to Maimonides' version).

III.
SHAVUOT DAY CUSTOMS

THE BOOK OF RUTH

The custom of reading the Book of Ruth on Shavuot dates from the talmudic era. The practice seems to have been well established by the time of Rabbi Tanchuma, a Palestinian amora of the fourth century. According to Rabbi Tanchuma, the object of the reading of Ruth is to point out a similarity in the backgrounds of Ruth and the Jews who had received the Torah. Ruth had suffered trials and tribulations before her conversion to Judaism. The Jews who stood at Mount Sinai had also been subjected to much suffering and oppression before receiving the Law (*Yalkut Shimoni* 596).

The message of Rabbi Tanchuma's comment was an admonition to Jews of all generations that allegiance to the Torah frequently entails anguish and pain and that one must be prepared to pay the price for bearing the word of God. Rabbi Tanchuma was a famous homilist and his message is a fitting example of his expertise in the field of homiletics. However, it is doubtful whether one can find in his comment the historical reason for the reading of Ruth on Shavuot.

Avudrahim (14th cent.) suggested two historical explanations. Ruth came to Bethlehem "in the beginning of the barley harvest season" (Ruth 1:22). The harvest season, according to Avudrahim, coincides with Shavuot. It is therefore appropriate to read the Book of Ruth on Shavuot, the anniversary of her arrival in Bethlehem. Our only reservation about his suggestion is the assumption of a coincidence of time. The barley harvest begins at the Passover season, whereas Shavuot marked the beginning of the wheat harvest. Avudrahim's second explanation for the association of Ruth with Shavuot is based on the propriety of reading the story of Ruth's conversion to Judaism on the anniversary of the Sinaitic revelation.

Subsequent commentators attributed the link between Ruth and Shavuot to the fact that Ruth was the ancestress of King David (Ruth 4:22). According to a talmudic tradition, David died on Shavuot (*Yalkut Shimoni* 735).

It is our custom to read the Book of Ruth on the second day of Shavuot, prior to the reading of the Torah. That was not always the practice. According to *Masechet Soferim* (edited in the eighth cent.), the first half of Ruth should be read at the end of the first day of Shavuot, and the second half at the end of the second day. However, it noted a common practice to read the book at the end of the Sabbath preceding Shavuot.

AKDAMOT

It was customary in the Middle Ages to translate the Shavuot Torah portion into Aramaic for the benefit of worshippers who did not understand the Hebrew text. The need for a translation derived from the intrinsic significance of the Sinaitic revelation in the Jewish religion. Accordingly, the Aramaic translation was read alternately after each verse (*Machzor Vitry* 299, 12th cent.). This custom emerged first in Babylonia, where Jews were conversant in Aramaic.

An introduction to the Aramaic translation of the text was added in the eleventh century when Rabbi Meir b. Isaac Nehorai of Orleans composed a prefatory Aramaic hymn named *Akdamot millin* ("At the beginning of his words"). The poem is a paean of praise to God, creator of heaven and earth, who has chosen Israel to give them the Torah. It is therefore their duty to proclaim the majesty of God to the nations of the world. Israel has paid a price for this mission, but the day of redemption is close at hand.

After the inclusion of the hymn into the liturgy, the following custom was adopted by most congregations. The kohen pronounced the Torah benediction, following which the reader read the first verse of the portion (Exod. 19:1). Upon his conclusion, the poem of *Akdamut* was chanted, followed by a reading of the Aramaic translation of the first verse of the portion. Thereafter, the alternate reading and translation of each verse was continued to the end.

Most European Jews were not conversant in Aramaic. Nevertheless, the custom of reading an Aramaic translation persisted for some time for the sake of preserving a traditional practice. The author of *Machzor Vitry* (12th cent.) included the Aramaic translation in his book. He prefaced the translation with an announcement which was to be read to the congregation. The announcement was intended to alert the worshippers that the Decalogue was about to be read. Interestingly, the announcement was written in pure Hebrew because the congregants no longer understood the Aramaic version.

The Aramaic translation was still part of the ritual in the fourteenth century (*Kol Bo* 52). However, due to the acknowledged ignorance of that language, the rabbis instituted an additional translation and interpretation of the Decalogue in the vernacular.

The Aramaic translation was eventually eliminated, but the chanting of *Akdamot*, which had become very popular, was retained. However, beginning with the seventeenth century, *Akdamot* was chanted prior to the kohen's recitation of the first benediction so as not to interrupt the reading of the Torah.

A brief Aramaic hymn, *Yatziv pitgam* ("True are the words"), is chanted on the second day of Shavuot, at the conclusion of the first verse of the Haftarah.

Akdamot was never part of the Sephardic ritual. Rav Saadiah Gaon (10th cent.) mentioned a custom of reading *azharot* (poems listing various mitzvot of the Torah). The *azharot* which were composed by the noted poet Solomon Ibn Gabirol (11th cent.) were adopted into the Sephardic ritual. Poems pertaining to positive biblical commandments are read at the conclusion of Musaf of the first day. Poems dealing with negative injunctions are read on the second day.

THE DECALOGUE

It is customary for the congregation to rise when the Decalogue is read on Shavuot morning. Strange as it may seem, there was initial rabbinical opposition to this practice. The objection was based on a talmudic opposition to the inclusion of the Decalogue in the daily congregational liturgy.

The Decalogue had been part of the liturgy of the Temple morning service, preceding the recitation of the *Shema*. When it was suggested that the same order be followed outside of the Temple (probably after its destruction) the rabbis demurred, due to allegations of *minim* (Hebrew Christians) that the entire Pentateuch had lost its validity, except for the Decalogue (Samuel, 3rd cent. amora, *Berachot* 12a). To counter the allegation of the *minim*, the Decalogue was omitted from the daily order of the service.

Despite the initial opposition, the custom of rising for the reading of the Decalogue became firmly established. It was felt that the special honor accorded to this passage was permissible so long as it was done within the context of the regular reading of the Torah.

The Decalogue has also been included by some kabbalists in the *Keriat Shema* prayer prior to the retirement for the night (*Siddur Shelah*).

YIZKOR

Yizkor (memorial) services are conducted in the Ashkenazic ritual on Yom Kippur and on the last days of the pilgrimage festivals. The solemn mood of Yizkor is in full harmony with the austere spirit of Yom Kippur. However, Yizkor seems incongruous in the festive atmosphere of holidays, when sadness is normally eschewed. The paradox is particularly conspicuous in Israel, where Yizkor stands out in stark contrast to the joyous customs of Simchat Torah. One may justly wonder why Yizkor came to be associated with holidays and what historical process is responsible for it.

The modern version of Yizkor dates from the latter part of the sixteenth century. Its origin, however, may be traced to the Talmud, and its roots lie in the Bible. There are several reasons why an individual may feel inclined to mention the names of departed forebears in his prayers: (1) to recall virtues of ancestors for whose sake

God may favor their descendants; (2) to pray that God forgive ancestral sins which bring punishment upon their offspring; (3) to pray to God that he forgive ancestral sins so that their souls may attain repose in the hereafter. We will explore the historical backgrounds of these motivations.

ZECHUT AVOT

The Judaic doctrine of *zechut avot,* according to which children are rewarded for the virtues of their ancestors, is firmly based on several pentateuchal sources: "And showing mercy unto the thousandth generation of them that love me and keep my commandments" (Exod. 20:6, Deut. 5:10); "The Lord, the Lord, God merciful and gracious, long suffering and abounding in goodness and truth. Keeping mercy unto the thousandth generation, forgiving iniquity and sin . . . " (Exod. 34:6–7); ". . . the faithful God who keeps covenant and mercy with them that love him and keep his commandments to a thousand generations" (Deut. 7:9). The first quotation is from the Decalogue and represents God's own declaration of his attributes. The second and third quotations are from pronouncements by Moses and represent his perception of God's attributes.

The promise of a reward for children for the virtues of their ancestors seems to be qualified in the Decalogue by the clause which reads "of them that love me," i.e., if the children are also God-fearing, their reward is enhanced because of the added merit of their parents. Is parental virtue also an extenuating factor in the judgment of wicked children? That appears to have been the view of Moses when he recalled the merit of the patriarchs in his plea for mercy for the worshippers of the golden calf (Exod. 32:13). Indeed, the qualifying phrase "of them that love me" was omitted by Moses from his pronouncement of the doctrine of transferal of parental merit to their children (Exod. 34:7).

The Talmud seems to uphold the view that the qualifying clause in the Decalogue does not refer to the children and hence does not limit the transferal of virtue to righteous children only. " 'To them that love me,' that is Abraham our father" (*Mechilta* on Exod. 20:6, edited in the 2nd cent.). Accordingly, God promised that the credit of virtuous parents will accrue to all children for the sake of Abraham and other men of great merit.

Rabbi Jose b. Chanina (3rd–4th cent.) expressed a similar opinion. In his comment on the phrase *nose avon* ("forgiving sin"; Exod. 34:7), he

probed the literal meaning of the word *nose* ("carries"). "The sentence
does not read that he carries away sins but that he 'carries a sin.' The
Almighty snatches the record of one sin so that the virtues stand out in
the balance" (Jer. *Sanhedrin* 10:1).

This position was not upheld by the Qumran sect. The *Book of Hymns*
quotes the pronouncement of Moses (Exod. 34:7): "merciful, long
suffering and abounding in loving kindness and truth, forgiving
transgression . . ." It then interpolates the qualifying clause of the
Decalogue which Moses had omitted: "[unto them that love him] and
keep his commandments" (chap. 16). The hymn omits the phrase
"keeping mercy unto the thousandth generation" and reserves rewards only to those who keep his commandments and to penitents.

According to the rabbis, the virtues of departed pious men carry
greater weight than the virtues of the living. The reputation which the
departed left behind them is in no danger of ever being tarnished by
subsequent sins. "There were many contemporary righteous people in
the camp [when the transgression of the golden calf took place], yet he
[Moses] did not mention them but only the departed [the patriarchs]. If
not for them the Jews would have perished" (*Tanchuma, Ki Tisa* 24). In
another comment, the rabbis noted: "As soon as Moses mentioned the
merit of the patriarchs, God immediately responded: 'I have forgiven
as you have asked' " (*Deut. Rabbah* 3).

The merit of the patriarchs is stressed in the daily *Amidah*, which
opens with the benediction of *Avot*. The rabbis also noted the importance of the patriarchs in the context of judgment days. "Thus said
the Almighty to Israel: 'My children, if you wish to find merit in
judgment on this day, mention the merit of the patriarchs and you, too,
will be merited' " (*Lev. Rabbah* 29). The principle of *zechut avot* is also
reflected in the apocryphal Prayer of Manasses, for the contrite king
opens his prayer with an invocation to the "God of our fathers,
Abraham, Isaac and Jacob."

The redeeming power of *zechut avot* embraces all God-fearing
people, not only the patriarchs. Thus the rabbis declared: "Happy are
the righteous; not only do they acquire merit [for themselves] but they
bestow merit upon their children and children's children to the end of
all generations" (*Yoma* 87a).

There are enough precedents in Jewish tradition to warrant the
mentioning of one's departed parents in prayer, in the hope of deriving
the benefit of their merit. In addition, one may also appeal to departed
parents and invoke their names in prayer, in the hope that they will
intercede with God in behalf of their offspring (*Shabbat* 89b, *Taanit* 16a).

However, all such prayers are self-serving, and it is doubtful that they provided the background from which the stirring Yizkor prayer evolved.

A TRANSFERAL OF SIN

The second motivation, a prayer to be freed of punishment for sins committed by ancestors, also has ample basis in Jewish tradition. The doctrine of transferal of sins of parents to their descendants was proclaimed in the Bible (Exod. 20:5, 34:7; Deut. 5:9). There are strong indications that this doctrine was limited to the sin of idolatry, the context in which it was promulgated in the Decalogue, and in which, after the transgression of the golden calf, it was repeated by Moses. Furthermore, the severity of the doctrine is explained by the fact that God is an *El Kana* ("a jealous God"). This attribute is mentioned five times in the Bible (Exod. 20:5, 34:14; Deut. 4:24, 5:9, 6:15). In each case it is associated with the trangression of idolatry. Nachmanides, too, ascribed the severity of the punishment to the gravity of the sin of idolatry (on Exod. 20:5). However, the theory that the doctrine of transferal has a limited application is not reflected in the Talmud.

Due to the difficulty presented by this doctrine, from both the theological and the ethical point of view, the prophets and the rabbis softened its impact. Rabbi Jose bar Chanina, who had broadened the doctrine of transferal of virtue to include sinful children (see above), also modified the seemingly harsh doctrine of transferal of sin. "Four decrees were ordained by Moses, our teacher, for Israel. Four prophets came and annulled them. . . . Moses said: 'He visits the sins of parents on children.' Ezekiel came and annulled it. 'The soul that sins, it shall die' [Ezek. 18:4]" (*Makkot* 24a).

The allegation that it was Moses who originated the doctrine of transferal of sin is puzzling in view of its inclusion in the Decalogue. It is possible that Rabbi Jose assumed that Moses had expanded the doctrine to cover all violations, not only idolatry, and that it was the comprehensive doctrine that Ezekiel annulled. This explanation is questionable. There is no evidence that Moses ever attempted to broaden the doctrine. Indeed, there are indications to the contrary.

The Deuteronomic reassertion of the transferal of merit (7:9) is followed by a warning: "He repays them that hate him to their face, to destroy them" (7:10). However, the transferal of sin was not mentioned at all. A categorical new principle seems to have been proclaimed in the following verse: "The fathers shall not be put to death for the children, neither shall the children be put to death for the fathers" (Deut. 24:16). The Talmud gave this verse a legal interpretation: parents and children may testify against each other in a court of law. Yet the moral tone of the sentence is clear and emphatic.

A denial that children may suffer for the sins of parents was restated in II Kings 14:6, Jeremiah 31:29, and Ezekiel 18:18. Talmudic consensus limits the transferal of sins to instances where children persist in the evil ways of their fathers (*Mechilta* 20:8, *Yoma* 68a, Onkelos and Yonatan b. Uziel on Exod. 20:5).

Despite the narrowing down of the doctrine of transferal of sin, many people have accepted it in its most comprehensive connotation. This is also reflected in the apocryphal literature. Tobit prayed to God: "Punish me not for my sins and ignorance, and the sins of my fathers who have sinned before me" (chap. 3). Ben Sira declared: "The children of sinners are abominable children. . . . The inheritance of sinners' children shall perish, and their posterity shall have a perpetual reproach" (Ecclus. 41).

The rabbinical rationalization of the doctrine of transferal of sin has eliminated the need for any child to pray for exemption from punishment for ancestral sins. Indeed, this genre of prayer has practically disappeared from Jewish sacred literature and it could hardly have served as a model for Yizkor.

A PRAYER FOR THE REPOSE OF SOULS

It is the third motivation, a prayer that the souls of sinners may find repose in heaven, that ultimately developed into the modern Yizkor. The earliest mention of a prayer, or a sacrificial offering, for the forgiveness of departed sinners is found in the apocryphal II Maccabees (ca. 76–63 B.C.E.; chap. 12). After the defeat of Gorgias, the governor of Idumea, Judah and his men attended to the burial of the fallen Jewish soldiers. To their great dismay, they discovered pagan amulets under the coats of the soldiers. Their deaths were clearly in retribution for their sins. Nevertheless, Judah sent two thousand drachma to Jerusalem for the sacrifice of sin-offerings for the killed soldiers.

Judah's act of atonement for the dead appeared strange to the author of II Maccabees. He obviously assumed that man's fate in the hereafter is determined solely on the basis of deeds committed in his lifetime. However, he explained that Judah was motivated by a belief in resurrection (i.e., so that the killed soliders would be free of sin when they return to life). "For if he had not hoped that they that were slain should have risen again, it had been superfluous and vain to pray for the dead."

Several centuries later, a talmudic rabbi expressed an opposite view. Commenting on a verse in Deuteronomy (21:8): "Forgive, O Lord, thy people Israel whom thou hast redeemed," he stated: " 'Forgive thy people Israel' refers to the living. 'Whom thou has redeemed' refers to the dead. From this we learn that the living can redeem the dead. Hence our custom to mention the dead on Yom Kippur and to offer charity in their behalf. . . . One might think that charity does not redeem the dead, we learn otherwise from the phrase 'which thou has redeemed.' From this we infer that when charity is offered for them . . . they become clean and purified" (*Tanchuma, Vayelech* 1).

This midrashic passage established two principles. Prayers for the dead are effective and therefore one should pray for them on Yom Kippur. Prayers are more effective when associated with charity. Charity replaces the sin-offerings of the Temple. The importance of charity was also stressed in a scriptural text: "Charity delivers from death" (Prov. 10:2), i.e., from suffering in the hereafter after death. This interpretation of the verse was indicated in the Apocrypha. "Charity delivers from death, and suffers not to come with darkness" (Tobit, chap. 4). According to a talmudic interpretation, charity saves from an unnatural death and from the pains of hell (*Baba Batra* 10a).

The propriety of memorial prayers in conjunction with charitable contributions was thus established in *Tanchuma*, setting a precedent for Yizkor. The ancient prayer was confined to Yom Kippur. However, the Midrash also mentioned a custom of praying for the dead on Sabbaths, imploring God not to return the souls of the condemned to hell upon the expiration of the day of rest.

The source of these statements is the "new" or supplemental *Tanchuma*, which was edited approximately in the sixth century. It reflects a prevailing Palestinian custom of voluntary individual prayers for the dead. The custom did not spread to the diaspora, not even to neighboring Babylonia. *Siddur Rav Saadiah Gaon* (10th cent.) makes no mention of memorial prayers.

BEGINNINGS OF THE MODERN YIZKOR

The first Crusade (1096), which created thousands of Jewish martyrs, served as an incentive for the institution of memorial prayers in medieval German-Jewish communities. The names of the victims were inscribed in memorial books, and special prayers were recited on the Sabbaths between Passover and Shavuot (the period of Sefirah) for the repose of their souls. For the first time, liturgical authors introduced into a memorial prayer the phrase "may the soul be bound up in the bond of eternal life," which was to become standard in Yizkor and *Male Rachamim*. This phrase was originated by Abigail when she addressed King David and wished him long life upon this earth (I Sam. 25:29).

In addition to the memorial prayers for the martyrs whose names had been inscribed in the memorial books, a general prayer was composed for all martyrs who remained anonymous. This prayer, known as *Av HaRachamim*, implored God "to remember them for good with the other righteous of the world" and to avenge their deaths. The prayer was initially recited twice a year, on the Sabbaths preceding Shavuot and Tisha B'Av.

EMERGENCE OF YIZKOR

The gradual emergence of Yizkor is reflected in *Sefer HaChasidim* by Rabbi Judah HeChasid (d. 1217). The rabbi was a native of Speyer, Germany, the first city to be attacked by the Crusaders in 1096.

Rabbi Judah, an anthologist of Jewish ethical lore and customs, described the custom of a righteous Jew who offered charity in atonement for the souls of his kin. This was a departure from the prevailing practice of memorializing the souls of the victims of the Crusades. The martyrs were not in need of atonement because the manner of their deaths atoned for them. When the Jew was questioned about the reason for his innovation, he remarked that amongst his kin there were some righteous Jews whose merits benefited him. He would be an ingrate if he did not pray for the repose of their souls.

Rabbi Judah approved of the man's practice. He felt that it was in keeping with the talmudic tradition that the dead are in need of atonement (*Sifre* on Deut. 21:8) and that the offering of charity in their behalf is commendable (*Sefer HaChasidim* 170). His approval went a long way toward the popularization of memorial prayers.

When *Siddur Rashi* was written (12th cent.), the practice of making memorial contributions had become widespread. Thus it is stated in the siddur: "One makes a public contribution to charity in behalf of the dead and the living. However, in all of Germany, one does not contribute charity for the dead except on this day [Yom Kippur] alone" (214). What had started as an individual practice evolved, within a short period of time, into a congregational Yom Kippur ritual.

Machzor Vitry (12 cent.) quoted a midrashic passage (*Pesikta Rabbati* 20) which mentions the practice of praying for the dead on Sabbaths. It indicated that this be done after the prayer of *Mi sheberach avotenu*, when we pray for those who make contributions to the congregation or are active in congregational affairs. He recommended that we pray for community-minded people who are no longer among the living (190).

The next intermediary stage in the development of Yizkor was a newly adopted custom of making charitable contributions for the living on the three pilgrimage festivals. *Machzor Vitry* took note of this practice: "And charitable contributions are made in public [on the second day of Shavuot] for the living only because the Torah portion read on this day contains the phrase 'every man shall give as he is able' [Deut. 16:17]. Such is the custom on every last day of the holidays, when this portion is read, to give charity for the living only and not for the dead, so as not to grieve on a holiday" (312).

The final stage in the development of Yizkor shifts to Eastern Europe. Rema (16th cent.) included the custom of reciting Yizkor on Yom Kippur in his annotations to the code (*Orach Chaim* 621:3). The deteriorating position of Polish Jewry in the seventeenth century, and a new list of martyrs swelled by the Chmielnicki massacres, made Jews receptive to the new custom of reciting Yizkor on the pilgrimage festivals in addition to Yom Kippur. The charitable contributions normally made on those occasions were henceforth associated with the memorial prayers.

The *Levush* code (published in 1590) is the earliest source for the modern practice of Yizkor. It states: "It is our custom to memorialize souls on the holidays" (347). It repeated the reason offered by *Machzor Vitry* for the custom of making charitable contributions on holidays, except that the latter associated the charity with prayers for the living. Rabbi Shabbetai HaKohen (Shach) also approved of the recitation of Yizkor on the holidays (*Yoreh Deah* 347:3). His commentary was published in 1647, one year before the outbreak of the Chmielnicki pogroms.

It is customary for persons whose parents are alive to leave the synagogue for the duration of the Yizkor service. This practice was instituted so that those who had suffered bereavements should not be tempted to be envious of worshippers who do not recite Yizkor because their parents are alive. Some rabbinic scholars explain the practice of leaving the synagogue as a precaution against accidental recitations of Yizkor by worshippers who are not orphans.

In modern Israel, the traditional Yizkor service is also the occasion for memorial prayers for soldiers who gave their lives in defense of their country.

THE PRIESTLY BENEDICTION

The Priestly Benediction (*nesiat kapaim*), pronounced in the diaspora on all holidays, is an ancient ritual which survived the destruction of both Temples. It is based on the command to Aaron and his sons to bless the children of Israel (Num. 6:22–26). This command is appropriately followed by the chapter which deals with the dedication of the Tabernacle (Num. 7). The Priestly Benediction was performed first in the Tabernacle and later in the Temple.

All blessings emanate from God. Man's blessings are not self-fulfilling. They are merely prayers invoking God's blessings. This holds true even of the Priestly Benediction, which is couched in phrases that have been divinely prescribed. That is the significance of the biblical verse: "So shall they put my name upon the children of Israel, and I will bless them" (Num. 6:27).

God's first blessing was addressed to all the living creatures which he had created: "And God blessed them, saying: 'Be fruitful and multiply . . .' " (Gen. 1:22). This blessing was not different in substance from the previous divine commands issued in the course of the creation: "Let there be light" or "Let the earth put forth grass." However, the technical term "blessing" was not used on those occasions.

The creation of inanimate objects is completed with their emergence into existence. Thereafter they function automatically, governed by divinely programmed laws of nature. The performance of animate objects, however, is controlled by a free will. God's blessing constitutes a promise of assistance and support to those who make proper decisions and choose the right course.

Noah was the first biblical figure to express a blessing: "Blessed be the Lord, the God of Shem" (Gen. 9:26). Blessing God is merely an articulation of gratitude and praise. The first blessing addressed by one individual to another was uttered by Melchizedek, king of Salem, when he blessed Abraham (Gen. 14:19). Melchizedek, the Bible tells us, was a "priest of God" (Gen. 14:18). This comment, and the sequence of the verses, seems to imply that the function of blessing was the prerogative of priests.

God's early blessings were generally addressed to the procreation of the species (Gen. 1:22–28, 9:1). The same is true of God's blessing of

Abraham: "And I will make you a great nation, and I will bless you" (Gen. 12:2). The blessing of Sarah had a similar theme: "And I will bless her and she will be a mother of nations . . ." (Gen. 17:16). The second blessing of Abraham related to the same subject: "I will bless you and multiply your seed . . ." (Gen. 22:17). When Rebecca took leave of her family, "they blessed Rebecca and said unto her: 'Our sister, be thou the mother of thousands . . .' " (Gen. 24:60).

Abraham is not credited with having "blessed" anyone. Apparently he considered it a priestly function and left it to Melchizedek. Isaac received his first divine blessing after the death of Abraham (Gen. 25:11). The content of this blessing was not revealed. He received his second blessing after his encounter with King Abimelech, "And I will bless you and multiply your seed" (Gen. 26:24). Isaac was the first patriarch to bless his children (Gen. 27:27–29). This was a formal blessing which assumed the character of a last will and testament. It was not addressed to the proliferation of their progeny but to their prosperity and domination. In his informal blessing of Jacob, Isaac reverted to the theme of fruitfulness (Gen. 28:1–4).

When Jacob returned to Beth-El, he received God's first blessing: "Be fruitful and multiply . . ." (Gen. 35:9). In his blessing of Joseph and his sons, Jacob said: "Let them grow into a multitude in the midst of the earth" (Gen. 48:16).

After the Sinaitic revelation, the Jews received the following instruction: "An altar of earth thou shalt make unto me. . . . in every place where I cause my name to be mentioned, I will come unto you and bless you" (Exod. 20:21). God's blessings would henceforth be channelled through the Temple, and the kohanim would convey them.

An analysis of the early development of the use of blessings reveals the following: survival of the species was the prime concern and principal objective of the blessings; it was a priestly prerogative to dispense blessings; laymen gradually adopted this practice; it was common for parents to bless their children.

After the exodus, when the proliferation of the Jewish people had assured its physical existence, survival ceased to be the sole objective of God's blessing. Indeed the Priestly Blessing does not address itself to that subject. The traditional importance attached to the Priestly Benediction was due to the inherent promise that God will give this blessing due consideration.

The text of the Priestly Benediction is vague. It consists of six brief blessings couched in abstract terms of grace, illumination, and divine attention. Only the second and sixth blessings spell out specific

promises of protection and peace (Num. 6:24–26). The vagueness
might have been purposeful because the substance of God's blessing is
variable to fit exigencies of changing conditions.

The vagueness of the Hebrew text undoubtedly motivated the
rabbinic ban on giving the Priestly Benediction in the vernacular (*Sotah*
39b). A translation could not capture the exact nuance and subtlety of
the blessings and hence might prove misleading. For a similar reason
the Talmud prohibited the delivery of rabbinical interpretation of the
Priestly Benediction on the Sabbath when the portion of *Naso* is read in
public (*Megillah* 25b).

IN THE TEMPLE

The Priestly Benediction was pronounced in the Temple by kohanim
who assembled on a special platform *(duchan)*. Hence the vernacular
expression "to *duchan*," meaning to pronounce the benedictions.

It was customary for the kohanim to have their hands washed before
ascending the *duchan* (*Sotah* 39a). After they assembled on the platform, they faced the congregation and raised their hands above their
heads, where the *Shechinah* (God's spirit) was present in the Temple
(*Sotah* 38a). The raising of hands was a traditional prayerful posture
(Lev. 9:22).

The recitation of the benedictions was a daily ritual in the Temple.
The three verses which comprise the six benedictions were pronounced consecutively, without any pause at the end of each verse to
permit the congregation to respond Amen. The response of Amen was
not practiced in the Temple (Jer. *Taanit* 2).

IN THE POST-TEMPLE ERA

After the destruction of the Temple, the Priestly Benediction was
pronounced in synagogues. A number of changes were introduced in
the diaspora. The pronouncement was limited to holidays only. In
Jerusalem it is still recited once daily and twice on Sabbaths and
holidays. In the rest of Israel it is recited once on Sabbaths and
holidays.

Following a medieval custom, the kohanim part their fingers to form
an opening in the center of the hand, in the shape of a *V*, with two
digits on each side. Another gap is left between the digits and the
thumbs. When the two thumbs are joined at their tips, a total of five

gaps is created. This conforms to the midrashic interpretation of the scriptural verse: "He peers through the lattice [*hacharakim*]" (Song of Songs 2:9). The numerical value of *ha* is five.

Another change in the diasporic ritual was the height to which the kohanim raise their hands—up to the shoulders instead of above the head. Since the ineffable name of God, which was pronounced in the Temple in honor of the Shechinah, is no longer enunciated, it is not necessary to raise the hands to the higher level.

Beginning with the thirteenth century, the duty of washing the hands of the kohanim was assigned to the levites. The primary source for this custom is the Zohar. According to Maharil (14th–15th cent.), a firstborn may perform the function in the absence of levites.

Prior to the pronouncement of the Priestly Benediction, the kohanim recite a prayer: "Blessed art thou . . . who commanded us to bless his people Israel with love." Up to the second century this prayer was optional (*Sotah* 39a). The standard version of the prayer was published in the third century (ibid.).

Shortly after the destruction of the Temple, Rabban Yochanan b. Zakkai (1st cent.) ordained that the kohanim remove their shoes before the pronouncement of the Priestly Benediction (*Sotah* 40a). This was done to enhance the prestige and sanctity of the synagogue and as a demonstration of respect for the congregation.

Another diasporic change was the institution of pauses at the end of each of the three biblical verses, at which time the congregation responds Amen. The kohanim face the congregation, as was done in the Temple, but they must not look at the worshippers, nor may the worshippers look at the kohanim, so as to avoid distractions. The worshippers must face the kohanim and not stand in back of them (*Sotah* 38b).

The Priestly Benediction is pronounced at the end of the eighteenth benediction of the *Amidah*, the benediction of thanksgiving (*modim anachnu*). This association was based on a talmudic interpretation of a scriptural verse in Leviticus (9:22; *Megillah* 18a).

In a congregational service, the kohanim are prompted by the chazan, one benediction at a time. In that manner the kohanim will pronounce the proper benediction in its proper sequence. Before the recitation of the benedictions, the chazan alerts the kohanim by exclaiming in a loud voice "Kohanim!" This practice was instituted in talmudic times and continued through the geonic period.

In about the tenth century, a short prayer was added to the *Amidah* as an introduction to the Priestly Benediction, *Borechenu baberachah hameshuleshet* ("Bless us with the threefold blessing"). Initially, this prayer was recited by the chazan only when there were no kohanim present. The prayer thus took the place of the Priestly Benediction, which in effect was recited without the medium of kohanim. Eventually, the introductory prayer was adopted by medieval Jewish communities as a permanent part of the service, even when kohanim were present. There was therefore no longer any need to alert the Kohanim with a special exclamation by the chazan, inasmuch as the word *kohanim* is part of the last phrase of the prayer. However, the chazan still raises his voice when he reaches the last phrase. The prayer has become a permanent part of the daily liturgy in commemoration of the Priestly Benediction which was a daily ritual in the Temple.

SHAVUOT MENU

It is customary to serve dairy food on the first day of Shavuot. This medieval practice was based on the traditional simile which compares the Torah to milk and honey (Song of Songs 4:11).

Another medieval custom prescribed the baking of twin breads joined at the center (*Kol Bo* 52; 13th–14th cent.). The author suggested that this custom was adopted in remembrance of the two loaves of bread which were offered in the Temple on Shavuot (Lev. 23:16). It is also likely that the twin breads were designed to commemorate the two Tablets of the Law.

It is customary on Shavuot to serve triangular dumplings (kreplach) filled with cheese. This practice is part of the tradition of serving dairy on Shavuot. Rabbinic scholars suggested that the triangular shape of this delicacy reflects the three parts of the Bible: Torah, Prophets, and Hagiographa.

The number three seems to have had a special significance in Shavuot lore. Thus it was noted in the Talmud that God gave a threefold Torah to a threefold people (Kohanim, Levites, Israelites), through a third-born (Moses), on a third day *(sheloshet yeme hagbalah)*, in the third month (Sivan, *Shabbat* 88a). It is also mentioned in the Talmud that Rabbi Joseph used to order a third-born calf for his Shavuot meal (*Pesachim* 68b). It was assumed that his preference was based on the quality of the meat. However, one must not overlook the significance of the number three, which might have been a factor in Rabbi Joseph's selection of the menu.

RELIGIOUS EDUCATION

The anniversary of the Giving of the Law was deemed an appropriate occasion for the initiation of young children in the study of Torah. *Machzor Vitry* (12th cent.) described the custom of giving a token lesson to beginners on Shavuot. Following the lesson, the child was served cake baked with milk and honey. Some also served eggs because children are fond of eggs. In addition, there was a custom of smearing honey on the letters of the alphabet which the child was taught and to have him lick the honey so that he could savor the sweetness of the Torah.

An interesting comment in *Kol Bo* (13th–14th cent.) sheds some light on the habit of swaying to and fro in the course of study and prayer. Some sociologists have attributed this practice to the time when there was a scarcity of books and a single book had to serve the needs of many students. As a result, the students who were sitting at a distance were forced to sway back and forth in order to follow the lesson in the book. *Kol Bo* indicates that the custom of swaying was the result of deliberate inculcation and training. Thus he wrote: "And children are taught to sway when they study, as it is written on the occasion of the Giving of the Law: 'And they swayed' " (Exod. 20:15; *Kol Bo* 74).

KING DAVID'S YAHRZEIT

According to tradition, King David died on Shavuot (*Yalkut Tehilim* 735). Modern observances of the yahrzeit are held on the afternoon of the second day of Shavuot. It is customary to recite the entire Book of Psalms. Following the service, a collation is served, and the deeds and achievements of King David are extolled.

Jerusalemites visit King David's tomb on the occasion of his yahrzeit.

FORECASTING THE WEATHER

The folk-tradition that the weather of Shavuot forecasts long-range meteorological conditions has been widely circulated and believed. The origin of this popular belief can be traced to the Talmud. Achitophel, it was said, informed his children that if the weather on Shavuot is clear, it is an indication that good weather will prevail for the balance of the year (*Baba Batra* 147a).

9

Chanukah Customs

INTRODUCTION
CHANUKAH LIGHTS

CHANUKAH COMMEMORATES Judah Maccabee's rededication of the Second Temple in the year 165 B.C.E. Judah ordained the length of the festival, but he did not prescribe any specific rituals for it. His official proclamation included a request that the event be celebrated "with mirth and gladness" (I Macc. 4). It was obviously left to the individual Jew to express his joy in whatever manner suited him best.

By the beginning of the first century C.E., the ritual of candle-lighting had become widespread. Josephus referred to the Maccabean festival by the name of "Lights" (*Antiq.* 12:7). By the end of the first century the name Chanukah had come into vogue (Bloch, *Biblical and Historical Background of the Jewish Holy Days*, p. 61). At the same time, the talmudic rabbis began to give greater emphasis to the religious motif of the festival, based on the miracle of the cruse of oil, than to the Hasmonean military victories. This created a need for a new set of rituals. The final shape and dimension of Chanukah was several centuries in the making.

IN THE FIRST AND SECOND CENTURIES

The earliest rabbinic Chanukah enactment was the dispatch of couriers to inform the diaspora of the date of Rosh Chodesh Kislev, so that Chanukah could be observed at its proper time (*Rosh HaShanah* 18a). The mishnah lists six occasions when couriers were dispatched. Messengers were also sent off in the month of Iyar (to announce the date of the Minor Passover so that Jews who had failed to offer the paschal lamb in Nisan could do so in Iyar) "when the Temple was in existence." Apparently, the number of occasions when messengers were dispatched remained constant, before and after the destruction of the Temple. After 70 c.e. the couriers of Av (for Tisha B'Av) replaced the couriers of Iyar.

The practice of sending couriers was first introduced in the second half of the second century b.c.e. (Bloch, p. 208). About a century and a half later, the new custom of kindling Chanukah lamps became widespread and received rabbinical approval. It therefore became necessary to inform the diaspora of the date of Rosh Chodesh Kislev. The furnishing of this information, instituted in the early part of the first century, constituted the first rabbinic enactment relating to Chanukah.

One of the early tasks of the rabbis was to clarify the basic ritual of Chanukah, the kindling of the lights. How many lights are needed for the performance of the mitzvah? On how many nights does one kindle lights? The ground rules were expounded in a series of four beraitot. The first beraita discusses the time of the kindling of lights. The second discusses the number of lamps and the days when they are to be kindled. The third deals with the location of the lamps, and the fourth (which was probably the oldest) explains the origin of the festival (*Shabbat* 21b).

The first beraita significantly begins with the word *mitzvato* ("its mitzvah"). Thus the lighting of the candles was raised to the level of a mitzvah, a higher theological degree than a mere obligation (*chovah*). One recites a benediction prior to the performance of a mitzvah, not a chovah. The exact wording of the Chanukah benediction was published in the third century (*Shabbat* 23a). On the other hand, Sabbath lights were termed a chovah (*Shabbat* 25b), and no benediction for Sabbath candles was ever published in the Talmud.

The time of kindling Chanukah lamps, according to the beraita, is "from sunset until the foot [pedestrians] disappears from the street." This was subsequently interpreted to mean a minimum of half an hour. The association of the Chanukah lamp with pedestrians in the street is an early reflection of the rabbinic emphasis on the need to publicize the miracle of the cruse of oil. Although streets might be more crowded in the daytime, daytime kindling of the menorah was ruled out because candlelight does not show up in the daytime.

It seems to have been the common practice in the first century to kindle only one light on each night. The rabbis considered such practice adequate to meet the requirements of the law. The effect of

Chanukah lights depended upon mass participation of the people. Poor people could not afford multiple lights, and some had difficulty meeting the expense of even a single light (*Shabbat* 23b).

While the single light was acceptable to the rabbis, they undoubtedly preferred the festive appearence of multiple lights. They therefore noted with great satisfaction the practice of some devout people to kindle a single light for each member of the family. Even more praiseworthy, they said, were those who used a different number of lights on each night. The gradual spread of that custom claimed the attention of the Schools of Shammai and Hillel. According to the School of Shammai, one should begin with eight lights and nightly decrease the number by one. The School of Hillel held the opposite view. One should begin with one light and end with eight. The latter view is the prevailing law. Yet as late as the third century there were still some scholars who followed the custom prescribed by the School of Shammai (*Shabbat* 21b).

The reason for the difference of opinion between the two schools was discussed several centuries later. According to one rabbi, the number of candles serves as a calendrical index of the days of Chanukah which are yet to come (Shammai) or which have already passed (Hillel). According to other opinions, the School of Shammai patterned the Chanukah ceremony after the decreasing order of sacrificial offerings on Sukkot. The School of Hillel subscribed to the principle that "one must increase but not decrease sanctity."

Regardless of the rationales, it appears that both schools wanted to make sure that the festival would be observed for the full eight days. When a single light is kindled, it is easy to stop short of the completion of the festival, by mistake or otherwise. By instituting a descending or ascending scale of lights, one must end the festival with either one or eight lights. As we will discuss later, since the custom of Chanukah lamps was of comparatively recent origin, it required rabbinic vigilance to obtain uniform compliance.

The third beraita prescribed the location of the Chanukah lamp. "It is incumbent to place the Chanukah lamp by the door of one's house, on the outside. If one dwells on an upper floor, he places it at the window nearest the street. But in times of danger it is sufficient to place it on the table." The need for publicizing the miracle of the cruse of oil dictated the choice of the outdoor location, in full view of passing pedestrians. The proximity to the door pointed to the owner of the lamp and was proof of his compliance with the mitzvah of Chanukah. The order to display one's menorah to the public was at the same time instrumental in the use of public opinion in enforcing obedience to the Chanukah law.

The reference to "times of danger" is a pathetic reminder of the persecutions by Emperors Trajan and Hadrian. When the publicizing of the story of Chanukah was fraught with danger, the message of Chanukah was even more important to the survival of the Jewish home and family.

IN THE THIRD CENTURY

The amoraim of the third century elaborated upon the laws of Chanukah. Any oil, they said, may be used in a Chanukah lamp. However, it is preferable to use olive oil because of its purity and because the little cruse discovered by the Hasmoneans contained olive oil (*Shabbat* 23a).

Three benedictions are recited on the first night and thereafter only two. The text of the benedictions was published for the benefit of those who perform the mitzvah (ibid.).

The kindling of lights is equally incumbent upon men and women. The obligation of women is based on the fact that "they too were included in the miracle" (ibid.). According to Rashi, women were prime victims of the repressions, and the valor of a woman (Judith) was instrumental in bringing about salvation.

The festival of Chanukah should be mentioned at the conclusion of the thanksgiving benedictions of the Shacharit and Musaf *Amidot* and in the prayer of Grace (*Shabbat* 24a).

If a house has two doors opening to the street or court, the owner must light two lamps (*Shabbat* 23a). This rule was designed to preclude false assumptions that the second door leads to a second apartment whose owner had failed to kindle Chanukah lights. The creation of misleading impressions was always an important consideration in the legislation of rabbinic law.

Third-century rabbis discussed at length the question of the permissibility of using Chanukah lights for illumination and other uses in the home. In many poor homes, there were no lights in the evening, except for Friday nights. In the long winter evenings people did their work by the light of a fireplace. Why not take advantage of the Chanukah light for some reading or for examining the denomination of a coin? Several rabbis were inclined to permit such practices, but the opposing opinion prevailed (*Shabbat* 21b). It was felt that the sanctity of the lights must not be diminished by mundane uses, which might convert the Chanukah lamp into another house fixture. Even the reading of a prayer by the light of the menorah was prohibited (Jer. *Shabbat* 2:1).

Despite the urgency of publicizing the miracle of the cruse of oil, particularly under the demoralization of increasing persecutions, the economic condition of the poor was not overlooked. Cheap oils are acceptable. Lamps which have two spouts may be used by two people (*Shabbat* 23b). Another indirect benefit to the poor was the rule which released people from the obligation of rekindling a lamp whose flame had accidentally gone out. The remaining oil may be used on the following night (*Shabbat* 21b).

Even with all these accommodations, there must have been considerable numbers of people who could not afford the Chanukah lamp. As an extra incentive, the rabbis proclaimed that all regular observers of the ritual of lights would be rewarded by heaven with scholarly children (ibid.). It speaks nobly of the traditional ambition of the Jewish people to raise scholarly children.

The broad scope of the mitzvah of Chanukah lights was reemphasized by the third-century rabbis. A boarder who spends the week of Chanukah away from home must light his own menorah or be a partner in the host's menorah by sharing in the expense of the oil. However, if the boarder has a wife who lights the menorah in her own home he is exempt (*Shabbat* 23a).

The clear visibility of the menorah was also stressed. It must not be placed on a platform which is more than twenty yards above ground. Most people will not notice a lamp perched at that height (*Shabbat* 22a).

IN THE FOURTH CENTURY

A wave of persecutions hit Babylonian Jewry in the fourth century. King Sapor II (310–382) was embroiled in many wars, in the course of which many parts of the country, including those which were heavily populated by Jews, were devastated. The city of Machuza, the birthplace of Rava, the most illustrious scholar of his generation, and his academy were burned down. Rava used his wealth and his influence with the king's mother to alleviate the condition of the Jewish population. However, he also felt the need for raising Jewish morale through a scrupulous observance of rituals and ceremonies which bore a message of perseverance and hope. In pursuit of this goal he contributed much to the laws of Chanukah.

Most Chanukah lamps of the period did not have a distinctive appearance to differentiate them from ordinary light fixtures. Individual lamps were combined and put in a row to produce the required number of lights on a particular night. When lamps were placed on the outside, near one's door, the location identified them as a Chanukah menorah. In times of danger, however, the menorah was kept in the house, thus losing its special identity.

Rava enunciated a new principle. The Chanukah menorah must be easily identified even in the home. This could be accomplished by having an extra light, separate and apart from the menorah, illuminate the home whenever the Chanukah lamp was kindled (*Shabbat* 21b). Thus people would immediately recognize the latter as a memorial to a miracle rather than another light fixture. As for the poor people who could not afford an extra light, the light produced by the fireplace would serve the same purpose.

Out of this principle evolved the medieval practice of using a shamash (serving candle) in addition to the required number of candles. This custom will be discussed later in the chapter.

Rava also clarified the exact position of the Chanukah lamp when kindled outside the home. It should be placed within ten handbreaths above ground where people would notice it best (*Shabbat* 21b).

Despite Rava's promotion of the mitzvah of Chanukah lights, he conceded that there may be times when other interests take precedence. Thus if a poor person must make a choice between Chanukah lights and Sabbath lights, the latter have priority because they are essential to domestic peace (*Shabbat* 23b). However, if the choice is between Chanukah lights and wine for Kiddush, the former get precedence (ibid.).

A rule promulgated by Rabbi Jeremiah provided for the recitation of a benediction (*sheasah*) by a person who sees a lighted menorah (*Shabbat* 23a). This rule was primarily intended for travelers who are away from home and have no opportunity for kindling their own lamp.

IN THE POST-TALMUDIC ERA

The earliest post-talmudic source of Chanukah customs is *Masechet Soferim* (edited 8th cent.). The prayer of *Al HaNisim* ("For the miracles") was first published in that book. It reflects a reassessment of the significance of the festival by highlighting the Hasmonean military victory as one of its central themes.

The original text of the thanksgiving prayer concluded with the

sentence: "Just as you have performed miracles in the former generations may you likewise do in the later generations and you will help us
in these days as [you have done] in those days." This sentence was
quoted with approval by Rav Amram Gaon (9th cent.) and Rav
Saadiah Gaon (10th cent.). It was disapproved, however, by Rabbi
Meir of Rothenburg (13th cent.) on the ground that supplication may
not be included in a prayer of thanksgiving. As a result of his objection,
the sentence was eventually eliminated.

Masechet Soferim disapproved of the use of clay menorahs because
they become unattractive after one night's use. It recommended metal
or glass menorahs. However, a clay menorah may be used if it is
thoroughly cleaned each night. A demand for beautifying ceremonial
objects emerged in the talmudic era with regard to the Seder and the
sukkah. In the post-talmudic era the same trend affected the
Chanukah menorah and, a few centuries later, the holiday of Shavuot.

Modern Chanukah decorations have become very elaborate, particularly in the American Jewish community. This continues, in a
sense, a development of a traditional trend for beautification. However, it also reflects influences of the pervasive Christmas pageantry
which is widely exhibited in the same season.

Clay menorahs were the cheapest lamps available in antiquity. Most
of them were homemade. Archaeologists have uncovered Chanukah
lamps made of stone, clay, and ceramics, dating from the period of the
Talmud. They are flat menorahs, measuring several inches in height.
However, it appears from a beraita (*Menachot* 28b) that there were
branched Chanukah menorahs, patterned after the Temple menorah.
Craftsmen were forbidden to duplicate a menorah with seven
branches. However, the Talmud permitted the creation of a menorah
with five, six, or eight branches. The latter was apparently produced
for use on Chanukah. The infinite variety in designs and shapes of
Chanukah menorahs has from the very beginning provided an unlim-
ited opportunity for artistic originality and expression. The most
poignant of these was the imprint of a menorah on the frosted window
of a concentration-camp bunk made with the bloodied finger of a
Jewish inmate.

Masechet Soferim also published the short prayer which is recited after
the kindling of the lights (*HaNerot Halalu*). The prayer mentions the
miracles as well as the Hasmonean wars. In addition, it emphasizes the
sanctity of the lights as well as the prohibition of putting them to other
uses.

The popular hymn *Maoz Tzur* (Rock of Ages) was composed in the thirteenth century by a liturgical poet, Mordecai. Nothing is known of his origin and life story. It is a prayer for the restoration of the Temple and the end of persecution. The poem has become the central hymn of Chanukah.

THE ORDER OF CANDLE-LIGHTING

Medieval sages adopted different procedures of lighting the menorah. Some begin with the left side of the menorah, placing each additional candle to the right of the preceding light. Others began with the right side of the menorah, as is our custom. Each additional light was placed to the left of the preceding candle. The latest candle, which signifies the number of the day of the festival, is kindled first, and the kindling then proceeds from left to right.

THE BENEDICTIONS

The Talmud ordained the recitation of three benedictions on the first night, *lehadlik, sheasah,* and *zeman.* The first benediction, "Blessed art thou who commanded us to kindle the light of Chanukah," established the text for all subsequent candle-lighting benedictions. In view of the traditional requirement that benedictions must precede the perform- ance of the mitzvah, the first night's three benedictions are recited prior to the kindling of the light.

On the second night, one recites the benedictions prior to the kindling. According to a medieval custom, the second benediction, "Blessed are thou . . . who performed miracles in those days at this time," was chanted before the kindling of the second candle, which marks the miracle of the second day. The modern practice, however, is to chant both benedictions before the kindling of the lights and to recite the prayer of *HaNerot Halalu* while lighting the rest of the candles. The third benediction *(Shehecheyanu)* is a seasonal prayer which is recited but once in a season. It is therefore omitted after the first night.

THE SHAMASH

The shamash ("servant") is an extra candle with which the Chanukah lights are kindled. The name *shamash* was first introduced in the Middle Ages (*Tur, Orach Chaim* 673). Initially, people added an extra candle as a precaution against an accidental violation of the law of Chanukah. If someone inadvertently happened to read by the light of the menorah, he committed no violation because the extra candle provided illumination for his reading.

In time a second extra candle was used for the sole purpose of kindling the Chanukah lights. This candle was given the name *shamash*, a "servant" of the Chanukah candles. Eventually, the functions of both extra candles were performed by a single candle, which retained the name *shamash*. In order to distinguish it from the other Chanukah lights, the shamash was heavier and longer than the normal Chanukah candles. Another distinction was introduced in the fifteenth century when the shamash was placed in a higher receptacle, above the Chanukah lights.

ELECTRIC MENORAHS

The use of electric Chanukah menorahs has become widespread in modern times. They are given prominent display and are visible from a considerable distance. Electric bulbs have also been used on occasion in place of Sabbath and yahrzeit candles.

In the opinion of many rabbis, electricity is an acceptable source of light which may be used on traditional occasions when light is required. Yet even if it meets the religious qualification, an electric menorah fails to preserve the spirit of "kindling lights," which has been central to the Chanukah tradition for nearly two thousand years. Because of this objection, some families have adopted the custom of lighting candles in addition to the electric Chanukah menorah, which is used only for display purposes.

WOMEN ABSTAIN FROM WORK

According to Avudrahim (14th cent.), it was the custom of some women to abstain from work during the entire festival of Chanukah. The purpose of this practice was to memorialize the role of the apocryphal Judith, whose slaying of Holofernes contributed to the Hasmonean victory.

It is inconceivable that women, charged with domestic obligations, could ever abstain from work for eight days. The Avudrahim text is undoubtedly erroneous. *Kol Bo's* text (13th–14th cent.) limits the abstention from work to the time when the Chanukah candles are burning. Sephardic women have adopted this custom.

IN THE SYNAGOGUE

The custom of lighting a Chanukah menorah in the synagogue was introduced in the Middle Ages. It was motivated by the need for publicizing the miracle of the cruse of oil and by a concern for transients who spend the night in the synagogue.

In many congregations the menorah is placed near the southern wall, duplicating the location of the menorah in the Temple.

It has become a modern practice to light a menorah in all places of public assembly.

SHACHARIT

The complete *Hallel* is chanted on each day of Chanukah. The inclusion of *Hallel* in the observance of Chanukah is mentioned in the original proclamation of Chanukah, issued, according to I Maccabees (chap. 4), by Judah Maccabee together "with the whole congregation of Israel." The proclamation was ostensibly published in 165 B.C.E.

The Talmud describes a different scenario. The miracle of the oil, which lasted for eight days, occurred in 165 B.C.E. "The following year [164 B.C.E.] these [days] were proclaimed a festival with *Hallel* and thanksgiving" (*Shabbat* 21b). The proclamation was not attributed to the Hasmoneans. It might have been ordained by rabbinic authorities.

Megillat Taanit (chap. 9) explained the reason for the chanting of *Hallel*. "For every salvation which God had wrought for Israel they responded with *Hallel*, songs, praise and gratitude, as it was written: 'And they sang one to another in praising and giving thanks unto the Lord' [Ezra 3:11]."

The complete *Hallel* is recited on every day of Chanukah, as is the custom on every day of Sukkot. On the other hand, only part of *Hallel* is recited on the last six days of Passover. Medieval rabbinic scholars ascribed the difference to the fact that each day of Sukkot has a distinctive feature, since the number of festival offerings differed from day to day. Each day was therefore treated as a distinct holiday. The same is true of Chanukah, since the number of candles differs from day to day. The Temple Passover ritual, however, was uniform throughout the holiday. It was therefore treated as a single unit. For that reason there was no need to repeat the entire *Hallel* on each day of the holiday.

Torah selections dealing with the dedication of the Tabernacle (Num. 7) are read daily at the Shacharit service. Three persons are given aliyot. The concluding passage, *Zot chanukat hamizbeach* . . .

("This was the dedication of the altar") is read on the eighth day of Chanukah. The last day has therefore come to be known as *Zot Chanukah*.

On the eve of the Sabbath, the Chanukah menorah is lighted before the kindling of the Sabbath lights. On the expiration of the Sabbath, the congregational menorah is kindled before Havdalah for the sake of advertising the miracle of the oil. In the home, however, the procedure is reversed.

CHANUKAH MENU

It is traditional to serve a cheese dish on Chanukah in memory of Judith, who lulled Holofernes to sleep by feeding him milk. This custom originated in the fifteenth century.

It is also traditional to serve potato latkes (pancakes) fried in oil, in memory of the miracle of the oil.

Feasting is not part of the Chanukah tradition. However, many people have adopted the custom of serving a festive meal in honor of the occasion. In the American Jewish community, Chanukah has assumed the proportions of a major festival as a result of the general festive atmosphere at that time of the year. It is marked by social events and celebrations, and has become an occasion for family gatherings.

CHANUKAH GIFTS

The tradition of giving money (Chanukah gelt) to children is of long standing. The custom had its origin in the seventeenth-century practice of Polish Jewry to give money to their small children for distribution to their teachers. In time, as children demanded their due, money was also given to children to keep for themselves.

Teen-age boys soon came in for their share. According to *Magen Avraham* (18th cent.), it was the custom of poor yeshiva students to visit homes of Jewish benefactors who dispensed Chanukah money (*Orach Chaim* 670). The rabbis approved of the custom of giving money on Chanukah because it publicized the story of the miracle of the oil.

Modern public institutions use the tradition of Chanukah gelt as a theme for fund-raising.

GAMBLING ON CHANUKAH

Children used their Chanukah money to play the game of spinning tops (dreidel). Since the amount of money involved in this pastime was insignificant, the game escaped rabbinic censure. The fact that the four Hebrew letters engraved on the sides of the top formed an acrostic for the sentence "A great miracle happened there" *(nes gadol hayah sham)* further legitimized the dreidel.

The practice of some adults to indulge in card-playing on Chanukah met with vehement rabbinic and communal opposition. Gambling was banned as a violation of religious law.

Ever since the introduction of card-playing in Europe in the fourteenth century, it had been an attractive pastime for Jews and non-Jews alike. The number of Jewish card-players, however, was small because most Jews found little time for such games. Their only days of leisure, Sabbaths and festivals, were too sacred to be profaned by card-playing.

There were several occasions, however, when Jews had some leisure time on weekdays. These included Chanukah, Purim, and Chol Hamoed, when workdays were shortened. Some utilized this opportunity for card-playing, despite rabbinic opposition. The famous Rabbi Chaim Yair Bacharach (17th cent.) took note of the practice and rendered a practical decision. One may play cards on Chanukah, Purim, and Chol Hamoed, but not for money.

10

Purim Customs

I.
THE MONTH OF ADAR

"WITH THE BEGINNING of Av rejoicing is curtailed, with the beginning of Adar rejoicing is increased" (*Taanit* 29a). Thus the rabbis of the Talmud contrasted the month in which the greatest disaster had occurred with the month of the most felicitous salvation.

Based on this observation, Rav Papa (4th cent.) offered the following advice: "A Jew who is involved in litigation with a pagan [before a judge who may be prejudiced] should avoid a trial in the month of Av, when his luck is bad. He should set his trial in the month of Adar, when his luck is good" (*Taanit* 29b). This advice reflected a Jewish tradition that God times happy events on happy historical days and unhappy events on unhappy historical days (*Taanit* 29a).

The unfortunate reputation of the month of Av was well deserved, considering the multiple tragedies of that month (*Taanit* 26b). On the other hand, Adar owes its good reputation to the events of Purim and, to a lesser degree, to the fact that the seventh of Adar is the traditional birthday of Moses (*Megillah* 13b).

One may argue that the month of Chanukah, Kislev, should rank equally in the scale of luck and good fortune with the month of Adar. However, the rededication of the Temple had little practical relevance to Jewish life in the post-exilic diaspora, whereas the downfall of Haman was repeatedly held up as an omen of a happy ending to the threat of perennial petty Hamans.

The grief which clung to Av inspired halachic restrictions in that period (*Yevamot* 43a). No special halachic rules were enacted for the month of Adar to reflect the joyous character of that month.

SHABBAT PARASHAT SHEKALIM

Sabbath Rosh Chodesh Adar, or the Sabbath preceding Rosh Chodesh Adar, is known as Shabbat Parashat Shekalim ("the Sabbath of the portion of the shekels"). In honor of this occasion, an additional portion of the Torah, prescribing a contribution of a half-shekel (Exod. 30:11–16), is read at the Sabbath morning service.

In the days of the Temple, the Bet Din used to dispatch messengers in the month of Adar to remind the people that contributions of the half-shekel were now due (*Shekalim* 1:1). The proceeds of these contributions were used for the purchase of cattle for public sacrificial offerings. Nisan marked the beginning of a new fiscal year. Thereafter, all purchases of cattle had to be paid for with the proceeds of the new annual contributions of the half-shekel (ibid.). Announcements on the first of Adar gave the people a month's notice to send in the money. Resh Lakish (3rd cent.) offered a homiletical explanation as to why the half-shekel was due in the month of Adar: "It was well known to the Almighty that Haman would someday pay shekels for royal permission to destroy Israel. He therefore anticipated Haman's shekels with the shekels of Israel" (*Megillah* 13b).

After the destruction of the Temple and the cessation of sacrificial rites, Jews of the diaspora continued to send the half-shekel to the Palestinian patriarchate for the maintenance of religious institutions. The reading of *Parashat Shekalim* served two purposes. It reminded the people of the need for contributions. It also served as a memorial to the ancient practice of the half-shekel in the days of the Temple.

The practice of reading *Parashat Shekaim* was most likely instituted in the second century. It seems that the custom did not become widespread for some time. In fact, amoraim of the fourth century were still debating the question whether the portion of *Shekalim* was to replace the reading of the regular portion of the week or merely supplement it (*Megillah* 30b). However, in Rashi's opinion, the reading of *Parashat Shekalim* was instituted when the Temple was still in existence (*Megillah* 29a; *korin beparshat shekalim*).

SHABBAT PARASHAT ZACHOR

The Sabbath preceding Purim is named Shabbat Zachor. The portion of *Zachor* (Deut. 25:17–19) enjoins Jews to remember the deeds of Amalek and to erase his memory. Haman is described in the Book of Esther as "the son of Hammedatha the Agagite" (3:1). Tradition assumed that Haman was a descendant of Agag, king of Amalek (I Sam. 15:9). The portion of *Zachor* forewarned Jews of the consequences of the failure to eradicate the memory of the Amalekites.

The readings of *Parashat Zachor* and *Parashat Shekalim* were most likely instituted at the same time.

DATES OF MEGILLAH READING

The mitzvah of reading the Book of Esther (the Megillah) on Purim was ordained, according to the Talmud, by the prophets or the Men of the Great Assembly. However, there is little evidence that this ordinance was observed prior to the third century B.C.E. In its early stages, the "reading" consisted of an informal recounting of the story of Purim. In Jerusalem, parts of the Hebrew text of the Megillah were read on Purim in the first century C.E. (Bloch, *Biblical and Historical Background of the Jewish Holy Days*, pp. 92–99).

According to a mishnah (*Megillah* 2a), the Megillah was initially read on different days, depending upon the history and location of a given community. In Shushan and other walled cities dating from the time of Joshua, the Megillah was read on the fifteenth of Adar (Esther 9:18). However, if the fifteenth of Adar occurred on a Sabbath, the reading of the Megillah was advanced to the fourteenth.

In large open cities (i.e., where ten men were always available to form a minyan and to attend to public activities), the Megillah was read on the fourteenth of Adar. However, if the fourteenth of Adar occurred on a Sabbath (prior to the fixing of the permanent calendar), the Megillah was read on the thirteenth of Adar (*Megillah* 5a).

Farmers, who normally attend a market on Mondays and Thursdays, had the Megillah read to them on the market day, if a rabbinic court was in session in that town. Farmers were not competent to read the Megillah on their own. Accordingly, if Purim occurred on Sunday, the Megillah was read to them on the eleventh of Adar (the preceding Thursday). If Purim occurred on a Tuesday or Wednesday, the Megillah was read on the twelfth or thirteenth of Adar.

The leeway granted to farmers was due to the essential service rendered by them "in providing water and food for their brethren in the cities" (*Megillah* 4b). The divergent dates of reading of the Megillah did not affect other Purim customs. Feasting and *shalach manot* were observed in Shushan and walled cities on the fifteenth of Adar and in all other places on the fourteenth of Adar.

ABOLITION OF DIVERGENT DATES

When was the special dispensation for farmers abolished? Rabbi Judah said: "When did this rule [of divergent dates] hold good? When the years were properly established and Israel dwelt in its land. But in these days, since they watch it [the date of the reading of the Megillah], it is read only in the proper time [on the fourteenth]" (*Megillah* 2a).

According to Rashi's interpretation of Rabbi Judah's statement, farmers enjoyed a special privilege only when the Sanhedrin's messengers could reach distant communities and inform them of the date of Passover. However, when the messenger service was disrupted (because Jews no longer dwelt on their land) farmers began to watch (*mistaklin*) the date of the reading of the Megillah and observe Passover thirty days later. Such calculations could lead to serious error if the Megillah is read on the eleventh, twelfth, or thirteenth of Adar. It was therefore necessary to impose a uniform date of reading the Megillah, the fourteenth of Adar, except for Shushan and walled cities.

Rashi's view that the farmers' divergent dates of reading the Megillah were abolished for fear of a miscalculation of the date of Passover raises some questions. If the fourteenth of Adar occurred on a Sabbath (prior to the fixed calendar of the fourth century), the Megillah was read on the thirteenth of Adar. Apparently the rabbis had no apprehension that this might lead to a miscalculation of the date of Passover. Furthermore, Rashi's opinion that the old rule was abolished due to the disruption of the service of the Sanhedrin's messengers is not in accord with his view that the old rule was abolished upon the destruction of the Temple (*Megillah* 2a, Rabbi Akiva). Messengers continued to be dispatched by the Sanhedrin for at least a century and a half after the destruction of the Temple.

Rabbi Yochanan (3rd cent.) discussed a law relating to the dispatch of messengers in his time (*Rosh HaShanah* 21a). Yet the same Rabbi Yochanan quoted the *chachamim* (tannaim of a previous century) to the effect that the farmers' divergent dates were abolished because they "watched [*mistaklin*] it" (*Megillah* 2a). Obviously, the abolition of the old rule was not linked to the availability of messengers.

A noted medieval scholar, Ritva, mentioned another version of Rabbi Judah's statement in which the element of a miscalculation of the date of Passover is eliminated. In place of *mistaklin* ("watch") his version reads *mistakanin* ("endanger"; *Megillah* 2a, *ika deamri*). According to Ritva, multiple dates of Megillah reading may enhance the resentment of non-Jews and provoke them into prohibiting the observance of Purim. The abolition of the old rule was motivated by the deterioration of political conditions after the destruction of the Temple.

Kol Bo (14th cent.) retained the original version of Rabbi Judah's statement but offered a different interpretation of the word *mistaklin* ("watch"): poor people "look forward" to the reading of the Megillah because of the charity which is distributed at that time, and it would be a grave disappointment to them to come to a synagogue on the fourteenth of Adar only to discover that the Megillah had been read at an earlier date. Apparently the number of poor people had greatly increased after the destruction of the Temple and that is why the new rule was established at that time.

There is a consensus of opinion that the uniform law was established after the destruction of the Temple. This is corroborated by a talmudic definition of the time reference inherent in "when Israel dwelt in its land," the phrase used by Rabbi Judah. The Talmud (*Baba Batra* 25b) defined the application of this phrase to the period of time up to the destruction of the Temple.

FEASTING AND SHALACH MANOT

According to the Book of Esther, the Jews of Persia rested on the fourteenth of Adar and made it a day of feasting (9:17). The Jewish community of Shushan did the same on the fifteenth of Adar (9:18). This celebration was a spontaneous expression of joy, not dictated by a formal proclamation. Gift-giving (*shalach manot*) was not part of the original festivities.

The Purim celebration was quickly institutionalized. This too seems to have been a spontaneous act, without the incentive of a special directive. Jews began to celebrate the anniversary of Haman's downfall (Esther 9:19) before Mordecai publicized his ordinance (Esther 9:20). A new feature was added to the celebration of the anniversary of Purim, *shalach manot*. The sending of food or cooked meals was a common ancient practice on festive occasions. On the memorable Rosh HaShanah (458 B.C.E.) when the assembled Jews were dismissed by Ezra to celebrate the holiday, they went home "to eat and to drink and to send portions (*leshalach manot*; Neh. 8:12). The Hebrew technical term for this type of sending portions is identical in Nehemiah and the Book of Esther.

After the institutionalization of Purim by the local Jews, Mordecai requested the Jews of all the Persian provinces to establish an annual Purim festival (Esther 9:20–22). He asked that Jews adopt the local

Purim customs of feasting and *shalach manot* and also added a new feature, *matanot laevyonim* ("gifts to the poor"; 9:22). Gifts to the poor were also associated with the celebration of pentateuchal pilgrimage festivals (Deut. 16:11, 14). With the establishment of Purim as a permanent festival, its celebration was similarly to be marked by the giving of charity.

Mordecai also stipulated that "these days be remembered and kept" (Esther 9:28). Remembrance implies an awareness or knowledge of the history of Purim. The Talmud did not attribute to him the ordinance of Megillah reading. Josephus (1st cent.) described Purim as a day when Jews feast and send portions to one another (*Antiq.* 2:6). He did not mention the reading of the Megillah. However, the Talmud mentions the reading of the Megillah in Jerusalem when the Temple was still in existence (*Megillah* 3a).

II.
IN THE SECOND CENTURY

THE INTERCALATION OF ADAR

The second century was a period of great intellectual ferment and creativity. The rabbinic leadership of the era set itself the task of binding national wounds and forging a viable religious community. Holidays and ceremonials were invested with new meaning to generate hope and faith in an eventual restoration. The festival of Purim, with its obvious potential for morale-lifting, became a significant tool in the recuperative process. Rabbi Joshua b. Karchah (2nd cent.) noted that there are weightier reasons for celebrating Purim than Passover (*Megillat Taanit*, chap. 12).

The growing practice of public Megillah reading required an authoritative adjudication of the procedure to be followed in an intercalary year (when there are two months of Adar). Should the Megillah be read in the first or the second Adar? This question was not so pressing in the previous centuries, when Purim was primarily a family festival (see Rashi on Esther 9:28). Since careful measures were taken to inform the diaspora of the intercalation of Adar, many Jews must have celebrated a second Purim in the second Adar. However, the recitation of benedictions before the reading of the Megillah, which became widespread in the second century, might constitute a religious violation if the reading is premature or past due. Rabban Simon b. Gamliel, head of the Sanhedrin of Usha, ruled that all Purim customs must be observed in the second Adar (*Megillah* 6b).

The schedule of intercalations was fixed in the permanent calendar published in 359. Prior to that, intercalations depended on a proclamation by the Sanhedrin, usually announced in the month of Adar. There was a practical reason for the choice of Adar as the only month to be intercalated. Passover must be celebrated in the spring season (Exod. 13:4). When the lunar calendar falls behind the solar calendar to the point where Passover might occur before spring, an extra month is added to the calendar. This resulted in the postponement of Passover by a month. The Sanhedrin normally waited until the month of Adar (the month before Nisan) to determine whether climatic conditions dictated an additional Adar.

Avudrahim offered another explanation. Adar must always be the twelfth month of the year. It was designated as such in the Bible (Esther 3:7). If Adar is intercalated, the first Adar is still the twelfth month. However, if any other month were to be intercalated, Adar would no longer be the twelfth month of that year.

READING FROM MEMORY

The Hebrew text of the Book of Esther was not readily available in the early part of the second century. This was particularly true prior to its inclusion in the canon. A parchment Megillah commanded a very high price. Some people might have been tempted to memorize the book and to read it from memory. The rabbis' prohibition of this practice was probably motivated by a desire to increase the demand for Megillot and thus lower the price. There was also a legitimate apprehension that a reader who does not have the text before him may inadvertently make mistakes.

THE TIME OF READING

When the reading of the Megillah became widespread in the second century, crowds flocked into the synagogue to fulfill the mitzvah of *mikra Megillah*. Since work was permitted on Purim, there were many people who were eager to hear the Megillah before they began the day's chores. How early may one read the Megillah? It was ruled that it may not be read before dawn (*Megillah* 20a). However, those who could not attend the early service were permitted to read the Megillah at any time during the day (*Megillah* 20b).

THE MESSAGE OF THE MEGILLAH

In addition to determining the time when the Megillah is to be read, the second-century rabbis also had to decide what part of the Megillah is to be read. To understand the nature of this problem, it is important to bear in mind that the Megillah was a valuable instrument for lifting the people's morale. The opening paragraph of a story usually has the greatest impact upon a reader. It was therefore deemed prudent to begin the reading of the Megillah with the paragraph which conveys the most constructive Purim message.

Four rabbis, all veterans of the Hadrianic persecutions, addressed themselves to this question (*Megillah* 19a). In Rabbi Simon b. Yochai's opinion, one should commence with chapter 6 ("On that night the king could not sleep"). When the crisis had reached its darkest point and all appeared lost, God intervened to deny sleep to the king. This seemingly unimportant event led to the unraveling of Haman's plot. The message of this sentence is: Do not lose faith in God's salvation even when hope is at its dimmest. Indeed, Rabbi Simon himself had been forced to stay hidden in a cave for thirteen years, but his hope for ultimate salvation had never flagged (*Shabbat* 33b).

Rabbi Judah said that one should begin with chapter 2, verse 5 ("There was a certain Jew in Shushan the castle, whose name was Mordecai . . ."). Rabbi Judah naturally agreed with Rabbi Simon that faith in God is essential to survival. However, he stressed the importance of self-help. One must not stand by idly in the face of danger and leave the problem up to heaven. It was Mordecai, the social and political activist, who, with the aid of God, frustrated Haman's design.

Rabbi Jose suggested that the reading of the Megillah begin with chapter 2 ("After these things, when the anger of King Ahasuerus had assuaged, he remembered Vashti . . . "). Apparently, to Rabbi Jose the most important Purim lesson is the warning against reliance upon sympathetic expressions by even the most benign rulers. When wisdom is slanted by anger or influenced by cupidity and ambition, even murder is condoned.

Rava (4th cent.) later analyzed the motives of friendly officials and frequently found them wanting. He pointed to the officials who had reported to Ahasuerus that Mordecai was never rewarded for saving the king's life. Why did they delay their report for such a long time? Rava's brief comment was: "They acted out of hate of Haman rather than out of love for Mordecai" (*Megillah* 16a).

Rabbi Meir disagreed with his colleagues. It was his opinion that the entire Megillah should be read. The book begins with an account of a lavish banquet tendered by King Ahasuerus. Jews, like all the other nationalities of Persia, had cause to rejoice. In times of peace and prosperity there is a tendency to relax vigilance. However, bigotry occasionally appears when it is least expected, and even the most auspicious events may trigger serious problems. Furthermore, the rabbis viewed the Jewish participation as an index of their rapid assimilation.

MEGILLAH BENEDICTIONS

With the universal adoption in the second century of the practice of reading the Megillah in public, the need for special benedictions came up for discussion. A mishnah advised congregations to follow local custom (*Megillah* 21a). According to a fourth-century interpretation, the mishnah referred only to the benediction which is recited after the reading of the Megillah. The benedictions which precede the reading had always been considered obligatory (*Megillah* 21b).

WORK ON PURIM

Despite the growing festive status of Purim, physical labor was not prohibited on that day. Rabbi Judah HaNasi was reported to have planted shoots on Purim (*Megillah* 5a).

A PURIM FUND FOR THE POOR

Every Jew, rich or poor, must be involved in the festivities of Purim, if the festival is to have its maximal theraputic effect. The Purim *seudah* (meal) has a much longer history than the reading of the Megillah. The same is true of the mitzvah of giving charity on Purim. The two basic mitzvot were fused with the establishment of a Purim fund for the poor. The proceeds were to be used exclusively for the expense of Purim meals (*Baba Metzia* 78b).

III.
IN THE THIRD CENTURY

NEW CUSTOMS

Further progress in the increasing importance of Purim was made in the early part of the third century. Rabbi Joshua b. Levi, a patron of the underground Jewish freedom fighters, held up Purim as an omen of ultimate victory over Rome. He was the first rabbi to declare the events of Purim a "miracle" (*nes; Megillah* 4a). Miracles have a way of rising above reality in achieving ultimate triumph. He broadened the mitzvah of Megillah-reading to include women (ibid.). He also ordained that the Megillah be read on Purim eve as well as Purim day so as to give the utmost exposure to the miracle of Purim (ibid.). For the same reason he requested rabbis to discuss the laws of Purim in the synagogue if the festival occurs on a Sabbath (ibid.).

The question of what part of the Megillah is to be read on Purim, a point of contention among the tannaim of the second century, was finally resolved. The entire Megillah must be read (*Megillah* 19a). Feasting on Purim was made obligatory (*Pesachim* 68b). However, attempts to prohibit labor on Purim were rejected (*Megillah* 5b).

SHALACH MANOT

The law of *shalach manot* was clarified in the third century. To fulfill this mitzvah properly, one must give at least two portions to one friend and charitable contributions to two poor people (*Megillah* 7a).

There is a talmudic record of a *shalach manot* of Rabbi Judah Nesiah (3rd cent.). It set a precedent for the law regulating *shalach manot*. It must consist of at least two items of food or drink (*Megillah* 7a). It was later expounded that the food must be cooked (if cooking is required) and ready to eat, without requiring any preparatory work on the part of the recipient.

THE IMPORTANCE OF SYMBOLISM

To enhance the effect of the Megillah, symbolic customs were introduced in the third century and given great emphasis. Rav (3rd cent.) ordered the scribes to write the names of Haman's ten sons on ten separate lines, forming a symmetrical column of names, each name directly under the name above it (Jer. *Megillah* 3:7). According to Rav, this format symbolizes the collapse of the ten wicked sons. In the construction of a brick wall, each brick is laid astride two bricks beneath it. If bricks were laid directly, one brick over the other, the wall would collapse.

Another symbolic innovation was the requirement that the reader of the Megillah recite the names of the ten sons in one breath (*Megillah* 16b). This symbolized the simultaneous expiration of the sons. The exact time when this custom was introduced cannot be ascertained. We assume that it dates from the third century, when many other symbolic practices were adopted.

Scribes were also ordered to elongate the *vav* in Vaizatha (the name of Haman's tenth son) to make it resemble a long boat-pole. The long *vav* symbolizes the pole upon which the ten sons were strung up (*Megillah* 16b).

Rabbi Jose b. Avin (3rd cent.) prescribed the format which scribes must follow in the writing of the names of the ten sons. The name is to be written at the beginning of the line and *et* ("the") at the end of the line, with a blank space between them. The large beginning and the small ending symbolizes the fate of each son (Jer. *Megillah* 3:7).

Rav made it a custom to greet the reader's mention of the name of Haman with the whispered phrase, "Cursed be Haman and cursed be his offspring" (*Breishit Rabbah* 49). This innovation is of historical interest because it foreshadowed the medieval noisemaker.

IV.
IN THE FOURTH AND FIFTH CENTURIES

A JOYOUS CELEBRATION

Rava (4th cent.) continued to enhance the festive character of Purim. He was undoubtedly motivated by the deteriorating political situation of Babylonian Jewry under Sapor II. The same consideration directed Rava's attention to the festival of Chanukah (chap. 9, 4th cent.).

With the adoption of the practice of Megillah-reading on Purim eve, many people must have preferred to serve the Purim feast at night when the members of the family were at home. Rava, however, declared that the feast must be served on Purim day (*Megillah* 7b). He probably felt that Purim would become an ordinary workday without the festive meal to set it apart.

Rava also announced that every person should welcome intoxication on Purim to a point where he would be unable to distinguish between "cursed be Haman" and "blessed be Mordecai" (ibid.). In view of the traditional Jewish repugnance to intoxication, medieval commentators resorted to ingenious intepretations which have watered down the potency of Rava's pronouncement. However, Rava deserves to be taken literally. He realized that the comforting story of Purim will never completely lift the burden of Jewish anxieties. The only way to forget past and current tyrants is to numb one's awareness of their existence with a bit of liquor. Rava's criterion was carefully chosen. He hoped that there would be at least one day in the year when Jews would not be conscious of the need to curse Haman. Obviously, Rava had no apprehension that a bit of drinking on Purim would turn Jews into alcoholics.

Most Jews have recoiled from intoxication even on Purim, despite the inclusion of Rava's injunction in the code. Interestingly, a special *piyut* (liturgical poem), entitled "This is the Night of Drinking," was composed in the Middle Ages for the Maariv service of Purim (*Machzor Vitry*, p. 583).

Rabbi Pinchas, a disciple of Rava, requested Jews to offer a special prayer for Charvonah, the official who pointed out the gallows which Haman had erected for Mordecai (Esther 7:9, Jer. *Megillah* 3:8). The expression of gratitude to Charvonah was included in the medieval hymn *Shoshanat Yaakov* as a reminder of the debt which Jews owe to righteous Gentiles.

BENEDICTIONS AND TRANSLATIONS

The text of the three benedictions (*al mikra megillah, sheasah nisim, shehecheyanu*) which precede the reading of the Megillah, and the benediction which follows the reading (*harav et rivenu*), were published in the fifth century.

The importance of reading the Hebrew text of the Megillah, instead of a translation, received greater emphasis. The knowledge of Greek was no longer widespread in the fifth century, and there was no reason why Greek should retain its privileged legal position. Ravina expressed a preference for reading the Megillah in Hebrew exclusively. He felt that the Hebrew text, even if not understood by some people, is more conducive to the publicizing of the miracle of Purim (*Megillah* 18a).

V.
IN THE POST-TALMUDIC ERA

By the close of the talmudic era, the festival of Purim had taken on its modern form. There has been little halachic innovation since that time. However, additional prayers were composed, among them the popular *Asher Heni* ("who has brought to nought") which is recited after the reading of the Megillah.

While there was little further development in the halachic sphere, there was a tremendous upsurge in the dramatization, color, and pageantry of the festival. Jewish youths in the Orient introduced the custom of burning Haman in effigy to the accompaniment of songs and dances.

The custom of folding the Megillah, folio on folio, dates from the tenth century. It was intended to dramatize the letter *(iggeret)* which Mordecai sent to the Jewish communities of Persia.

The custom of choral reading of several sentences of the Megillah was also introduced at that time. Initially, only two verses were read out loud: *Ish yehudi* (2:5) and *Layehudim hayeta* (8:16). Subsequently, two more were added: *Umordecai yatza* (8:15) and *Ki Mordecai* (10:3).

The custom of giving Purim gifts to Christian servants prevailed in medieval Provence and France (*Siddur Rashi* 346). The custom grew out of the practice of poor Jews to send their small children on Purim to solicit donations. The parents were reluctant to accompany their children so they asked Christian servants to escort them. In the spirit of Purim generosity, the people gave gifts to the escorts as well as the children.

THE MEDIEVAL MACHATZIT HASHEKEL

The practice of putting *machatzit hashekel* money (half of a standard coin) in the synagogue's charity box, or plate, prior to the reading of the Megillah was introduced in the thirteenth century. It was customary to deposit three coins because the term *machatzit hashekel* is mentioned three times in the same biblical paragraph (Exod. 30:13, 15). The proceeds were given to the poor for expenses of the Purim meal. Thus the ancient biblical and talmudic practices were renewed.

In an ironic twist of this custom, King Ludwig of Bavaria, in 1342, imposed an annual tax upon the Jews of Munich. He called the tax *Opferpfennig* ("sacrificial coin"), named for the traditional *machatzit hashekel*. As the alleged heir of the Holy Roman Empire, he claimed proprietary rights to this tax. Emperor Vespasian had diverted the *machatzit hashekel* to the Roman treasury after the destruction of the Temple.

THE PURIM NOISEMAKER

The origin of the Purim noisemaker can be traced to the fourteenth century. Jews of Provence and France used to write the name of Haman on stones. When Haman's name was mentioned by the Megillah reader, children erased it by rubbing two stones against each other. Thus the spirit of the biblical injunction to erase the memory of Amalek was fulfilled.

Austrian Jews eliminated the name Haman. They encouraged their children to clap two stones in order to create a booing effect. Adults used to whisper *zecher tzadik liverachah* ("may the memory of the righteous be a blessing") after the mention of Mordecai's name, and *shem reshaim yirkav* ("may the name of the wicked rot") after the mention of Haman (Maharak, *Minhagim*). This practice was based on a midrashic statement (*Bereshit Rabbah* 49).

PURIM MASQUERADES

The practice of masquerading on Purim dates from the Middle Ages. At first it was customary to put on peasant clothes. This was probably a practical precaution against attacks by anti-Semitic mobs who might be provoked by the Purim hilarity. In time, the simple disguise was converted into a masquerade in colorful costumes. Eventually, men paraded in women's clothes, and vice versa. Although transvestism is a serious violation of biblical law, the noted author of responsa, Rabbi Moses Mintz (15th cent.) ruled that the practice may be tolerated on Purim.

The relaxation of austerity on Purim inspired humorous and artistic self-expression. Musicians and Purim jesters enlivened the medieval festival scene. In modern times, Purim has been celebrated with skits, masquerades, carnivals, clowns, "Purim rabbis," the crowning of Queen Esther, and so forth.

THE MEGILLAH ON SATURDAY NIGHTS

The Purim night service on Saturday night follows the following order: Maariv, Havdalah, Megillah.

11

Customs of Minor Festivals

I.
CUSTOMS OF ROSH CHODESH

IN BIBLICAL TIMES

THE DATE OF ROSH CHODESH is of extreme importance in the Jewish religious calendar because it fixes the time of all holidays except the Sabbath. Its religious significance dates from the establishment of the festival of Passover (Exod. 12:2). However, as a subdivision of lunar time, the monthly cycle marked a clearly defined segment of the year, which entered into the calculations of primitive man.

Days and lunar months are perceptible divisions of time of which ancient man was cognizant. The same is true of the solar year. On the other hand, the weekly cycle was the product of ecclesiastic innovation introduced long after the month had become a popular subdivision of time. Primitive creeds related the week to the cult of the moon, with each week marking a phase of the growing and waning moon. Since the week was not carved out by astronomical phenomena, its length varied from place to place. In a considerable part of the ancient world, the week consisted of ten days.

In Jewish tradition, the week is not a subdivision of the month. Its establishment rested on the historical account of the creation of the universe. The rationale for the seven-day period was mentioned in the Bible long before the month appeared in the text (Gen. 2:2).

An analysis of biblical sources is helpful in tracing the prominence of the month in Jewish life. The first unit of time mentioned in the Bible was the day (Gen. 1:5). Then came the week (Gen. 2:2). Unlike the

293

astronomical references in the terms *chodesh* ("renewal of the moon") and *shanah* ("repetition of the solar seasons"), the initial name of the week was *shavua*, derived from the Hebrew for the numeral seven. The next unit of time mentioned in the Bible was the year. It was used in the context of the chronological table of the genealogy of Adam's generations (Gen. 5:3). Man's life-span was measured in round figures of years, without any reference to birthdays. The month was mentioned for the first time in connection with the chronological dating of the flood (Gen. 7:11). The indication of months in historical chronicles was essential to a description of an exact date. However, in measuring the duration of a period, man prefered an index of years and days. This obviated the need for addition and subtraction. A period of time less than a year was reckoned in days. The flood waters prevailed for 150 days (Gen. 7:24). There are similar references to periods of 70 days (Gen. 50:3) and 66 days (Lev. 12:5). Only when the time reference coincided with the period of a month was the latter index used (Gen. 29:15).

It was a mark of human progress when people began to describe a duration of time in terms of years and months. This was reflected in the text which lists the time spent by David with the Philistines as "a year and four months" (I Sam. 27:7).

The importance of the week in the early history of Judaism was due to the centrality of the Sabbath in Jewish religious life. Indeed, the name *sabbath* became a synonym for a week (Lev. 23:15).

SABBATH AND ROSH CHODESH

The regular observance of the Sabbath at the end of each week lent the weekly cycle extraordinary importance. Similar religious considerations projected the monthly cycle into equal prominence. Mandated redemptions of firstborn humans and animals, at the age of one month, necessitated calculations in monthly terms. What was more important was the need for establishing the dates of festivals by counting the days of each month. Even in a much later period, when the Sanhedrin provided the needed information, its message was limited to the date of Rosh Chodesh and it was left to each Jew to fix the day of the holiday. Intimacy with the month was also essential for the performance of mitzvot relating to laws of purity and mourning.

The hard-and-fast rule that festivals must be linked to a specific day of the month, regardless of the day of the week on which it falls, has one notable exception. The biblical Shavuot occurs exactly seven weeks from the second day of Passover, regardless of the day of the month. This arrangement was considered so remarkable that the festival was named "Weeks." The exception may possibly be explained by the fact that Shavuot is not an independent holiday but an appendage of Passover, marking the cereal harvest, which bridges both festivals. As an indication of this continuity, Shavuot must fall on a specific day of the week, the day which follows the day on which Passover began. Thus if Passover falls on a Tuesday, Shavuot must fall on a Wednesday. This can only be achieved by measuring the interval between the holidays in terms of weeks.

Despite the importance of the month in the religious calendar and the consequent significance of Rosh Chodesh, the Sabbath was much more sacred and fundamental to the faith. However, in early popular peception Rosh Chodesh loomed as the major occasion of the two. Several factors might have contributed to this conception. There was an element of atonement in the Temple ritual of Rosh Chodesh which was absent from the Sabbath ritual. A sin-offering was brought on Rosh Chodesh for the atonement of sins. According to a rabbinic interpretation, the offering atoned for the sin of eating holy food which had become unclean (*Shavuot* 9b). Such violations were common and the people eagerly awaited the monthly forgiveness.

Rosh Chodesh, like the Sabbath, was considered a proper occasion for attending a prophet's lectures (II Kings 4:23). Although labor was permitted on Rosh Chodesh, business activities were suspended (Amos 8:5). According to a talmudic tradition, the custom of reading the Torah on Rosh Chodesh dates back to the days of Moses (Jer. *Megillah* 4:1). This tradition surely reflects the antiquity of the custom, which called for the assembly of congregations.

Whatever its theological significance, the popular appeal of Rosh Chodesh was based on its joyous character and on the festive meals, which were occasions for family gatherings. When David failed to appear at King Saul's Rosh Chodesh banquet, Jonathan explained David's absence by the latter's decision to attend his family's feast at Bethlehem (I Sam. 20:27, 29). The festive meals enhanced the social significance of Rosh Chodesh, but they were also encouraged as a means of publicizing the date of the beginning of a new month.

By comparison with Rosh Chodesh, the Sabbath was a much more austere and restrictive day. It is not surprising that when the ancients mentioned the two most frequent festivals, Rosh Chodesh, or just Chodesh as it was generally called, and the Sabbath, the former was mentioned first (II Kings 4:23; Isa. 1:13, 66:23; Hosea 2:13). Isaiah and

Hosea reflected the popular perception of these festivals common in the eight century B.C.E. A reversal in the status of the Sabbath and Rosh Chodesh emerged with the establishment of the Babylonian diaspora. Thereafter the Sabbath preceded Rosh Chodesh (Ezek. 46:3, Neh. 10:34, I Chron. 23:31, II Chron. 2:3, 8:13).

A few factors contributed to the restoration of the primacy of the Sabbath vis-à-vis Rosh Chodesh. On the one hand, the Sabbath began to assume an increasingly joyous character. On the other hand, the suspension of sacrificial rites in the period between the two Temples eliminated the element of atonement from Rosh Chodesh. Furthermore, the custom of serving festive meals on Rosh Chodesh gradually decreased in importance and popularity. The main purpose of the meal, the publicizing of the date of Rosh Chodesh, lost its urgency with the introduction of couriers sent by the Sanhedrin to bring vital calendrical information to the attention of the diaspora.

IN THE SECOND COMMONWEALTH

The proclamation of Rosh Chodesh by the Sanhedrin, formerly an exclusive jurisdiction of the high priest, became a source of vehement contention by all nonrabbinic Jewish sects. The sectarians insisted on permanently fixed calendars which leave no discretionary powers to a religious court.

The jurisdiction of the Sanhedrin to fix the calendar on a monthly basis was inherent in its judicial powers. The proceedings leading to a proclamation of Rosh Chodesh were guided by established rules of evidence. Testimony by witnesses who claimed to have seen the moon was subjected to the court's examination. Testimony contrary to astronomical calculation was disqualified.

The thirtieth day of the month was observed as Rosh Chodesh in anticipation of the arrival of witnesses. If none arrived, the Sanhedrin sat in session again on the following day to proclaim it Rosh Chodesh.

If testimony was received on the thirtieth day, that day was officially declared the first day of the new month, leaving the preceding month with twenty-nine days. In the event that the proclamation was made on the thirty-first day, there were two days of Rosh Chodesh, the thirtieth and thirty-first. Despite its being observed as Rosh Chodesh, the thirtieth day was actually the last day of the preceding month, which numbered thirty days. The second day of Rosh Chodesh was counted as the first day of the new month.

A twenty-nine-day month was known as *chaser* ("incomplete"), and a thirty-day month was called *male* ("complete"). The Sanhedrin's discretionary power to choose the date of Rosh Chodesh was circumscribed by a rule that there may be no less than four nor more than eight complete months in any given year (*Arachin* 8b).

According to a mishnah (*Rosh HaShanah* 23b), the Sanhedrin provided lavish meals to induce witnesses to come forward. This practice was most likely instituted in the first century, when turbulent conditions in Jerusalem contributed to the reluctance of potential witnesses to travel to that city. The Sanhedrin came to rely more and more on astronomical calculations, and the testimony of witnesses became a mere formality, with rules of qualification not strictly enforced. This was particularly true after the destruction of the Temple.

Relaxed application of rules of evidence occasionally led to subsequent impeachment of witnesses whose testimony had been admitted by the court. According to the provisions of the law, a court's decision based on false testimony is reversible. In the case of a proclamation of Rosh Chodesh, a reversal of the proclamation could lead to disastrous consequences. Jewish communities that did not hear of the reversal would celebrate the holiday on one date, and those that became cognizant of the reversal would celebrate it on another date.

While the Temple was in existence, the unity of the Jewish people was never seriously threatened. Under the changed circumstances of the post-Temple era, any divisiveness posed a danger to the viability of distant Jewish communities in the diaspora. It was urgent to maintain religious uniformity. Rabban Gamliel, the first head of the Sanhedrin of Hillel's house after the destruction of the Temple, established the irreversibility of the Sanhedrin's proclamation of Rosh Chodesh, even when based on erroneous judgment (*Rosh HaShanah* 25a). To lessen rabbinic opposition to his rule, Rabban Gamliel based it on a biblical text (ibid.).

The assumption of such absolute power was also legitimized by various homiletical assertions in the Talmud. Thus God was alleged to have yielded his own prerogatives to the judgment of the Sanhedrin in fixing the date of Rosh Chodesh. "When the heavenly tribunal perceives that the earthly tribunal has sanctified a new month, it also sanctifies it" (Jer. *Rosh HaShanah* 2:7).

There is another perplexing talmudic passage which apparently alludes to the difficulty presented by this instance of absolute rabbinic power. Moses is said to have evinced some difficulty in comprehending three laws which God had commanded: the construction of the menorah, Rosh Chodesh, and the identification of unclean reptiles.

Due to Moses' perplexity, these laws had to be clarified by the Almighty (*Menachot* 29a).

What was so unique about the aforementioned three laws? It seems to me that the talmudic passage is alluding to the supernatural and discretionary powers vested by God in the rabbinic leadership which had initially perplexed Moses.

The western light of the menorah burned for twenty-four hours, even though it contained the same amount of oil as the other lights, which lasted only through the night (*Sifra*, Lev. 24:2–3). The jurisdiction to proclaim Rosh Chodesh was an exercise of extraordinary discretionary power. Biblically prohibited reptiles had no visible distinguishing marks to guide the rabbis in identifying them.

In the Temple era, the Sanhedrin's chief preoccupation with regard to Rosh Chodesh was the proclamation of the new month and the dissemination of the information in the diaspora. After the destruction of the Temple, the rabbis concentrated upon the exposition of the laws of Rosh Chodesh and its rituals.

IN THE POST-TEMPLE ERA

Second-century Jewry, recovering from the disastrous loss of the Temple and national independence, was in greater need of feasts than fasts. Rabban Gamliel ranked Rosh Chodesh with Chanukah and Purim as festival days on which no fasts may be observed (*Taanit* 15b). This ordinance formalized a practice which had already been followed voluntarily by pious individuals in previous centuries. The apocryphal Book of Judith extolled its heroine, who "had fasted all the days of her widowhood, except for the eve of the Sabbath and the Sabbath, and the eve of Rosh Chodesh and Rosh Chodesh" (8:6, ca. 1st cent. B.C.E.). Rabban Gamliel's decree did not prohibit fasting on the eve of Rosh Chodesh.

Funeral lamentations and eulogies were also prohibited on Rosh Chodesh (*Moed Katan* 28b). Another second-century regulation set the number of Torah aliyot on Rosh Chodesh at four (*Megillah* 21a). The permissibility of labor on Rosh Chodesh was discussed and ruled in the affirmative (*Chagigah* 18a). It appears, however, that despite the ruling that the performance of labor on Rosh Chodesh is not legally prohibited, business and trade activity was largely suspended. This is the clear implication of the explanation for the addition of a fourth aliyah on Rosh Chodesh because "the people are not hindered from their work," i.e. they generally do not work on that day (*Megillah* 22b).

According to Rashi, this statement referred to women, who are accustomed to abstain from work. This comment is questionable for several reasons. It is doubtful that the custom of women abstaining from work dates back to mishnaic times. Congregational services on Rosh Chodesh were mainly attended by men, and it is their needs which had to be taken into consideration.

An effort was made in the third century to once again popularize the Rosh Chodesh festival meal. According to an early amoraic statement, "The entire sustenance of man is fixed for him from Rosh HaShanah to Yom Kippur, except for the expenditures for Sabbaths and festivals. . . . if he spends less he is given less, if he spends more he is given more" (Betzah 16a). In a somewhat later statement, Rosh Chodesh was added as a day for which an indefinite food allotment is granted (Pesikta deRav Kahana 28).

Another third-century enactment provided for the mention of Rosh Chodesh in the Amidah (Berachot 49a) and the prayer of Grace (Shabbat 24a). The recitation of the incomplete Hallel at the morning service of Rosh Chodesh was instituted in Babylonia in the third century (Taanit 28b).

THE BLESSING OF THE NEW MOON

The practice of blessing the moon upon its renewal was introduced in the third century (Sanhedrin 42a). The reappearance of the moon was regarded as a reminder of God's creation of the universe and a proper occasion for welcoming the presence of the Almighty. In deference to that perception, it was decreed in the fourth century that one must stand when reciting this prayer (ibid.).

The custom of blessing the moon originated in Palestine. At first the blessing consisted of a single sentence: "Blessed be he who renews the months [or moons]." A longer text was subsequently introduced and published in the Talmud (Sanhedrin 42a). The ritual was elaborated upon in the eighth century (Masechet Soferim 20) and further enlarged by the sixteenth-century kabbalists.

The Talmud ruled that the period for reciting the blessing of the moon ends when it reaches its full dimension (Sanhedrin 42a). There was no limitation upon the time when one may begin to recite the prayer. However, a limitation was introduced in the medieval period as a result of an interpretation of a phrase in Masechet Soferim (edited in 8th cent.). According to that text, the blessing of the moon should be offered on a Saturday night, "when he is perfumed [mevusam] with the fragrance of spices [the *besamim*] and attired in nice clothes" (chap. 20). This sentence obviously refers to worshippers who emerge from the synagogue on Saturday nights in their Sabbath clothes, bearing the fragrance of the Havdalah spices. According to a later interpretation, the word *mevusam* refers to the moon, which must be clearly visible before the prayer is offered. It was therefore ruled that one should wait at least three days after the nativity of the moon to recite the prayer (*Kol Bo* 43). According to another medieval custom, the new moon of the months of Tishri and Av should be blessed after Yom Kippur and Tisha B'Av. It was felt that one's frame of mind in the periods of atonement and mourning is incompatible with the joyous mood with which one should welcome the presence of God.

The reason for the introduction of the benediction of the moon has not been indicated. We can only conjecture that historical developments contributed to the popularity of this innovation. Ever since the wars of Emperor Septimius Severus, who visited Palestine in the year 200, the country had experienced the sting of exorbitant Roman taxation and hostility. Conditions improved somewhat with the rule of Alexander Severus (222–235). At about the same time, Judah II succeeded to the office of Patriarch. Due to his influence with Alexander Severus, some of Hadrian's repressive laws were removed. Judah transferred the seat of the patriarchate to Tiberias and ordered that the proclamation of new months be made in that city. It is likely that the renewal of the moon's cycle was highlighted with a popular ritual as an omen that the happy days of Judea would soon be renewed.

SHABBAT MEVORACHIM

The custom of announcing the date of the new month on the Sabbath preceding Rosh Chodesh originated in the geonic period. Some scholars traced the basis of the custom to a talmudic statement of Rabbi Jose that he made sure to ascertain the date of Rosh Chodesh before reciting the Sabbath Musaf prayer (Jer. *Sanhedrin* 5:3).

In a sense, the publication of a permanent calendar in the fourth century obviated the need for an official proclamation of the new month. Yet some geonim felt that there was still a need for a symbolic proclamation in memory of the ancient sanctification of the month.

Rav Amram Gaon (9th cent) mentioned a custom of announcing the beginning of the new month on the day of Rosh Chodesh (*Seder Rav Amram Gaon*). Subsequent geonim objected to the practice because it created the appearance of an official proclamation of a new month, which may only be done by a religious court in Palestine. It was therefore decided to advance the announcement of the date of the new month to the preceding Sabbath.

According to the medieval Ashkenazic rite, the ceremony began with the prayer of *Mi sheasa nisim* ("he who wrought miracles"). The *molad* (exact time of the appearance of the moon) was then announced. The molad is the same throughout the world. The announced molad in terms of hours and *chalakim* (a *chalak* equals 3 and ⅓ seconds) are those of Jerusalem's solar time. After the molad, the date of Rosh Chodesh was announced, and the ceremony was concluded with the prayer of *Yechadeshehu* ("may the Almighty renew it").

A special introductory prayer, *Yehi ratzon* ("may it be thy will"), was added in the Polish ritual in the eighteenth century. The entire composition, except for the first sentence, was originally written by Rav (3rd cent.) as a daily prayer (*Berachot* 16b)). The custom of holding the Torah during the announcement of the date of Rosh Chodesh was also introduced in the eighteenth century.

A ROSH CHODESH CUP OF WINE

It was customary in some medieval communities for the husband to present the cup of wine that is usually drunk after Grace to his wife in appreciation of the blessings which she brings to the home. Another cup of wine was then filled for the pronouncement of the benediction after Grace (*Machzor Vitry*, 12th cent.).

ROSH CHODESH TUITION FEES

According to a medieval custom, parents gave their children tuition money for the teacher on Rosh Chodesh (Bach, *Orach Chaim 419, Umah shekatav*). The custom was based on a talmudic statement (*Betzah* 16a).

IN THE SYNAGOGUE

The prayer of *Yaaleh veyavo,* in which Rosh Chodesh is mentioned, is inserted in the Shacharit *Amidah*. After the *Amidah* the congregation recites the incomplete *Hallel*. Four persons are called to the Torah for the reading of the selection dealing with the sacrificial ritual of Rosh Chodesh (Num. 28:1–15). The tefillin are removed prior to the recitation of the Musaf *Amidah*. The penitential prayer of *Tachanun* is not recited on Rosh Chodesh.

In some congregations the morning service is concluded with *Borachi nafshi*.

WOMEN ABSTAIN FROM WORK

The Jerusalem Talmud refers with approval of the custom of women abstaining from work on Rosh Chodesh (*Taanit* 1:6). Rav Hai Gaon (10th–11th cent.) cited the same talmudic reference as the source for the custom of women abstaining from meat and wine during the nine days of Av (Avudrahim, *Hilchot Taaniyot*). *Kol Bo* (13th–14th cent.) mentioned the custom of women abstaining from work when the Chanukah lights are burning.

The greater restrictions assumed by women seem to have originated in Palestine, whence they spread to Babylonia and subsequently to Europe.

Pirke deRabbi Eliezer (a midrashic work edited in the 9th century) offered a reason for the women's custom of abstaining from work on Rosh Chodesh. "The women had refused to surrender their rings to their husbands in the incident of the golden calf. The Almighty rewarded them therefore that they should observe Rosh Chodesh" (chap. 44).

The relevance of the incident of the golden calf to the observance of Rosh Chodesh is somewhat obscure. It may possibly be explained by the tradition that Moses ascended Mount Sinai on Rosh Chodesh Elul to receive the second Tablets of the Law (Rashi, Exod. 33:11). God's command that Moses ascend the mountain (Exod. 34:2) on Rosh Chodesh signaled his forgiveness of the sin of the golden calf. The women had greater reason for celebrating the day because they had never been guilty of that sin.

Avudrahim *(Seder Rosh Chodesh)* quoted another midrash which offered a different explanation for women's greater observance of Rosh Chodesh. They responded before the men to Moses' appeal for contributions for the Tabernacle (Exod. 35:2). The Tabernacle was erected on Rosh Chodesh Nisan (Exod. 40:17).

II.
ISERU CHAG CUSTOMS

The day following Passover, Shavuot, and Sukkot is called Iseru Chag, a supplemental holiday. It is based on a statement of Rabbi Simon b. Yochai (2nd cent.): "Whoever makes an addition [or 'binding'] to the holiday by feasting is regarded in the Scriptures as though he had built an altar and offered a sacrifice thereon. For it is said: 'Bind the sacrifice [*iseru chag*] with cord, even unto the horns of the altar' " (Ps. 118:27; *Sukkah* 45b). According to one of Rashi's interpretations, the recommendation of an extra day of feasting refers to the day following the holiday (ibid., *baachilah ushetiyah*).

The religious character of Iseru Chag was first mentioned in the Middle Ages (*Shibole HaLeket* 262). Rema (16th cent.) included in his annotations to the code (*Orach Chaim* 429:2) a suggestion that one should add some extra courses to his meal on that day.

Tachanun is omitted on Iseru Chag and no fast may be observed on that day.

The day after Shavuot, which is included in the category of Iseru Chag, is also known by the special name of Yom HaTavuach ("the day of slaughtering"). The single day of the biblical Shavuot could not accommodate the many pilgrims who wished to offer private thanksgiving sacrifices. They had no choice but to offer them on the day after Shavuot. Hence the name Yom HaTavuach. The day was considered a semi-festival in the tannaic period. The delivery of funeral eulogies was prohibited (*Chagigah* 18a).

III.
CHAMISHAH ASAR B'SHEVAT CUSTOMS

The semi-festive character of the fifteenth of Shevat derives from the tannaic designation of that day as the New Year of Trees (*Rosh HaShanah* 2a). The designation was more than just of social import. It was a major legal principle affecting the law of tithing and the prohibition of fruit of immature trees (*orlah*).

Fruit set aside as a tithe must be of the same season as the fruit which it redeems. Consequently, fruit which blossomed prior to the fifteenth of Shevat may not be used as a tithe for fruit which blossomed after that date.

A new tree enters into its second year upon reaching the fifteenth of Shevat. That determines the date when its new fruit may first be eaten.

According to an amoraic explanation, the winter rains, which begin after Tishri, generally come to an end in Shevat. The blossoms that appear after the fifteenth of Shevat have surely been nurtured by springs fed by waters of the current year. Earlier blossoms might have drawn their sustenance from waters of the previous year and are therefore regarded as the fruit of that year (*Rosh HaShanah* 14a).

The fifteenth of Shevat had no religious significance in the talmudic period. However, beginning with the thirteenth century, the rules which normally apply to semi-festivals—the omission of *Tachanun* and prohibition of fasts—were put into effect.

Major innovations in the celebration of the fifteenth of Shevat were introduced by the Palestinian kabbalists of the sixteenth century. Special liturgical compositions were written and the day was marked by the eating of indigenous fruits and the drinking of four cups of wine.

Some of these innovations had a far-reaching effect upon the celebration of this semi-festival throughout the diaspora. Jews in the cold European zones ate carobs and dried fruits of varieties that grow in Palestine.

According to a curious custom of more recent origin, Jews prayed on the New Year of Trees for success in obtaining a beautiful etrog for the coming Sukkot. There was also a practice of serving jam made from the etrogim of the previous Sukkot. These customs might have been inspired by a talmudic account of Rabbi Akiva's picking of an etrog on the first of Shevat (*Rosh HaShanah* 14a) and a subsequent discussion of the status of etrogim on the fifteenth of Shevat (ibid. 14b).

In the past several centuries, the fifteenth of Shevat has been declared a school holiday. In modern Israel schoolchildren strengthen their ties to the soil by planting trees on that day.

IV.
PURIM KATAN CUSTOMS

In an intercalary year, Purim is observed in the second Adar (*Megillah* 6b). Prior to the publication of the permanent calendar in the fourth century, there were some rare occasions when Purim was celebrated twice in the same year. If the court's decision to add an extra Adar was announced after Purim had already been celebrated, the festival was observed again in the second Adar (ibid.).

The possibility of celebrating Purim twice in the same year was eliminated by the permanent calendar. Medieval scholars, however, differed in their opinions as to whether the prohibition of funeral eulogies and fasts remains in effect in both Adars of an intercalary year.

The prevailing medieval custom retained these prohibitions in the first Adar, and the day was named Purim Katan ("Minor Purim"). Pious Jews served a festive meal on Purim Katan. Rema (16th cent.) endorsed this practice (*Orach Chaim* 697). Memorial prayers and *Tachanun* are omitted.

V.
YOM HAATZMAUT CUSTOMS

On the fifth of Iyar, 5708 (June 14, 1948), the State of Israel declared its independence. The rebirth of Zion represented the fulfillment of ancient prophetic predictions and the culmination of modern nationalistic aspirations. From both the religious and the secularist point of view, it was the most significant event in Jewish history since the year 70.

Yom HaAtzmaut (Independence Day) has been institutionalized as a national holiday in Israel from the very outset. It took a little time for a formal text of a religious celebration to be established. As a religious observance, the text has a place in the liturgy of the Jewish diaspora.

The observance begins on the evening of the fourth of Iyar. The service opens with the recitation of the One hundred and seventh, Ninety-seventh, and Ninety-eighth Psalms. This is followed by the fifth, sixth, and eighth stanzas of the hymn *Lecha Dodi*. The introductory phase of the service is followed by Maariv. Upon its conclusion, the ark is opened and the *Shema* is exclaimed three times, followed by the chazan's reading of verses 9 and 10 of Numbers 10. The shofar is blown and the congregation responds with *L'shanah habaah biyerushalayim habenuyah* ("next year in built-up Jerusalem"). The service is concluded with *Shir HaMaalot* to the tune of *Hatikvah* (Ps. 126) and *Ani maamin . . . bebiat hamashiach* ("I believe in the coming of the Messiah"). A festive meal is served at home and candles are lit in honor of the occasion.

Shacharit includes the *Pesukei deZimrah* of Sabbaths and festivals (Pss. 19, 34, 90, 91, 135, 136, 33, 92, and 93) and the complete *Hallel*. The Haftarah *Od hayom benov* (Isa. 10:32–12:6) is chanted. This is followed by a prayer for the government, a memorial for the fallen soldiers, and *Av HaRachamim*. The service is concluded with *Ani Maamin*.

Tachanun is omitted at Minchah services.

VI.
PESACH SHENI CUSTOMS

Jews who had been defiled by contamination were barred from offering the paschal lamb in the Temple. They were given an opportunity to sacrifice the lamb one month later, on the fourteenth of Iyar (Num. 9:10–11). *Hallel* was chanted during the ritual preparation of the offering but not in the course of the meal (*Pesachim* 95a). Obviously the day itself was not characterized by any holiness.

Jewish tradition has sought to preserve the memory of all ancient special occasions connected with the biblical festivals. The religious calendar therefore takes note of Pesach Sheni ("Second Passover"). The fourteenth of Iyar is not classified as a festive day and it does not suspend the mourning rituals of the Sefirah period. However, some congregations omit *Tachanun* on that day.

VII.
LAG B'OMER CUSTOMS

Lag B'Omer (thirty-third day of Omer) is celebrated on the eighteenth of Iyar. The restrictive mourning regulations which are in effect through most of the period between Passover and Shavuot are suspended on Lag B'Omer. Marriages and haircuts are permitted, and the prayer of *Tachanun* is omitted.

The special significance of Lag B'Omer was first mentioned in the fourteenth century. By the fifteenth century it was established as a semi-festival. Sixteenth-century kabbalists added a new dimension to the holiday by designating it the yahrzeit of Rabbi Simon b. Yochai, the traditional author of the Zohar. Pilgrimages are made to Meron, the burial place of the venerated sage. Many parents take their young sons to Meron on Lag B'Omer for their first haircuts. Rabbi Simon's tomb is illuminated with torches and elaborate festivities take place.

In some areas of Eastern Europe Lag B'Omer was declared a school holiday. Teachers related the heroic story of Bar Kochba's rebellion, and students would go out into the fields with bows and arrows to fight the Romans. (For a full discussion of the history of this festival, see Bloch, *Biblical and Historical Background of the Jewish Holy Days,* chap. 8.)

VIII.
YOM CHERUT YERUSHALAYIM

East Jerusalem was united with West Jerusalem on the twenty-eighth day of Iyar, 5727 (June 7, 1967). For the first time since the creation of the State of Israel, Jews gained access to the Western Wall and the site of the Temple, the hub of Jewish religious and national existence.

This day, like Yom HaAtzmaut, became a religious and national holiday. The religious aspect of the holiday finds its expression in the liturgy. *Tachanun* is omitted from the Minchah service on the twenty-seventh of Iyar. Maariv is chanted in the traditional melody of festival services. Shacharit on the twenty-eighth of Iyar includes the festival *Pesukei deZimrah* (see Yom HaAtzmaut) and the complete *Hallel*.

IX.
THE FIFTEENTH OF AV

The semi-festival of the fifteenth of Av is of ancient origin. It was discontinued and restored several times in the course of Jewish history. The rationale of the holiday similarly changed from time to time. It began as an agricultural festival, evolved into a youth (or matrimonial) carnival, and ultimately became a Temple holiday, associated with the offering of wood for the altar.

The fifteenth of Av is one of many semi-festivals listed in *Megillat Taanit* (chap. 12). All of them, with the exception of Chanukah and Purim, were discontinued, and they left no trace in the religious calendar. However, the fifteenth of Av is still commemorated, and the rules which regulate the liturgy of semi-festivals are in effect. *Tachanun* is omitted, beginning with Minchah of the fourteenth of Av (Polish rite). The same is true of the prayers of *LaMenatzeach* and *Kel erech apayim (Siddur Bet Yaakov)*.

The retention of the fifteenth of Av in the religious calendar was probably due to the extensive discussion of the festival in the Talmud (*Baba Batra* 121a) and the sweeping statement of Rabbi Simon b. Gamliel (2nd cent.) that "Israel had no festive days like the fifteenth of Av . . ." (ibid.).

Kol Bo (14th cent.) also devoted extensive space to a discussion of the festival of the fifteenth of Av and thus assured its continued commemoration *(Hilchot Tisha B'Av)*. (For a full discussion of the background of the fifteenth of Av, see Bloch, *Biblical and Historical Background of the Jewish Holy Days*, chap. 11.)

12

Tisha B'Av Customs

I.
INTRODUCTION

TISHA B'AV IS ONE of four memorial fasts established after the destruction of the First Temple in 586 B.C.E. (Zech. 8:19). According to tradition, Tisha B'Av was proclaimed a public fast, whereas the other three—the third of Tishri, the tenth of Tevet, and the seventeenth of Tammuz—were declared voluntary private fasts (*Taanit* 12b). There was ample reason for the differentiation. The voluntary fasts marked setbacks suffered in a tragic period. Tisha B'Av, on the other hand, commemorated the culmination of the national disaster.

The four memorial fasts were suspended shortly after the building of the Second Temple (518 B. C. E.; *Rosh HaShanah* 18b) and restored after its destruction (70 C. E.). Tisha B'Av was most likely reinstated by the Sanhedrin of Yavneh, under the presidency of Rabban Gamliel II (80–118 C. E.). The remaining fasts were reintroduced after the defeat of Bar Kochba (135 C. E.; see Bloch, *Biblical and Historical Background of the Jewish Holy Days*, pp. 232–233).

The restored fasts resumed their original status. Tisha B'Av once again became a mandatory public fast while the others retained their status as voluntary private fasts (*Rosh HaShanah* 18b). The Talmud attributed the stringency of Tisha B'Av to the multiple disasters which had occurred on that day (ibid.). However, of the four listed tragedies on that day, three related to events that had occurred in the period of the Second Temple and therefore could not have been a factor in determining the status of Tisha B'Av in the Babylonian diaspora. As we have previously indicated, the special solemnity of Tisha B'Av derived from its commemoration of the loss of the Temple (see Tosafot, *Hoil; Rosh HaShanah* 18b).

309

CATEGORIES OF FASTS

The rites of Tisha B'Av are made up of the traditional rituals of public fasts plus some of the mourning customs for a departed kin. A brief discussion of the rituals of public fasts in the talmudic era will help clarify the development of Tisha B'Av. Fasts fell into several categories, some of which were marked by graduations on an ascending scale of solemnity and restrictions.

CATEGORY A—PRIVATE SUPPLICATORY FASTS

Rationale: To arouse penitence through self-mortification.
  Objective: To secure salvation from an impending tragedy.
  Restrictions: Abstention from food beginning with sunrise.

CATEGORY B—PUBLIC SUPPLICATORY FASTS

Rationale: Same as category A. Also, to enhance awareness of a critical situation and create a sense of mutual responsibility. Theologically, congregational prayers are more effective than prayers in private.
  Objective: Same as category A.
  Restrictions: A graduated scale of prohibitions which increase as the emergency grows more critical. The graduations are best illustrated by the laws regulating public fasts for rain.
  First Stage. Mandatory fast from sunrise.
  Second Stage. Fast begins on preceding evening. Prohibition of the following pleasurable acts: washing with warm water, anointing of one's body, wearing of leather shoes, marital intercourse. Performance of labor, though not a pleasurable act, is prohibited. This restriction is based on a rabbinical interpretation of Joel 1:14 (*Taanit* 12b).
  Third Stage. Business shops are closed. A shofar is blown at a public assembly.
  Fourth Stage. Business transactions, building and planting, betrothals and marriages must be diminished. Personal greetings and salutations are not exchanged because people who have incurred the displeasure of God should shun the companionship of their fellowmen, in the manner of a person who has been placed under a ban (ibid.). Mourning customs are added to acts of self-mortification. The realization that God's grace has been turned away is cause for mourning.

CATEGORY C—PRIVATE MEMORIAL FASTS

Rationale: To arouse penitence through mourning.

Objective: To invoke God's mercies to the end that past tragedies not be repeated and that baneful consequences of past tragedies be annulled.

Restrictions: Same as Category A.

The major source of private memorial fasts is the concluding chapter of *Megillat Taanit*. In addition to the historical fasts, one may also adopt his own memorial fasts, such as on occasions of yahrzeit and anniversaries of past family disasters.

CATEGORY D—PUBLIC MEMORIAL FASTS

Rationale: Same as category C.

Objective: Same as category C.

Restrictions: The principal public memorial fast is Tisha B'Av. Its prohibitions include elements of the second and fourth stages of category B. It also includes some additional mourning rites. All of these will be discussed later in this chapter.

IN THE TALMUDIC ERA

The mournful tone of the commemoration of the loss of the Temple was set by Rabbi Yochanan b. Zakkai (1st cent.). As soon as the news of the tragedy reached him, "he rent his clothes and wept and lamented" (*Avot de Rabbi Natan* 4). He thus set a precedent for the inclusion of mourners' rites in the context of the observance of Tisha B'Av.

The laws governing Tisha B'Av were discussed and formulated in the second century, following the defeat of Bar Kochba. Rabbi Simon b. Gamliel, president of the Sanhedrin of Usha, was most responsible for the evolving laws.

The rabbis divided the time of mourning into four halachic periods: the nine days (beginning with the first of Av), the week of Tisha B'Av (beginning with the Sabbath preceding the fast), the eve of Tisha B'Av, and the ninth of Av.

IN THE SECOND CENTURY

The Nine Days. "When Av comes in, gladness must be diminished" (*Taanit* 26b). A beraita (*Yevamot* 43a) elaborates upon the details.

"Before this time [beginning with the first of Av] people diminish business activities, building, and planting [the same as in the fourth stage of category B]. Marriages are prohibited [they are merely diminished in stage 4 of category B]. Betrothals, without feasts, are permitted [they are diminished in stage 4 of category B]."

Betrothals per se were not deemed inconsistent with a state of mourning. Even a mourner in the shivah period was not restricted from betrothal (*Hilchot Avelot* 392:1; Rema prohibited it). In times of stress, such as drought, one must concentrate on prayer. All activities which lay a foundation for one's future, such as betrothals, must be diminished. However, mourning is the principal motif of the restrictions during the nine days. Betrothal, when not celebrated with a feast, merely establishes a legal status and is therefore permissible during the nine days. The exchange of social greetings and salutations (diminished in stage 4 of category B) was for practical reasons not restricted prior to the day of the fast.

The Week of Tisha B'Av. It is forbidden to cut one's hair and to wash laundry during the week of Tisha B'Av (*Yevamot* 43a). Rabbi Meir advanced this prohibition to the first of Av, and Rabbi Judah extended it to the entire month of Av. Rabbi Simon b. Gamliel, however, limited the prohibition to the week of Tisha B'Av (*Taanit* 29b). This restriction is a mourning rite and was never part of the observance of other public fasts.

The Eve of Tisha B'Av. The additional restrictions which were enacted for the eve of Tisha B'Av are confined to the pre-fast meal. Unlike the pre-fast meal of Yom Kippur, which may be lavish in its variety of courses, the pre-fast meal of Tisha B'Av must be limited to one cooked dish. No wine or meat may be served (*Taanit* 26b).

Wine and meat, according to tradition, generate lingering joy. Furthermore, wine and meat were part of the Temple's sacrificial rituals, which came to an end with the loss of the Sanctuary. It was therefore considered proper to abstain from them close to the fast. First-century zealots had advocated a permanent ban on wine and meat as a continuing expression of grief for the Temple (*Baba Batra* 60b, Rabban Yochanan b. Zakkai). The rabbis discouraged extreme forms of asceticism and sanctioned such a ban only at the pre-fast meal.

Tisha B'Av. There are five pleasurable acts which are prohibited on Tisha B'Av: eating, washing, anointing, wearing of leather shoes, and marital intercourse. The interdiction begins with the preceding evening (*Taanit* 30a). These restrictions parallel those of Yom Kippur and of a mourner. Similar prohibitions were enacted in the second stage of category B, in which, however, the restriction of bathing was limited only to warm water.

The study of Torah or Talmud is prohibited because intellectual pursuits produce joy. It is permissible, however, to read Lamentations, Job, and parts of Jeremiah.

With regard to the performance of labor, one should follow the custom of the community in which he resides. Scholars have been urged to abstain from work (*Pesachim* 54b).

In the opinion of Rabbi Judah, an advocate of stringent Tisha B'Av restrictions, one must abide by the rules of mourning and sleep on the ground. The majority of the rabbis disagreed (*Taanit* 26b).

The Three Weeks. In addition to the three halachic periods of mourning, there is a reference in the Midrash to a "period of stress" between the seventeenth of Tammuz and the ninth of Av (*Eichah Rabbati, Umerov Avodah* on Lam. 1:3). There is also a reference in the Jerusalem Talmud (quoted in *Tur, Orach Chaim* 551) to the twenty-one days between the two fasts. However, both references have a homiletical rather than a halachic significance.

INITIAL MODERATION

A review of Tisha B'Av enactments in the second century gives an impression of moderation. This is particularly true of the attitude of the patriarchate, which headed the culturally autonomous Jewish community of Palestine. In their efforts to make coexistence with Rome a viable policy, the patriarchs minimized commemorations of past conflicts.

In line with that policy, Rabbi Simon b. Gamliel publicized the festive character of the fifteenth of Av, an ancient Jewish youth festival (*Taanit* 26b). Thus he removed the impression that the entire month of Av is a solemn period, a view upheld by Rabbi Judah (*Yevamot* 43a). Rebbe, the son of Rabban Simon b. Gamliel and editor of the Mishnah, deliberately inserted his father's statement about the fifteenth of Av immediately following the discussion of the laws of Tisha B'Av (*Taanit* 26b).

The policy of moderation is also reflected in Rabban Simon b. Gamliel's explanation as to why the rabbis of his generation were not inclined to compose a record of the trials and tribulations of their time, similar to *Megillat Taanit*, which had been published after the destruction of the Temple. "We too cherish our troubles but what can we do? If we attempted to put them in writing, we could not accomplish it"

(*Shabbat* 13b). He obviously felt that too much preoccupation with past troubles would not serve the cause of the people.

It is apparent that Rebbe also favored the toning down of the extreme solemnity of Tisha B'Av. He favored the cancellation of Tisha B'Av when it falls on a Sabbath, in disagreement with the prevailing law that in such an event Tisha B'Av is postponed but not canceled (*Megillah* 5b).

IN THE THIRD AND FOURTH CENTURIES

The laws of Tisha B'Av continued to be defined in greater detail in the third and fourth centuries. On the whole, the spirit of moderation evident in the tannaic period persisted. Samuel (3rd cent.) announced that Tisha B'Av was the only memorial fast to attain the status of a public fast in the Babylonian diaspora (*Pesachim* 54b). Rav Papa (4th cent.) confirmed the optional nature of the other three memorial fasts: "If they wish they fast, and if they wish they do not fast" (*Rosh HaShanah* 18b).

Despite the persisting spirit of moderation, some restrictions were added in this period. New clothes may not be made beginning with the first of Av (Jer. *Taanit* 1:6). One rabbi expressed an opinion that betrothals should be prohibited during the week of the fast (*Yevamot* 43a, Rashi, *Kodem d'kodem*). The tannaic admonition that joys be diminished from the first of Av led Rav Papa to the conclusion that this period is marked by bad luck. He therefore advised Jewish litigants to avoid litigation in non-Jewish courts at that time (*Taanit* 29b). Rabbi Yochanan (3rd cent.) cautioned teachers not to administer corporal punishment during the three weeks after the seventeenth of Tammuz because it might endanger the health of the students (*Midrash Eichah Rabbati* on Lam. 1:3). Walking alone on a road at this time of the year was also discouraged (ibid.).

IN THE POST-TALMUDIC ERA

The gradual emergence of a set of halachic laws affecting the three-week period reflects the post-talmudic revision of the moderate talmudic policy. *Eichah Rabbati*, edited approximately in the seventh century, was an early harbinger of a new trend of imposing more stringent Tisha B'Av restrictions. This Midrash drew most of its material from the Jerusalem Talmud. The Palestinian amoraim had good reason to favor harsher restrictions, for they were subjected to more severe persecutions than their Babylonian colleagues. The ruins of Jerusalem were never out of their sight.

The new trend was reflected in *Masechet Soferim* (edited in the 8th cent.), which describes a contemporary Tisha B'Av custom of placing an empty Torah Scroll case on the floor as if it were a corpse. Some people then performed the rite of *keriah* (rending of clothes) and wailed in the manner of bereaved. Others left their benches and lay down on the ground. Such innovations had no basis in the Talmud but emerged out of an impulse to dramatize the ancient tragedy and to ventilate Jewish frustrations and grief.

Progressively deteriorating conditions contributed to the development of the new trend. Nachmanides (13th cent.) took note of the worsening situation of the Jewish people in his comment on the three optional memorial fasts. "And now they [the Jews] have already made it a practice to fast and they have obligated themselves. Therefore no individual may breach the fence, especially in these generations when the afflictions of Israel have multiplied and there is no peace" (quoted by Avudrahim).

THE PROHIBITION OF WINE AND MEAT

The prohibition of wine and meat during the nine days is based on a quotation of Rav Hai Gaon (10th–11th cent.) from the Jerusalem Talmud (*Taanit* 1:6): "It is the practice of women to abstain from wine and meat, beginning with the month of Av until the end of the fast." He concluded with the statement: "And this is the prevailing custom in Babylonia" (quoted by Avudrahim *Hilchot Taaniyot*). The prohibition of wine and meat during the nine days was slow in acceptance. The Talmud had excluded them only from the pre-fast meal. The extension of the prohibition was adopted later by Babylonian Jewry. Avudrahim (14th cent.) stated that "in these lands [Spain] this custom did not spread and only individuals follow it." *Kol Bo* wrote somewhat later that it had become the practice of Spanish Jewry to abstain from wine and meat from the first of Av. According to the *Tur* (13th–14th cent.), the Jews of Germany abided by the new custom. Some, it noted, abstain from wine and meat beginning with the first of Av, and others, from the seventeenth of Tammuz (*Orach Chaim* 551).

Asheri, the father of the author of the *Tur*, is also quoted as having said: "And I have noted that there are some precious women who abstain from eating meat and drinking wine from the seventeenth of Tammuz to the tenth of Av. They assert that this tradition was handed down to them from their mothers in every generation. I believe that the custom was instituted as a memorial to the offering of the Tamid and the libation of wine which were discontinued [on the seventeenth of Tammuz]. Some of the earlier sages adhered to this custom" (quoted by *Kol Bo*).

The earliest source which mentions the prohibition of wine and meat during the nine days is Rav Hai Gaon, whose statement was previously quoted. His opinion was based on a text in the Jerusalem Talmud. However, our version of the text does not mention this prohibition. It reads as follows: "It is the practice of women not to weave [to make new clothes] . . ." This version of the text was known to the medieval sages, but they also quoted Rav Hai's version, which credited women with the prohibition of wine and meat. This leaves us with two questions. What historical or theological reason prompted women to institute such a prohibition? How did the variant version come about?

Most variant versions result from copyist's oversights—interchanging of letters, for instance, and accidental omission of sentences. Interpolations of new phrases or sentences, however, point to a deliberate insertion by a copyist. Scholarly copyists of the early post-talmudic period did not make marginal notes. They corrected the text whenever it appeared corrupt or unintelligible.

It is quite obvious that in the case of Rav Hai's version, some copyist felt the need for an interpolation in order to clarify a seemingly obscure passage. The troublesome phrase in the original text read *lo l'hishtaye* ("not to weave," derived from *sheti*). In the absence of vowel marks, the word can easily be mistaken for the Aramaic "not to drink" (*lo l'mishte*). A blanket prohibition of drinking must have appeared puzzling to the copyist, so he supplied the clarifying phrase, "not to drink wine and eat meat." Such a prohibition was mentioned in the Talmud (*Taanit* 26b) for the pre-fast meal. In the talmudic prohibition meat is mentioned first and then wine. In the emended Jerusalem text wine is mentioned first because it followed the injunction "not to drink."

The copyist left intact the introductory phrase of the sentence: "It is the practice of women . . ." Consequently, the abstention from wine and meat during the nine days came to be associated with the initiative of women. No one offered an explanation for this initiative. However, the original text dealt with the restriction on making new clothes, a custom which had come into vogue in the third or fourth century.

Since the production of new clothes was in the hands of women, the prohibition mainly affected women.

The prohibition of wine and meat during the nine days would have become the accepted practice with or without the emended version of the Jerusalem text. Since the trend in the sixteenth century was to extend all restrictions beyond the period of time set by the Talmud, it would have also affected the restriction on meat and wine.

The restriction on meat and wine does not apply to the Sabbath or a *seudat mitzvah*, the collation served on the occasion of a circumcision, Pidyon Haben, or *siyum* (the completion of a talmudic tract).

Fowl is not considered meat, but it may not be served for the pre-fast meal (*Tur, Drach Chaim* 552). Subsequent rabbis banned fowl in the nine-day period.

LAUNDERING

The Talmud prohibits laundering in the week of Tisha B'Av (*Yevamot* 43a). Rema (16th cent.) extended the prohibition to the beginning of the month of Av (*Orach Chaim* 551:3). Medieval custom (13th cent.) prohibited the wearing of newly laundered clothes, even if laundered prior to the month of Av (*Tur, Orach Chaim* 551). The wearing of new clothes, beginning with the month of Av, is also prohibited.

HAIRCUTS

The Talmud prohibits the cutting of hair during the week of Tisha B'Av (*Yevamot* 43a). Rema extended the prohibition to the three weeks between the seventeenth of Tammuz and the ninth of Av (*Orach Chaim* 551:4).

BATHING

The Talmud prohibits bathing on Tisha B'Av. Rema extended the prohibition to the nine days (*Orach Chaim* 551:16). Some contemporary rabbis permit swimming instruction when the immersion is not intended for bathing pleasure.

WEDDINGS

The Talmud prohibits weddings and betrothal banquets during the nine days (*Yevamot* 43a). Rema extended the prohibition to the three weeks (*Orach Chaim* 551:2).

SHEHECHEYANU

One does not eat a new fruit which requires the benediction of *Shehecheyanu* (the blessing upon reaching a new season). Such a benediction is inappropriate in a season of sorrow. The prohibition covers the three weeks (*Orach Chaim* 551:17).

BLESSING OF THE NEW MOON

The blessing of the new moon, normally done after Rosh Chodesh, is delayed until the evening of the tenth of Av (Rema, *Orach Chaim* 551:8).

SHABBAT CHAZON

The Sabbath preceding Tisha B'Av is called Shabbat Chazon after the opening phrase of the Haftarah, *Chazon Yeshayahu* (Isa. 2:1). One does not wear Sabbath clothes on this Sabbath.

When Shabbat Chazon falls on the eve of Tisha B'Av, the Havdalah is limited to the blessing over the light *(bore meore haesh)*. The blessing over the wine is recited on the following night, after the expiration of the fast.

When Tisha B'Av falls on a Sabbath, the fast is postponed to the following day (*Megillah* 5a).

THE PRE-FAST MEAL

The pre-fast meal must be limited to one cooked dish. According to tradition, the meal is eaten in individual privacy. The prayer of Grace should not be introduced by *zimmun* (an invitation to other members to join in the prayer).

According to a medieval custom, some people sat on the ground when eating the pre-fast meal (*Machzor Vitry* 264, 12th cent.).

TISHA B'AV EVE

The principal Tisha B'Av restrictions are listed in the Talmud (*Taanit* 30a). They are discussed at the beginning of this chapter.

The evening service is followed by the reading of *Eichah* and the recitation of prayers of lamentation *(kinot)*. To heighten the doleful atmosphere, one sits on the ground and reads by candlelight.

The Tisha B'Av practice of sitting on the ground was first mentioned in *Masechet Soferim* (edited in the 8th cent.). The medieval custom of darkening the synagogue is based on a passage in *Eichah Rabbati*, according to which the Almighty darkened the sun and the moon as a demonstration of his grief over the destruction of the Temple (Avudrahim).

SHACHARIT

According to the twelfth-century custom, tallit and tefillin are not worn at the morning service. The omission of the tallit is based on the implication of the phrase *bitza emrato* (Lam. 2:17), which was translated in the Targum as "he rent his tallit." Tefillin are omitted because they are called *pe'er* ("glory"), and there is no glory on Tisha B'Av.

The parochet (curtain) which adorns the ark is removed on Tisha B'Av. It was customary in some medieval congregations to place the Torah Scroll used for the reading of the morning's portion on a low lectern as a sign of mourning (Avudrahim). Three individuals are called to the Torah. Prayers of lamentation *(kinot)* are recited after the reading of the Torah.

It was customary in some medieval communities to assemble in the synagogue to read the Book of Job.

It is customary to visit cemeteries on Tisha B'Av. In Jerusalem, Jews visit the Western Wall to see the ruins of the Temple.

MINCHAH

Tallit and Tefillin are worn at the Minchah service. Once again three individuals are called to the Torah: kohen, levi, and maftir.

An additional prayer, *Nachem* ("comfort"), is inserted in the *Amidah* after the fourteenth benediction (the rebuilding of Jerusalem; *Siddur Rav Amram Gaon*, 9th cent.). Unlike the special prayer of *Anenu* ("answer us"), which is recited on all public fasts in the morning and afternoon, *Nachem* is recited only as part of the Minchah *Amidah* on Tisha B'Av. A prayer of consolation was considered inappropriate at the height of the day's grief and lamentation.

AFTER TISHA B'AV

The prohibition of bathing and the cutting of one's hair is customarily extended to midday of the tenth of Av. This is done out of respect for some Palestinian amoraim who fasted on the ninth and tenth of Av (Avudrahim) and in memory of the flames which continued to rage in the Temple on the tenth of Av.

SHABBAT NACHAMU

The Sabbath following Tisha B'Av is called Shabbat Nachamu, after the opening phrase of the Haftarah, *Nachamu, nachamu ami* ("comfort ye, my nation"; Isa. 40:1). The same prophet whose chastisement ushered in the week of the fast now provides words of comfort for the mourners. For the next six weeks, up to Rosh HaShanah, the Haftarah selections are taken from Isaiah's comforting prophecies. This custom is based on the tradition that seven comforting messages were conveyed to Jerusalem after the destruction of the Temple (Kitov, *Sefer HaTodaah*, p. 416).

Shabbat Nachamu officially concludes the saddest chapter in ancient Jewish history, which has given rise to numerous mournful customs. We have finished the discussion of these customs with Shabbat Nachamu because it ends the tragic period on a happy note. Yet as the Midrash indicates (*Pesikta Rabbati* 29), Jerusalem had repeatedly rejected all efforts at consolation. Unless the nation learned the meaning of the tragedy—why it happened and how a recurrence could be avoided in the future—all consolations would be vain. Judaism must also probe the theological implications of the disaster.

An effort to provide some answers was made in the famous elegy dedicated to the Ten Martyrs, whose deaths exemplified the grief which flowed from the loss of the Temple and divine protection. The second part of this chapter is devoted to an analysis of this poignant selichah, which is recited on both Yom Kippur and Tisha B'Av.

II.
THE TEN MARTYRS

INTRODUCTION

The flames of the burning Temple, set by a defiant Roman soldier, consumed the last vestiges of Jewish autonomy under the Romans. Henceforth the destruction of the Sanctuary was to become the indelible symbol of the end of national independence. The episode of the Ten Martyrs was the first tragic reminder of the sorrows and hazards of the *galut* and in time became its symbolic epitome.

The Jewish people were profoundly stirred by the fate of the Ten Martyrs. Numerous martyrs had preceded them. King Jannai is alleged to have executed hundreds of rabbis. That, however, was the result of religious factionalism and political family quarrels. Rome, on the other hand, made Judaism its target. The Jews were never to forget that in the diaspora their physical as well as spiritual security was always in jeopardy.

Several historical sources preserved an account of the Ten Martyrs. Some of them were written centuries after the Hadrianic persecution. It was not until the end of the eleventh century, after the first crusade had left a trail of Jewish blood along its European route, that an eloquent elegy describing the tragic death of the Ten Martyrs was included in the prayerbook. As a result of this elegy, the story of the Ten Martyrs became the most familiar chapter in the chronicles of Jewish martyrology.

ABSENCE OF ELEGY FOR SECOND TEMPLE

The destruction of the Second Temple did not produce an elegy comparable in sorrowful grandeur to the Book of Lamentations, which bewailed the loss of the Solomonic Temple. There were a number of reasons for this literary sterility. The creative genius of the sages was concentrated on the task of producing the monumental talmudic literature. Unlike the prophets, the rabbis were primarily teachers and not preachers. Practical theological problems had to be given urgent and immediate attention. Liturgical rituals and forms had to be fixed to make it possible for the synagogue to replace the ancient Sanctuary as the center of Jewish religious life. It was more important to establish occasions for rejoicing than to surrender to weeping and dismay. For psychological reasons, greater emphasis was given to the popularization of morale-building customs and rituals. While the old fast-days commemorating the end of the First Commonwealth were revived, great stress was also placed upon the heroic past and its numerous minor festivals. Among the early books published during that critical period was *Megillat Taanit*, which listed all ancient festivals, and the *Scroll of Antiochus*, which related the miracles of the Hasmonean triumph. We must also bear in mind that any criticism of Rome was fraught with real danger. The rabbis found it much more expedient to confine their comments to the Book of Lamentations. While ostensibly referring to Babylonia, they actually alluded to Rome. The fact that the Second Temple, like the first, was destroyed on the ninth of Av, gave this date a dimension of timelessness as a day of national grief. The Book of Lamentations therefore remained the true and immortal voice of Jewish sorrow.

The absence of a clearly defined theological explanation for the national catastrophe in the year 70 was very likely another contributing factor in the failure of the post-Temple generation to produce another Book of Lamentations. The prophet Jeremiah saw clearly a divine retribution in the destruction of Judea. He presented the religious justification in cogent and unequivocal terms. "For the iniquity of the daughter of my people is greater than the sin of Sodom" (Lam. 4:6). "It is because of the sins of the prophets and the iniquities of the priests that have shed the blood of the just in the midst of her" (ibid. 4:13). "Run ye to and fro through the streets of Jerusalem and see now and know, and seek in the broad places thereof, if you can find a man, if there be any that does justly, that seeks truth and I will pardon her" (Jer. 5:1). The picture portrayed by Jeremiah was one of total darkness and corruption. He emphatically repudiated the notion that his generation might have suffered for other people's sins. "In those days [after the restoration] they shall say no more: 'The fathers have eaten sour grapes and their children's teeth are set on edge' " (ibid. 31:28). Since the captivity of Judea was the result of its sinfulness, only penitence could help regain the favor of the Almighty. "Let us search and try our ways and return to the Lord" (Lam. 3:40). The rabbis later confirmed Jeremiah's view in justifying the destruction of the Solomonic Temple. Thus they cited a dialogue between the Almighty and Abraham on Tisha B'Av night. Abraham inquired why the Jews were not spared. The Almighty informed him that they had transgressed the entire Torah (*Pesichta Eichah Rabbati,* Rabbi Jonathan Patach).

What explanations could the sages offer for the destruction of the Second Temple? The moral climate of Jerusalem's masses on the eve of the Roman siege was high. The city was the seat of renowned scholars and a great academy. According to a talmudic tradition there were 480 synagogues in Jerusalem and each one had a school attached to it (Jer. *Megillah,* chap. 3). According to another source there were 394 courts of law in the holy city (*Ketubot* 105a). The bulk of the people were God-fearing, and they were even ready to sacrifice their lives to prevent the Romans from desecrating the Sanctuary. Surely that generation was not filled with iniquity.

In subsequent generations, however, many sages continued to probe into the moral aspects of the period in order to shed some light upon the national catastrophe. One talmudic source listed many conditions which apparently reflected the moral decline of the people: "Jerusalem was destroyed because of violation of the Sabbath, the failure to recite the *Shema* mornings and evenings, the closing down of Hebrew schools, the lack of humility, the absence of deferential treatment of the great, the lack of shame, and the disrespect for scholars" (*Shabbat* 119b). This list carries a serious indictment of Jerusalem's Jewry on the eve of the destruction of the Temple. However, such conditions prevailed only in besieged Jerusalem, in the grip of military zealots. Those were critical years when famine was king and the sword was the arbiter, when all normal peacetime pursuits and amenities were suppressed. Jeremiah's charges, leveled against the people of his generation, could not apply to the generation of Rabban Yochanan b. Zaccai.

MORAL IMPLICATION OF MARTYRDOM

The theological explanation for the tragedy of the Ten Martyrs was even more difficult to arrive at. The moral implication of this martyr-dom crystallized only gradually as the account of the death of the ten sages, executed over a period of a few generations, was skillfully woven into a simple episode. In its final form it conveyed a message of profound religious and national significance.

The list of the Ten Martyrs is headed by Rabbis Simon and Ishmael. Their martyrdom was commemorated long before the phrase "Ten Martyrs" came into being. The earliest account of the death of the two rabbis was associated with a deathbed prophecy made by Shmuel Hakatan. The latter, a scholar at Yavneh in the days of Rabban Gamliel II, died in the year 130 c. e. His colleagues had praised him unstint-ingly and said that he was worthy of prophecy. The fact that his prophetic utterances on his deathbed came true gave this story wide circulation and assured its place in history through oral transmission by succeeding generations.

Samuel Junior is said to have prophesied that Simon and Ishmael would die by the sword, other rabbis would be killed, and violence was to follow (*Sanhedrin* 11a). Who were the Simon and Ishmael mentioned in the prophecy? They were apparently two rabbis killed in the Bar Kochba rebellion, which broke out a few years after Shmuel's death, or in the Hadrianic persecution, which followed the rebellion. One historian identifies this Simon with Rabbi Simon, the son of Rabbi Chananiah Segan Hakohanim (Levi). Another historian identifies Simon with Simon Bar Kochba (Brill). One may also suggest Simon b. Azai, who was included among the Ten Martyrs on several rabbinic lists. Ishmael may be identified with Rabbi Ishmael b. Elisha, the colleague of Rabbi Akiva.

An early beraita, quoted in *Mechilta,* relates the story of "Rabbi Ishmael and Rabbi Simon who were led to their execution." The author of this early source thus identifies Samuel's "Simon and Ishmael" with two rabbis. The fact that this author further reports that Rabbi Akiva had received word of their execution dates the two martyrs as contemporaries of Rabbi Akiva.

The beraita in *Mechilta* holds special interest for us because it attempts to deal with the theological aspects of this martyrdom. Why were they killed? Since their deaths were attributed to minor, personal, social sins, we may assume that the subsequent explanation of major errors in religious policy had not yet been formulated. The *Mechilta's* account of the martyrs' personal guilt is based on a text in Exodus (22:21): "If you afflict them in any wise [the stranger, the widow, and the orphan], for if they cry at all unto me I will surely hear their cry. My wrath shall wax hot, and I will kill you with the sword . . ." This biblical admonition is utilized to demonstrate that the punishment of the martyrs fits their alleged crime. "When Rabbi Ishmael and Rabbi Simon were led to the execution, the latter said to the former: 'Rabbi, my heart is faint, for I know not why I am being killed! . . . Said Rabbi Ishmael: 'Perchance a widow came to you for judgment or to ask a question and you kept her waiting until you finished drinking your beverage. It is written in the Torah, "if you will afflict them" . . . It is the same whether it is a substantial affliction or a minor one.' Said he, 'Rabbi, you have comforted me.' " By attributing the rabbi's martyrdom to personal guilt, this whole chapter is divested of any real theological or national significance. We may note in passing that the author of *Mechilta* appended a postscript to the older beraita. We are informed that Rabbi Akiva received a report of the execution of the two rabbis. He does not mention, however, the martyrdom of Rabbi Akiva. We may assume, therefore, that this passage of the *Mechilta* was written prior to the death of Rabbi Akiva (ca. 132 C.E.). At this point there was as yet no clear and discernible policy of calculated martyrdom imposed by Rome on the Jewish religious leadership. The executions of Rabbis Simon and Ishmael must have appeared to their contemporaries as two isolated cases. Their execution did not immediately endow them with the crown of martyrdom. It was not until after the death of Rabbi Akiva and the tragedies of the Hadrianic reign of terror that the expression *harugei malchut* came into vogue (*Pesachim* 50a).

FOUR MARTYRS (SEMACHOT)

The next source in chronological order, listing the names of four executed rabbis, is found in the tractate *Semachot*. Although this work was edited after the close of the Talmud, it includes many old beraitot dealing with rituals attendant upon death. It is in connection with this subject that the beraita describes the rituals following the death of Rabban Gamliel the Elder (ca. 50 c. e.). The mention of the death of this great sage is followed by an account of the execution of four sages: Rabbi Simon b. Gamliel, Rabbi Ishmael, Rabbi Akiva, and Rabbi Chananiah b. Tradyon. The chapter concludes with an account of the martyrdom of Pappus and Julianus of Laodicea (chap. 8).

There are a number of pertinent observations to be made on the passage in *Semachot*, which forms an important link in the development of the chronicle of the Ten Martyrs.

The four names listed in *Semachot* are identical with the four names listed in the concluding chapter of *Megillat Taanit*. Both draw on sources dating from a period shortly after the execution of Rabbi Akiva and prior to the execution of his younger colleagues. *Megillat Taanit* mentions the additional name of Chananiah Segan Hakohanim.

The historical authenticity of the execution of the four sages whose names are listed in *Semachot* is well established. There are independent talmudic sources which confirm the martyrdom of these rabbis: Rabbi Simon and Elisha (*Sanhedrin* 11a), Rabbi Akiva (*Pesachim* 50a), and Rabbi Chananiah b. Tradyon (*Avoda Zarah* 18a). *Megillat Taanit* even preserved the date of the execution of these rabbis.

The identity of Simon and Ishmael mentioned by Shmuel Hakatan was changed for the first time by the author of the passage in *Semachot*. According to this list, Simon is identified with Rabbi Simon b. Gamliel (obviously not the Simon in Shmuel Hakatan's prophecy), who had been the *nasi* in Jerusalem during the rebellion against Rome. We know from Josephus that he had taken an active part in the insurrection and had opposed Josephus, whom he had suspected of partiality toward Rome. The absence of any historical reference to Rabbi Simon b. Gamliel in the period following the destruction of the Temple leads us to the assumption that he had been executed by the Romans.

Semachot offers no clue to the identity of Rabbi Ishmael. Since he is described as a contemporary of Rabbi Simon b. Gamliel, we must conclude that he was not the Rabbi Ishmael b. Elisha who was a colleague of Rabbi Akiva.

Why did the author of the *Semachot* list of martyrs change the identity of the original Simon and Ishmael in the traditional account of Shmuel Hakatan's prophecy? The change may represent the desire of the author to confirm a historical fact—the execution of Rabbi Simon b. Gamliel. Since he was a prominent person and the bearer of a revered title, the addition of his name would enhance the dramatic effect of the list of martyrs. It is also possible that the change resulted either from a scribal or a historical error. According to the text in chapter 8 of *Semachot*, Rabbi Gamliel the Elder and Rabbi Elazar b. Azariah eulogized Shmuel Hakatan upon his death. This is an obvious error. Rabbi Gamliel the Elder died prior to the birth of Rabbi Elazar b. Azariah. The Rabbi Gamliel who eulogized Shmuel Hakatan was Gamliel II of Yavneh, a grandson of Rabbi Gamliel the Elder. It is very likely that the erroneous mention of Rabbi Gamliel the Elder led the author of the *Semachot* list to believe that Shmuel Hakatan was a contemporary of Rabbi Gamliel the Elder and that the reference to Simon in his deathbed statement was to Rabbi Gamliel the Elder's son, the martyred Rabbi Simon b. Gamliel. Whatever the reason for the mention of Rabbi Simon b. Gamliel in the list of martyrs in the text of *Semachot*, it established a precedent which was followed by all subsequent sources.

The text in *Semachot* is the sole source which includes the names of Pappus and Julianus among the martyrs. Pappus and Julianus had apparently organized a rebellion against the Roman Emperor Trajan. They were executed approximately in the year 117 c. e. Their personal piety and virtue was greatly extolled by aggadic authors. Yet like Bar Kochba, who was killed in Palestine a few decades later, they were essentially political and not religious martyrs. The prevailing opinion of the talmudic sages was opposed to the inclusion of political victims among the martyrs. This opinion crystalized during the Roman siege of Jerusalem, when the rabbis objected to the useless bloodshed resulting from the hopeless rebellion. This opinion hardened with rabbinic opposition to Bar Kochba's rebellion. The inclusion of Rabbi Akiva among the martyrs was due to his defiance of the Roman ban on religious instruction and not to his support of Bar Kochba. His political activities must have been indeed very discreet, for the Romans did not molest him for his political activities and were apparently ignorant of this phase of his public life. There were, however, some rabbis who undoubtedly felt that fighters for freedom deserve the rank of martyrdom, even if such struggle was foredoomed to failure. Rabbi Joshua b. Levi, a resident of Lud, a center of anti-Roman activities, and a patron of Palestine's patriotic youth, favored the granting of the status of martyrdom to the patriots. The Talmud preserved an account of a vision reported by Rabbi Joseph, the son of Rabbi Joshua b. Levi. In this vision Rabbi Joseph had witnessed the favorable treatment accorded in heaven to Jewish martyrs.

The sages later sought to identify these martyrs. At first they were identified as "Rabbi Akiva and his colleagues." This opinion was refuted because Rabbi Akiva's outstanding merits and his heavenly rewards did not depend upon his martyrdom. The rabbis therefore concluded that the martyrs in Rabbi Joseph's vision were the "martyrs of Lud," i.e., political martyrs (*Pesachim* 50a). It is conceivable that the names of Pappus and Julianus were appended to the beraita quoted in the eighth chapter of *Semachot* by some rabbis in the early part of the third century, when there was a favorable climate for such an opinion among some of the leading Palestinian amoraim. Rabbi Judah HaNasi, who pursued a policy of peaceful coexistence with Rome, excluded the list of martyrs from the Mishnah and surely made no mention of Pappus and Julianus, who were executed for insurrectionist activities against Rome. No subsequent list of martyrs ever included the names of these two heroes. Jews, however, continued to revere their memory. Rabbi Jacob Bar Acha (3rd cent.) canceled an ancient holiday because the anniversary of the martyrdom of Pappus and Julianus fell on the same day (Jer. *Taanit*, chap. 2).

TEN MARTYRS (MIDRASH EICHAH RABBATI)

The next in the chronological order of sources listing the martyrs is found in *Midrash Eichah Rabbati* (2:2). The list of martyrs is included in this work as an elaboration of the account of Jewish sorrows in the context of the framework of the Book of Lamentations. It does not purport to establish the theological justification of these martyrdoms but merely to chronicle historical events.

Eichah Rabbati mentions ten martyrs. It is apparently the earliest source containing a complete list. We must note, however, that it attaches no special significance to the number of the martyrs nor does it coin the phrase "Ten Martyrs." It repeats the four names listed in the earlier beraita in *Semachot*, whose deaths had also been recorded in

other talmudic sources. There is an obvious error of omission in the
second name listed in *Eichah Rabbati.* Our version reads "Rabbi
Gamaliel." It should read "Rabbi Simon b. Gamliel."

In addition to the four names—Rabbis Ishmael, Simon b. Gamliel,
Akiva, and Chananiah b. Tradyon—there are the names of three more
sages whose deaths were also recorded in other talmudic sources:
Rabbi Judah b. Baba (*Sanhedrin* 14a), Rabbi Chutzpas HaMeturgeman
(*Kiddushin* 39b), and Rabbi Judah HaNachtum (Jer. *Chagigah* 2). The
martyrdom of the preceding seven sages was considered an established historical fact, and their names reappeared on all subsequent
midrashic and post-talmudic lists. The only exception is Rabbi Judah
HaNachtum, whose name was omitted from the post-talmudic lists.
This omission might be attributed to the discovery of an identical
dramatic account of the severed tongues of Rabbi Chutzpas and Rabbi
Judah HaNachtum lying in the dust. In view of Rabbi Chutzpas's
reputation as an interpreter and preacher with a "silver tongue," the
touching account was most poignant in the story of his tragic end. It
was consequently assumed that the inclusion of Rabbi Judah
HaNachtum in the martyrs' list was in error.

In addition to the preceding seven sages, *Eichah Rabbati* mentions the
following: Rabbi Yeshevav, Ben Azai, and Rabbi Tarfon. The author
seems uncertain about the authenticity of the latter's martyrdom and
notes the fact that some scholars substitute Rabbi Elazar Charsona for
Rabbi Tarfon.

We do not know the sources from which *Eichah Rabbati* drew its
information. It is possible that some ancient records no longer extant
had supplied the names of the remaining three sages. However, it is
more likely that the information was based on some oral tradition,
emanating from speculation and association of personalities.

Rabbi Yeshevav, the first rabbi in this last class of names, was a scribe
and apparently the secretary of the academy of Yavneh. As an
important rabbinic official he would be a prime target of the Romans.
His name was retained on all subsequent lists of the Ten Martyrs.

We may suggest the following reasons for the inclusion of the name
of Ben Azai on the martyrs' list in *Eichah Rabbati:*

1. Ben Azai was a close colleague of Rabbi Akiva. When the term
   harugei malchut was initially used, it applied to "Rabbi Akiva and his
   colleagues" (*Pesachim* 50a). Ben Azai's name might have been
   included by virtue of his association with Rabbi Akiva.
2. Ben Azai's first name was Simon. It might have been assumed that

Shmuel Hakatan's deathbed prophecy of the death of Simon referred to Ben Azai, inasmuch as he could not have been referring to Rabbi Simon b. Gambliel, who had died in the lifetime of Shmuel Hakatan.

3. Rabbi Akiva's last statement, proclaiming his acceptance of a martyr's death, was based on the verse in Deuteronomy: "And thou shalt love God thy Lord, with all thy heart and with all thy soul, and with all thy might" (6:5). The phrase "with all thy soul," according to Rabbi Akiva, meant even if the enemy takes one's life (*Berachot* 61b). A similar statement is attributed to Ben Azai (*Sifre*, Deut. 6:5). In his interpretation he seems to have exceeded even the zeal of Rabbi Akiva. One must demonstrate his love for God by seeking an opportunity to sacrifice his life in the service of the Almighty. This statement might have led to the belief that he, too, was among the martyrs. However, another talmudic source indicates that he died a natural death (*Chagigah* 14b). His name was omitted from the post-talmudic lists of the martyrs.

It seems that the inclusion of Rabbi Tarfon's name was also due to his close association with Rabbi Akiva. He was one of the sages who had participated with Rabbi Akiva in the famous "Seder" in Bnai Brak. He was also a resident of Lud, a center of anti-Roman agitation. It was probably assumed that he had died a martyr's death. At the time of the composition of the *Eichah Rabbati* list, it was apparently impossible to verify the facts. Eventual research must have led to the elimination of his name from all subsequent lists. The same is true of Rabbi Elazar Charsana, a disciple of Rabbi Akiva, whose name did not reappear in the later sources.

The *Eichah Rabbati* list is the most significant link in the creation of the epic of the "Ten Martyrs." Though it was composed later than the abridged list in *Semachot,* both cover the same historic period between the fall of Jerusalem and the Hadrianic persecution (70–135 c. e.).

TEN MARTYRS (MIDRASH TEHILIM)

The martyr's list in *Midrash Tehilim* (chap. 9) was incorporated into a midrashic comment on Psalms 9:13, "For he that avenges blood has remembered them. He has not forgotten the cry of the humble." One must not read a sense of vindictiveness into this sentence. Retribution is an essential ingredient of law and order. No one can believe that destiny is guided by divine principles of right and wrong without allowing for the ultimate punishment of the wrongdoer and compassion for the innocent victim. The same human emotions which prompted the victims of the crusades to compose the *Av harachamim* also inspired the composition of *Shefoch chamatcha* ("pour out thy wrath").

Like the earlier *Eichah Rabbati, Midrash Tehilim* does not mention the number ten, nor does it attach any significance to it. Its list is practically a copy of its predecessor's, with the exception of a few variations which indicate an attempt at a more critical historic evaluation. Rabbi Ishmael is identified more clearly by the addition of his father's name—Elisha. We are thus to assume that the reference is to Rabbi Ishmael b. Elisha, the colleague of Rabbi Akiva, and not to a contemporary of Rabbi Simon b. Gamliel. It places Shmuel Hakatan's reference to Ishmael in its proper historical perspective. It also corrects the erroneous version of *Midrash Eichah Rabbati,* which names Rabbi Gamliel instead of Rabbi Simon b. Gamliel. The latter's martyrdom was based on oral traditions antedating the prophecy of Shmuel Hakatan. The names of Rabbi Tarfon and Rabbi Elazar Charsana were omitted because their martyrdom could not be substantiated by historical evidence. One new name is introduced for the first time—Rabbi Jose. The tanna Rabbi Jose is generally identified as Rabbi Jose b. Chalafta, one of the five disciples of Rabbi Judah b. Baba who were ordained by him prior to his martyrdom. Rabbi Jose was also a student of Rabbi Akiva. The inclusion of his name extends the martyrdom period covered by this list to the post-Akiva generation.

A text in the Jerusalem Talmud cites a tradition which might have been the source for the belief that Rabbi Jose died a martyr. The text reads as follows: "When Rabbi Jose b. Chalafta died, blood streamed from the waterspouts at Lud. They said it was because he had given his life over the decrees" (Jer. *Avodah Zara* 3). It was probably taken to mean that he had sacrificed his life in defying the Roman anti-religious decrees and that the miraculous and symbolic stream of blood appeared at Lud, Palestine's center of anti-Roman activity. However, this version is at variance with the Babylonian version of this tradition, which reads: "At Rabbi Jose's [death] the waterspouts of Sepphoris expelled blood" (*Moed Katan* 25b). Sepphoris was the seat of Rabbi Jose's academy. It was not identified with the rebellion against Rome, nor was it stated that Rabbi Jose "gave his life." The Tosefta (chap. 1) explained this tradition by stating that Rabbi Jose devoted his whole life to the preservation of the mitzvah of circumcision (see Tosafot, *Shafu; Moed Katan* 25b). In the post-talmudic lists of the martyrs, the name of Rabbi Jose is omitted and in his place appears the name of another student of Rabbi Akiva, Rabbi Elazar b. Shamua.

POST-TALMUDIC SOURCES

The versions of a "post-talmudic midrash, *Ele Ezkera* and *Asarah Harugei Malchut,* present the ultimate development of the heroic story of the Ten Martyrs. The authors of this midrash were not interested in history per se but rather in the theological doctrines which it reflected. They blithely ignored historical perspective as they converted this chapter of Jewish martyrology into a stirring tale of sublime destiny, wherein the self-sacrifice of the sages stands out against the background of inexorable divine purpose which determines the fate of all mankind.

An examination of the list of martyrs in this midrash reveals three new names in substitution for the three other names which had been dropped. Rabbi Jose's name was dropped for reasons previously discussed. Rabbi Elazar b. Shamua, whose name was substituted, was, like Rabbi Jose, among the five sages who had been ordained by Rabbi Judah b. Baba, shortly before his martyrdom. The five newly ordained rabbis were hunted by the Romans and had to go into hiding or flee the country. There might have been a tradition that one of the five sages was caught and executed. There is no evidence, however, in support of such a tradition. As to Rabbi Elazar b. Shamua, he is said to have reached a ripe old age, with the implication that he died peacefully (*Megillah* 27b). Rabbi Chananiah b. Chachina, a student of Rabbi Akiva and a colleague of Ben Azai, replaces the latter on the martyr's list. Ben Azai's name was dropped for reasons previously indicated. The choice of Rabbi Chananiah might have been motivated by the fact that he was Rabbi Akiva's student and the belief that he had shared the fate of a great many of Rabbi Akiva's students. Rabbi Judah b. Damo (or b. Teima) replaces Rabbi Judah b. Nachtum. I have already discussed the reason for the dropping of the latter's name. The author might have assumed that the Rabbi Judah, to whom martyrdom had been attributed, was Rabbi Judah b. Teima whose piety was expressed in his saying "Be bold as a leopard and light as an eagle, swift as a gazelle and strong as a lion to do the will of your father in heaven" (*Avot* 5:24). Such zeal surely imposes a duty to surrender one's life in the service of the Almighty.

Midrash Ele Ezkera is the first source to identify Rabbi Ishmael as "Rabbi Ishmael Kohen Gadol," thus definitely placing him in the period when the Temple was still in existence. The Talmud makes mention of a Rabbi Ishmael b. Elisha who was a high priest (*Berachot* 7a). His father, Elisha, is also alleged to have been a high priest (*Avot deRabbi Natan* 38:3). Rabbi Ishmael b. Elisha the High Priest was possibly the grandfather of Rabbi Ishmael b. Elisha, the contemporary of Rabbi Akiva. Some confusion is created by the subsequent midrashic reference to Rabbi Ishmael's father as Rabbi Jose. This was probably due to an accidental slip through an erroneous association with the name of a later tanna, Rabbi Ishmael b. Jose, a colleague of Rabbi Judah HaNasi. This slip was corrected in the second version of the midrash, where the martyr is identified as "Rabbi Ishmael b. Elisha Kohan Gadol." The reason for this positive identification will become clear as the tale of the Ten Martyrs in its final heroic form unfolds itself.

The Ten Martyrs are portrayed by the post-talmudic midrash as contemporaries who were summoned by the king to hear themselves charged with responsibility for the sale of Joseph by his brethren. This crime was punishable by death, according to the laws of the Torah. The sages are alleged to have subsequently sent one of their colleagues as an emissary to heaven to intercede with the Almighty. The identification of one of the sages as a high priest serves the purpose of the author by lending greater dramatic effect to the story. By virtue of his position as a high priest, he had been in close communion with God. He was therefore the logical choice for a mission which required an ascent to heaven.

Was there any historical basis for the inclusion of a high priest among the martyrs? There were several martyred high priests in Jewish history. There was Zechariah the son of Jehoiada, who was killed in the Solomonic Temple (II Chron. 24:21); Seraiah, the last high priest of the Solomonic Temple, was martyred by the order of Nebuchadnezzar at Riblah (II Kings 25:20). The Hasmonean Jonathan and Simon were killed in battle, and Chananyah b. Chizkeyahu was assassinated by the extremists shortly before the destruction of the Temple. The high priest who conceivably could have given rise to the post-talmudic tradition of a martyred high priest by the name of Ishmael was Ishmael b. Favi (*Yoma* 9a), who was martyred in Cyrene, Africa. This Ishmael had held the high priesthood for ten years (48–58 C. E.) In the year 58 he went with a Jewish delegation to Rome to intercede with Emperor Nero against the desecration of the Temple. He was retained by Nero as a hostage in Rome (Josephus, *Antiq.* 20, chap. 8:11). According to Josephus he was ultimately beheaded in Cyrene (*Wars* 6, chap. 2:2). The date and circumstances of his beheading were not indicated. It is doubtful, however, whether the martyrdom of Ishmael b. Favi was known to the author of *Midrash Ele Ezkera*.

The list of martyrs in *Midrash Ele Ezkera* was copied by the author of the elegy *Ele Ezkera* and was ultimately incorporated into the Yom Kippur liturgy. Thus it became the most familiar and widely accepted version of the story of the Ten Martyrs. The real significance of the post-talmudic midrash, however, lies not in its list of martyrs but in its treatment of the theological aspects of martyrdom and its reaction to early Jewish contributions to Christianity.

AN ANTI-TEMPLE PARTY

Midrash Ele Ezkera finds the justification of the martyrdom of the ten sages not in any fault in their personal lives but in the collective guilt of the rabbinic leadership for its failure to effectively combat a widespread ideological deviation. Thus it states: "After the destruction of the Temple, the transgressors of that generation said boastfully, 'What did we lose by the destruction of the Sanctuary? There are in our midst great scholars who train the people in the observance of the Torah and its commandments.' Thereupon the Almighty inspired the king of Rome to seek instruction in the Torah of Moses from [Jewish] scholars and elders . . . then he summoned ten Jewish scholars."

Who were the transgressors who did not deplore the destruction of the Temple? We are precluded from identifying them with Hellenists by the claim of the "transgressors" to continued loyalty to the Torah. They must, therefore, be classified as a dissenting minority whose views were never reflected in the post-Temple rabbinic literature. Among the eighteen benedictions fixed by the academy of Yavneh there was included a prayer for the restoration of the sacrificial rites in the Sanctuary. A special prayer, *Sheyibane bet hamikdash* ("may the Sanctuary be rebuilt"), was appended to the end of every service. It was added also to the conclusion of the preliminary service which was recited privately each morning prior to the morning service. It was also inserted at the end of *Avot*, which had originally concluded with chapter 5, verse 23 (see Herford, *Avot*). Indeed, throughout the talmudic era, the hope for the restoration of the sacrificial rites remained a fixed tenet of rabbinic Judaism. When the sages referred to the Temple they generally appended the phrase: "May it be speedily rebuilt in our days." The technical laws of sacrificial rites continued to serve as a subject of widespread discussion and interpretation throughout the talmudic period. All this would seem to indicate a unanimity of opinion on the desirability and need for the restoration of the Temple. Yet one might argue that the very persistence of the rabbis in stressing the prayer for the restoration of the Temple might indicate the presence of a sizable body of opinion which did not consider the existence of the Temple essential to the development of Judaism and the rabbis were thus attempting to counteract its influence.

We may point to a veiled statement at the conclusion of _Eicha Rabbati_ which possibly alludes to the existence of two schools of thought. The statement is in the form of a comment on the last prayer in the Book of Lamentations: "Restore us, O Lord, unto thee and we shall return, renew our days as of old." This verse is the epitome of our classical post-Temple prayer for restoration. The verse speaks first of a personal restoration of the individual to God and it concludes with the vague request for a renewal of conditions "as of old." One midrashic opinion states: " 'Renew our days as of old'—like unto Adam, as it is written: 'and he banished Adam and he sojourned east of the Garden of Eden.' " The prime objective of the Jewish people after the destruction of the Temple, according to this commentary, was the restoration of the blissful state that existed prior to the banishment of Adam from the Garden of Eden. The Temple played no part in the perfection of the initial era of Genesis. Pursuance of the laws of the Torah by a personal restoration to God would lead to a renewal of the original perfection of the creation. A dissenting comment, however, states: " 'Renew our days as of old'—as it is written: 'Then shall the offering of Judah and Jerusalem be pleasant unto the Lord, as in the days of old, and as in ancient years' " (Mal. 3:4). This opinion, in opposition to the broad universalist overtones of the first commentators, makes the restoration of the sacrificial rites at Jerusalem the ultimate goal of our prayer. It is significant that it was this verse from Malachi which was appended by the rabbis to the prayer of _Sheyibane beit hamikdash_ and thus made part of our liturgy. In effect this prayer limits its objective to the restoration of the Jewish state as it existed prior to the destruction of the Temple.

The primacy of social justice is emphasized in the Bible. The following verse in Proverbs (21:3) is highly illustrative: "To do righteousness and justice is more acceptable to the Lord than sacrifice." Rabbi Samuel bar Nachman, a third-century Palestinian amora, seems to have reflected a lingering anti-Temple sentiment in his description of a dialogue between God and King David. The Almighty sought to reassure David that his life was meritorious even though he was not permitted to build the Temple. He quoted the verse from Proverbs and concluded: "The justice and righteousness which you perform is more pleasant to me than sacrifices" (Jer. *Berachot*, chap. 2).

If we are correct in assuming that there was an anti-Temple party within Judaism, who were its leaders and where was it centered? There were apparently several parties opposed to the dominance of Jerusalem for divergent reasons. Some were motivated by piety, sickened by the reappearance of Sadducean high priests. Others were moved by patriotism, in rebellion against the Herodian influence in the appointment of political high priests. Still others, like the Essenes, and the Qumran sect, turned equally against the Jerusalem priesthood and the rabbinical academy, creating a favorable climate for the ultimate emergence of Judeo-Christianity.

THE ELDERS OF BETEIRA

The city of Betar was probably one of the centers of an anti-Jerusalem party and the B'nai Beteira, or Zikne Beteira, were its proponents. Historians have not succeeded in identifying with any degree of certainty the Elders of Beteira.

Josephus mentions a Beteira, founded in the northeast by Babylonian Jews in the days of King Herod (*Antiq.* 17, chap. 2:3). It is impossible to connect the Elders of Beteira with this newly established community. It is inconceivable that the religious leaders of a new community could assert their leadership over the entire Palestianian Jewry in so short a time. The B'nai Beteira were the religious heads of the Palestinian Jewish community in the interim between the deaths of Shemaya and Avtalion and the appointment of Hillel as the head of the academy in Jerusalem. During that period, when the academy in Jerusalem had apparently lost its primacy for lack of leadership, all important religious problems were referred to the Elders of Beteira (*Pesachim* 66a). The Beteira mentioned by Josephus was never identified by the Talmud as the seat of an academy. It stands to reason that the residence of the Elders of Beteira would also be the center of an institution of learning. The midrash, however, does mention the existence of many schools in Betar: "There were five hundred schools in Betar, and the smallest of them had no less than three hundred students" (*Eichah Rabbati*, chap. 2). Even if we allow for an aggadic exaggeration, this statement reflects the reputation for learning enjoyed by Betar. Betar also had a reputation for fierce patriotism and anti-Roman feeling. They undoubtedly viewed with disfavor the political domination of Jerusalem by Herod. They must have disapproved of the tacit mutual noninterference pact between Shemaya and Avtalion and Herod. They also must have opposed the permission granted by the Jerusalem sages to Herod to rebuild the Temple. "Herod's Temple" might well have been anathema to all anti-Herodians. Through his appointment of high priests Herod secured complete control of the administration of the Temple. The rabbinic leadership of the Jerusalem academy had rightly felt that they must support the Temple because the masses continued to venerate the Sanctuary as a religious and national symbol. It had thus become an invaluable asset in preserving the unity and loyalty of the nation. With the support of the masses the rabbis were able to prevent the Sadducean high priests from violating traditional ritual observances. Yet there must have been pious men who questioned the propriety of allowing Sadducean priests to supervise and conduct sacrificial rites.

This background material may shed some light on an enigmatic passage in the Talmud (*Pesachim* 66a): "This law was obscure to the B'nai Beteira. Once the fourteenth of Nisan fell on the Sabbath and they did not know whether the Passover rite takes preference over the Sabbath. . . . It was reported that there was one man [Hillel] who had studied under the two great sages of that generation, Shemaya and Avtalion, and he knew whether the Passover rite takes preference over the Sabbath. So they summoned him . . . he was immediately placed at the head and appointed *nasi*. All day long he expounded the laws of the Passover rite. Then he reproved them: 'What led to this state of affairs that I should arrive from Babylonia and become your *nasi*? Is it your laziness that you did not study under the two great men of this generation, Shemaya and Avtalion?' " How can one explain the ignorance of the B'nai Beteira of a law affecting the religious function of an entire people? The coincidence of the fourteenth of Nisan with the Sabbath occurs at least ten times in a century. Surely there must have been enough precedents for the rabbinic leadership to follow. Why did the B'nai Beteira relinquish their leadership as a result of their forgetfulness? Why did Hillel embarrass them so soon after they had so graciously relinquished their leadership to him? How does one reconcile Hillel's attitude with his reputation for modesty, patience, and gentility? The talmudic passage mentions another legal question which was put to Hillel on the day of his appointment as *nasi*. Hillel replied: "This law I once learned and have forgotten . . ." Why did he not feel that such forgetfulness disqualified him from leadership?

The entire passage takes on new meaning if it is read against the background of a much more serious ideological conflict. When the problem of the sacrificial rite was presented to the B'nai Beteira, they were faced with the challenge of their own convictions against Herod's Temple. They hesitated and offered Hillel the opportunity to assert his leadership by supplying the answer to the masses who were eager to bring the paschal lamb. Hillel thereupon expounded the laws of this rite all day and concluded with a criticism of the school which had rejected the leadership of Shemaya and Avtalion and their policy of moderation and accommodation with the government. Their alleged ignorance of the law of the paschal ritual when the fourteenth of Nisan falls on the Sabbath (according to the calendar of the Book of Jubilees it always falls on the Sabbath) might have erroneously also placed them under the suspicion that they were secret followers of the anti-rabbinic Essenic calendar, according to which the fourteenth of Nisan always falls on a Tuesday. The B'nai Beteira, realizing that popular opinion supported Hillel, relinquished their leadership to him and retreated gracefully to their own center of influence in Betar outside of Jerusalem.

A later midrash indicated in its customary veiled style that the residents of Betar had suspended their pilgrimages to Jerusalem and in effect had severed their relations with the Holy City. It relates that when a resident of Betar would go to Jerusalem to pray (apparently prayer pilgrimages to Jerusalem continued for a while after they had ceased offering sacrifices at the Temple), the leading laymen of the city would taunt them with the question: "Do you seek leadership in Jerusalem?" Then they would inform him that it was rumored than he intended to sell his property (in preparation for departure from the country or the joining of anti-government forces). In the end they would deprive him of his land (through forced sale or outright confiscation on charges of anti-government activities). This harsh treatment caused the man from Betar to stop coming to Jerusalem and even led to his prayer for the destruction of the Temple (*Eichah Rabbati*, chap. 2). The rabbis subsequently considered the destruction of Betar a retribution for having lit candles in celebration of the destruction of the Temple (ibid.). This would seem to indicate that the opposition of the Betar people to the Temple and its administration continued to linger even after the Temple had been destroyed.

THE ESSENES

It is doubtful, however, that the reference in *Midrash Ele Ezkera* to the "transgressors of the generation" who felt that Judaism had lost nothing as a result of the destruction of the Temple could apply to people who were motivated by anti-Herodian and anti-Sadducean feelings. Surely so odious a label as *pritze hador* would not be attached to any pious followers of the school of B'nai Beteira. It is more likely to have embraced such anti-Jerusalem parties as the Essenes, with whose views we are now more familiar thanks to the Dead Sea Scrolls, and also the early Judeo-Christians.

According to Philo the Essenes abstained from the sacrifice of animals, "regarding a reverent mind as the only true sacrifice." Such an attitude would naturally orient them against the Temple and its priesthood. The opposition to sacrificial rites was not adhered to by all the Essenic sects. The dwellers of the Qumran caves, who were undoubtedly members of an Essenic sect, specifically authorized the brethren to bring offerings as prescribed by Mosaic law (*Zadokite Document*). Yet this concession to Jerusalem did not alter their opposition to the Jerusalem priests and to society generally. Only priests who had gone through the sectarian rites of purification and had accepted its strict discipline could become sacred and were to be known as Zadokites.

The Qumran sect did not recognize the authority of the rabbis to interpret the law. The historic struggle between the rabbinate and the priesthood for supreme religious authority had culminated in favor of the former, ever since the days of Rabbi Simon b. Shatach. The Qumranites did not accept the outcome as the final verdict of an evolutionary process. They insisted on the primacy of the priesthood as it had been established in the days of Moses and Aaron. Every person who wished to join the sect had to take a binding oath "to abide with all his heart and soul by the commandments of the Law of Moses, as that law is revealed to the sons of Zadok—that is, to the priests who still keep the Covenant and seek God's will" (*Manual of Discipline*). This view brought them in direct conflict not only with the Temple and its priests, a great many of whom were Sadduceans, but also with the Jerusalem academy and its rabbinic leadership.

A study of the *Zadokite Document* reveals a number of rabbinic traditions adhered to by the sect. Water drawn in a vessel could not be used for ritual ablutions (the document deals with sectarian purification). The observance of the Sabbath is to commence prior to sunset. No one is to walk outside of a city beyond a prescribed distance. No food prepared on the Sabbath may be eaten on that day. No one may engage a Gentile to transact business for him on the Sabbath. These are some of the traditions which they shared in common with the

Pharisees. However, the acceptance of such traditions did not reflect a recognition of rabbinic authority. It was, rather, due to the very ancient origin of these customs. The sectarians were essentially anti-rabbinic. They specifically stated that no one had the right to "advance the statutory times or postpone the prescribed season" *(Manual of Discipline)*. This was a denial of the basic right of the Sanhedrin or the rabbinic academy to fix the calendar. They diverged from rabbinic traditions in many respects: marriage of an uncle to a niece was prohibited; polygamy was prohibited; testimony of a single witness was admissible even in a capital offense, if such an offense was repeated and each instance witnessed by a single witness; no clean beasts were to be sold to heathens; no fish was to be eaten unless it was ripped open while still alive and its blood drained; and so forth.

It is commonly assumed that the Essenes were the forerunners of the early Judeo-Christians. Their hostile attitude to the Temple and the Pharisees was the climate in which Christianity began to grow. Scholars have pointed to many striking parallels between the teachings of the Dead Seas Scrolls and the doctrines of the early Christians. There is a similarity in their sacraments and organization. The Scroll of Habakkuk refers to the faithful being redeemed by God because of their "faith in the Teacher of Righteousness." Both emphasize baptism. Both awaited the "anointed one." Both were people of the "New Covenant" (the Christians rendered the term "New Testament"). There were many other parallel practices, but this is not the place to discuss them.

In spite of the clearly anti-rabbinic attitude of the Essenes, the Talmud mentions no polemics between the rabbis and the Essenes, in contrast to the common disputations with the Sadducees. It is possible that the rabbis considered them devoid of any influence. Their total number is estimated to have been about four thousand. They lived mainly in villages and did not engage in active proselytizing. Furthermore, the Essenes prohibited their members from debating the meaning of the law with "men of ill-repute," anyone who was not a member of the sect *(Manual of Discipline)*. A de facto truce therefore existed between the rabbis and the Essenes. This probably spared the Essenes from attack by the masses and enabled them to thrive unmolested. Their survival indirectly contributed to the rise and spread of the early Judeo-Christians. The author of *Midrash Ele Ezkera,* mindful of the persecutions of Jewry under Christian Rome, viewed in retrospect the gentle treatment accorded to the Essenes *(pritze hador)* as sinful and directly responsible for the ultimate tragedies which had befallen the

Jewish people and filled its chronicles with chapters of martyrdom. A similar opinion was expressed by Rabbi Simon bar Abba in *Midrash Eichah Rabba* (chap. 1): "The great men of Israel saw a sin committed and they turned their heads the other way. To which the Almighty responded: 'The time will come when I will do the same to you.' "

INDIRECT CONTRIBUTION TO THE RISE OF CHRISTIANITY

The second version of this midrash *(Asara Haruge Malchut)* omits the reference to the anti-Temple party (the Essenes) and proceeds immediately to the indirect guilt of the rabbis in contributing to the rise of Christianity by teaching the Torah to some of the men who became the leaders of the movement. It spells out more clearly the moral of the parable, quoted also in the first version. "When God created the trees, they grew sturdy and tall and they greatly rejoiced. As soon as the Almighty created iron the trees were saddened and they said: 'Alas! the Almighty has created iron which will cut us down.' [Upon reflection they said: 'If we withhold our wood from the iron so that it will have no wooden handle, it will be unable to do us harm.'] So Israel, too, if they had not taught Torah to Caesar, they would not have come to this."

The contents of the Torah first became known to the pagan world through the Septuagint, a work of Jewish sages, initially commended by the rabbis. Many of the early church fathers who left a heritage of enmity toward Judaism originally acquired their knowledge of the Bible from rabbinical scholars. It was the teaching of the Torah to non-Jews, resulting in the rise of an offspring religion filled with hate for its mother faith, which forms the basis for the guilt of the rabbis.

The midrash describes the Torah instruction given to the Roman Caesar. When he learned about the biblical capital offense of kidnapping, he summoned ten Jewish sages and informed them that they would be held guilty for the offense of the ten sons of Jacob, who had kidnapped and sold Joseph (hence the significance of *ten* martyrs). What basis was there for the legendary account of a king's charge against Jews, based on a violation of a scriptural law? The pagan kings of Rome were ignorant of the Torah. No pagan king ever accused the Jews of crimes based on an alleged violation of the Bible, nor of a crime allegedly committed by their forefathers. It is obvious that the author of the midrash, ignoring historical perspective as usual, described conditions under Christian Rome in a setting of pagan Rome.

The doctrine of the "first sin" originated with Christianity. The responsibility of children for the sins of their fathers is compatible with this doctrine. On the same theological grounds, Jews of all generations could be held liable for the alleged crime of Christ-killing committed by their forefathers. Jews were also accused of rejecting Christianity in violation of prophetic utterances which allegedly had predicted a new testament. The post-talmudic authors of the midrash, living under the repressive conditions of the Christian Roman Empire, skillfully camouflaged current conditions by putting in the mouth of a Roman pagan emperor a charge, placing responsibility upon Jews for crimes which had been committed by their forefathers. The emperor bolstered his charge with a quotation from the Scriptures. Caesar's charge that Jews were responsible for the sale of Joseph by his brethren was but a thinly disguised version of Christian claims of Jewish responsibility for Judas's betrayal for money. The author of the midrash then reflected: who was responsible for this state of affairs? He concluded that the Jews themselves must bear a share of the blame for having introduced the Gentiles to the Torah.

In the midrashic account of the ascent of Ishmael, the high priest, to heaven to discover whether the emperor would be allowed to carry out the executions, the angel Gabriel informed him that the sages would have to die for the sins of Joseph's brothers. This statement is not to be taken as a theological sanction of the Christian doctrine of the responsibility of children for the sins of their fathers. It is merely an affirmation of the fact that Jewish religious leaders will at times suffer martyrdom as a result of such a doctrine, espoused by non-Jews. The decree of martyrdom of the ten sages was issued, according to the midrash, at the insistence of Samael, the guardian angel of Rome. Their martyrdom was the direct result of their sin of teaching Torah to Caesar.

Having concluded that the Ten Martyrs were not entirely blameless, the author of the midrash still has to explain the bloody chapter of Jewish martyrdom throughout the ages. What about the thousands of innocent martyrs? Can the burden of blame be attached to all of them? Both versions of the midrash crystalize a doctrine which was culled from earlier talmudic and midrashic sources. The reaction of the ten sages to their impending martyrdom was voiced by Rabbi Ishmael, according to the midrash, in the following words: "If it is a decree [*gzeirah*] decreed by heaven, we will accept it. If not, we may be able to void it [through prayer]." When Rabbi Ishmael reported that the martyrdom was decreed in heaven, Rabbi Simon b. Gamliel remarked: "The Lord of Israel will accept our souls as an offering, and he will thereafter avenge our lives by punishing wicked Rome."

THEOLOGICAL DOCTRINE OF MARTYRDOM

The emerging theological doctrine on martyrdom and suffering may be summed up as follows:

1. Martyrdom (or privation) may be the result of a heavenly decree (*gzeirah*) due to the fault of an individual. A *gzeirah* is irrevocable, and the martyr should accept his fate with resignation. The martyrdom will advance the cause of justice by speeding the eradication of those who inflict martyrdoms upon mankind.
2. Some martyrdoms are not the result of a direct heavenly decree, and no blame need attach to the martyrs. The world is filled with evil powers which seek the destruction of the innocent. The free will granted to all human beings gives free rein to evil impulses. Normally righteous people, unless they deliberately expose themselves to danger, are protected by the vigilance of the Almighty. There are times, however, when the Almighty turns his face away and removes his vigilant protection (*Eicha Rabbati* 1). This happens when evil is rampant and most people are corrupt and a majority of Jews neglect the Torah. The unchecked evil forces will then engulf everybody. The righteous will also suffer, like the innocent child who will get hurt when the vigilant eyes of an adult have been removed from him.
3. Suffering and martyrdom which flow from the removal of God's protection may be averted by means of prayer and penitence. They may also be resisted by means of self-defense and counterattack.
4. We have no means of knowing whether a tragedy is the result of a *gzeirah* or the removal of God's protection. There is always the hope that prayers and penitence will arrest the tragedy. By the same token one may always resist aggression by force.
5. There are some major catastrophes in which the religious leadership can, through divine inspiration, discern the force of a *gzeirah*. Under such circumstances one must learn to accept the inevitable while the sages seek to discover the faults and errors which contributed to the issuance of the decree. Prayer and penitence are always in order as an atonement for one's mistakes.

The destruction of both Temples was due to a *gzeirah* according to the rabbis (*Pesichtah de Eichah Rabbati*). The destruction of Betar was also considered the result of a *gzeirah*. The rabbis thus condemned by implication the futile resistance to Rome. On the other hand, the assault of Haman was not due to a *gzeirah* and resistance to him was proper. The martyrdom of the ten sages was also due to a *gzeirah*, and the martyrs therefore meekly accepted their fate.

The use of the term *gzeirah* in the midrash of the Ten Martyrs had a far-reaching effect on the religious attitudes of the Jewish people fated to martyrdom. This term was incorporated into the selichah *Ele Ezkera* and consequently became a familiar concept to every Jew. It was a refuge to the multitudes of pious Jews who did not wish to probe the implication of great national and individual tragedies. If fasting and prayers were of no avail, they realized that a *gzeirah* had been issued. Since no man is blameless, it would be futile to question heavenly justice. Like the ten martyred sages, they would meekly accept their fate in the hope that the cause of righteousness would somehow thereby be advanced.

13

Customs of Minor Fasts

I.- III.
TZOM GEDALIAH, TENTH OF TEVET, AND SEVENTEENTH OF TAMMUZ

THE DESTRUCTION of the Temple is commemorated by four fasts. The principal fast, Tisha B'Av, is discussed in the preceding chapter. The Fast of Gedaliah is observed in memory of the assassination of Gedaliah on the third of Tishri (Jer. 41:1–2). The fast of the tenth of Tevet commemorates the siege of Jerusalem by the Babylonians (II Kings 25:1). The fast of the seventeenth of Tammuz marks the day of the breaching of the wall of Jerusalem. This fast was originally observed on the ninth of Tammuz, the anniversary of the day when the Babylonians penetrated into the city in 586 B. C. E. (II Kings 25:3–4), but was later changed to the seventeenth of Tammuz, the day when the Romans allegedly breached the wall in the year 70.

The fasts which are linked to events which preceded the destruction of the Temple are known by the dates when these events occurred. The Fast of Gedaliah, a post-Temple tragedy, is known by the name of the martyr.

When and where did these fasts originate? It is commonly assumed that they were established in the Babylonian diaspora. Ezekiel, the leader of the Babylonian Jewish community, was informed of the dates of the siege of Jerusalem (Ezek. 24:2) and of the destruction of the Temple (ibid. 33:21). Yet in neither case does the text indicate that the prophet followed up the information with a declaration of a fast. In any event, it is unlikely that Ezekiel initiated the Fast of Gedaliah in view of his opposition to Gedaliah's policies.

Nebuchadnezzar appointed Gedaliah governor of Judea (Jer. 40:5). He was assigned the task of reorganizing the Jewish community and of heading a pro-Babylonian administration. Gedaliah set up his head-

345

quarters at Mitzpah, a historic city with an ancient shrine (ibid. 41:5). Jewish refugees who had remained in Palestine flocked to Mitzpah. Gedaliah advised them to seize and occupy abandoned estates (ibid. 40:10). He thus hoped to repopulate the desolate province. According to Professor Klausner, Ezekiel vehemently opposed the seizure of abandoned estates because it would dampen the hopes of the expatriates for a speedy return to their homes (Ezek. 33:24; *Hist. Shel HaBayit HaSheni*, vol. 1, p. 55).

The fasts of Gedaliah and the ninth of Av were instituted within a year of the destruction of the Temple (Zech. 7:5). An analysis of various biblical texts leads to the conclusion that these fasts were instituted by Palestinian Jews. A state of mourning had spontaneously been adopted by the survivors (Jer. 41:5). The tragic events of the ninth of Av were known to them long before the news reached the Babylonian community. Their grief was compounded by the assassination of Gedaliah, an event nearly as tragic in their eyes as the destruction of the Temple. His death spelled the end of the reconstruction of the Palestinian Jewish community. Furthermore, the "House of the Lord" in Mitzpah, where sacrificial rites were performed (ibid.), had become a hopeful omen of God's salvation. The end of this shrine was a crushing blow to their morale.

After the flight of prominent Jews to Egypt (Jer. 41:17), there still remained a considerable number of Jews who continued to live in scattered areas of the country. To these Jews, the fasts of the ninth of Av and Gedaliah became the principal memorial days of the tragic era. The other two fasts were most likely considered minor memorials observed only on a voluntary basis.

The fast of Tisha B'Av was eventually adopted by the Babylonian diaspora as a public fast. The secondary fasts of the tenth of Tevet and the seventeenth of Tammuz became private fasts, the observance of which was discretionary with individual Jews. As was indicated before, it is doubtful whether the Fast of Gedaliah was ever observed in Babylonia at all.

The restoration of the Jewish community in Judea did not immediately affect the status of the memorial fasts. In 518 B.C.E. a Babylonian Jewish delegation arrived in Palestine to inquire whether the fast of the ninth of Av should remain in force (Zech. 7:3). No mention was made of the other fasts because, being private fasts, they had not become widespread. As for the ninth of Av, the delegates reported that it had been observed in Babylonia "these so many years" (ibid.).

Interestingly, they did not claim that the fast had been observed ever since the destruction of the Temple.

The delegates addressed their question to "the kohanim of the House of the Lord of Hosts and to the prophets" (Zech. 7:13). The kohanim obviously did not have the answer. Zechariah, too, did not immediately respond to the question. Instead he was provoked into delivering a discourse to the local population, "the people of the land and the kohanim" (Zech. 7:5). He mentioned the fact that in the past seventy years (since the end of the Temple) they had been fasting in the months of Av and Tishri (ibid.). He took no note of the other two fasts because of their secondary and private character. Zechariah questioned the sincerity of their fasting.

Eventually Zechariah answered the question posed by the Babylonian delegates. The four fasts were to be discontinued henceforth (Zech. 8:19).

Talmudic tradition confirmed the fact that Tisha B'Av was the only public memorial fast in Babylonia (*Pesachim* 54b). The Talmud also introduced a new rationale for the Fast of Gedaliah to make it more acceptable to Babylonian Jewry when the fasts were restored after the destruction of the Second Temple. That fast was instituted, according to the Talmud, "to teach you that the death of righteous people is as weighty as the burning of the House of our Lord" (*Rosh HaShanah* 18b). Indeed, *Megillat Taanit* listed several anniversaries of the deaths of righteous men and recommended that those days be observed as fast days.

The exact date of the assassination of Gedaliah is not mentioned in the Bible. It is merely stated that it had occurred in "the seventh month" (Jer. 41:1). The Talmud provided the information that the assassination took place on the third of Tishri (*Rosh HaShanah* 18b). Rabbenu Yerucham (14th cent.) suggested that the tragedy occurred on Rosh HaShanah but that the fast was postponed to the day after the holiday (*Bet Yoseph, uma shekatuv, Tur, Orach Chaim* 549).

Ever since the thirteenth century all minor memorial fasts were made obligatory. In the words of Nachmanides: "And now they [the Jews] have already made it a practice to fast and they have obligated themselves" (quoted by Avudrahim).

CUSTOMS

When a memorial fast occurs on a Sabbath, it is postponed to Sunday.

When the tenth of Tevet occurs on a Friday, it is observed on the same day. This is the implication of the biblical expression *beetzem hayom* ("in the same day"; Ezek. 24:2; Avudrahim, *HaTaaniyot*).

All pleasurable acts forbidden on Tisha B'Av are permitted on the minor fast days, except for eating and drinking. The fast begins at dawn.

The chazan recites the prayer of *Anenu* ("answer us") in the *Amidah* of Shacharit, at the conclusion of the seventh benediction.

The portion of *Vayechal* (Exod. 32:11–14, 34:1–10) is read at the Shacharit and Minchah services.

The third aliyah at the Minchah Torah reading is maftir. The Haftarah of *Dirshu* (Isa. 55:6–56:8) is chanted by the maftir.

The congregation recites the prayer of *Anenu* in the Minchah *Amidah* in the middle of the sixteenth benediction, following the phrase *al teshivenu*.

Selichot (penitential prayers) for fast days are recited by the congregation.

IV.
THE FAST OF ESTHER

The Fast of Esther, observed on the thirteenth of Adar, dates from the eighth century. It was instituted by the Babylonian Jewish community. In the Palestinian rite, the fast was spread over three days, on Monday, Thursday, and the next Monday following Purim. The three-day fast approximated the length of the fast which was ordained by Queen Esther (Esther 4:6).

For a review of the history of the Fast of Esther, see Bloch, *Biblical and Historical Background of the Jewish Holy Days*, chap. 12.

CUSTOMS

The Fast of Esther begins at dawn.

If Purim occurs on a Sunday, the fast is advanced to the previous Thursday. Fasts are not scheduled on Fridays unless the date of the fast falls on that day. If a fast date falls on a Sabbath, it is generally postponed to Sunday. This is impossible in the case of the Fast of Esther because it is followed by a holiday. The fast is therefore advanced to the previous Thursday.

The reason for not favoring fasts on Fridays is the need to avoid interference with the time-consuming preparations for the Sabbath.

Kol Bo (14th cent.) mentions another reason for the reluctance to schedule fasts on Fridays. A Friday fast might create the impression of an imitation of a non-Jewish rite (*Hilchot Taanit* 62). Friday, the day of the Crucifixion, was a traditional Christian fast-day. Interestingly, *Masechet Soferim* (edited in the 8th cent.) mentions a time in Jewish history when Jews were hesitant about declaring fasts on Sundays because Christians might be offended by Jewish fasts on a day when they are happy (chap. 17).

All congregational rituals pertaining to minor fasts are in effect on the Fast of Esther.

V.
TAANIT BECHORIM

The Fast of the Firstborn, observed on the fourteenth of Nisan, commemorates the escape of firstborn Jews from the death of the tenth plague. Jews had been spared the afflictions of all the other plagues. According to *Kol Bo* (58), firstborn Egyptians served as priests of their families. Some firstborn Jews acted in the same capacity and therefore deserved the same penalty. Taanit Bechorim is a fast of gratitude to mark their escape.

There was no formal Fast of the Firstborn in the talmudic era. However, there were some individuals who voluntarily observed such a fast. Thus it was noted that Rabbi Judah HaNasi (d. 220) ate neither chametz nor matzah on the eve of Passover (Jer. *Pesachim* 10:1). There is no clear indication that Rabbi Judah abstained from all food, yet that is the implication of the talmudic comment that his abstention was due to the fact that he was a firstborn. Nevertheless there was no general practice of fasting. Rabbi Mana (end of 3rd cent.) observed that his father was a firstborn but had never fasted on the eve of Passover (ibid.).

Masechet Soferim (edited in the 8th cent.) is the earliest source of a formalized Fast of the Firstborn (chap. 21).

CUSTOMS

All firstborns, including kohanim and leviim, fast on the fourteenth of Nisan.

If the first day of Passover occurs on a Sunday, the fast is observed on the preceding Thursday (see "Fast of Esther"). However, if it falls on Saturday, the fast is observed in the proper time, on Friday.

In some medieval Jewish communities firstborn females also observed the fast. Rema (16th cent.) ruled that females have no obligation to fast on the eve of Passover (*Orach Chaim* 470:1).

It is customary for fathers of firstborn minors to fast in their behalf.

A firstborn present at a mitzvah-meal (following a circumcision or the completion of a talmudic tract) is exempt from fasting.

Many congregations arrange to have a mitzvah-meal on the morning of the fourteenth of Nisan for the convenience of firstborn.

VI.
YOM KIPPUR KATAN

Sixteenth-century kabbalists considered Rosh Chodesh a minor day of judgment and atonement for sins committed in the preceding month. Since fasting is forbidden on Rosh Chodesh, they instituted a fast on the eve of Rosh Chodesh and named it Yom Kippur Katan. If Rosh Chodesh occurs on a Sabbath, the fast is observed on the preceding Thursday.

A special order of liturgy was arranged for the occasion. One version of this order was published in *Siddur Shelah*. A slightly modified version was printed in the Siddur of Rabbi Jacob Emden. Surprisingly, one of the selected lead compositions, *Yom Zeh* ("this day"), was composed by Rabbi Leo da Modena (16th–17th cent.), known for his anti-kabbalist stance.

Yom Kippur Katan is not mentioned in the code. Nevertheless it spread throughout the Diaspora. In some areas this fast was observed on the day of the molad (nativity of the moon), if it occurred prior to Rosh Chodesh. Those who followed this custom terminated the fast at the time of the molad.

VII.
TAANIT BEHAV

Behav is an acronym of the letters *bet, he, bet* (Monday, Thursday, and Monday). Mondays and Thursdays were considered propitious occasions for prayers and fasts because the Torah is read on those mornings. Another explanation was provided by the tradition that Moses ascended Mount Sinai on Thursday to receive the second Tablets of the Law and came down on Monday. God's forgiveness was thus linked to those two days (*Tur, Orach Chaim* 134). The concluding chapter of *Megillat Taanit* also noted a rabbinic tendency in talmudic times to decree fasts on Mondays and Thursdays. A similar tradition is indicated in *Masechet Soferim* (chap. 21).

The *Tur* code (13th cent.) is the earliest source for the three Behav fasts, which are observed after Passover (in the month of Iyar) and after Sukkot (in the month of Cheshvan, *Orach Chaim* 497). The timing of the Behav fasts was based on a talmudic statement, *sakba dishata rigla* ("the sorest spot of the year is a festival"; *Kiddushin* 81a). According to a tosafist commentary, men and women gather on holidays and have the opportunity to eye each other. This contributes to an infraction of the strict code of moral behavior. The tosafist added that for this reason fasts have been instituted after Passover and Sukkot (ibid., *sakba dishata*).

Behav fasts attained great popularity in the sixteenth and seventeenth centuries. A guest at a mitzvah-meal on the day of a Behav fast is exempt from fasting (Rema, *Orach Chaim* 568:2).

VIII.
TAANIT SHOVAVIM TAT

Shovavim Tat is an acronym for eight biblical portions *(Shemot, Vaera, Bo, Beshalach, Yitro, Mishpatim, Terumah, Tetzaveh)*. The portion of *Ki Tisa* was not included because of its account of the golden calf. Sixteenth-century kabbalists instituted a fast in each of those weeks. The most prevalent custom was to fast on eight Thursdays but only in an intercalary year. This was due to the long interval between the two Behav periods in an intercalary year, during which time there were few penitential fasts. Religious instincts had dictated a need for additional fasts for the good of the soul.

IX.
THE FAST OF THE TWENTIETH OF SIVAN

The fast of the twentieth of Sivan was originally decreed by Rabbenu Tam, the celebrated tosafist (12th cent.), in memory of the Jews who were burned in Blois, France, on May 26, 1171, in the first blood libel on the European continent. The fast was observed by Western Jews. However, the expulsion of Jews from England and France led to the discontinuance of the fast.

Seventeenth-century Polish Jewry renewed the fast of the twentieth of Sivan in memory of the martyrs of the Chmielnicki massacres.

X.
A YAHRZEIT FAST

It is customary to fast on a parent's yahrzeit day as an expression of grief and respect for the memory of the deceased.

Talmudic practice merely called for abstention from meat and wine on a yahrzeit day (*Shevout* 20a). The connotation of this statement was a prohibition of feasting on an anniversary of a parent's death. However, medieval scholars gave the prohibition a narrower interpretation. Maharil (14th–15th cent.) construed the talmudic practice as a total abstention from food. Rema (16th cent.) followed his opinion in the annotations to the code (*Yoreh Deah* 402:12).

The fast is waived if the yahrzeit occurs on a day when *Tachanun* (penitential prayer) is omitted.

XI.
PRIVATE FASTS

Private fasts were common among Jews from biblical times on. In the medieval period, communities frequently assumed annual fasts to commemorate narrow escapes from disaster. Individuals occasionally assumed fasts in penance for sins.

The most common private fast was Taanit Chalom (a dream fast). Dreams have been regarded as omens of events to come. Under the stress of religious persecution and economic deprivation, nightmares disturbed the sleep of the weary. To prevent such nightmares from becoming a reality, people resorted to fasts. This practice was considered so urgent that one was permitted to fast even on a Sabbath (*Berachot* 31b; Tosafot, *kol hayoshev*). However, this dispensation was limited in the Middle Ages (*Orach Chaim* 288:2).

XII.
HOLOCAUST DAY

National disasters are traditionally commemorated by fasts. Modern Jewish communities, however, are not receptive to new fasts. The Chief Rabbinate of Israel therefore declared the ancient fast of the tenth of Tevet a memorial day for the victims of the Nazi Holocaust. A special memorial prayer for the souls of the martyrs is recited after the reading of the Torah portion of *Vayechal*.

The twenty-seventh of Nisan was proclaimed a national Holocaust Day (Yom HaShoah) by Israel's Kneset in memory of the Nazi victims and the uprising in the Warsaw Ghetto.

14

In Remembrance of Historical Events

"REMEMBER THE DAYS OF OLD, consider the years of many generations" (Deut. 32:7). History shapes the development of individuals and nations. Childhood experiences are decisive in the formation of adult attitudes, and national traits are similarly conditioned by historical events.

Memories of past glories and triumphs produce a sense of self-reliance and a relaxation of tensions. They also serve to bolster national morale in periods of stress and confrontation. On the other hand, recollections of past hardships, struggles, and martyrdoms harden a national resolve to survive and heighten a nation's alertness to hostile plots.

As an ancient people, Jews can look back to numerous triumphs and defeats. The Bible stresses the importance of remembering the good as well as the bad. "Remember his marvelous works that he has done" (I Chron. 16:12), but also "Remember what Amalek did unto thee on the way as ye came forth out of Egypt" (Deut. 25:17). In its broader context, this exhortation encompasses all the highways traversed by the Jewish people in their long and eventful history—on the way to the Promised Land, on the way to Babylonia, on the way to Rome, on the way to the four corners of the earth, on the way to Treblinka, and on the way back to the Promised Land.

When history is forgotten it ceases to influence the course of the present or the future. Ancient events normally fade from man's memory. Can Jews be expected to remember events which are three thousand years old? Indeed, the world urges Jews to forget the Holocaust in the short span of three decades.

Jewish tradition has built-in safeguards against the obliteration of

355

the past. The very first chapter of the *Shulchan Aruch*, the religious code which delineates the full dimensions of Jewish life, calls upon every Jew to constantly remember the destruction of the Temple in the year 70 and the many tragedies which resulted from it. Judaism seeks to perpetuate ancient memories through customs and prayers. The sages asked all generations to relive the exodus and the revelation on Mount Sinai. They must also identify with the captives of Judea who were forced to leave Jerusalem by the legions of Rome.

TEN REMEMBRANCES

Rabbi Jacob Emden (1697–1776) included in the liturgy special prayers inspired by ten historical events which, according to the Bible, should be remembered by Jews. Each prayer begins with the words: "I recall . . ." The recollections are based on a list of events drawn up by Rabbi Isaac Luria (1534–1572), the famous kabbalist, who suggested that Jews should meditate upon the significance of those incidents. Rabbi Emden felt that meditation alone was insufficient to meet the biblical dictate of an active remembrance. He therefore composed the special prayers in order to articulate the duty to keep those memories alive.

The following are the ten historical events highlighted in Rabbi Emden's prayers: the exodus (Exod. 13:3), the Sabbath (Exod. 20:8), Mount Sinai (Deut. 4:9–10), the covenant (Deut. 8:18), the golden calf (Deut. 9:7), the manna (Deut. 8:2–3), Miriam's transgression (Deut. 24:9), Amalek's treachery (Deut. 25:17–19), Balaam's hypocrisy (Micah 6:5), the fall of Jerusalem (Ps. 137:5–6).

The events in Rabbi Emden's list follow, with one exception, the order in which they appear in the Bible. The gist of the short prayers that he affixed to each event may be summed up as follows: A plea to God that he extend his protection to the Jewish people to assure their survival, that he promote harmony in their ranks so that they may present a united front, that he strengthen their loyalty to the Torah and their faith in an ultimate redemption, that he forgive their sins whenever they confess and repent.

The objective of Rabbi Emden's prayers fits into a theological framework which covers man's relations to God. History is used as an incentive to greater religious fervor and dedication to prayer. Rabbi Emden overlooked, however, the equally important biblical aim to allow historical influences to shape Jewish psychological development.

Rabbi Emden's ten biblical incidents may be consolidated and reduced to three major events, the most far-reaching in Jewish history—the exodus, the Torah, and Jerusalem. The process of the exodus, which lasted forty years, encompasses the manna, the golden calf, Miriam, Amalek, and Balaam. The comprehensive topic of the Torah covers the Sabbath, Mount Sinai, and the covenant. The topic of Jerusalem permeates Jewish life throughout the ages.

IN REMEMBRANCE OF THE EXODUS

"Remember the day in which ye came out from Egypt out of the house of bondage" (Exod. 13:3). The exodus is part of ancient history, beyond the normal national memory span. God commanded, however, that the memory of the exodus be kept fresh for all time (Exod. 12:14). Its importance in the preservation of the faith and the development of the Jewish character may be gauged from the fact that there are at least fifty references to the exodus in the Bible. Its centrality in Judaic theology is basic because it marked the finalization of the covenant God concluded with Abraham (Gen. 15:18). That covenant was to go into effect upon the departure of the Jews from Egypt. The exodus, therefore, marked the establishment of a covenant between God and the Jewish people (Deut. 29:24).

The experience of enslavement in Egypt affected Jewish socio-ethical laws and concepts. Thus the injunction to provide generous gifts to servants whose term of employment had expired was motivated by the ancient experience of bondage in Egypt (Deut. 15:15). The same motivation inspired the commandment to love the stranger (Deut. 10:19) and to deal justly with the orphan (Deut. 24:15). The injunction to provide for the servant, Levite, stranger, orphan, and widow so that they may rejoice on the holidays is based on the same historical experience (Deut. 16:12). A similar reminder is appended to the law which mandates owners of vineyards to leave some grapes on the vine "for the stranger, for the orphan and the widow" (Deut. 24:22). The biblical stress on charity and compassion for the underprivileged is undoubtedly a contributing factor to the Jewish propensity to champion liberal causes. It also conditioned the Jewish practice to take care of their poor, even in countries where governments have enacted comprehensive social legislation.

In addition to the humanitarian impact of the exodus on Jewish social commitments, it has also served the theological purpose of bolstering Jewish faith in God. The miracle of the exodus is frequently invoked as proof of the existence of God. Divine proclamations are often preceded by an identification of God as the redeemer of the Jews in Egypt. The first commandment of the Decalogue opens with the proclamation: "I am the Lord, thy God, who brought thee out of the land of Egypt, out the house of bondage" (Exod. 20:2). This identification was repeated by the psalmist: "There shall be no strange deity in thee, neither shalt thou worship a foreign god. I am the Lord thy God who brought thee up out of the land of Egypt" (81:10–11).

The first Jewish affirmation of faith in God came in the wake of the exodus. "And Israel saw the great work which the Lord did upon the Egyptians, and the people feared the Lord; and they had faith in the Lord and his servant Moses" (Exod. 14:31). The third section of the *Shema*, which proclaims the unity of God, also links God to the exodus from Egypt. The generation of Jews which entered the Promised Land expressed their conviction to Joshua that they would never lose faith in God because of their recollection of the miracles of Egypt (Josh. 24:16–17).

The prospect that Jews may someday forget the story of Egypt led Moses to issue a warning: "Then thy heart may be lifted up and thou wilt forget the Lord thy God who brought thee forth out of the land of Egypt, out of the house of bondage" (Deut. 8:14). Moses also warned against a false prophet "because he has sought to draw thee away from the Lord, thy God, who brought thee forth out of the land of Egypt" (Deut. 13:11).

In addition to serving theological ends, the memory of the exodus also sustained Jews in time of adversity and bolstered hopes of survival and ultimate salvation. The scriptural promise that the God who had taken them out of Egypt would never totally reject them gave new hope to a people beset by doubts and apprehensions. "And yet for all that, when they are in the land of their enemies, I will not reject them. . . . I will for their sakes remember the covenant of their ancestors, whom I brought forth out of the land of Egypt" (Lev. 26:44–45).

The memory of Egypt also inspired Jews to be sanguine in the face of the greater numbers and superior strength of the enemy. "If thou shalt say in thy heart: 'These nations are more than I, how can I overcome them?' Thou shalt not be afraid of them; thou shalt well remember what the Lord, thy God, did unto Pharaoh and unto all Egypt" (Deut. 7:17–18). If Jews must have recourse to war to defend themselves against their enemies, they must not be discouraged by the heavy odds favoring their foes, "for the Lord, thy God, is with thee, who brought thee out of the land of Egypt" (Deut. 20:10).

CUSTOMS COMMEMORATING THE EXODUS

Various customs and rituals have been ordained to keep the memory of the exodus alive. The first and foremost reminder of that fateful incident is the festival of Passover, the observance of which was commanded while the Jews were still in Egypt. The annual reinactment of the drama of the exodus and the recitation of the many wonders which transpired at that time served to perpetuate the memory of that great epoch. "Remember the month of spring, and keep the Passover unto the Lord, thy God; for in the month of spring the Lord, thy God, brought thee forth out of Egypt by might" (Deut. 16:11).

The Sabbath day, on which man, his servant, and his beast must rest, is another memorial to the exodus. The Hebrew slaves were not entitled to a day of rest. It was only after their delivery from bondage that they could rest from their labor one day each week. "And thou shalt remember that thou wast a slave in the land of Egypt, and the Lord, thy God, brought thee thence by a mighty hand, by an outstretched arm; therefore the Lord, thy God, commanded thee to keep the Sabbath day" (Deut. 5:15). According to a rabbinic tradition, Jews were ordered to observe the Sabbath three days after their crossing of the Red Sea (*Sanhedrin* 56b). Thus this important memorial to the exodus was given priority over all the other festivals (with the exception of Passover).

The festival of Sukkot is also a memorial to the exodus. "You shall dwell in booths seven days . . . that your generations may know that I made the children of Israel to dwell in booths, when I brought them out of the land of Egypt, I am the Lord thy God" (Lev. 23:42–43).

The ritual of tefillin is another daily reminder of the exodus. This law was ordained simultaneously with the institution of the festival of Passover, several days prior to the departure from Egypt. The biblical sequence is highly enlightening. "Seven days thou shalt eat unleavened bread . . ." (Exod. 13:6). "And thou shalt tell thy son in that day, saying: 'It is because of that which the Lord did for me when I came forth out of Egypt' " (Exod. 13:8). "And it shall be for a sign unto thee upon thy hand, and for a memorial between thine eyes" (Exod. 13:9). A repetition of the ritual of tefillin is stated in the same chapter. "And it shall be when thy son asks thee in time to come: 'What is this?' " (referring to the firstlings of animals). The passage is concluded with the injunction: "And it shall be for a sign upon thy hand and frontlet between thy eyes, for by strength of hand the Lord brought thee forth out of Egypt" (Exod. 13:14, 16). The sequence of the text clearly links the ritual of tefillin to the exodus.

The above-quoted passages are inserted into the tefillin boxes. They are thus to serve as reminders of the exodus and also as educational tools in transmitting the lesson of the exodus to the young and the skeptics. In the words of Nachmanides: "Since the Almighty does not perform miracles in every generation for all the wicked and disbelievers to see, he commanded us to make a memorial and a sign to that which our eyes had seen and that we should transmit that fact to our children, and our children to their children to subsequent generations" (Exod. 13:16).

Eventually, the role of the tefillin was expanded to serve as a memorial to the Torah (Deut. 6:8, 11:18). The added commandments were also associated with the parental obligation to teach the Torah to the young (Deut. 6:7, 11:19).

PRAYERS COMMEMORATING THE EXODUS

The memory of the exodus is daily refreshed by numerous prayers of our liturgy and by many biblical excerpts included in the prayerbook. A few illustrations will suffice. "God, our Lord . . . who helped us overcome our enemies . . . who wrought for miracles and retribution upon Pharaoh and brought forth the people Israel from among them to everlasting freedom . . ." *(Emet VeEmunah)*. The ancient ode of *Nishmat (Pesachim* 118a), a song of thanksgiving, gives praise to God who redeemed us from Egypt and released us from the house of bondage. In the blessing of the new month, we invoke God, who "wrought miracles for our fathers and redeemed them from slavery to freedom, may he speedily redeem us and gather our exiles from the four corners of the earth." Indeed, the Jewish liturgy is unique in providing source material on important historical events.

The Kiddush ("sanctification"), recited on Sabbath eve and holidays, calls to our attention the fact that these special days have been ordained "in remembrance of the departure from Egypt." As a result of such frequent reminders, the Hebrew phrase *zecher liyetziat mitzrayim* has become a household expression in every traditional Jewish home.

IN REMEMBRANCE OF THE TORAH

"Remember the Torah of my servant Moses" (Mal. 3:22). The exhortation of the prophet Malachi was not addressed to any specific ordinance in the Torah but to its entirety. It is the aggregate of all its provisions which define the Jewish way of life. To that end God commanded Joshua "to observe to do according to the entire Torah. . . . thou shalt meditate upon them day and night that thou mayest observe to do according to all that is written therein" (Josh. 1:7–8). Malachi was witness to the ravages of assimilation and skepticism which undermined the viability of the people. "For Judah has profaned the holiness of the Lord which he loveth, and has married the daughter of a strange god" (2:11). His appeal to the Jews to remember the Torah was another way of saying: "Remember that you are Jews."

To assure the remembrance of the Torah, Joshua was ordered to set up stones on the west side of the Jordan upon which the text of the Torah was to be engraved (Deut. 27:8). A public reading of the Torah (or of Deuteronomy) was to be given in Jerusalem at the end of the first day of Sukkot in the first year of the sabbatical cycle (Deut. 31:11; *Rosh HaShanah* 12b). The need for such measures reflected the fear uppermost in the minds of Moses and subsequent leaders that some Jews might forget the Torah and their distinctiveness from other nations. The relapse of the people after the death of Moses was predicted in the Scriptures (Deut. 31:16, 29).

The fundamental law designed to counteract the pressures of assimilation was the life-long obligation to study the Torah and to teach it to the young (Deut. 6:7). Initially this obligation devolved upon the father. It was soon realized, however, that the cause of religious education would make little progress unless the community assumed the responsibility for the education of the young. A school for children was established in Jerusalem in the period of the Second Temple, most likely after the emergence of the Hasmoneans. When this too proved inadequate, additional schools were set up in each district. Finally, Joshua b. Gamala, a high priest who officiated in 64 C. E., set up a net of schools in each town and village and ordered that all children from the age of six and up attend school (*Baba Batra* 21a). The existence of an academy for advanced studies probably dates back to the days of Ezra (5th cent. B. C. E.).

CUSTOMS PERPETUATING THE TORAH

The spread of religious education substantially reduced the threat of assimilation. However, as the size of the Jewish diaspora expanded and Jews settled in remote lands, far removed from centers of learning, the problem of estrangement grew more acute. Not only were some Jews ignorant of the Torah but many were in danger of forgetting their descent. The rite of circumcision was an indelible seal stamped upon the flesh as a permanent reminder of one's Jewishness. As long as the rite was practiced, Jewish identity was assured.

It was also important to have identifiable and visible Jewish distinctiveness displayed in public. The biblical commandment of *tzitzit* ("fringes"), attached to the outer garment, was designed to serve as a reminder of one's Jewishness and the Torah. "And it shall be unto you for a fringe, that you may look upon it and remember all the commandments of the Lord and do them" (Num. 15:39).

The mezuzah attached to the doorposts of Jewish homes similarly served as a reminder of the Torah and the parental obligation to transmit its traditions to the children. The two biblical excerpts written on the parchment of the mezuzah (Deut. 6:4–9, 11:13–21) stress the importance of the study of the Torah and the education of the young.

Tefillin are also memorials to the Torah. The two excerpts in the mezuzah are also inserted into the tefillin boxes. A third excerpt from Exodus (13:9) also stresses the importance of Torah study. "And it shall be for a sign unto thee upon thy hand, and for a reminder between thine eyes that the law of the Lord may be in thy mouth . . ."

The custom of Torah reading at public assemblies of worship is very ancient. Tradition attributes to Moses the provision for the reading of a scriptural portion on Sabbath mornings. This tradition reflects the antiquity of the practice. Ezra (5th cent. B. C. E.) is credited with being the originator of the custom of reading the Torah on Mondays and Thursdays and on Sabbath afternoons.

A few holidays have also been designated as memorials to the Torah. Beginning with the second century, Shavuot was declared a holiday in celebration of the anniversary of the giving of the law on Mount Sinai (see Bloch, *Biblical and Historical Background of the Jewish Holy Days*, p. 188). Simchat Torah, the day on which Jews celebrate the completion of the reading of the Torah, is another memorial instituted in post-talmudic times.

PRAYERS COMMEMORATING THE TORAH

The liturgy includes numerous references to the Torah and to the Jewish commitment to obey its commandments. We will quote but a few. The twelfth-century hymn *Yigdal*, which formally opens the morning service, includes the verse: "A Torah of truth has God given to his people." The first blessing after the purification benediction reads: "Blessed art thou, O Lord, our God, king of the universe, who has sanctified us by thy commandments and commanded us to study the words of the Torah." The first petition of the morning service reads: "Make pleasant therefore, we beseech thee, O Lord our God, the words of thy Torah in our mouth . . . may all know thy name and learn thy Torah . . ."

In addition to the many references to the Torah, excerpts from the Bible and the Talmud have been made part of the liturgy, so that study of the Torah and the recitation of prayers are intermingled. After the benediction over the Torah, which is read shortly after the opening of the morning service, one intones an entire mishnah: "These are the commandments which have no fixed measure . . . but the study of the Torah leadeth them all" (*Peah,* chap. 1).

IN REMEMBRANCE OF THE DESTRUCTION

"By the rivers of Babylon, there we sat down, yea, we wept, when we remembered Zion" (Ps. 137:1). The very first chapter of the *Shulchan Aruch* code stresses the need for being constantly aware of the loss of the Temple. The same chapter also suggests that the end of the second trimester of the night is the moment when prayers for the restoration of Zion are most acceptable. The Talmud stresses the need for customs commemorating Jerusalem (*Sukkah* 41a).

The fact that the remembrance of the destruction of Jerusalem is mentioned in the first chapter of the code does not necessarily mean that it has priority over all the other remembrances to which Jews are committed. The code's selection was based on the fact that it opens with a citation of religious practices which one must perform at the beginning of the day. The call for pre-dawn prayers consequently takes precedence.

Unquestionably, the remembrance of the destruction of the Temple holds a place of centrality in the unconsciousness of the Jewish Diaspora. The cheerful phrase *zecher liyetziat mitzrayim* thus has its counterpart in the doleful *zecher l'churban*.

What purpose does the memory of the loss of Jerusalem serve? One of the principal tenets of Judaism is the belief in the ultimate redemption of Israel, the reestablishment of a Jewish homeland, and the return of God's glory to Zion. This ancient belief did not stem from a mood of nationalistic irredentism but from a yearning for religious fulfillment in the Holy Land, inherent in the scriptural promise of a messianic age.

The deuteronomic prediction of a restoration was never considered an idle utopian dream. "And the Lord, thy God, will turn thy captivity

. . . and gather thee from all the peoples, whither the Lord, thy God, has scattered thee" (Deut. 30:3). The tragic prophet Jeremiah, a contemporary of the destruction of Jerusalem, left a message of hope even as he lamented the destruction. "Thus says the Lord: 'Refrain thy voice from weeping, and thine eyes from tears, for thy work shall be rewarded,' says the Lord, 'and they shall come back from the land of the enemy' " (31:15). The memory of the destruction kept the belief in the restoration alive.

Maimonides lists thirteen principles of faith to which every Jew must subscribe. The twelfth principle reads: "I believe with perfect faith in the coming of the Messiah; and though he tarry, I will wait daily for his coming." The conditions which will prevail in the messianic age have never clearly been defined. However, it has been assumed that a description of that age is reflected in a vision of Micah: "And it will come to pass in the end of days that the mountain of the Lord's house shall be established . . . and many nations shall go and say: 'Come ye and let us go to the mountain of the Lord . . . he will teach us of his ways . . . and he shall judge between many peoples . . . and they shall beat their swords into plowshares . . .' " (4:1–5). Jews eased the pain of waiting for the Messiah with continued dreams of a return to Zion in a world of peace.

If Jews had ceased mourning for Zion, they would have given up all hopes for its restoration—the trickle of Jewish pilgrims to a land which had turned into a desolate wilderness would have dried up, modern Zionism could not have seen the light of day, and the State of Israel would never have emerged. Without the expectation of an ultimate redemption, Jews would have been crushed by the iron crown of martyrdom.

Jerusalem was destroyed by the Babylonians in the year 586 B. C. E. The hope for a return to the ancestral land was articulated by the captives as soon as they reached foreign land. With the memory of their loss fresh in their minds, they took an oath: "If I forget thee, O Jerusalem, let my right hand forget her cunning . . ." (Ps. 135:7).

To reinforce the yearning for Zion, the religious leaders of the diaspora immediately decreed four fast-days in commemoration of the destruction. There was no apprehension that Jews might in time forget Zion. The prophet had predicted that the captivity would return after seventy years (II Chron. 36:21). The prophecy was fulfilled, and upon the restoration of Jerusalem the exilic fast-days were promptly discontinued (Zech. 8:19).

The second destruction of Jerusalem took place in the year 70 C. E., when Titus ordered the burning of the city and the Temple. Rome was infinitely more powerful and stable than Babylonia had been six and a half centuries earlier. There was no prophet to offer reassurance that the exile would be of short duration. There was a strong undercurrent of hope at the beginning. Eventual disappointment, however, led to disturbances, culminating in the insurrection of Bar Kochba (132–135).

There were a few rabbinic leaders who shared the early optimism of the masses. Rabbi Akiva was one of them. When a rabbinic delegation visited Rome, they were deeply saddened by the contrast between that prosperous metropolis and the desolate Jerusalem. Rabbi Akiva, however, retained a cheerful mien. "If God is so kind to transgressors of his will, how much more compassionate will he be with those who abide by his will" (*Makkot* 24b).

The overwhelming majority of the rabbinic leadership took a much more sober view of the immediate prospect of a restoration of Jerusalem. They were resigned to the reality of a prolonged Roman domination and planned for the survival of Jewry as a religious community. At the same time they never surrendered their belief in a messianic intervention at the end of days.

RABBAN YOCHANAN B. ZAKKAI

The burden of leadership at the time of the destruction of Jerusalem fell upon the shoulders of Rabban Yochanan b. Zakkai, who was the *av bet din* ("head of the court") in the Sanhedrin, which was presided over by lineal descendants of Hillel. Due to the political attributes of the presidential office, the president of the Sanhedrin was considered a persona non grata by the Romans. The onus of negotiating an agreement of coexistence had to be assumed by the head of the court. Rabban Yochanan succeeded in obtaining concessions from Titus which were crucial to the future development of Judaism. He received permission to establish an academy in Yavneh. Implied in that permission was the privilege of religious autonomy of the Jewish community. He also persuaded Titus to permit the successors of the hierarchy of Hillel to continue in the presidency of the Sanhedrin (*Gittin* 56a). Titus' consent made it possible for Rabban Gamliel to serve as *nasi* (president) and to set up a religious organization with the power to regulate the ecclesiastic affairs of the nation.

Having entered into a pact with Titus, Rabban Yochanan gave up the use of force as a means of regaining independence. Salvation must henceforth come from God, and the Jewish people must prove itself worthy of it. The task of the religious leadership was to rekindle the piety of the nation. To his disciples, Rabban Yochanan put it this way: "You are fortunate, O Israel, whenever your performance is acceptable to the Almighty, no nation can dominate you. But when you transgress his will, he hands them over into the hands of a contemptible nation" (*Ketubot* 66b).

When the news of the destruction of the Temple reached Rabban Yochanan at Yavneh, "he rent his clothes and his disciples did likewise and they wept, screamed, and lamented the loss" (*Avot deRabbi Natan* 4). By this action Rabban Yochanan indicated that the loss of the Temple is to be treated as a loss of a kin and that the laws of mourning (*avelut*) should be observed (*Taanit* 30a, *Moed Katan* 26a). The fast of Tisha B'Av was most likely reinstated in the same year. The remaining three fasts (Tzom Gedaliah, Asara B'Tevet, and Shiva Asar B'Tammuz) were reinstated after the disastrous end of Bar Kochba's insurrection in 135 (see Bloch, *Biblical and Historical Background of the Jewish Holy Days*, p. 232).

The end of the Temple's sacrificial rites troubled many Jews. How would they atone for their sins? Rabban Yochanan reassured them. Charity, he said, is just as effective as sacrificial rites (*Avot deRabbi Natan* 4). Henceforth, charity and prayers replaced the ritual offerings in the religious prescription for atonement. The charity box was thus established as an important adjunct of the worship service.

Rabban Yochanan introduced some new customs in order to keep the memory of the Temple alive. Thus he decreed that the shofar be blown in Yavneh on a Rosh HaShanah day which falls on the Sabbath, as it had been previously done at the Temple (*Rosh HaShanah* 29b). He also ordained that the lulav be used at services on all the days of Sukkot, a practice previously confined to the Temple only (*Rosh HaShanah* 30a). He explained his ordinance with the need for *zecher l'mikdash* ("in memory of the Temple"). Another custom introduced at that time and labeled *zecher l'mikdash* was the eating at the Seder of a sandwich of matzah and maror, just as Hillel had done at the time of the existence of the Temple.

Rabban Yochanan's grief at the loss of the Temple was not shared by all the people. The Essenes, opponents of the priestly caste in the Temple, were not saddened by its destruction. The Judeo-Christians viewed the disaster as a vindication of their doctrines. However, there were also some traditional Jews in whose eyes the Temple had lost its sanctity in its declining years. A rabbinic author noted that "Betar existed for fifty-two years after the destruction of the Temple. Why was it destroyed? Because they lit candles [celebrated] in memory of the destruction of the Temple" (*Eichah Rabbati Pesichta* 4).

Despite the error of the date in the preceding passage (Betar was destroyed in 135, 65 years after the destruction) and its obvious prejudicial tone against Bar Kochba, the statement undoubtedly reflects an ancient belief that the people of Betar did not mourn the loss of the Temple because they saw greater hope for the future of Judaism in the academy than in the strife-torn Temple. One wonders about the possible connection between the B'nai Beteira, who opposed Rabban Yochanan's shofar ordinance in memory of the Temple, and the city of Betar.

The Talmud also mentions other Jews who "do not mourn for Jerusalem" (*Taanit* 30b). In another account, the Talmud describes the people of Kefar Sechanya, who were punished for their refusal to mourn for Jersualem (*Gittin* 57a). It is possible that these anti-Jerusalemites were the Judeo-Christians, who are said to have had an important cell in Kefer Sechanya (*Avodah Zara* 27b).

At the other end of the spectrum were the Pharisees, who advocated a permanent state of asceticism and mourning in memory of Jerusalem (*Baba Batra* 60b). Such a stance would have put a blight upon the orderly growth of rabbinic Judaism by concentrating the nation's attention upon mourning for the past.

We thus get a view of three reactions to the loss of the Temple— indifference, moderate grief, and excessive mourning. The majority followed the lead of Rabban Yochanan. Zion must not be forgotten, and the hope for its eventual restoration must be retained. To aid that process, it is important to observe the new customs and rituals which had been introduced in commemoration of the Temple. The main thrust of rabbinic planning, however, must be directed toward the adjustment of Judaism to the new conditions created by the destruction of the Temple. Religion must remain a viable force in the long exile which lay ahead.

THE PHARISEES

Who were the Pharisees (*perushim*), the chief mourners of Zion? Some scholars assume that the name is derived from a Hebrew term meaning "interpreters [of the law]." This is erroneous for two reasons. The Hebrew term for "interpreters" is *mepharshim* or *parshanim*. Furthermore the majority of the Pharisees were not scholars and did not interpret the law, as I will try to point out later. It is regrettable that as a result of this error there seems to be a consensus among historians that the *chachamim* (rabbinic leaders) and the *perushim* are identical. The fact is that the rabbis and the Pharisees did not always see eye to eye.

Another school of scholars assumes that the name Pharisees means "separatists," those who separated themselves from the *amei-haaretz* (the ignorant and the nonobservant). This too is erroneous. The Pharisees admittedly did not trust the ignorant Jews insofar as their observance of the laws of tithing and purity was concerned. However, they did not sever their contacts with these Jews and were actually regarded with great respect by everyone. Josephus states that "the cities give great attestation to them on account of their entire virtuous conduct" (*Antiq.* 18:1).

The true meaning of *perushim* is "abstainers," those who abstain from sin and acts of doubtful legality. The word is derived from *prishut*, ("abstention"), frequently mentioned in the Talmud (*Yoma* 74b, *Ketubot* 60a, and many others). One example of their abstinence was their refusal to touch the garments of an *am-haaretz* who was lax in his observance of the laws of defilement (*Hagigah* 18b). Similar restrictions were practiced by individuals who bore the title of *chaver* ("associate"; *Demai*, chap. 2). A *chaver* was known for his strict adherence to the laws of tithes and purity. He also abided by the rabbinic ordinance against the breeding of small cattle to avoid damage to a neighbor's property. There were some *chaverim* who were more extreme in their conduct. They made no vows and were not given to laughter. They avoided defilement by contact with the dead. They also set aside regular hours for study. Those who excelled in their scholastic work eventually joined the ranks of the *chachamim* (*Baba Batra* 75a).

The *chaver* and the *parush* held similar views, except that the *parush* was more of a proselytizer, while the *chaver* was content to keep to himself. According to Josephus, "the Pharisees are able greatly to persuade the body of the people and whatsoever they do about divine worship, prayers and sacrifices, they perform them according to their direction" (*Antiq.* 18:1). The Pharisees, most likely, were in the vanguard of those who engaged the Judeo-Christians in debate and in turn became the prime target of the Christian counterattack. We may describe the Pharisees as a popular activist group which wielded great influence among the people.

To become a *chaver* one had to make a public declaration to that effect in the presence of three other *chaverim* (*Bechorot* 30b). It is very likely that a *parush*, too, had to follow a similar procedure of initiation in order to acquire the title of *parush*.

The Pharisees were among the staunchest supporters of the rabbis. To quote Josephus again: "They [the Pharisees] also pay respect to such as are in years [the elders], nor are they so bold as to contradict them in anything which they have introduced" (*Antiq.* 18:1). However, unlike the non-Pharisaic followers of the rabbis, they were zealots and extremists. According to Josephus, they lived frugally and despised delicacies. There is ample evidence that a few rabbis were sympathetic to their leaning to asceticism. Rabbi Ishmael b. Elisha is a notable example (*Baba Batra* 60b). Most rabbis, however, viewed the tendency with disfavor.

A revealing mishnah reflects the rabbinic displeasure with Pharisaic extremism. "Rabbi Joshua said: 'A woman prefers one *kav* [poverty] and a love-life to nine *kav*s [luxury] and continence.' He used to say: 'A female Pharisee and the wounds of Pharisees wear out the world' " (*Sotah* 20a). Within the context of the mishnah, Rabbi Joshua's objection to this specific type of female Pharisee is her preference for celibacy on religious grounds. A woman who chooses to devote her time to praying and fasting while neglecting her God-given function of child-bearing is pursuing a course which is detrimental to society.

The meaning of the phrase "the wounds of Pharisees" is obscure. A subsequent talmudic passage which lists seven types of Pharisees may offer a cue to the meaning of Rabbi Joshua's phrase. The following are the seven types: one who circumcises himself for the sake of marrying a Jewish woman and joins the Pharisees to impress the people with his piety (his sincerity is in doubt); the Pharisee who repeatedly boasts of his religious zeal (he may be engaged in a cover-up); the Pharisee who serves God out of love (truly pious); the Pharisee who serves God out of fear (deficient); the Pharisee who is guilty of exaggerated humanity (seeks to make an impression); the Pharisee who shuts his eyes to avoid gazing at women (he stumbles into walls and frequently wounds his head); the Pharisee who walks with his head down (excessive humility) (*Sotah* 22b). The thrust of Rabbi Joshua's criticism was aimed at extremism, which may lay an individual open to charges of folly or insincerity.

The types of Pharisees who were singled out for criticism were not representative of the majority of the Pharisees, who were sincerely pious, albeit extremist. The Talmud quotes a deathbed statement of King Jannai (d. 76 B.C.E.) to his wife: "Fear not the Pharisees or the non-Pharisees but only the hypocrites who ape the Pharisees" (*Sotah* 22b).

It was to be expected that some hypocrites would infiltrate the ranks of the Pharisees. Scholarship was not a requisite for membership in the Pharisaic sect, only piety and zeal. As a result it was easy for unscrupulous individuals who craved popular adulation to join the Pharisees by masquerading extreme piety.

Not a single rabbi was ever identified in the Talmud as a Pharisee. There was a clear terminological distinction between the two. A rabbinic disciple was called a *chacham,* which distinguished him from the *chaver* and the *parush* (*Bechorot* 30b).

Gradually the distinction began to blur in the eyes of the world, primarily due to the deliberate deception of the Judeo-Christians who clashed with the Pharisees. They used their attack upon the Pharisees as a means of discrediting the entire rabbinic leadership. There were two steps in this campaign. First the rabbis were identified with the Pharisees. The repeated bracketing of the "scribes" (rabbis) with the Pharisees (Matt. 5:20) established that identity. Thus Rabban Gamliel, the first-century president of the Sanhedrin, was called a Pharisee (Acts 5:34). That was a historical distortion. The next step was to discredit all the Pharisees. Luke singled out an ostentatious Pharisee to whom he attributed a boastful prayer: "I fast twice a week, I give the tenth of all things I acquire . . ." (18:11). Such ostentation and insincerity was then attributed to all Pharisees and by extension to all rabbis. Hence the familiar salutation: "Scribes and Pharisees, hypocrites" (Matt. 23:23).

The impact of this deception of Christendom was explosive. The myth that the Talmud is a product of hypocrisy received widespread acceptance. The word Pharisee became a synonym for "hypocrite." Even so eminent a scholar as Herbert Danby was subconsciously trapped by this deception. In his excellent translation of the Mishnah, he rendered the Hebrew *isha perusha* ("female Pharisee"; *Sotah* 20b) into "a woman that is a hypocrite."

The sincere zeal and extremism of the Pharisees influenced their stance in favor of excessive mourning for the Temple. According to the Talmud, "when the Second Temple was destroyed there was an increase in the number of Pharisees who refused to eat meat and drink wine" (*Baba Batra* 60b). This ascetic tendency might have spread beyond the confines of their sect to the detriment of the Jewish people. It was Rabbi Joshua (ca. 40–125), the popular and beloved leader who had previously criticized Pharisaic excessive zeal (*Sotah* 20b), who saved the day by his skill in moderating their extremism through logical persuasion.

Still, the sentiment in favor of extreme mourning did not entirely disappear. The famous Rabbi Ishmael b. Elisha (a grandson of the martyr by the same name) exclaimed during the Hadrianic persecutions: "We should take it upon ourselves not to marry and bring children into the world, so that the seed of Abraham may come to an end. However, such a decree would not be accepted by most people" (*Baba Batra* 60b). A suggestion of national suicide was never seriously considered by him, and his tragic remark was uttered in a moment of deep despair.

AVELE ZION

The persisting tendency in some quarters to indulge in undue mourning gave rise early in Jewish history to the formation of a loosely knit group known as Avele Zion ("the mourners of Zion"). This brotherhood was not bound by any defined rules and regulations of conduct. They devoted most of their time to prayer and lamentation and lived an ascetic life in great poverty.

The name Avele Zion was derived from Isaiah (61:3), who comforted the "mourners of Zion" who place ashes upon their heads. Isaiah, of course, was not referring to a specific group by that name but to all Jews who mourn for Zion.

The principal seat of the Avele Zion was Jerusalem, except for the periods when Jews were barred from that city. They did not engage in any work and depended on charity for their subsistence. Groups by the same name also emerged in the Middle Ages in Germany, Italy, and some countries of the Orient. They were beneficiaries of individual charity grants and bequests.

The name Avele Zion was perpetuated in a prayer which is recited on Tisha B'Av: "Comfort [*nachem*], O Lord, our God, the Avele Zion and the Avele Jerusalem and the mourners of the desolate city . . ." The ancient prayer of *Nachem* is mentioned in the Jerusalem Talmud (*Berachot* 4:3), however, the name Avele Zion was not yet part of the prayer at that time. There was also another slight variation in the opening of the prayer. In place of *nachem* the prayer began with *rachem* ("Have mercy"). The plea for compassion upon Jerusalem is frequently mentioned in the Scriptures. The same expression is retained in the *Birkat HaMazon (rachem na)*. A plea for mercy, however, does not reflect the fact that the supplicant is in a state of mourning.

Every Jew is in a state of mourning on Tisha B'Av, and a prayer for heavenly comfort is appropriate. The classic prayerbook of Rav Amram Gaon (9th cent.) is the first record of the substitution of *nachem* for *rachem*. That brought it closer to our modern version. However, the name Avele Zion was not yet included in the prayer. Obviously they were not much in evidence in that period in Babylonia. *Machzor Vitry,* the popular work completed in France in 1208, is the first source in which the name Avele Zion was included in the Tisha B'Av prayer. It is likely that some groups went by the name Avele Zion and others by the name Avele Jerusalem. Both are mentioned in the prayer. The formula for comforting a bereaved mourner combines both names: "May the Almighty comfort you together with the Avele Zion and Jerusalem." The prayer inserted in the *Birkat HaMazon* in the house of a mourner mentions only the Avele Jerusalem. The special prayers for the Avele Zion reflect a common awareness of the existence of groups of people who are in a constant state of mourning for Jerusalem.

CUSTOMS COMMEMORATING JERUSALEM

The first custom in commemoration of the critical situation in Jerusalem predated the destruction of the Temple. According to a mishnah, "when the Sanhedrin ceased to function, song ceased from the place of feasting" (*Sotah* 48a). Dr. Sidney B. Hoenig dates the cessation of the Sanhedrin to the year 66 C.E., the time of the outbreak of the rebellion against Rome (*The Great Sanhedrin,* p. 113). It appears that the banning of vocal music for entertainment resulted from a spontaneous reaction to the turmoil in Jerusalem. The initial restriction applied only to music in public in "places of festivities." After the destruction of the Temple the restriction was extended to instrumental music at weddings (*Sotah* 49a). The Babylonian sage Mar Ukva (3rd cent.) prohibited vocal music as well (*Gittin* 7a). However, he did not specifically prohibit vocal music at weddings, and no such prohibition was ever enacted (see *Gittin* 7a, Tosafot, *Zimra*).

The following ordinances in memory of the Temple were enacted after the destruction of Jerusalem: when a house is stuccoed a small area should be left blank; in preparation of a full-course banquet an item or two should be left out; women should omit a few pieces when they put on ornaments (*Baba Batra* 60b). These restrictions were ordained by the *chachamim* (ibid.), which implies that the ordinances reflected the rabbinic consensus. It was obviously felt that such restrictions did not constitute an undue burden and were within the guidelines laid down by Rabban Yochanan and Rabbi Joshua.

The new customs were at first slow in getting universal compliance. Babylonian Jewry of the Patrician period (160 B.C.E.–226 C.E.) were enjoying a golden era of freedom and growth and it hardly considered itself in exile. It was not until the Neo-Persian period (226–640), when Jewish autonomy declined, that Babylonian Jewry was in a mood for mourning. It was in the time of Rav (d. 247), Rav Chisda (d. ca. 309), and Rav Papa (d. 375) that the old restrictions were once again discussed in detail. Rabbi Joseph (a younger colleague of Rav Chisda) clarified the dimensions of the blank area in a newly stuccoed wall. Rav Chisda added that the bare spot should be in a visible location near the door. Rav Papa suggested that the hors d'oeuvre of salted fish be omitted from the menu. Rav said that a woman who applies cosmetics should not remove the hair on her temples (*Baba Batra* 60b).

Another custom instituted in Babylonia at that time was the daubing of ashes on the groom's forehead on the spot where the tefillin usually rest (*Baba Batra* 60b). Later halachists ordained that an empty seat with no setting be left when a table is set (Maimonides, *Hilchot Taaniyot* 5:13; *Orach Chaim* 560:2).

Beginning with the fourth century, most of the restrictions listed above became part of the Jewish tradition. However, efforts to skirt some of these customs were common. The famous Rabbi Isaiah Horowitz (d. 1628) vehemently protested against the practice of some people to cover the bare spot on the wall with an inscription: "This spot is left bare in memory of the destruction." Nevertheless, the custom gradually fell into disuse as a result of the prohibition of Jewish ownership of real estate in most medieval countries.

A substantial number of mourning customs in memory of the Temple were linked to marriage ceremonies and the apparel of the bridal couple. This practice was inspired by the psalmist's verse: "If I set not Jerusalem above my chiefest joy" (137:5). Weddings are mankind's chiefest joy, and the memory of Jerusalem might dissolve in the heady atmosphere of the occasion.

The earliest of these restrictions were enacted shortly after the destruction of the Temple. "During the war with Vespasian, they decreed against crowns worn by bridegrooms and against drums [musical instruments at festivities]. During the war of Quietus [the Roman general who invaded Babylonia in 116; see Soncino, *Sotah* 49a] they decreed against crowns worn by brides. . . . During the final war [Bar Kochba's insurrection in 132] they decreed that a bride should not be transported in a palanquin [a decorated conveyance borne on the shoulders] in the midst of the city" (*Sotah* 49a).

The three restrictions which went into effect between 70 and 135 C. E. apparently were not ordained by the rabbis but stemmed from the pressure of zealots. The usual attribution "the rabbis decreed" is missing in this instance. Indeed, the rabbis took exception in the matter of bridal transportation. "Our rabbis decreed that a bride may go out in a palanquin" (ibid.).

The prohibition of the wearing of the groom's diadem initially received only sporadic compliance. The exilarch in Babylonia searched for a biblical source for this restriction. Rav Chisda based it on the verse in Ezekiel: "The mitre shall be removed and the crown taken off" (21:31; *Gittin* 31b). The discovery of a biblical source gave the custom traditional authority.

In addition to the mourning wedding customs which date from talmudic times, new ones were introduced in the Middle Ages. Thus in Spain bride and groom wore wreaths made of olive leaves. The bitter taste of the leaves commemorated the destruction. In Germany grooms put on hooded cloaks, popularly worn by the general population as a mourning garb. German Jews also instituted the custom of eating eggs on the Seder night. Eggs are traditionally part of a mourner's first meal. The reason for recalling Zion on Passover night was attributed by some rabbis to a calendrical coincidence. Tisha B'Av and the first day of Passover fall on the same day of the week. In addition to this solemn reminder, Jerusalem is also recalled at the Seder in a happier mood, with the exclamation "Next year in Jerusalem!"

Most of the previously mentioned customs have disappeared. However, many other customs, including the exilic fast-days, still persist. The breaking of a glass under the canopy is widely observed. This practice is not mentioned in the Talmud, but the significance of the breaking of a dish as a shock deterrent against levity was well understood in antiquity. The sages were normally apprehensive that undue levity and hilarity in public might lead to a violation of the bounds of moral propriety. It was for this reason that women were segregated from men during the hilarity of Simchat Bet HaShoavah (*Sukkah* 51b).

To stop excessive levity at a wedding reception, Mar the son of Ravina broke a precious cup, worth four hundred zuz (*Berachot* 31a). On a similar occasion, Rav Ashi (d. 427) used the same method to sober the guests (ibid.). The breaking of the dishes took place during the festivities, not under the canopy, and in both cases it was the father of the groom who did the breaking. The tosafists (12th and 13th cent.) attributed the practice of breaking a glass under the canopy to this talmudic passage. *Kol Bo,* a medieval anthology of customs, is the first source to associate the breaking of the glass with a display of mourning. Rabbi Joseph Caro did not mention this custom in the *Shulchan Aruch* because it was not widespread among the Sephardim. Rabbi Moses Isserles (16th cent.), however, included this Ashkenazic custom in his annotation to the code (*Orach Chaim* 650) and thus assured it universal compliance.

Other customs instituted in talmudic times in commemoration of Jerusalem are still observed in modern times. Thus we face Jerusalem when we recite the *Amidah*, and the ark is placed on the eastern wall. The ark in the ancient synagogue uncovered at Massada faces west because Jerusalem is west of Massada. The custom of facing east is mentioned in the Talmud (*Berachot* 30a). It was based on the biblical verse: "and they will pray unto thee toward their land" (I Kings 8:48).

The prayer for rain (*morid hageshem*) is recited in the winter season when Palestine is in need of rain (*Taanit* 2a). It may not be said in the summer, when rain would be harmful to the Palestinian harvest.

In the distribution of charity, when funds are limited, priority must be given to the poor in the Holy Land (*Sifre*, Deut. 15:7).

A man may force his wife to move to Palestine. If she refuses, she may be divorced and she forfeits her ketubah. Likewise, a wife may force her husband to move to Palestine. If he refuses, she is entitled to a divorce and to collect the ketubah (*Ketubot* 112b). Maimonides included this law in his code (*Hilchot Ishut* 13:20). The tosafists, however, aware of the hazards of a trip from medieval Europe to Palestine, considered the law no longer operative (*Ketubot* 112b, *Hu omer*).

PRAYERS COMMEMORATING ZION

The *Shulchan Aruch* recommends in its very first chapter that prayers for the restoration of Jerusalem be recited at the end of the second trimester of the night. This was based on a talmudic statement that the Almighty expresses his own sorrow and grief at that time (*Berachot* 3a). Eventually special prayers were composed for the occasion.

The kabbalists introduced the custom of midnight prayers for Jerusalem. These prayers, known at the *Tikkun Chatzot*, became very popular with the spread of Kabbala in Europe.

Prayers for the restoration of Zion are prominently highlighted throughout the liturgy. Petitions for the ingathering of the Jewish people are included in the preliminary prayers. To quote but a few: "O bring us back from the four corners of the earth . . . "; "And to

Jerusalem thy city return in mercy . . . "; "May it be thy will that the Temple be speedily rebuilt."

The Bible and the Talmud, festivals and fast-days, customs and prayers sealed the memory of Zion in the hearts of all Jews.

Bibliography

Abarbanel, Isaac. Commentary on the Haggadah. New York, 1947.

Ach Letzarah, by Yekutiel Greenwald. St. Louis, 1938.

Against Apion, by Flavius Josephus. Translated by Havercamp.

Alfasi. Vilna, 1893.

Antiquities of the Jews, by Flavius Josephus. Translated by Havercamp.

Apocrypha. Edited by Manuel Komroff. New York, 1936.

> Ecclesiasticus
> I Maccabees
> II Maccabees
> Tobit

Avudrahim Hashalem, by David Avudrahim. Jerusalem, 1963.

Baer Hatev. Commentary on *Shulchan Aruch*. Warsaw, 1878.

Bayit Chadash. Commentary on *Tur* code. Warsaw, 1867.

Bet Yoseph. Commentary on *Tur* code. Warsaw, 1867.

Bible

> Pentateuch. Vilna: Mikraot Gedolot, 1930.
> Genesis
> Exodus
> Leviticus
> Numbers
> Deuteronomy

> The Former Prophets. Warsaw, Kitve Kodesh.
> Joshua
> Judges
> I Samuel
> II Samuel
> I Kings
> II Kings

> The Later Prophets. Warsaw, Kitve Kodesh.
> Isaiah
> Jeremiah
> Ezekiel

Hosea
Micah
Zephaniah
Malachi

Hagiographa. Warsaw, Kitve Kodesh.
Psalms
Proverbs
Song of Songs
Lamentations
Ecclesiastes
Esther
Nehemiah
I Chronicles
II Chronicles

Biblical and Historical Background of the Jewish Holy Days, by Abraham P. Bloch. New York: KTAV, 1978.

Chashmonaim. Divre Ketuvim Acharonim. Tel Aviv, 1956

Chaye Adam, by Abraham Danzig. New York

Chinuch, by Aaron Halevi of Barcelona. Lemberg, 1889.

Concordance, by Julius Fuerst. Leipzig, 1932.

Daat Zekenim Baale Tosafot. Commentary on the Pentateuch. Vilna: Mikraot Gedolot, 1930.

Daily Prayer Book, by Joseph H. Hertz. New York, 1948.

Days of Awe, by S. Y. Agnon. New York, 1965.

Dead Sea Scrolls. Edited by Theodor H. Gaster. Garden City, N.Y. 1956
      Manual of Discipline
      Zadokite Document

Divre Chibah. Commentary on Ritva, *Moed Katan,* by Rabbi Chaim I. Bloch. New York, 1935.

Encyclopaedia Judaica. Jerusalem, 1972.

Great Sanhedrin, by Sidney B. Hoenig. Philadelphia, 1953.

Historia Shel Habayit Hasheni, by Joseph Klausner. Jerusalem, 1951.

History of the Jews of Italy, by Cecil Roth. Philadelphia, 1946.

Jewish Life in the Middle Ages, by Israel Abrahams. London, 1932.

Kitzur Shulchan Aruch. Abridged code. Lemberg, 1910.

Levush, by Mordecai Jaffe. Berdichev, 1918.

Maadane Shmuel. Commentary on *Kitzur Shulchan Aruch* by Samuel Borstein. Lemberg, 1910.

Machzor Roma Haggadah. Italy, 1540.

Machzor Vitry, by Rabbi Simchah. Nuremberg, 1923.

Magen Avraham. Commentary on *Shulchan Aruch.* Warsaw, 1879.

Masechet Soferim. New York, 1936.

Midrashim

> *Midrash Rabbah Al HaTorah VeChamishah Megillot.* New York, 1925.
>
> > *Shemot Rabbah*
> > *Vayikra Rabbah*
> > *Bamidbar Rabbah*
> > *Devarim Rabbah*
> > *Shir HaShirim Rabbah*
> > *Eichah Rabbah*
>
> *Mechilta.* Vilna: Chamishah Chumshe Torah, 1891
>
> *Midrash Ele Ezkerah.* Edited by J. D. Eisenstein. New York: Otzar Midrashim, 1928.
>
> *Midrash Shochar Tov.* Jerusalem, 1960.
>
> *Pesiktah Rabbati.* Vienna, 1880.
>
> *Pirke deRabbi Eliezer.* Edited by D. Luria. Warsaw, 1852.
>
> *Seder Eliyahu Rabbah VeSeder Eliyahu Zuta.* Jerusalem, 1959.
>
> *Sifra, Vayikra.* Warsaw: Chamishah Chumshe Torah, 1879.
>
> *Sifre, Bamidbar and Devarim.* Warsaw: Chamisha Chumshe Torah, 1879.
>
> *Tanchuma (Midrash Yelamdenu).* New York, 1925.
>
> *Yalkut Shimoni.* New York, 1944.

Mishnah. Translated by Herbert Danby. London, 1933.

Mishneh Torah, by Moses b. Maimon. Berlin, 1926.

Moadim Behalachah, by Shlomo J. Zevin. Tel Aviv, 1954.

Nachalat Shivah, by Samuel b. David Halevi. Warsaw, 1902.

Nachmanides. Commentary on the Pentateuch. Vilna: Mikraot Gedolot, 1930.

New Testament

> Acts
> Luke
> Mark
> Matthew

Nissim Geronidi (Ran). Commentary on Alfasi. Vilna, 1893.

Personalities and Events in Jewish History, by Cecil Roth. Philadelphia, 1953.

Philo the Alexandrian. *Works of Philo Judaeus.* Translated by C. D. Younge, London, 1854.

Rema. Annotations to *Shulchan Aruch* by Moses Isserles. Berlin, 1918.

Responsa of Solomon b. Adret. Vilna, 1881.

Seder Rav Amram Gaon. Jerusalem, 1971.

Sefer Charedim, by Judah Chasid. New York, 1953.

Sefer HaMinhagim, by Abraham Klausner. Jerusalem, 1978.

Sefer HaMitzvot, by Moses b. Maimon. Edited by Chaim Heller. Jerusalem, 1946.

Sefer HaTodaah, by Elijah Kitov. Jerusalem, 1976.

Sefer Kol Bo. Tel Aviv.

Sefer Maharil, by Jacob Moellin. Jerusalem, 1968.

Shibole HaLeket, by Zedekiah b. Abraham of Rome. Venice, 1546.

Shlomo Yitzchaki (Rashi). Commentary on Pentateuch and Talmud.

Shulchan Aruch. Berlin: Chorev, 1927.

Siddur Bet Yaakov, by Jacob Emden. Lemberg, 1904.

Siddur Otzar HaTefilot. New York, 1946.

Siddur Rashi. Edited by Jacob Freimann. Berlin, 1911.

Siddur Rav Saadiah Gaon. Edited by I. Davidson, S. Assaf, and B. I. Joel. Jerusalem, 1978.

Talmud (Babylonian). Vilna, 1880.

    Berachot
    Peah
    Demai
    Terumot
    Bikkurim
    Shabbat
    Eruvin
    Pesachim
    Shekalim
    Yoma
    Sukkah
    Betzah
    Rosh HaShanah
    Taanit
    Megillah
    Moed Katan
    Chagigah
    Yevamot
    Ketubot
    Nedarim
    Sotah
    Gittin
    Kiddushin

    Kallah
    Baba Kama
    Baba Metzia
    Baba Batra
    Sanhedrin
    Makkot
    Shevuot
    Eduyot
    Avodah Zarah
    Avot
    Horayot
    Avot deRabbi Natan
    Semachot
    Menachot
    Chulin
    Bechorot
    Arachin
    Keritot
    Tamid
    Ohalot
    Niddah
    Yadayim
Talmud (Jerusalem). Vilna, 1926.
    Berachot
    Peah
    Bikkurim
    Shabbat
    Pesachim
    Shekalim
    Yoma
    Sukkah
    Rosh HaShanah
    Taanit
    Megillah
    Moed Katan
    Chagigah
    Ketubot
    Sotah
    Baba Batra
    Sanhedrin
    Avodah Zarah

Targum Onkelos. Pentateuch.

Targum Yonatan b. Uziel. Vilna: Mikraot Gedolot, 1930.

Targum Rav Yosef. Chronicles. Vilna: Mikraot Gedolot, 1930.

Torah Temimah. Commentary on Pentateuch by Baruch Epstein. New York, 1928.

Tosafot. Commentary on Talmud Bavli.

Tosefta (appended to Alfasi). Vilna, 1893.

Treasury of Jewish Letters. Edited by F. Kobler. London, 1952.

Tur code. Warsaw, 1863.

Tzavaat Rabbi Judah, by Judah Chasid. New York, 1953.

Venice Haggadah. Venice, 1609.

Wars of the Jews, by Flavius Josephus. Translated by Havercamp.

Washington Haggadah, by Joel b. Simon. Italy, 1470.

Yam Shel Shelomo, by Solomon Luria. Stettin, 1861.

Zichronot Eretz Yisrael, by Abraham Yaari. Jerusalem, 1947.

Zohar. Vilna, 1894.

Index

Compiled by Robert J. Milch, M.A.

I. Biblical Passages

II. Names and Subjects